REAR ADMIRAL GEORGE W. MELVILLE, U. S. A. (Retired).

The survivor of three Arctic expeditions, who was given a gold medal by Congress for his distinguished services. He was a member of the De Long Expedition, and when the "Jeannette" was crushed in the ice, marched with part of the crew to the coast of Siberia at the mouth of the Lena River. He led an expedition to search for De Long and found the relics of the ill-fated leader. Admiral Melville is one of the most experienced Arctic explorers and is an authority of the first rank on the subject of Arctic travels.

FINDING THE
NORTH POLE

DR. COOK'S OWN STORY OF HIS DISCOVERY, APRIL 21, 1908

THE STORY OF COMMANDER PEARY'S DISCOVERY, APRIL 6, 1909

———TOGETHER WITH———

THE MARVELOUS RECORD OF FORMER ARCTIC EXPEDITIONS

EDITED BY

CHARLES MORRIS

Member of the Geographical Society of Philadelphia

WITH AN INTRODUCTION BY

GEORGE W. MELVILLE

REAR ADMIRAL U. S. NAVY, RETIRED

The Survivor of Three Arctic Expeditions who Recovered the Records of the Jeannette Expedition, and also the Remains of De Long and his Companions and was Given a Gold Medal by Congress for his Distinguished Services

ILLUSTRATED

THE LYONS PRESS
Guilford, Connecticut
www.lyonspress.com
An imprint of The Globe Pequot Press

Special contents of this edition copyright © 2003 by The Lyons Press
Originally published in 1909 by W. E. Scull

All rights reserved. No part of this book may be reproduced or transmitted in any form by any means, electronic or mechanical, including photocopying and recording, or by any information storage and retrieval system, except as may be expressly permitted in writing from the publisher. Requests for permission should be addressed to The Lyons Press, Attn: Rights and Permissions Department, P.O. Box 480, Guilford, CT 06437.

The Lyons Press is an imprint of The Globe Pequot Press.

10 9 8 7 6 5 4 3 2 1

Printed in the United States of America

ISBN 1-59228-072-2

Library of Congress Cataloging-in-Publication Data is available on file.

Finding the North Pole

By George W. Melville,
Rear Admiral U. S. Navy, Retired

NOT only the people of the United States of America, but the whole civilized world were electrified by the announcement on September 1, 1909, through the public press that despatches had been received from Dr. Frederick A. Cook, claiming that he had the great honor, on April 21, 1908, of reaching the long-sought-for goal, the physical North Pole of the earth.

Nor had the resulting excitement subsided before Commander Robert E. Peary, U. S. N., cabled to the Associated Press on September 5, 1909, that he had planted the Stars and Stripes upon the North Pole on April 6, 1909. The sensation was without parallel in the history of polar discovery. Where men had for centuries striven in vain it suddenly was told to the world that two Americans had independently achieved the supreme goal of their ambitions.

Those who have most keenly felt the extremities of the Arctic, and who are best acquainted with the history of men's baffled attempts to set foot upon the earth's axis, can only gasp in wonder at the achievement as recorded in Dr. Cook's own story of his discovery of the North Pole. Having, then, occasionally noted that news is often later modified before it becomes history, and particularly scientific history, I have decided to await the examination of Dr. Cook's own evidence, and naturally with intense interest. If the information given to the world is verified and accepted by the best qualified men, how great is the honor! Not only to the man but to the nation he represents this glory is all but immeasurable.

FINDING THE NORTH POLE

Robert E. Peary's expedition was equipped in the most thorough and scientific manner for making the conquest of the North Pole. He was an Arctic traveler of large experience, and had rendered valuable aid to science by his explorations of the regions north and east of Greenland. He was one of the first to demonstrate to the scientific world that Greenland is an island, and had sailed on his latest voyage confident that he would return successful.

When we take into consideration the time, treasure and life that has been spent in this seemingly impossible feat of toil; patient suffering of hunger, cold and self-denial, not to speak of the personal danger to life and limb, it must be considered one of the greatest feats of human endurance of modern times. Almost alone, after leaving the main base of his supplies in Grinnell Land, and with but two Eskimo natives and dogs and provisions sufficient for his journey and return, it was a courageous heart and stout body with endurance beyond the common run of mortals for Dr. Cook to start across the unknown ice of the Arctic Ocean, which is always in motion, never at rest, in all seasons. That ice which had turned back so many brave hearts in utter defeat, that ice which had defied some of the best equipped expeditions and the strongest men of soul and body, aye and buried, too, in its frozen bosom, so many of the best blood and brains of the human race, who for more than three hundred years have been fighting to attain that Ultima Thule, the north polar axis of the earth.

The quest and sacrifice began away back in Sir Hugh Willoughby's time, in 1553, when, striving to make a much coveted northeast passage for a short route to the East Indies, he and his whole ship's company perished to a man in the vain endeavor. Then followed a long line of the ancient mariner and fisherman class, their ships fitted out by merchant princes of their country, including some of those best known for their valor, perseverance and loyalty to the problem they had in view: Frobisher, Davis, Barrentes, Behring, Parry, Ross and Franklin; a frequent relay of hardy spirits has persevered down to our present day and generation where many of these, both officers and men, laid down their lives on the altar of science and Arctic discovery; not for money, but that the world might know what was beyond the great unknown.

But considering the present day, with the experience of men still living, who have done heroic service in the Arctic, we can with confidence quote the work done by Captain MacClintock, Royal British Navy, one of the latest and best authorities on Arctic travel or sledging in his search for relics of the ill-fated last Franklin expedition. He made the best marches on record of one thousand miles continuous sledging. This, it is true, was done by the aid of supporting sledges laying out provision depots, and so well did Sir Leopold MacClintock do his work and so well made were his sledges that they have been copied ever since in all well-equipped Arctic expeditions. Heretofore all great sledging was advisedly done in the summer time, notwithstanding the handicap of snow blindness and the difficulties of wading at times waist deep in water, from the melting snows, that covers the floe. Such water cannot always run off freely into the open lanes of water, both because of the depressions in the center of the floe and also because the dike-like ridges, thrown up through the crushing and grinding of the ice by the immense pressure of the moving floes, make lakes in places, or a series of them, from a mile or two to three miles in width. These the sledging party must go through, as the detours would be interminable. Herein lies the question, whether it is best to travel by night or day, or during the winter season or summer season. Heretofore all Arctic travelers have preferred the summer, notwithstanding its many drawbacks. It has been considered heretofore that it was impossible to travel during the long winter night of cold and darkness which seems to have been chosen in part by Dr. Cook.

This was a serious question in one of the councils preceding the loss of the "Jeannette" by Captain George W. DeLong, U. S. N., of which council I had the honor of being a member. The question was whether we should abandon the ship in the springtime and take the summer march as the ship was drifting beyond any known march of record, and try to reach a place of succor, or whether we should remain by the ship and "eat her out" and take the chances of the march in the long winter night.

The arguments against the winter night march were as follows: That we could not procure fresh water to drink by melting the snows with our alcohol lamps because the snow where we found it in the winter season was saturated with salt; the grinding and pulverizing of the salt-water hummocks, by the wind-driven snow acting as a sand blast, mixed the salt ice with the snow. As a point to remember I will here state the fact that during the whole of the drift of the "Jeannette," twenty-two months, we were never able to procure one pound of fresh-water snow, not even out of the ship's tops, that was fresh enough when melted to make potable water. Every ounce of water used in the "Jeannette" for drinking purposes was distilled.

To travel in the Arctic darkness heretofore had always seemed impossible because of the inability to see how to go, or follow a compass course.

The cold, being more intense in the winter time, would require warmer clothing and foot gear to prevent frost bite; the searching winds that neither man nor beast can stand up against would necessitate the usual camping down in a hole dug in the snow until the cessation of the storm. There was, and is, greater danger from possibility of frost bite disabling the whole party, because no man can be abandoned on the march while he is alive. I have personally had the majority of a boat's crew disabled from frost bite in the month of October. With heavier clothing the party is handicapped in marching and hauling the sledges which is constant, besides the inability to sleep at night even in the warmest reindeer sleeping-bags. For as the chill of death comes upon the sleepers all hands must break out and thrash about to put the blood into circulation before again trying to turn in to sleep.

ESKIMOS ON BOARD THE "JOHN R. BRADLEY."

These guides are here shown on the deck of the schooner which carried Dr. Cook to Greenland, where he was left to make his dash to the Pole.

Photos by Paul Thompson, N. Y.
ARCTIC SCENES TAKEN ON THE COOK-BRADLEY EXPEDITION

Trapping a Walrus.
John R. Bradley and Eskimos in front of Eskimo huts. Photographed before Dr. Cook was left to himself.

Scene on the "J. R. Bradley."
Scene in the Far North, showing penguins on the ice floe at the right and heads of walrus swimming at the left.

The body can only supply a certain amount of natural heat. These calories must be kept up by adding fuel to the human furnace; this means a larger supply of food per ration per man, all of which means greater weight to be carried or hauled. The same applies to dogs. The natives when possible house their dogs in winter, never in the summer. Again, the health of the party must be preserved if possible. Short rations, bitter cold, tremendous labor of sledge hauling, or even marching, with salt or brackish water to drink, in a very few weeks would bring on scurvy. In fact, these are the ideal conditions to cause scurvy, especially after some time in the Arctic.

In summer time most of these adverse conditions disappear. The greatest objections are: the softer snow to travel over, the deep ponds of water on the floes that are to be traversed and the snow blindness, which, however, need not trouble the travelers if they will wear colored goggles on the march. Less food, less clothing and freedom from frost bite are advantages, but greatest boon of all is the fresh water to be obtained from the top of every conical or sloping piece of ice that is covered with melting snow, for the melted snow water on the floe and in the ponds is too salt to be used for drinking purposes. But when the spring sun comes on the temperature rises to about 32 or 34 degrees Fahrenheit. The salt in the snow on the slopes of the hummocks begins to melt at about 29 degrees F., this super-salted water first falls down on the surface of the hummock and at each increasing fraction of a degree a larger volume of the salt water flows away until the temperature of 32 degrees or more is reached. When all the super-salted water has thus run off on the surrounding floe, it leaves the fresh water snow on the top and sloping sides of the hummocks.

The summer traveler then gathers this soft snow into the kettles and about three-fourths of a pint of alcohol will melt thirteen pints of slushy snow and water and bring it to a boil. Then by throwing in a couple of ounces of tea it supplies not only a refreshing and invigorating drink, but adds an immense amount of heat to the body and acts as so much food. When traveling in the summer, on the ice-floe there is generally to be found an abundance of game, such as walrus, seal and bear, with occasionally a fox which follows after the bear to eat the crumbs that fall from his feast. And if the ice-floe is near land or islands there is also numerous water fowl of all kinds, to kill which, of course, it is necessary to have shotguns, though the army repeating rifle is the proper arm for killing all large game.

The reasons above set forth are those usually advanced by all Arctic explorers for and against summer and winter travel, and it was the opinion of Captain DeLong and his officers that we should abandon the ship in the summer time. Fortunately for us we were saved making the decision, as our ship was crushed under us and we were obliged to make the march in midsummer. Of this march much has been written, and as a march cut off from all base of supplies it has been considered one of the most heroic in Arctic literature.

I regret to have to be compelled to refer to the retreat from the "Jeannette," but it is necessary to do so, as also to refer to many of the other recorded marches in the Arctics in the past. At times the progress made by the "Jeannette's" retreating party amounted to but two and a half miles per day, although each day the distance traveled was from twenty-five to thirty miles, but because of the many trips made back and forth and the routes necessarily taken to avoid water lakes and impassable ice ridges, our net advance on some days was very small. The surface of the floe was so broken and ridged up by the pressure of the ice masses, that we cut, by means of pickaxes and shovels, a road nearly all the way to open water, where we could launch our boats. Then it was ice and water navigation as occasion offered to open water, and the remainder of the journey was made in open boats until we reached the land. The rest of that pitiable story and the most heroic endeavor of Captain DeLong with his boat's crew has been told in his Ice Journals by his devoted wife, Emma DeLong. The final part of the retreat resulting in the death of DeLong and his loyal boat's crew, the particulars of which are copied from the Ice Journals of DeLong, is the most heroic and, at the same time, the most soul-stirring tale of Arctic adventure.

The retreat of the "Jeannette's" crew and the recorded marches of some of the best Arctic travelers, including Captain MacClintock, R. N.; Robert E. Peary and Cagni, show that some of the best records have been from three to seven miles per day.

When we take into consideration that the distance and time as reported by Dr. Cook's despatches would amount to between twelve and fifteen miles per day, it seems incredible, but for the fact that it is the statement of a veracious man. If verification proves these reports correct, it shows the greatest effort ever made by man on the face of the globe.

Nothing can be more interesting or inspiring than the story of the men who have braved the hardship and perils of the Arctic regions, and apart from Dr. Cook's report of his expedition, which, of course, must stand or fall on its own merits, this book will be found to contain interesting accounts of Peary's and other important polar discoveries and experiences.

ARCTIC NIGHT

O ye thick-ribbed ice!
O ye everlasting ice and snows!
The cold that eats into the vitals and kills,
The sun that has lost its heat and settled behind the ice-clad hills.
O Nature, cold and frost laden, will ye ne'er relent?
Will the hills never melt?
Will the sun never return to cheer the soul of the heart-sick mariner?
Whose body trembles with the dread disease,
Whose eyes are dimmed, whose teeth chatter like the castanette,
The blood thinned by foul disease, and poisoned limbs too weak to carry the frail body hence.

Ye strong, brave hearts, fail not,
But believe that life and light and heat will again return,
The body and mind shaken by the frost and dread disease, and the life-blood frozen will again melt and the heart beat strong.
The brave hearts that faced the ice king and demon of death in his lair, will again rejoice with the returning sun,
O Frost, where is thy victory?   Behold, again
The sun with heat and light and life is king, and the heart of the mariner again rejoices.

Table of Contents

	PAGE
FINDING THE NORTH POLE By GEORGE W. MELVILLE, Rear Admiral U. S. Navy, Retired.	3

CHAPTER I.
THE DRAMATIC ANNOUNCEMENTS OF COOK AND PEARY 17

CHAPTER II.
COOK'S STORY OF HIS DISCOVERY OF THE NORTH POLE 28

CHAPTER III.
THE STORY OF PEARY'S GREAT EXPLOIT 48

CHAPTER IV.
SIDE-LIGHTS ON THE PEARY EXPEDITION 67

CHAPTER V.
EARLY LIFE AND EXPERIENCES OF DR. FREDERICK A. COOK... 84

CHAPTER VI.
COOK IN THE ANTARCTIC AND IN ALASKA 93

CHAPTER VII.
BRADLEY'S ACCOUNT OF THE COOK EXPEDITION 111

CHAPTER VIII.
ROBERT E. PEARY, THE INDOMITABLE POLAR EXPLORER 123

CONTENTS

CHAPTER IX.
Peary Crosses Greenland 138

CHAPTER X.
Peary's Farthest North of 1905-6 152

CHAPTER XI.
Europe Gives Honor to Dr. Cook 168

CHAPTER XII.
Receptions of Cook and Peary on American Soil 179

CHAPTER XIII.
The Controversy Between Cook and Peary 194

CHAPTER XIV.
Interesting Scientific Work in the Arctic 203

CHAPTER XV.
Animals of the Arctic Region 216

CHAPTER XVI.
Terrors and Mysteries of the Polar Regions 225

CHAPTER XVII.
The Search for the Northwest Passage 233

CHAPTER XVIII.
The Ross and Parry Polar Voyages 245

CHAPTER XIX.
The First Franklin Expedition 253

CHAPTER XX.
The Terrible Fate of the Sir John Franklin Expedition 259

CONTENTS

CHAPTER XXI.
Dr. Kane's Famous Arctic Voyage 277

CHAPTER XXII.
Hayes, Hall and Other Hardy Adventurers 298

CHAPTER XXIII.
Nordenskiold and the Northeast Passage 318

CHAPTER XXIV.
The Horrors of the "Jeannette" Expedition 325

CHAPTER XXV.
Melville Finds the Remains of the DeLong Party 339

CHAPTER XXVI.
Greely's Arctic Winter of Starvation 351

CHAPTER XXVII.
Nansen's Memorable Voyage in the "Fram" 369

CHAPTER XXVIII.
Andree's Fatal Flight Northward in a Balloon 390

CHAPTER XXIX.
Modern Vikings in the Arctic Seas 402

CHAPTER XXX.
Abruzzi, the Royal Italian Explorer 415

CHAPTER XXXI.
The Problem of the Antarctic Zone 428

CHAPTER XXXII.
Shackleton on the Threshold of the South Pole 441

CHAPTER I

Dramatic Announcements of Cook and Peary

THE world has been making history fast within the twentieth century, and this has been especially the case in the matter of polar research. In this regard the first week of September, 1909, was in its way the most extraordinary in the history of mankind. In that one week there came to us from the frozen north two of the most surprising announcements ever received by man. The North Pole, the goal sought for centuries, the quest of which had given rise to endless adventures and untold sufferings, with little result except an unceasing tale of misfortune, misery, disappointment and death, had been reached at last, and strangely enough the honor of the discovery came from two separate sources and was claimed by two men.

On the first day of that eventful month the world was startled by the undreamed of announcement, flashed over the electric wires from the far-off Shetland Islands, that the long-sought goal had been reached on April 21, 1908. And while the world was still struggling in the throes of the astounding news, belief in the story mingled with doubt and incredulity, there came five days afterwards a similar claim, one received without doubt, that a second explorer had reached the same goal, the date of discovery in this case being April 6, 1909.

The first to announce the great discovery was Dr. Frederick A. Cook, a polar explorer of long experience, who for two years had been lost to sight in the icy seas, so utterly removed from human ken that men had given up the hope of ever seeing him again, fearing that the demon king of the ice realm had made him its victim, and that death had claimed him as its own. With little hope that the dauntless adventurer would ever reappear, a relief expedition had been prepared, its purpose being to find him if alive, or trace the record of his fate if dead, when the tidings that he had accomplished the great feat and set foot on the northern extremity of the earth's axis, came over the wires, and the world stood still in astonishment at the startling statement.

The second to lay claim to this great triumph was the well-known and famous polar explorer, Commander Robert E. Peary, who for twenty-three years had devoted his life to the work of research, and who, in the summer of 1908, had made a last and desperate journey to the icy north, bent on success if it lay within the powers of man.

On September 6th, while the world of geographical science was doing its utmost to honor the intrepid Cook, and the King of Denmark was feasting him within his palace as the worthiest of guests, the man who stood foremost in the annals of geographical research, there flashed down from Labrador a second announcement to the same effect, in the following significant words:

"HAVE NAILED THE UNITED STATES FLAG TO THE NORTH POLE.   PEARY."

Again over the whole realm of civilized mankind flashed the astounding news, and the world, which was slowly digesting the tidings so lately received, had laid before it a new feast of wonder and astonishment.

Never in the history of man had two such surprising items of news been received in such brief succession. To the people of the United States they brought not only astonishment but pride. Both these men were citizens of our own country, true-born Americans the pair, and to feel that the honor of this discovery, to whichever of the two men it belonged, appertained to the United States, was a source of heartfelt gratification. The North Pole was ours! Our flag waved over it! The polar region belonged to our country!

There was much here to be proud of and grateful for, and that this new section of the earth would be claimed as part of our great country was beyond reasonable doubt.

To those who might ask what did it all signify, of what use was such a discovery to mankind, what had been really gained by the long search, we may reply in the one word, "Knowledge." Since man first came upon the earth knowledge has been his continual quest. Knowledge about the earth, the air, the sea, the stars of heaven; knowledge of all nature's doings, of the trees, the rocks, of storm and calm, summer and winter, of everything that falls before the human eye or appeals to the human mind.

Man came upon the earth as a new tenant of a great unknown universe, full of mysteries and marvels, and the desire "to know" was early born within him. Whatever the purpose of this desire, it was there. No doubt one leading purpose was to aid and benefit himself, to obtain something that would be to his advantage, to explore new realms in search of food or something else of use to him in his task of subduing and fitting for his own ends the animal and vegetable life of the earth.

But it was not this alone. In time there developed within the mind of man the thirst for knowledge for its own sake, the wish to widen his store of information, to develop his intellect, to grasp all that the world had to offer him of mental food. This was the birth of the spirit of science, the basis of which is knowledge, its superstructure the conception to which knowledge leads.

Geographical discovery was long in becoming a main object to man. The primitive tribes spread over the earth simply through the nomadic instinct or as the result of the increase and crowding of population. So far as we are aware, it was not until the palmy days of the Greek civilization that travelers—like the historian Herodotus, for example—first set out to discover what was worth seeing and knowing in the rest of the world. And not until within the last few centuries has the desire to know what the remote regions of the earth had to offer become insistent in the human mind.

Columbus was one of the chief pioneers in this field. It was not so much personal benefit that he had in view as the wish to learn what secrets the great western ocean might hide in its mysterious depths. It was this that spurred him to his mighty task, the *wanderlust* of which to-day we hear so much, the thirst to discover, the fame he might gain, that moved this famous navigator. And it is this same spirit that has moved the Cooks and Peary and others of like type in our own day to cross a new unknown ocean to learn what secrets lay hid in its mystic depths.

Never before as within the last and the present centuries was this eagerness to penetrate the unknown regions of the earth so vital in men's minds. During the few centuries before there was something like it in the eagerness with which the new-discovered continent of America was explored. But in this it was the search for gain that chiefly moved the explorers. The Spanish conquerors traversed the south in search of gold, the French adventurers explored the north in quest of furs, the British in the mid-realm were engaged in making themselves new homes in the western wilderness. Few of all these were moved by that pure desire to learn the secrets of the earth which has been largely the inspiring spirit of recent discovery.

Within the past hundred years this spirit has manifested itself as never before. As if ashamed to admit that there was so much of our little planet remaining unknown, after the many millenniums of man's esistence upon the earth, adventurers set out on all sides burning with the desire to discover the earth—so far as it was still unrevealed. There was much still to discover. Of the great continent of Africa, almost nothing was unknown beyond the immediate coast. Asia, the greatest of the continents, held a multitude of mysterious secrets. Even America, actively as it had been trodden and explored for four centuries, had vast areas on which the foot of man had never been set. And apart from these, in the far north and south, were two great regions, continental in extent, those of the Arctic and Antarctic zones, almost as unknown as if they belonged to the planet Mars instead of to the earth. Indeed, if we may judge from the dicta of some astronomers, far more was known about the general surface of the remote Mars than about the earth. Thus great prizes remained for the discoverer, and on all sides he went abroad to make the earth his own.

It is not our intention here to go into the record of the work of discovery here alluded to. It is that of polar research and the significance of the recent results with which alone we are concerned. Yet it is well to say that the activity of recent geographical research and its brilliant results have been phenomenal. Within little more than half a century the unknown center of Africa—all Africa indeed within a hundred miles or so of the sea-coast—has been made known and nearly all taken possession of by the nations of Europe. Civilization has invaded the Dark Continent to its darkest recesses, and the railway, man's distance destroyer, is fast threading it from north to south, from east to west. Asia, too, has been traversed in all directions and great part of it taken possession of by European nations. These have introduced civilization where only barbarism existed before and have awakened the long dormant empires of China and Japan to reach out for a place among the leading nations of the earth. As regards America, the hitherto untraveled areas are fast becoming known.

As may be seen from what has been said, the activity of the traveler and discoverer has been extraordinary within the period named, a period through all of which many now on the earth have lived. The great prizes of the explorer were largely won, and little of the earth's surface remained to be traversed except the icy regions surrounding the North and South Poles.

In these regions, and especially in that of the North Pole, man had not been idle during the period in question. Indeed, for great part of four centuries daring adventurers had been seeking this region, some drawn to it by the elusive lure of the Northwest Passage, their purpose being one of commercial gain; some in quest of the whale and the seal, drawn directly by the love of gain; some by efforts to reach the Pole, the pure spirit of discovery animating these.

One by one, step by step, these great men advanced nearer the goal of their desires. It is an interesting fact that among the earliest to make a high northern record was Henry Hudson, the discoverer of the Hudson River and Manhattan Island, on which the great city of New York was afterwards to rise. In the north his name survives in Hudson Bay. More than two centuries later came Captain Parry, who made a high north record not reached again until half a century after his time. It is interesting that this early voyager adopted the method of sledging over the ice by which the Pole was finally reached, and which is spoken of frequently as if it was a discovery of our own day.

We may hastily run over the roster of those who followed. Prominent among these were Sir John and James Ross, who located the Magnetic Pole, and the unfortunate Sir John Franklin, whose tragic fate, with that of his crew, was the most deplorable event in the record of Arctic discovery. After him for many years came a series of voyagers in search of the remains of his expedition, some of whom made important discoveries. Chief among these was Captain McClure, who crossed from Bering Strait to the Atlantic and was the first to traverse the long-sought Northwest Passage.

Prominent among the searchers for the Franklin expedition were several Americans, the first of whom, Dr. Elisha Kane, made the best northing achieved to that time by an American ship. Following him came the expeditions of Dr. Hayes and Captain Hall, each making an important record, and then that of the unfortunate Greely, who was left for a winter in the Arctic wilds almost without food, and was finally rescued when on the very verge of death by starvation. We must mention here another American, the still more unfortunate DeLong, whose ship was sunk in the Siberian seas, and who with many of his followers perished by starvation on the bleak Siberian coast.

This rapid résumé of explorers' names and feats is given merely by way of introduction, as the story of where they went and what they achieved is given at length in the later sections of this work. It is our purpose here merely to introduce them by name, and make a running record of achievements up to the present year. To complete the list given must be added a few other names, who bring the roll up to our own immediate times.

Chief among these were the following: Sir George Nares, an English explorer, who followed the American route in 1876 and reached latitude 83 degrees 20 minutes, the highest north of his time. This was done by laying up his vessel in winter quarters and sledging over the frozen waters north of Greenland. Then followed the Austrian Payer, the discoverer of the Franz Josef Islands; Nordenskiöld, who traversed the Northeast Passage; Andrée, the unfortunate, who perished in an attempt to reach the Pole in a balloon; Nansen, the Norwegian explorer, who let his ship be frozen in the ice of the Siberian seas and sledged to latitude 86 degrees 14 minutes, a new "highest north." In 1900 came an Italian explorer of royal descent, the Duke of the Abruzzi, who sent a sledge expedition northward from the Franz Josef Islands and made a record of 86 degrees 34 minutes, twenty geographical miles higher than Nansen. The last two whom we shall name here were Norwegians, Captain Sverdrup, who remained for years in the far north and discovered new islands west of Greenland, and Captain Amundsen, who completed the work of McClure in discovering the Northwest Passage, and surpassed him by taking his ship through that long-sought passage. The feats of all these adventurers will be given in detail in later chapters.

While the latter of those named were doing their work, the two with whom we are specially concerned, Robert E. Peary and Frederick A. Cook, were engaged in their pioneer Arctic adventures. Peary had explored the inland ice-cap of Greenland, east of Disco Bay, in 1886, and in 1892 crossed the north of that island to Independence Bay, in latitude 81 degrees 31 minutes north. He made a second voyage in 1893-95, in 1897 brought back an immense meteorite discovered at Cape York, Greenland, and in 1898 went north and devoted a number of years in an effort to reach the Pole by the aid of dogs and sledges. On this occasion he reached latitude 84 degrees 17 minutes, and in his next expedition, 1905-6, surpassed all previous records by his "highest north" of 87 degrees 6 minutes. His final expedition in 1908-9 led him to the Pole itself in April of the latter year.

Dr. Frederick A. Cook has a record of polar adventure almost as long as that of Commander Peary. He went north first as surgeon of Peary's expedition of 1891, gaining much experience in sledging work. A few years later he was made surgeon of the Belgian Antarctic expedition, in which he added materially to his knowledge of the realms of ice. He had previously gone to Greenland as the leader of the unlucky "Miranda" expedition, and subsequently he climbed the difficult slopes of Mt. McKinley, the highest mountain not only of Alaska, but of America. In 1907 he went north again, and in 1909 the world received from him the startling announcement above mentioned.

We may complete this résumé by briefly noting down the course of south polar discovery. Comparatively little was done in this field prior to the period 1838-40, when three expeditions were sent to the Antarctic, a French, an American and a British. Of these, the American discovered the seemingly continental stretch of Wilkes Land and the British reached Victoria Land and sighted the volcanoes Erebus and Terror.

For over fifty years afterwards this region was neglected. Then Antarctic exploration was resumed and became active. A Belgian expedition, that on which Dr. Cook went as surgeon, was despatched in 1897, and had the severe experience of drifting about

JOHN R. BRADLEY IN THE ARCTIC REGIONS

John R. Bradley, the friend and backer of Dr. Frederick A. Cook, is shown in this picture reclining behind an Eskimo companion, and was thus photographed by Dr. Cook, or a member of the party, on the Cook-Bradley Polar Expedition of 1907-1909.

BEAR KILLED BY BRADLEY-COOK PARTY

John R. Bradley is here shown on the deck of his vessel, which carried him and Dr. Cook to Greenland on their famous expedition.

BRINGING A WALRUS ASHORE

The monster shown in the picture between the group of men is being hauled on the ice floe with a tackle after it had been harpooned in open water. The inflated skin seen in the foreground was used as a buoy attached to the end of the harpoon line in order that the hunters might follow their prey's progress.

HAULING A WALRUS ABOARD

The ship's crew is here seen hoisting a dead walrus on to the deck of the "J. R. Bradley" while on the Cook-Bradley Expedition.

for an entire year frozen in the ice. Three expeditions, German, Swedish and British, were sent south in 1901, of which the Swedish had a very severe experience, while the British, under Captain Robert E. Scott, made a sledge trip over the ice to latitude 82 degrees 17 minutes south, 250 miles nearer the Pole than had before been reached.

With Scott's party was Lieutenant Shackleton, of the British Navy, who went again in 1907 and had the remarkable good fortune of reaching, in January, 1909, a point 111 miles from the South Pole. Instead of a sea as in the north, he found here a continental extent of land, the Pole being situated on a plateau 10,000 to 11,000 feet high. His signal success gave such impetus to the spirit of south polar research in England that Captain Scott began preparations for a second venture, proposing to take with him Manchurian ponies, Arctic dogs and a motor car, as Shackleton had done, with a fixed determination of planting the British flag on the Pole, if possible. He is now actively engaged in preparations for this expedition.

Such is a preliminary statement of the leading events in polar research. As may be seen, the year 1909 ranks high in the record, the triumph of Peary and Shackleton being made in that year, and also the announcement of Cook's prior success. It is of great interest to be able to state that man's conquest of the air made its greatest progress in the same year, since it saw Count Zeppelin's phenomenal voyage in an air-ship of over eight hundred miles, and Bleriot's striking feat of crossing the English Channel in an aeroplane, which latter flying machine broke all previous records in the same year.

With this brief digest of the progress of polar discovery, as preliminary to the full treatment that follows, we may return to the question already asked: What does it all signify? Of what use or utility is it? Shall we answer this insistent question again, using Dr. Franklin's reply to a somewhat similar question: "Of what use is a baby?"

The utility of polar research needs to be considered from two points of view, that of its benefit to mankind from the economic status, and that of its intellectual significance, its usefulness in extending the boundaries of human knowledge. Before the result was achieved, we were ignorant what the advantage might be in either of these cases. When Alaska was purchased from Russia for a few millions of dollars, there were many who looked on the transaction as a sheer waste of the public money. But the baby has grown since then, and it has not done growing since. No one can venture to say how many hundreds of millions of dollars Alaska may yet be worth.

As regards the North Pole area, no one knew what might be found there. Shackleton has found veins of coal near the South Pole; for all that any one could say, land containing veins of gold or diamonds might be found at the North Pole. Though this was improbable, it was not certain, and though the event has proved that no land exists there, this could not be known until the Pole was actually reached. Dr. Cook tells us that he found a large new island on the route to the Pole; who knows of what value this may prove? Here is what Evelyn B. Baldwin, commander of the Baldwin-Ziegler expedition to the Arctic realm, says of the possible output in wealth of the polar lands:

"Up on one of the lonely shores of Greenland huge deposits of cryolite are being mined by hardy Americans. At another point Dr. Chamberlin and I saw quartz formations with unmistakable signs of rich gold deposits. And there is a great cliff composed of almost solid iron ore of the finest quality which was discovered by Peary. It is but logical to suppose that in this region of extraordinary magnetic phenomena we should find ores and other minerals with unique properties and of exceptional purity.

"I, as well as other polar searchers, know that there are coal beds enough in the so-called frozen north to be of inestimable value to future generations, especially when the deposits in other parts of the globe have become exhausted. Many times have I encountered outcroppings upon the surface that would have meant an almost limitless fortune if they had been farther south.

"It is not at all improbable that where such resources abound we shall also find remarkable deposits of crystal formations. I do not think it is out of the range of possibilities that some day gems of various descriptions will be brought from the polar regions. It is true that under existing conditions the ice presents apparently insurmountable physical barriers. But just as I am convinced of the ultimate utility of the resources of the north, so am I convinced that after more scientific investigation we will discover how to utilize the extraordinary terrestrial magnetism or electricity and devise means to serve us in overcoming the apparent barrier that nature has seemingly provided."

Aside from the somewhat sordid view of the material benefits which the Arctic realm is likely to yield, lie the indubitable ones of its possible scientific and mental benefits. The extension of our knowledge of the earth's surface is not lightly to be contemned. Until man becomes acquainted with the full extent of the planet which has been bequeathed to him, knows its shape, its conditions, everything regarding it, he has not made full use of his inheritance. Around the North Pole lay a great unknown area. To-day it is known. That domain can be set aside as fenced in and done with so far as knowledge of its general conditions are concerned. This, in itself, is something worth gaining.

But next comes in the scientific value of the discovery, and it is not safe to decide as yet how great this may be. There are meteorological phenomena to be observed and studied; there are the movements of currents, the range of temperature, the possibly important electrical and magnetic conditions. No one knows what may be there of service to mankind, and until an exhaustive investigation has been made no one can know. We may close this consideration of the subject by repeating Dr. Franklin's question: "Of what use is a baby?"

CHAPTER II

Cook's Story of His Discovery of the North Pole

THE first announcement to the world by Dr. Frederick A. Cook that he had discovered the North Pole came like a lightning flash from a clear sky. If it had come from Commander Robert E. Peary, there would hardly have been a moment of surprise. Everyone knew that he had gone north splendidly equipped for a polar dash and with the benefit of many years of experience, and it was widely hoped and trusted that he would crown his present effort with success.

But from Dr. Cook the world at large was expecting nothing. It was known that he was somewhere in the North; lost apparently; a relief expedition for his rescue had been prepared and sent out. That the prize of the Pole, persistently sought for centuries, attempted by many well advertised and well equipped expeditions, the struggle for which had so far led chiefly to suffering and death, should be attained in this sudden and unexpected manner, by a man who had gone north apparently only on a hunting trip and to whom few besides his special friends gave a thought, was a matter to fill everyone with astonishment. Therefore when, on the 1st of September, 1909, from Lerwick, the capital of the Shetland Islands, there flashed over land and under sea this surprising telegram:

"Reached North Pole April 21, 1908. Discovered land far north. Return to Copenhagen by steamer 'Hans Egede.'
"FREDERICK COOK."

the world stood astounded as if it had received an electric shock and for the moment people fairly stopped breathing, so startled were they by the stupendous character of the unlooked-for news.

To his wife, wired to her former address in Brooklyn, came also a message, thus worded:

"LERWICK, Shetland Islands, September 1.
"MRS. FREDERICK A. COOK,
"No. 693 Bushwick Avenue, Brooklyn, N. Y.:
"Successful and well. Wire address to Copenhagen.
"FRED."

Simultaneous with these was the following despatch, sent to Copenhagen from an inspector of the Greenland government, who was on board the "Hans Egede":

"We have on board the American traveler Dr. Cook, who reached the North Pole April 21, 1908. Dr. Cook arrived at Upernavik in May of 1909 from Cape York. The Eskimos of Cape York confirm Dr. Cook's story of his journey."

These brief messages only whetted the public taste. What did it all mean? How did he succeed in this wonderful discovery where so many had failed? Who was this Frederick Cook? What had he done to make his word worthy of credence? What reason had any one to accept his astounding statement? Was the telegram a "fake," a falsehood manufactured to deceive the world?

Who Frederick Cook was soon appeared. His name and exploits were well known to geographers. For seventeen years he had been before the world, mainly in the work of polar research. In 1891 he had sailed with Lieutenant Peary in his first polar expedition. In 1893 he had gone north on the yacht "Leta," and in 1894 on the steamer "Miranda." These were but summer excursions, but he was learning the secrets of the North. In 1897 he had gone to the Antarctic region as surgeon of the Belgian expedition and for a year had remained in this vessel frozen in the heart of a heavy ice-pack, drifting two thousand miles over the Antarctic Sea. In 1903 he had made a vigorous attempt to ascend Mt. McKinley, the loftiest of American mountains, and in 1906 had tried again and succeeded.

Dr. Frederick A. Cook was evidently far from unknown. He was a man hardened in polar explorations and mountain climbing. Few living men had better fitted themselves to dare the perils of the North. Finally, in 1907, he had gone north again, had plunged into the depths of the polar mystery, and for two years had been lost in the white silence of the sea of ice. Where was he? No one knew. The feeling was widespread that he had perished. A relief expedition was prepared to search for him, with little hope of finding more than his frozen corpse. It was under such circumstances as this that the world received the news above given and stood stunned with surprise and admiration at the astounding tidings of the great event.

We propose to give here Dr. Cook's own story of the admirable feat he thus claimed to have accomplished, but these introductory remarks are of importance as indicating the significance of the story. Later in this work the reader will be able to acquaint himself with the details of the centuries of exploration of the Arctic region and search for the Pole. He will also find chapters descriptive of Dr. Cook's earlier career and of the beginning of the special expedition which was now announced to be crowned with such splendid success. He will be told how Dr. Cook had gone north from New York in what was expected to be merely a hunting expedition, the fact that it might end in a dash for the Pole being kept secret from the general public. He will be able to read how, with the financier of the expedition, Mr. John R. Bradley, a landing had been made at the Eskimo settlement at Etah, and Dr. Cook, finding conditions well suited for the purpose, announced to Mr. Bradley his intention to "try for the Pole."

Back went Bradley, leaving his late guest on shore with the Eskimos and with an ample equipment for the sledge journey he had in view, only one white man remaining with him. This was Rudolph

Copyright 1907 by Harper & Bros.,   Copyright 1907 by F. A. Cook.
From "To the Top of the Continent" published by Doubleday, Page & Co.

A REMARKABLE PHOTOGRAPH

This is the photograph which Dr. Frederick A. Cook brought back with him to show the world that he had placed the American Flag on Mt. McKinley in the western part of frozen Alaska, the highest peak on the American continent, 20,300 feet high.

DR. FREDERICK A. COOK IN ESKIMO COSTUME

Dr. Cook gave as the great secret of his success the fact that he made friends of the Eskimos and lived as they lived while in the Polar regions.

Copyright 1909 by Underwood & Underwood, N. Y.

THE LAST GLIMPSE OF PEARY

This view of "The Roosevelt" shows Peary's ship on her departure from Etah for the North Pole. No word was received from her gallant leader until September 5, 1909.

Franke, one of the Bradley crew, who aided him in his preliminary work, but did not go with him on his long journey.

On August 27, 1907, Mr. Bradley bade good-bye and wished good luck to his late companion and sailed away to the south. The first week after his departure was spent by Dr. Cook and Franke in building a house, aided by Eskimos. By the middle of September they had comfortable quarters built and then proceeded to lay in a stock of meat to last them through the long winter. The whole of the next month was devoted by Dr. Cook and Franke to hunting. At the beginning of the long Arctic night the temperature was between thirty and forty degrees below zero.

Notwithstanding the intense cold the ice was not always firm, according to Franke, and traveling was dangerous, especially in the morning and evening. Dr. Cook and Franke found a new way to prepare dog food, the secret of which Franke afterwards refused to disclose, but said Dr. Cook counted upon it giving him a big advantage over other explorers. Furs, clothing such as the Eskimos use, and harness for the dogs, were purchased by Dr. Cook on trips he made at great risk and personal danger to Inglefield Gulf and North Star Bay. The house they lived in during the winter of 1907-08 was built of boxes and consisted of one room, twelve feet square. In this room was done the carpentering, meat curing, baking, cooking, living and sleeping. It was also the reception hall for visiting Eskimos.

Ever since his first trip to the Arctic Dr. Cook had declared that the only way to reach the Pole was to make a start in the height of the Arctic winter, and thus get the advantage of a continuous ice passage. He also declared that compressed or tabloid foods were useless—that the only way to do was to live as the Eskimos do and eat their food. He had no faith whatever in balloons or other modern schemes for reaching the Pole, contending that the only effective method was by walking and hard work.

For years his fellow members of the Explorers' Club had been made familiar with his ideas on the subject, one of which was that it was useless to attempt to reach the Pole with several white men in the party; the fewer the white men the better the chances of success.

That he had faith in his own convictions was shown when he asked only for a single volunteer from the crew of Mr. Bradley's schooner. And he proved it again when he started on the perilous journey with Franke as his sole white companion.

On February 19, 1908, the start north was made. The first night was spent in three snow-houses on an ice-floe in Kane's Basin. Cape Sabine was reached late the following evening and the next day the party was stormbound. The next march brought the party to Rice Strait, ten miles northwest of Greely's memorable winter quarters of 1883-84. Finally Flagler Bay was reached. There the rigors of the march exhausted Franke, and on March 3, 1908, Dr. Cook, not wishing to be encumbered with a sick man, ordered him back to Annootok to watch the supplies.

It should be stated here that Mr. Bradley, on his return from the north brought with him the following letter to Mr. Herbert L. Bridgman, secretary of the Peary Club:

"I have hit upon a new route to the North Pole and will stay to try it. By way of Buchanan Bay and Ellesmere Land and northward through Nansen Strait over the Polar Sea, seems to be a very good route. There will be game to the eighty-third degree, and here are natives and dogs for the task. So here is for the Pole with the flag."

This was the first definite statement of Cook's intention, but it cannot be said that it aroused much expectation in men's minds. For a single adventurer, with no ship or base of supplies awaiting his return and with only a few Eskimo companions to make such an attempt, looked to the members of the club like "midsummer madness," and the stone which Cook had thrown in their midst started hardly a ripple of interest in the geographical waters.

DR. COOK AND HIS LITTLE DAUGHTER

This photograph was taken shortly before Dr. Cook left home in August, 1907, on his world-famous expedition with John R. Bradley, and shows him playing with his little daughter.

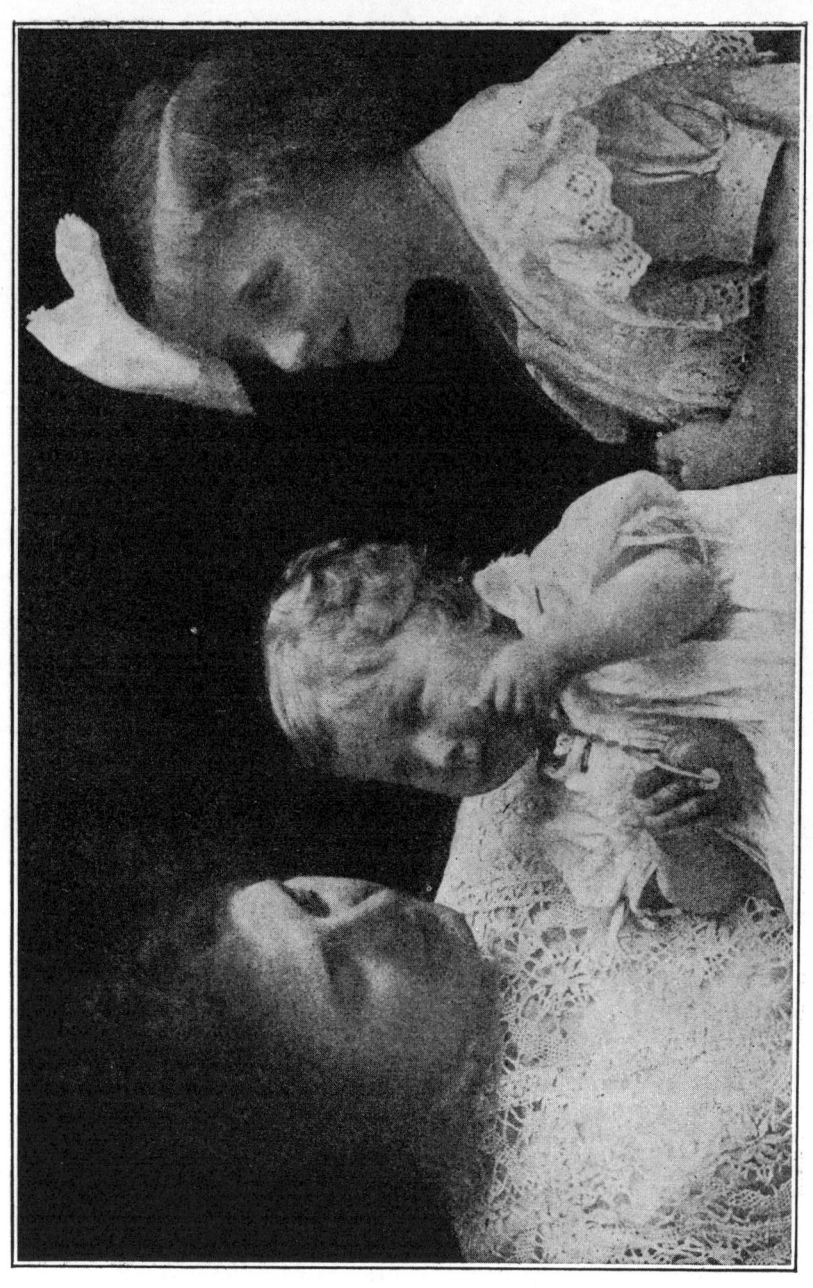

DR. COOK'S WIFE AND DAUGHTERS

Mrs. Cook's confidence in her husband's ultimate success, even after his friends had given him up for dead in the frozen fastnesses of the North, moved the sympathies of the entire world.

SUPPLIES ON THE "J. R. BRADLEY"

This photograph shows the deck of the schooner "J. R. Bradley," which her owner, Mr. John R. Bradley, said was equipped in the most complete and modern manner for the expedition to the North Pole. It proved to be the intention of the ostensibly simple hunting party to land Dr. Cook with an outfit for his hazardous journey. Mr. Bradley said that these provisions were deposited along the shore of Greenland for a distance of five miles in the haste of the skipper to get his vessel out to sea before the ice closed in upon her.

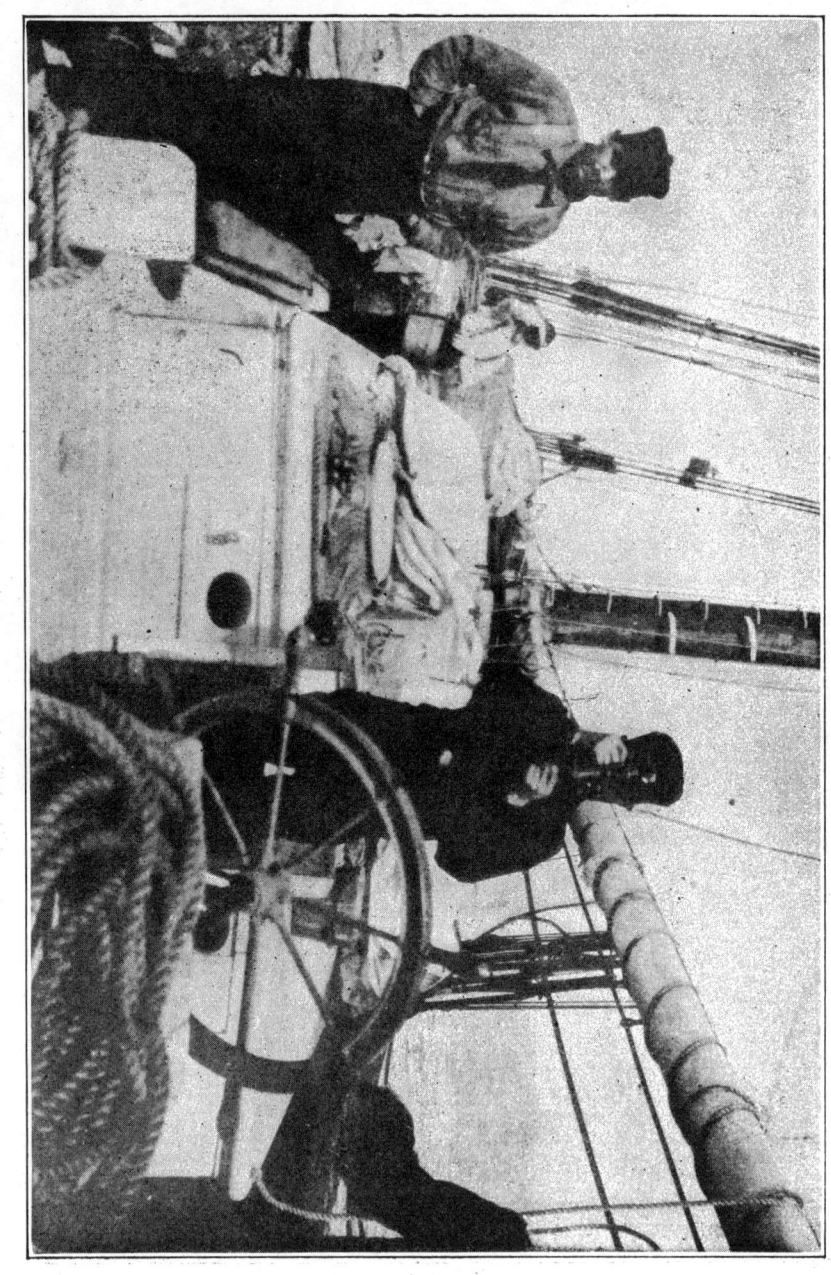

TAKING OBSERVATIONS WITH THE COOK-BRADLEY INSTRUMENTS

This photograph shows the master of the "J. R. Bradley," on which Dr. Cook and his outfit sailed to the extreme shores of Greenland before he was left there by his friend and backer, John R. Bradley, to make his dash for the Pole.

Cook also wrote to his wife under date of December 6, 1907, that part of the letter of public interest being as follows:

"I have this opportunity to send a letter to Upernavik by Ramussen during this month, and I must hasten to report our progress to the present. I have 100 dogs, and as many more as I desire, with fifteen of the best men of the tribe assembled here for the attack over the new route across Ellesmere Land, out by way of Nansen Sound and back by Kennedy Channel [the channel between Greenland and Ellesmere Land], thus using to good advantage the drift and the musk oxen, so abundant in Ellesmere Land.

"All of my equipment is ready and we hope to start for the goal late in January. With men and dogs well fed and under normal conditions, like my predecessors, I feel confident, as our equipment means perfection. When we return we will push southward at once to Cape York and Upernavik."

With these introductory pages we leave the stage to Cook himself, letting him give his narative of the journey. It is a plain, terse story, going little into details, but bearing the aspect of truth upon it. We fill it out here with illustrative comments and additions:

"After a prolonged fight with famine and frost, we have at last succeeded in reaching the North Pole. A new highway with an interesting strip of land has been found and big game haunts which will delight sportsmen and extend the Eskimo horizon. Land has been discovered on which rest the earth's northernmost rocks. A triangle of 30,000 square miles has been cut out of the terrestrial unknown.

"The expedition was the outcome of a summer cruise in the Arctic seas on the schooner 'Bradley,' which arrived at the limits of navigation in Smith Sound late in August, 1907. The expedition cost $50,000, of which my friend John R. Bradley gave about $30,000, the rest being my own money.

"Here conditions were found to launch a venture to the Pole. J. R. Bradley liberally supplied from his vessel suitable provisions for local use and my own equipment for emergencies served well for every purpose of Arctic travel. Many Eskimos had gathered on the Greenland shores at Annootok for the winter bear hunt, immense quantities of meat had been collected, and about the camp were plenty of strong dogs. The combination was lucky, for there was good material for equipment. When I reached Etah I really had no definite idea of striving to reach the North Pole that year, but there I found that everything was ready in the way of equipment, and so I decided to risk the adventure at once. This time we started out to reach the Pole and everything else was of a secondary consideration. It was not possible to carry certain apparatus, and it was impossible also to study the deep sea or take soundings. We carried all necessary simple instruments for astronomical observations and we were very lucky to obtain observations virtually every day. The positions noted must have been nearly correct. We had three chronometers, one watch, compasses and pedometers. All were carefully controlled by each other from time to time; the watch, however, got out of order. We had all the modern instruments which other explorers have had, including thermometers, barometers and sextants of the latest models. I think that all explorers will be satisfied with my data.

"All that was required was conveniently arranged for at a point only 700 miles from the boreal center. A house and workshop were built of packing boxes by willing hands, and this northernmost tribe of 250 people set themselves to the problem of devising a suitable outfit. Before the end of the long winter night we were ready for the enterprise and plans had matured to force a new route over Grinnell Land northward along its west coast out on to the Polar Sea. The campaign opened with a few scouting parties being sent over the American shores to explore the way and seek the game haunts, but their mission was only partly successful because of the storms.

"At sunrise of 1908 (February 19th), the main expedition

embarked on its voyage to the Pole. It consisted of eleven men and 103 dogs, drawing eleven heavily laden sledges. The expedition left the Greenland shore and pushed westward over the troubled ice of Smith Sound. As we pushed over the ice fields some dogs had to be killed to provide food for others, so that on one stage of the journey there were forty-eight left, and on the last stage only twenty-six, with one sledge and my two most faithful Eskimos. Other explorers have always done their expeditions with tremendous impedimenta and all sorts of luxuries. I journeyed with two Eskimos and lived as an Eskimo. After leaving land, with its animals and birds, I lived entirely on pemmican, dried meat and fat, thus abandoning everything which belongs to civilized life. It was with faint hope of seeing my friends again that I plunged into the land of eternal loneliness in winter, of endless night. It was always the same, one day like another, going onward to the North with nothing in sight upon the great white desert, with no sound, with no sun. The gloom of the long night was relieved only by a few hours of daylight. The chill of the winter was felt at its worst.

"As we crossed the heights of Ellesmere Sound to the Pacific slope the temperature sank to minus 83 Fahrenheit, the coldest of the journey. Several dogs were frozen and the men suffered severely, but we soon found the game trails, along which the way was easy. In this march we secured 101 musk oxen, seven bears and 335 hares. My favorite meat was musk ox. I dislike bear, seal, walrus and dog. I tired of fox, which the Eskimos like very much. For three months I lived on eider ducks and gulls alone. The musk ox has a hump back and low horns, so a lasso falls off. He charges everything that gets near him, so we formed a loop from ropes and he put his head in. It took us two months to learn that trick.

"We missed the depots which previously had been established, but we came accidentally upon one of Sverdrup's depots, where we found provisions and instruments in a most excellent state of preservation. Owing to the smallness of my expedition our requirements were not large. For the same reason we were able to proceed most quickly. We were working with a full equipment and on the preliminary work of 200 men, women and children. There seems to be an impression that I was not properly outfitted. If I started again I would do practically the same thing. Our motive force was men and dogs. The men were accustomed to the life, not amateurs dragged in for a year. These men's life is that of men who seek the Pole. No one who does not know the true Eskimo can appreciate his force. I regard the Eskimos as much more intelligent than we are when it comes to finding positions in the Arctic without instruments. They know where they have not been. They have a name for the Pole, the "Big Nail." They know the earth is round, and they appreciate the spirit in which Arctic expeditions are undertaken.

"Going northward I struck first a westerly course from Greenland and then moved northward. We pushed out into the Polar Sea from the southern point of Heiborg Island on March 18th. Six Eskimos returned from here. With four men and forty-six dogs moving supplies for eighty days, the crossing of the circumpolar pack was begun. Three days later two other Eskimos, forming the last supporting party, returned and the trials had been now reduced by the survival of the fittest. The furthest land north found by us is between the parallels of 84 and 85, and near the 102d meridian. There was no game observed beyond Heiborg Island. I saw a bear track in latitude 83 and surface life in the water algæ. The drift of the ice during the entire trip was northward. The wind was south and west.

"For the last part I was able to have a choice in picking the best men and best dogs until the final selection, which explains our rapid progress. Besides, travelers in the north are accustomed to man-drawn sleds and heavy loads, and are not used to expert drivers and quick dogs. We averaged a little less than fifteen miles a day. The ice gave an open route. The loads were light. Then again we did not wait until the middle of March, but set out in February, practically in the night. Our first hundred miles was through a game country. We had abundant fresh meat to feed the dogs. The men when we reached the Polar Sea were thoroughly accustomed to the life and were well fed on fresh meat instead of starting half starved for the final dash, as many do. This was the greatest element in our success. We traveled four hundred miles through a game country and reached the Polar Sea fat and in good trim."

The men who were sent back brought with them a letter addressed to Rudolph Francke, which is of some interest in this connection. It read as follows:

"March 17. The Polar Sea, north of C. Hubbard.

"DEAR RUDOLPH: Thus far it has gone very well, but the weather has been awful cold. We got no musk ox until we crossed Ellesmere Land, but since we have secured 102 musk ox, five bears and about 150 hares.

"The Eskimos will probably return slowly, for they like this land very well. I do not expect them to reach you until the middle of May. If we are lucky, we will take a short cut back and get to Annootok by the end of May.

"When the natives get back give them all one block of tobacco and nothing more till I get back, except those who go away. Picodlima and Egingwah will go away. Give them a knife and a hatchet each and anything else we can spare which they want. If you get a chance send to Igloodohoming, and also to the island off North Star, a box of biscuit and a can of alcohol.

"To the present we have seen nothing of Crocker Land, and I am taking a straight course for the Pole. The boys are doing well, and I have plenty of dogs. I hope to succeed. At any rate, I will make a desperate attempt.

"While I expect to get back to you by the end of May, still I wish you to be ready to go to Acponie, the island off North Star, where the whalers' steamers come, by the 15th of June, and if I am not back go home with the whalers. I think, however, we will be back.

"Gather all the blue fox skins you can. These must be our money on the return trip. If you can get a few bear skins take them, also narwhal and walrus tusks, but do not give too much for them.

"The dogs that come back that belong to us turn over to Ponicpa to feed and work. If Kudnu (the Dane) is still there, urge him to wait for our return either at Annootok or at North Star, for I am anxious to go to Upernavik at once on our return, and he can be of much use to us.

"There is likely to be much open water between you and Etah, so you had better send the trunk with narwhal tusks and all things for the return to Etah at least, if not further, as soon as you can.

"I have regretted many times that you are not with us, but at the moment it seemed best to send you back, and on the whole you are of more assistance to me at the house to guard and care for our things than here in the field in this awful cold and wind. I trust you are of the same opinion.

"So good-bye and now to the Pole.   Yours cordially,

"FREDERICK A. COOK."

Dr. Cook's narrative continues:

"The two best men and twenty-six dogs were picked for the effort. There before us in a line of 460 miles lay the goal. The first days provided long marches and we made encouraging progress. A big lead which separated the land from the ice of the central pack was crossed with little delay. The low temperature was persistent and the winds made life a torture. But, cooped up in our snow-houses, eating dried beef tallow and drinking hot tea, there were some animal comforts occasionally to be gained. We used a silk tent when the cold was too great, because it takes an hour and a half to build a snow-house. The tent was also more pleasant.

"For several days after the sight of known land was lost the overcast sky prevented an accurate determination of our positions. On March 30th the horizon was partly cleared and new land was discovered to the westward. Our observations gave our position as latitude 84.47, longitude 86.36. There was urgent need of rapid advance. Our main mission did not permit a detour for the purpose of exploring the coast. Here were seen the last signs of solid earth; beyond there was wothing stable to be seen. We advanced steadily over the monotony of moving sea-ice and now found ourselves beyond the range of all life—neither footprints of bears nor the blow-holes of seals were detected. Even the microscopic creatures of the deep were no longer under us. The maddening influence of the shifting desert of frost became almost unendurable in the daily routine. The surface of the pack offered less and less trouble and the weather improved, but there still remained the life-sapping wind which drove despair to its lowest recess. The extreme cold compelled physical action. Thus day after day our weary legs spread over big distances. Incidents and positions were recorded, but adventure was promptly forgotten in the next day's efforts.

"The night of April 7th was made notable by the swinging of the sun at midnight over the northern ice. Sunburns and frost bites now were recorded on the same day, but the double day's glitter infused quite an incentive into one's life of shivers. Our observation on April 6th placed the camp in latitude 86.36, longitude 94.2. In spite of what seemed long marches we had advanced but little over a hundred miles. Much of our work was lost in circuitous twists around troublesome pressure lines and high irregular fields. A very old ice drift, too, was driving eastward with sufficient force to give some anxiety. Although still equal to about fifteen miles daily, the extended marches and the long hours for traveling with which fortune favored us earlier were no longer possible. We were now about 200 miles from the Pole and sledge loads were reduced. One dog after another went into the stomachs of the hungry survivors until the teams were considerably diminished in number, but there seemed to remain a sufficient balance for man and beast to push along into the heart of the mystery to which we had set ourselves.

"I was always in the lead with the compass. We did not ride in the sledges. We had a team of thirteen dogs when the sledges were lightened, and the dogs were not all needed. The disabled dogs and the dogs that were not of much use made food for the other dogs. As I approached the Pole the Eskimos with me were utterly scared at the meteorological conditions.

"Then came April 21st. That was the great day. We looked for the sun. As soon as we got it I made careful observations. Great joy came over us. We were only sixteen miles from the desired spot. I said to myself: 'Bully for Frederick.' At our next observation we reached 89 degrees 59 minutes 46 seconds. The Pole was in sight. Then we went on. The last stretch was the easiest I ever made in my life, although I had still to make two observations, and the ice was very broken. But my spirits were high, and I shouted like a boy. The Eskimos looked at one another, surprised at my gayety. They did not share my joy. I felt that I ought to be there. I told Etukishook and Ahwelah, the accompanying Eskimos, that we had reached the 'Great Nail.'"

"I made my last observations and found that I was standing on the Pole. I was too tired really to feel any sensation. When at last I reached the North Pole and when every line was south and I stood on the summit of the world, I put up a sign that my journey was at an end and that the victory had been gained for my country. I planted the Stars and Stripes upon that spot which had been the goal of centuries of exploration, and which I was destined to reach at last. I did not leave the flag flying, but I buried one in a tube. We reached the Pole at seven o'clock in the morning. I had taken daily observations for a whole fortnight before arriving there. Everywhere we turned was south. With a single step we could pass from one side of the earth to the other; from midday to midnight. At last the flag floated to the breezes at the Pole. It was

April 21, 1908. The temperature was minus 38 Fahrenheit; barometer, 29.83; latitude, 90; as for the longitude, it was nothing; as it was but a word. I knew when I reached the Pole by astronomical observations. I am satisfied that any competent scientific explorer can see it from these observations. I am sure I was within the circle of the Pole where there was no north or east or west, but only south. I do not claim to have put my finger on the exact spot; I do not claim to have put my foot on it, but personally I think we have been at the spot. When the observations have been figured out again it is possible that there will be found slight errors and differences, but I am certain that a gunshot fired from where we were would have passed over the Pole.

"Although crazy with joy, our spirits began to undergo a feeling of weariness. Next day, after taking all our observations, a sentiment of intense solitude penetrated us while we looked at the horizon. Was it possible that this desolate region, without a patch of earth, had aroused the ambition of so many men for so many centuries? There was no ground, only an immensity of dazzling white snow, no living being, no point to break the frightful monotony. There was nothing to see but ice, ice, ice; no water, only ice. Concerning the ice around the Pole, so far as I could see, it was slightly more active there than at one or two degrees south. It drifted somewhat more to the south and east. Its general character was not very different from that at other places. There were more holes here than at the eighty-seventh degree, which shows there is more movement and drift here, but this and other observations I made afterwards when I got more settled. I stopped two days at the Pole, making many observations, and I assure you it wasn't easy to say good-bye to the spot. I should have stayed there longer had it not begun to freeze us in our idleness. The Eskimos were uneasy and the dogs howled fearfully.

"At the Pole I did not leave the usual examples of currency, but a tube, not a brass tube, containing a small silk flag and a very brief report of our trip to the Pole, the day and year it started and a record of the journey. I have brought back the most exact observations absolutely proving my statement. I have kept a diary throughout my entire expedition, in which I recorded the most minute details.

"On April 23d we started on our return. We were forced to take a more westerly route, and the first ten days I took observations daily and recorded them. I was unable to measure the depth of the sea, as I had not the necessary instruments. The coming back was much harder in every way. It took us only from February 19th to April 21st to reach the Pole. We were a year coming back, including the delay in summer. The daily distance covered on the northward trip was slightly less than fifteen miles; on the southward trip it was ten miles. The ice was broken up by pressure and traveling was far more difficult. There were open leads. We ran short of nothing going out, but on the return trip our provisions rapidly decreased in quantity, and the food for man and dog was reduced to a three-quarter ration, while the difficulties of the route increased until they became disheartening. After passing the eighty-fourth parallel there remained on our sleds scarcely enough food to reach our caches on Nansen Sound unless we averaged fifteen miles daily, but with our reduced strength and the hostile conditions we were hardly equal to ten miles daily.

"We took a straight course for the musk-ox lands, but after a twenty days' struggle through thick fog we found ourselves far down in Crown Prince Gustav Sea, with open water and impassable small ice as a barrier between us and Heiborg Island. The drift had carried us far out of our intended course. Food and fuel were now exhausted, but polar bears came along as life savers and for a time the dread of starvation left us. With them we went into Wellington Channel, hoping to be able to reach the whalers in Lancaster Sound, but we were soon stopped by failing food supplies and jammed small ice.

"Without game this short route to an early ship was no longer possible, and to satisfy the pangs of hunger we sought Jones Sound, where after a long run of hard adventures by boat and sled a cruel necessity forced us into winter quarters in September in Sparbo, without food, fuel, ammunition or winter clothing.

"With no dogs, no shelter and no guns our outlook was nearly hopeless. But fortune came our way, bows and arrows, harpoons, lances and other implements were made from the wood of our sleds. The musk ox and bear were taken with lance and knife, small game was secured with the bow and arrow and slingshot. Foxes were trapped in stone traps. The wolves and the seal were attacked and secured in our folding canvas boat, an underground den was built and the winter of 1908 and 1909 was passed with a taste of savage life, for we had not a morsel of civilized food, not even salt.

"At one point in our journey, when no animal life was visible, and for three days we had nothing to eat, fortune came to our aid. In a crevice of the ice we caught sight of several walruses. I had only a few cartridges left. I crept along the ice on my stomach, approaching the animals slowly so as not to scare them. I expended all my cartridges, and as a result got two of the walruses. Our lives were saved.

"During the expedition we ate all kinds of meat. I like musk ox best, but would eat bear or fox if the other was not available. Everything tastes good when one is starving. On one occasion a dead seal was greedily eaten. We brought ten dogs back with us, the others having been eaten by their companions. Those saved were given the freedom of their wolfish propensities and allowed to forage for themselves.

"On February 18th we left our winter cave. As the sun rose over the hills of North Devon, we started for Annootok, dragging musk-ox meat as food and molded tallow for fuel. Deep snow, bad ice, open water and continued storms made the return slow and arduous. We reached Annootok after a run of hard luck, April 5th. Here we were met by Mr. Whitney, only to find that the Peary men had misused our station with its equipment, under the protest of Mr. Whitney."

The Mr. Whitney above mentioned was a sportsman from New Haven, who had gone north on a hunting trip and made Annootok his headquarters, and was consequently on hand to meet and greet him on his return. As the story is told, Commander Peary had put Murphy, his boatswain, in charge of Cook's supplies at Annootok.

"The Commander gave Murphy instructions to use Cook's supplies first," says Whitney, "because he said they were improperly packed and would spoil earlier than Peary's. We built our box house at Annootok and used the Cook provisions. I read the instructions to Murphy and they were clear. He was not ordered to start out in search of Cook, who was believed to be somewhere in the region. If Dr. Cook came through, however, the instructions to Murphy were to let him have what supplies he wanted and to take a receipt for them. Dr. Cook was shown the instructions, and he was given what supplies he asked for."

It appears, however, that Murphy was a burly, hot-headed Newfoundlander, who did not know Cook and was not inclined to treat with courtesy the half-famished claimant of the goods in his charge. Whitney told his friends of many months of bickerings and quarrels with Murphy, of Murphy's bulldozing and bullying methods and of the final quarrel over Cook's stores and the Peary provisions at Etah in which the boatswain flared up with savage fury and seized an axe with what seemed a palpable desire to attack him. The cabin boy, Pritchard, it seems, was on Whitney's side and seized a gun as Whitney did. By threatening to shoot the fiery boatswain they succeeded in bringing about more amicable relations. In the end, as we are told, Murphy consented to shave the returned explorer, and for the few days that Cook remained more amicable conditions existed.

Shortly afterwards Dr. Cook left Annootok and made his way southward to Upernavik, hoping to find there some means of transportation to Europe or America. He was received by the governor of Greenland in a somewhat peculiar manner. Here is Governor Kraul's report of the interview:

"It was in the middle of the night when natives came to my house crying that foreigners had arrived from the Far North. I was somewhat surprised, because I had not heard anything of a solitary man's northward trip. Nevertheless I rose from bed and called to the man, who was standing at a short distance from my house, 'Are you suffering from vermin?' Dr. Cook modestly replied, 'No, sir.' 'Then you can come in.'"

Dr. Cook entered the house, and Governor Kraul said: "For every reason it will be best for you to take a bath." Dr. Cook obeyed in silence, and after bathing, Kraul reports, "We talked together for more than half an hour before Dr. Cook, after having shown me his route on the map, in reply to my inquiry, 'Then you have been at the North Pole?' quietly said 'Yes, I have.'"

From Upernavik the "Hans Egede" took him as passenger and brought him to Copenhagen, his arrival preceded, as we are aware, by the world-awakening telegram from Lerwick.

It seems worth while here to supplement Dr. Cook's narrative with a few particulars given by him in response to the questions of interviewers, and covering interesting details of his momentous journey. Here is one such remark:

"A great fissure opened up behind us as we reached the Pole," he said, "and it seemed as if we were isolated from the world. My two Eskimos threw themselves at my feet, and, bursting into tears, refused to continue either one way or another, so paralyzed were they with fear. Nevertheless, I calmed them, and we resumed our journey.

"You ask my impression on reaching the Pole. Let me confess I was disappointed. Man is a child, dreaming of prodigies. I had reached the Pole, and now, at a moment when I should have been thrilled with pride and joy, I was invaded with a sudden fear of the dangers and sufferings of the return."

Asked about the food supply, he said:

"One should live on the country as long as possible, and to do this every advantage must be taken of the land route, where game may generally be found. When the land is left and the ice-clad sea is entered upon, pemmican, biscuits and tea are the main elements of subsistence. One pound of pemmican per day for man and dog will support life. Pemmican, properly prepared from dried raw beef, pounded into powder and mixed with tallow, carries more nutritive and heat-making powers for the same bulk than any other preparation of meat. It is packed in six-pound tins and these enclosed in wooden cases, convenient for handling.

He went on to say that he took no stimulant with him but tea, never using tobacco and using the undrinkable wood-alcohol for fuel. As regards tea, his story is rather surprising, as he states that he took only two pounds of it in his dash to the Pole, and did not use all that. Yet tea was made every day, each man being given two or three cups on each occasion. This made twelve or eighteen cups a day, all brewed out of two teaspoonfuls of tea. It was far from strong, but it served the purpose, making palatable the hot water which added so much to their bodily warmth.

No vegetable food was taken and no salt. In his opinion neither are necessary, as the Eskimos use neither salt nor vegetables, yet never suffer from scurvy. With pemmican no salt is needed, but when he got back to Greenland, as he says, he ate salt like sugar. Also they went with scarcely any medicine, and as for soap, only one cake was taken, and that was lost on the route. It was not wept for, as washing in the Arctic is pure misery.

Dr. Cook says further:

"In our journey we were almost always wet with ice water, and often had wet feet. We slept in damp situations, in wind-swept clouds, or wet snow, surrounded by conditions that should have caused colds, rheumatism and all kinds of cold-weather ills, yet our health was good throughout. Yet when we got back to civilization, with warm, dry beds to sleep in, good shelter, varied food and little exercise, there promptly appeared headaches, colds, tonsilitis, neuralgia and other such unwelcome visitations."

Dr. Cook was obliged to abandon his sledge twenty miles back from Annootok and to totter on with his two equally worn-out companions. It was sent for and brought in, where Whitney saw it and gave his testimony as to its condition. When asked if it looked as if it had been used in so hard a journey as that to the Pole, he replied:

"It looked as though it had been subjected to hard usage, and its appearance to my mind confirmed Dr. Cook's story of his experience. The sledge was badly cut up. Some of the wooden strips had been slivered for firewood, for the doctor had no other material for a fire. The base of the frame had been cut down for arrows or harpoons with which he and his Eskimos killed Arctic hare for food. The Eskimos had taken off the steel runners to make knives."

As Peary has said that no explorer could achieve the Pole unless he had one of the Peary design, Whitney was asked if there was any resemblance between the Cook and Peary sledges.

"No," he answered, "there was not. Dr. Cook's sledge was patterned after the type that Dr. Wilbur Grenfell uses in his work. Cook adapted the Grenfell sledge because, I suppose, he thought Grenfell's experience had been extensive enough to enable him to judge of the most effective pattern for rough work."

When told of the assertion of Hensen and others that Cook's two Eskimos were too young and inexperienced to have accompanied any navigator to the Pole, Whitney said:

"I employed both on my musk ox hunting trip and found them capable. They are bright young fellows and they were the best dog drivers and sledge handlers in my outfit. These two Eskimo boys that Dr. Cook had would get their sledges over the ice faster than any other drivers, pushing and lifting and jumping them."

"Were they intelligent?"

"Yes, very intelligent. I would not want any better Eskimos."

CHAPTER III

The Story of Peary's Great Exploit

IF the 1st of September, 1909, had been a great day in the history of polar research, the 6th of September was a greater one. The startling tidings which had so disturbed the world on the former date were repeated on the latter from another and, as many considered, a more trustworthy source, and the public pulse was set throbbing again at feverish speed.

On the latter day came over the wires from Indian Harbor, Labrador, via Cape Bay, Newfoundland, the following astounding despatch:

> "STARS AND STRIPES NAILED TO THE NORTH POLE.
> "PEARY."

What did it mean? Could it be correct? Was this fanciful way of expressing a great fact the one that would be chosen by a dignified naval officer like Robert E. Peary? Such were the questions that many asked. It was far from certain that this was not a hoax, the outcome of the sense of humor of some fantastic individual at Indian Harbor.

Men waited in suspense—hope mingled with doubt. They had not long to wait. An hour later a second message was received by Herbert L. Bridgman, Secretary of the Arctic Club of America. It was to the following effect:

> "Pole reached. 'Roosevelt' safe.
> "PEARY."

These startling and laconic messages, flashed from the coast of

Labrador to New York and thence to the four corners of the globe at the moment when Dr. Frederick A. Cook was being acclaimed by the crowned heads of Europe and by the world at large as the discoverer of the North Pole, added a remarkable chapter to the narrative of a grand achievement.

Bridgman's comment on the message settled the question of its source in the mind of the multitude. On seeing the text of the message, he exclaimed:

"That settles it without a doubt. Peary has reached the North Pole. He and I fixed upon a secret code in which he was to convey to me his success or failure. Translation of the code words in his dispatch means that he has at last achieved his greatest ambition.

"There were a lot of words in the code. Several began with the word 'sun,' and these were to indicate that he had been successful in his quest of the Pole.

"I have left my list of code words at Northampton, but I think that the word 'sunshine' was the code word we agreed upon for 'Pole reached. Roosevelt safe.' There were several words beginning with 'moon,' which were to signify that Commander Peary had not reached the Pole."

A second message to Mr. Bridgman read:

"Kindly rush following: Wire all principal home and foreign geographical societies of all nations, including Japan, Brazil, etc., that the North Pole was reached April 6th by Peary Arctic Club's expedition, under Commander Peary.   PEARY."

This was but the beginning of despatches from the returning explorer. Soon they began fairly to rain down the wire. To Henry F. Osborne, of the American Museum of Natural History, came the following:

"The Pole is ours. Am bringing large amount of material for museum.   PEARY."

Before the explorer left on his trip a year ago he had assured Mr. Osborn that if he reached the Pole he would come back with a sack full of curios that would probably make some interesting exhibits. Mr. Osborn cabled his thanks to Peary upon receiving the message, and despatches came to Peary from other sources, conveying the congratulations of foreign and American geographical societies and former polar explorers on the accomplishment of the great feat, including one from the International Polar Commission, signed by Cagni, Nordenskiöld and Lecointe, officials of the commission.

Going back a little, let us tell from its beginning the story of the final expedition of the persistent explorer, the claim of whose success followed so quickly that of Dr. Cook. When Commander Peary planned the trip with which we are here concerned he announced that he would remain in the ice until the Pole had been reached, even if it took the three years for which his ship was provisioned, to succeed. His experience on his former trips was such that he now felt sure of accomplishing the design to which so many years of his life had been devoted. With this in mind, he set out to raise the money necessary to equip the expedition.

He needed $50,000, and this he had considerable difficulty in obtaining. He put in all the money he had himself, and relied upon popular subscription and his friends to furnish the remainder. Zenas Crane, of Dalton, Mass., gave $10,000, and others contributed liberally. Even when he lacked half of the necessary amount Peary went ahead characteristically to get his ship in order, feeling sure that the money would come. It came, and when it did the explorer was all ready to weigh anchor and proceed north.

The ship, the "Roosevelt," which the Peary Arctic Club built for the explorer for his journey north in 1905, was completely overhauled. New engines and boilers were installed and many changes, suggested by the explorer's previous experience, carried out. The "Roosevelt" was first launched in Bucksport, Me., on March 23,

THE STORY OF PEARY'S GREAT EXPLOIT

1905. The designer was William E. Winant, of New York, who worked from Peary's own suggestions. She is 182 feet in length, with a beam of 35.5 feet, a depth of 16.3 feet, and a mean draught, with stores, of 17 feet. Her gross tonnage is 614 and her estimated displacement about 1,500 tons. She is a three-masted fore-and-aft schooner-rigged steamship. She was built entirely of white oak, with treble frames close together, double planked. Her walls are from 24 to 30 inches thick. The keel, 16 inches thick, is reinforced with false keels and keelson. Her heavy bow is backed by twelve feet of solid deadwood. Her stern, reinforced by iron, had a long overhang, to protect the rudder from the ice, but the rudder itself was so arranged that it could be lifted out of the water when jammed or entangled.

It had been Peary's purpose to set out in 1907, but the ship could not be got ready in time, so that it became necessary to defer the trip till 1908. This failure in his plans prevented the possibility of a very interesting event, which might have taken place if he had got off at the time originally intended. In that case his dash to the Pole would probably have been made in 1908, and the strange contingency might have happened of the two rival explorers, Cook and Peary, meeting at the end of the earth's axis. In such a possible case what else would have occurred? Would the bad blood which has since developed have manifested itself there, and the Pole have been the scene of a royal battle for its possession? Or would the rivals have consented to bury the hatchet with their records and drag back the coveted prize in friendly union? No one can say; but in such event, in any case, the present unhappy controversy could not have arisen.

At any rate, this interesting possibility was prevented by Peary's year's delay, it being on July 6, 1908, that the "Roosevelt," with a picked crew and thoroughly stocked for a three years' stay in the North, set sail from New York. The scientists on board were the following: Dr. John W. Goodsell, of New Kensington, Pa.; Professor Donald B. McMillan, of Worcester, Mass.; Professor George Borup, of Yale University; Professor Ross G. Marvin, of Yale University; Dr. John Scott, surgeon.

The scientific equipment which Commander Peary took with him on his voyage was said at the time to be the most complete ever taken to the polar regions. It consisted of all the instruments needed in meteorological, astronomical and tidal observations.

Forty guests of the Peary Arctic Club escorted the ship as far as City Island, and it then proceeded to Oyster Bay, where Mr. Peary had arranged to have President Roosevelt inspect the boat. Just before leaving Commander Peary discussed his journey with the newspaper men.

"I'll not promise anything before I start," he said, "except that I am going to put into it every bit of energy, moral, mental and physical, that I possess. I feel confident that in any case I shall carry the American flag further north than ever. Unless the unforeseen happens I shall plant the Stars and Stripes at the Pole. If conditions are no worse in the next season than they were during the last voyage I shall hope to accomplish the object of the expedition and return in about fifteen months—that is in October, 1909. I am prepared, however, for a stay of three years.

"The attainment of the North and South Poles by American expeditions would be worth to this country many times the few thousands expended just for the closer bond, the deeper patriotism resulting when every one of the hundred millions of us could say, 'The Stars and Stripes float at both ends of the earth's axis and the whole earth turns about them.'"

All the way to Oyster Bay the vessel got an ovation, and when it reached there President Roosevelt, his wife and family went on board and inspected it.

"Well, Peary, good-bye, and may you have the best of luck," said President Roosevelt as he gave the explorer's hand a hearty grasp.

"Thank you," responded Peary with a smile, "I never felt so confident of success in all these years as I do now."

The President expressed himself as being heartily pleased with everything and everybody about the ship, and shook hands with all the crew. Captain Bartlett, shaking hands with the President and bidding him farewell, said, "It's ninety or nothing; the North Pole or bust this time."

It is not necessary to describe the trip north other than to state that the "Erik," the convoy of the "Roosevelt," was injured by striking an iceberg when off Etah, which place the "Roosevelt" left on August 18th, with excellent prospects of making her way farther north. The "Erik" was repaired and set out on her return voyage.

On October 9th last Henry Johnson, an able seaman of the "Roosevelt," arrived in New York from Greenland, bringing the first oral news of the expedition. He returned because of an injury to his knee. He brought a letter from Peary to the Arctic Club, telling of the progress the ship had made, with photographs and other data. Johnson stated that the "Roosevelt" was hit by a hurricane off the coast of Greenland on July 29th. It opened the seams of the ship's bow to such an extent that several of the crew felt her to be practically unseaworthy for a rough voyage among icebergs. While she was being repaired at Etah, Johnson said, her leaky bow caused apprehension among some of the crew. When the "Erik" reached St. John's, however, her commander reported that she had left the "Roosevelt" in good shape.

At Etah, the northernmost Eskimo settlement, Peary obtained the necessary aid from these people, and before the "Roosevelt" steamed out of that harbor it had taken on board forty-nine Eskimos, men, women and children, 226 dogs and the meat of more than forty walrus. The trip north proceeded with comparative ease, with the ordinary obstructions from fog and broken ice, and Robeson Channel was navigated as far as Lady Franklin Bay without meeting either of these.

Farther north trouble began, heavy ice being met, the "Roosevelt" being driven ashore twice by the ice and somewhat injured. On September 2d they succeeded in getting past Cape Union, at which these troubles had occurred, and northward until Cape Sheridan was reached on the 5th. They were now through Robeson Channel and in the Polar Sea, at the northeast extremity of Grant Land, opposite Greenland, which here trends off to the east, while Grant Land trends to the west. Here the ship was put into winter quarters, at a point close to the position at which it had wintered three years before, and which was reached on the same day as on that occasion.

It had been Commander Peary's desire to winter at some point much farther west, to avoid the difficulties which had formerly imperilled his expedition. On that occasion he was greatly impeded by the rapid drift of the ice to the east, which a little retarded his progress north, and, worse still, carried him so far to the east on his return that he had to make his landing on the coast of North Greenland, many days' march from the "Roosevelt," his base of supplies, and put him in imminent danger of starvation. As it happened, however, the ice conditions obliged him to put the "Roosevelt" into nearly her old quarters of three years before.

Cape Columbia, a point on the northern coast of Grant Land at a considerable distance westward from Cape Sheridan, was now selected as the starting point of the northward trip, and after the work of landing stores and erecting a house and workshop had been completed, sledging trips westward were inaugurated for the purpose of conveying supplies to the chosen starting point. This continued from September 17th to November 5th, by which time a large store of supplies was collected at Cape Columbia, ready for the northward journey in the coming spring. Hunting parties were also kept busy and much game was brought in. Meanwhile the ice lifted the "Roosevelt," listing her eight or ten degrees to port, and all winter she remained with her decks at a considerable slant.

THE STORY OF PEARY'S GREAT EXPLOIT

The long winter months were broken somewhat by excursions for hunting and other purposes, and were not without their alleviations in the way of home pleasures. Christmas was especially celebrated and in a style all its own. Captain Bartlett thus tells us what they had for dinner:

"Well, we began with soup, oxtail soup, musk oxtail soup. Then we had a saddle of Cape Sheridan musk ox; beats planked steak all hollow. We wound up with Washington pudding, Washington pie, plum pudding, fruit, raisins and nuts."

Every man on the ship received a box of candy from Mrs. Peary, and there were Christmas boxes for every one. Captain "Bob" had a box which had been entrusted to the commander, while the commander's box had been in care of the skipper. Neither knew of the other's trust, proposed by a loving wife. Toddy, in not too liberal measure, tobacco or cigars, was there for every one.

After the feasting came the races, which had been arranged by Professor McMillan. There were races for men, women and children. There were races for women with children strapped to their backs, races for boys and girls and a tug of war. The course was laid on ice and lighted by lanterns, for the time was the middle of the Arctic night. The temperature was 20 degrees below zero.

Karkelleah, "Jimmy" in the vernacular, won the boys' race, Sigloo was first at the finish for men Eskimos, while Marvin won the 100-yard dash for the whites.

Lacumah, a sturdy married bride, with her first born upon her back, proved speediest in the married women class, and won first prize. This was a cake of scented soap. She had the choice of a kit containing thread, scissors and thimble and a frosted cake. To the surprise of all she chose the soap.

The final work of conveying supplies to Cape Columbia began on February 17th and continued until the 22d, and by the 27th everything was in order for the dash to the Pole, the stores all at hand, the sledges in best order, and the dogs in prime fitness for hard work, well fed and their harness in excellent shape.

Despite Peary's wish to start much farther west than on his former excursion, he seems to have been obliged to accept nearly the same starting point as before. But he may have overcome this by heading northwestward over the sea-ice until a considerably more westward longitude was reached before heading due north. The party which left the "Roosevelt" for the final journey consisted of seven white men, over fifty Eskimos, twenty-three sledges and one hundred and forty dogs.

The end of February arrived and the time for the final great dash was at hand. What might lie before them no one could tell. There might be wide leads, or stretches of open water, such as were encountered in former polar journeys, and long lines of ridged and jagged ice were sure to be encountered, which it would be necessary to climb over or cut pathways through. It was all a problem, as is always the case in Arctic travel. Fortunately for the explorers, on this occasion the ice conditions proved unusually favorable and remarkably rapid progress was made.

The plan adopted was to send forward successive detachments, following each other at fixed intervals, and each turning back after a certain northing was reached, Peary's own detachment being left for the final dash to the Pole. This plan was adhered to throughout, Bartlett taking the lead with the pioneer party on February 27th and the others following in due succession.

The dreaded troubles soon developed, several sledges being ruined by the rough ice in the first march, while open water soon added its quota to the difficulties. The worst of the open water leads was encountered on March 4th, this being almost a lake of dark, threatening water stretching far to east and west and holding the travelers unwilling captives for a full week. During this week the sun lifted its round, red face above the horizon, to the joy of the explorers, this being the first time they had seen it for more than five months.

During the weary waiting at the lead there was anxiety con-

THE STORY OF PEARY'S GREAT EXPLOIT

cerning the whereabouts of Marvin and Borup, who failed to come up at the expected time and who had with them the supply of alcohol and oil, indispensable in polar travel. It was three days after the lead was crossed before the missing men reached the camp, they having been delayed by misadventures. Their arrival with the oil and alcohol was, as may be imagined, warmly welcomed.

On March 14th Dr. Goodsell turned back, in accordance with the original plan, and McMillan, whose foot was badly frost-bitten, was sent back the next day. Thus it went on, day after day, the difficulties of traveling growing less as the distance to the Pole decreased. Borup was the second to turn back with a supporting party, leaving at latitude 85 degrees 23 minutes, while Marvin followed him on the backward track at 86 degrees 38 minutes, and Bartlett at the eighty-eighth parallel, two degrees from the Pole and higher north than man had ever before been. In each case the supporting party reinforced the supply of those still going forward

Shortly before Bartlett's departure the explorers passed through the one great danger of their journey, the ice suddenly opening so near their sleeping place as to put them in great peril, while two of their dog teams narrowly escaped being dragged into the water or crushed by grinding ice blocks. Rushing hastily from their igloos, the dogs were hitched to the sledges and their effects drawn at all speed to a safer place. All night and the next day the groaning ice continued to open and close, then the danger passed, all became fair sailing again, and the forward march was resumed.

After Bartlett's departure about one hundred and forty miles remained to be covered. Peary remained the only white man in the party. With him was his negro servant Henson and four of the Eskimos, the pick of the party, while the dogs taken with him were the best of the pack and the sledges all in good condition and well laden with all things needed. From this time forward all went well, the progress being great, as much as twenty-five miles in a day being covered. It was twilight all the way, the sun appearing above the horizon for only a short time each day.

As he neared the Pole, Peary declares, the going got better and better and the temperature rose. This is not surprising, for temperature, as one goes farther north, often rises considerably for a time and conditions are less severe on the body. This, however, cannot be depended upon, for without warning the thermometer will shoot downward again.

The Pole was finally attained on April 6th, and Peary's exultant words about his arrival at that goal make one's blood tingle as he reads them. He must have acted like a school boy in his delight. In his journal he wrote exultantly: "The Pole at last! The prize of three centuries, my dream and goal for thirty years; mine at last! I cannot bring myself to realize it." His movements after reaching the Pole, in going ten miles back of his camp and eight miles to the right of it, making observations all the time, were advisable and show his determination not to make any mistake about his discovery. It isn't likely that he could be certain that he stood on the exact center of the earth's axis, but by going off at various angles and using his sextant, he could come very near locating it.

What enjoyment it must have been for him to take photographs, as he says he did, at the earth's summit! For thirty hours, he states, he took observations, planted flags and studied the horizon. On the afternoon of the following day he set out on the return trip to Cape Columbia.

Matt Henson, who, as stated, formed one of the party, gives his story of the triumph in the following words:

"We arrived at the Pole just before noon on April 6th, the party consisting of the Commander, myself, four Eskimos, and thirty-six dogs, divided into two detachments equal in number and headed respectively by Commander Peary and myself. We had left the last supporting party at 87 degrees 53 minutes, where we separated from Captain Bartlett, who was photographed by the Commander. Captain Bartlett regretted that he did not have a British flag to erect on the ice at this spot, so that the photograph might show this as the farthest north to which the banner of England had been advanced. I kept a personal diary during this historic dash across the ice field.

"Our first task on reaching the Pole was to build two igloos, as the weather was hazy and prevented taking accurate observations to confirm the distance traveled from Cape Columbia. Having completed the snow-houses we had dinner, which included tea made on our alcohol stove, and then retired to rest, thus sleeping one night at the North Pole.

"The Arctic sun was shining when I awoke and found the Commander already up. There was only wind enough to blow out the small flags. The ensigns were hoisted toward noon from tent poles and tied with fish lines.

"We had figured out the distance pretty closely and did not go beyond the Pole. The flags were up about midday April 7th and were not moved until late that evening. The haze had cleared away early, but we wanted some hours to take observations. We made three close together.

"When we first raised the American flag its position was behind the igloos which, according to our initial observations, was the position of the Pole, but on taking subsequent observations the Stars and Stripes were moved and placed 150 yards west of the first position, the difference in the observations being due perhaps to the moving ice.

"When the flag was placed Commander Peary exclaimed in English:

" 'We will plant the Stars and Stripes at the North Pole.'

"In the native language, which I thoroughly understood, I proposed three cheers, which were given in the Eskimos' own tongue. Commander Peary shook hands all around, and we had a more liberal dinner than usual, each man eating as much as he pleased.

"The Eskimos danced about and showed great pleasure that the

Pole at last was reached. For years the Eskimos had been trying to reach that spot, but it was always with them 'tiquelgh,' which, translated, means, 'get so far and no closer.' They exclaimed in a chorus, 'Ting neigh tim ah ketisher,' meaning, 'We have got there at last.'"

The flags raised at the Pole, as stated by Commander Peary, were the following: The first flag to be thrown to the breeze was a silken American emblem presented to him by his wife fifteen years ago. He had carried this flag on every one of his expeditions to the North, leaving a piece of it at the highest point he attained. The last remnants were raised and left at the Pole.

He then raised the navy ensign, the flag of the Navy League, then the flag of the Delta Kappa Epsilon Fraternity, and finally a flag of peace. Tent poles and snow lances were used as flagstaffs, and when all had been raised the Commander took a number of photographs of the group.

After this ceremony Peary inclosed records of his trip and other documents and personal papers in a box, and buried this in the ice. The documents were placed in watertight coverings, and the box itself was watertight, so that it would float if the shifting or melting ice brought it to water. Of the solar eclipse which took place while he was at the Pole and which was visible from that point, he failed to get a good view, on account of clouds, the sun being much obscured.

This accomplished, the successful explorers set out on their southward route. At the start of the homeward journey Peary told his men that the marches were to be longer and sleep less. No time was to be lost in making needless observations, and the thing to do was to get back to Cape Columbia, away from their perilous position on treacherous ice. Back near the eighty-seventh parallel, he says, was a stretch, fifty miles wide, that made him very uneasy, for a prolonged easterly or westerly gale would make it an open sea.

It was just after leaving the Pole that he made his last sounding of the ocean depth. Five miles from the Pole he came across a deep crack in the ice and by chopping away part of the new surface ice that had recently formed, he was able to let down his lead and wire. For 1,500 fathoms it went down, and when the line was exhausted, with no bottom having been reached, he started to pull it up again. In doing this, the wire caught and was broken and the apparatus sank and was lost.

Three marches brought Peary to the igloos where Captain Bartlett had turned back. The last of the three was accomplished with a northerly gale blowing snow and ice in their faces. Nobody knows, who has not been there, what it means to travel under such conditions, with the temperature away below zero. It seems that one's blood would freeze solid.

Mile after mile Peary hurried toward Cape Columbia, more than four hundred miles away. Good fortune met him at every step, and, though he frequently encountered open leads, the new ice was sufficient to support his sledges. The face of the landscape had been much changed, however, since he passed over it before. Many of the igloos built by his supporting parties had vanished. This was probably due to the shifting ice-floes. The return, in fact, was made with remarkable ease and speed, the rate of progress being almost doubled. The old trail was visible throughout and they went back on their outward track, undisturbed by any eastward drift and heading straight for their starting point.

It must have been a joyful moment when, on April 23d, the tired Eskimos came in sight of Cape Columbia and danced about on the ice as though crazy with delight. In spite of their primitive intellects, Eskimos can speak forcibly and appropriately at times.

One cannot blame Peary and his men, after their reunion with the comrades who had parted from them at intervals on the trip, for spending the two days following their arrival at the cape in sleep. The reaction of both mind and muscle must have been overpowering.

It is interesting to note that he attributes his success in great measure to a new type of sledge, which, he says, reduced the work of both dog and driver, and a new type of camp cooler, which added to the comfort and sleep of the men. His account of the southward journey of the "Roosevelt" from Cape Sheridan is interesting, but many explorers have accomplished that trip, so there is no need to give any details of the homeward voyage, of which the world became apprised on September 6th, when the messages came speeding downward from Indian Harbor, Labrador, conveying the news of Commander Peary's signal success.

With all these tales of good fortune, there is one of ill fortune to relate, that of the unfortunate death of a prominent member of the expedition, Ross Marvin, who was drowned on his return journey. It is thus described in an extract from Dr. Goodsell's diary:

"Ross Marvin is gone, the Polar Sea has claimed him. The 'Roosevelt's' flag is flying at half-mast. Our hearts are sorrowful for the loss of a dear comrade. I had retired last evening and had not fallen asleep when I heard the cry 'The comatees (sledges) are coming.' Marvin was overdue several days and we were expecting him. Borup came to the door and said, 'Marvin is gone; he went through the ice.' Two Innuits (Eskimos) had started back with Marvin.

"Koodlooktoh related how Marvin had gone ahead in the morning with the comatees. Ross came to the big lead and attempted to cross. The thin ice gave way with him. The broken surface showed that he had made a gallant struggle to penetrate the thin ice to a firmer ice a few yards beyond.

"The icy water and the colder air together in a few minutes must have benumbed his hands and rendered all efforts unavailing. The Eskimos arrived too late. They observed the footsteps terminating at the edge of the broken lead, the back of a koolatah (Innuit jacket) showing above the surface of the water. The following morning the body disappeared. As is the Innuit's custom, a bag containing Marvin's clothing was left at the edge of the ice."

"Alas! poor Marvin!" was Peary's answer when questioned about him. He went on to say:

"All of my parties are composed of one leader, and four or five Eskimos. The leader has breakfast, then goes on ahead, leaving the Eskimos to pack and break camp. This is what Marvin did. He was several miles ahead of his sledges, when he came to a lead covered with young ice. Either he did not examine it carefully or was incautious, for when his Eskimos came up they found a great hole in the ice, in the center of which they saw Marvin supported by the air in the back of his kapeth, or blue fox coat. He had made a brave fight for his life. He had broken a big circle of ice, but the frigid cold soon chilled him, and his was one more life paid in tribute to the search for the Pole."

When the Eskimos discovered him in the water they placed all of his clothing behind the pool and then made haste back to the ship, where they reported his death to McMillan and Borup. They made all haste to the scene of the tragedy, but on their arrival the body had disappeared, nor was it discovered.

In answer to questions of newspaper correspondents concerning his trip, Peary gave the following information:

"What was it that specially favored you on this trip?" asked one.

"It was the wind principally, or rather the absence of it," Peary answered. "With no wind one is able to follow up the trail on the way back, and can return in half the time that it takes to go. Wind will shift the trail or fault it, as we say. This makes it necessary to break a new trail or lose time hunting for the old one. Without wind there is no waste of time on the return trip. The dogs and men feel better and the way is easy. They know they are going home, and they will go two miles with the Pole at the back to one while facing it. I make it a rule to travel north until two-thirds of my supplies are exhausted, knowing that I can return to my base of supplies in half the time."

"To what do you attribute your success?" was the next question. "Was it luck in having better conditions or was it that you were better equipped for the work?"

Commander Peary replied: "I expected that question. "It was a combination of both. The absence of strong, continued winds at right angles to my line of march helped me greatly. That was what always bothered me in former expeditions. Headwinds or winds from the south don't bother me a bit. Of course, the wind in your face makes bad sledging, but the cross-winds cause the ice to drift east or west and throw you out of your calculation. This time we had the wind dead ahead. That pressed the ice against the land which we had left and made good footing."

"How about your equipment?"

"It was far superior to what I have had in former expeditions," answered the explorer. "The sledges were of a new type, with special features which made the work easier."

"What were their special features?" he was asked.

"They were improvements similar to those which a yacht builder would develop in a yacht, after he had been building racing craft for ten years. The strain on the dogs was reduced, the sledges were stronger, less liable to breakage, and went over the ice with twenty to thirty per cent less resistance.

"You must understand that there is no riding in sledges when you go to hunting the Pole. If the man with the sledge is able to walk beside it, without any further work than the driving of the dogs, he considers himself lucky. The man with the sledge must bend over the handles, guiding it away from the rough places, lifting it by main strength over them sometimes, reducing the strain on the dogs or sledge wherever possible. He must have muscles of steel. He must be tireless. He must have a wind that does not give out. The nearest thing that I can think of to sledge driving is breaking up virgin soil behind a plow drawn by horses or oxen."

DR. COOK IN ARCTIC COSTUME ON SKIS

This picture shows the heavy furs which must be worn to keep out the terrible cold, and the Norwegian skis, or wooden strips twelve feet long and four inches wide, which are of great value in traveling over snow.

Photograph, Underwood & Underwood, N. Y.
DR. FREDERICK ALBERT COOK

Who reported on September 1, 1909, that he had reached the North Pole on April 21, 1908. Dr. Cook when shown this picture said he had not worn a beard for many years. The change in his appearance caused by privation in the Arctic is noticeable.

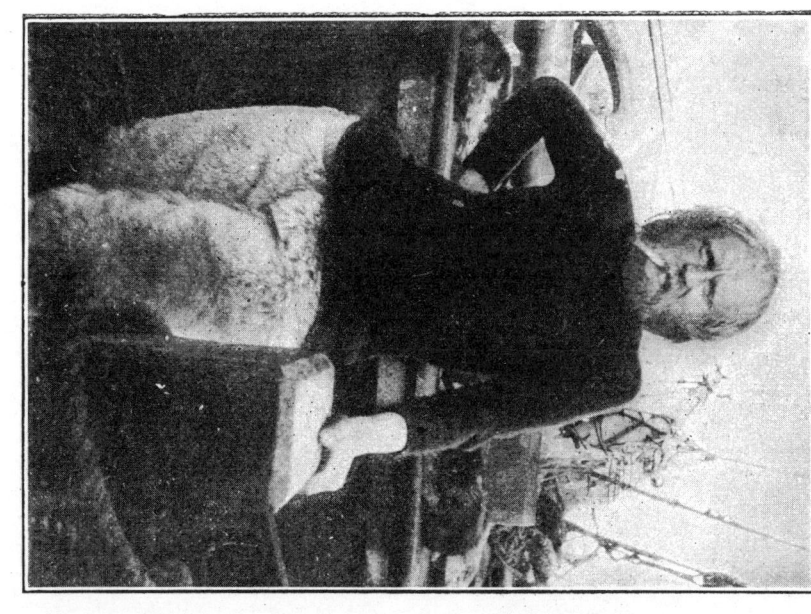

Photo by Paul Thompson, N. Y.
RUDOLF FRANCKE
Who said he was the last white man seen by Dr. Cook before he started for the Pole.

DR. FREDERICK A. COOK
As he appeared before his last Polar journey.

ESKIMOS AND THEIR SLEEPING DUGOUT

The mound of snow seen in the middle of this group is the doorway of the cave under the snow made by the Eskimos, and used by them for sleeping purposes in the most intense cold of the northern regions. Frequently ice and snow shut them in completely, but this method of keeping warm, curious as it may seem to us, has doubtless been tested by the use of centuries.

THE STORY OF PEARY'S GREAT EXPLOIT 65

"What training is necessary for the work?" somebody asked the Commander.

"One can train for Arctic exploration as one would train for a prize fight," was the reply. "The training consists of good habits, with sound, healthy body as a basis to work on. One must be sound of wind and limb, to use the horseman's phrase, and he must not be a quitter. That's the kind of training that finds the Pole."

Reverting to the program which he had followed, Commander Peary said:

"After leaving the ship, every five or six marches, depending on the distance covered, a supporting party would be turned back, the best Eskimos and sledges continuing forward with the strongest men. In going up each man has a loaded sledge, while the returning men have one sledge, the other three being broken up to repair the broken sledges or the ones that are discarded. This was done at the end of the seventh, twelfth, seventeenth, and twenty-second marches, a march, going up, consisting of twelve to sixteen hours, and returning eight to twelve hours.

"On the final dash from 87.57 degrees north latitude to 90 degrees. It took five men, five sledges, and forty dogs. The five sledges were the pick of twenty-five which had started from the ship, and these five had been practically rebuilt. We had the forty best dogs and the four best Eskimos, three of whom had been on previous expeditions with me. They knew the ropes; they knew how to handle the sledges, how to overcome open leads.

"Did the Eskimos express any emotion on reaching the Pole?" Commander Peary was asked.

"Not at that time," he replied, "but when we got back to the ice fringe of the Cape Columbia, when they knew there was no more leads to cross, no more broken ice to be fought, you would have thought they had all gone crazy."

"Well, how did you feel, Commander?" asked one interviewer. Commander Peary rose from his seat. He drew himself up to his full height. His voice was steady and solemn as he turned and faced the questioner.

"Can't you imagine how a man feels after spending twenty-three years of the best years of his life, who had given parts of his body, the body God gave him, in accomplishing his ambition, when he attains it?"

CHAPTER IV

Side-Lights on the Peary Expedition

WHILE Commander Peary was winning the great prize of his life, some of his companions were having their share of experiences and adventures, and some of these, as told by the parties concerned, were so full of spice and vital spirit that they will serve as illuminating side-lights upon Peary's own story. Especially bright and boyish is that given by young George Borup, a Yale professor and athlete, the photographer of the expedition. It is given in a letter written to his father and given by him to the press. Good wine needs no bush, and the young fellow's graphic account of his adventures may speak for itself.

"DEAR DAD: Gee whiz! I've had a wonderful trip, and wish in many ways we had been stuck up here for another year. The Commander has been just great to me from start to finish. He is kindness and consideration personified, and we fellows would do anything for him. After we got to Cape Sheridan last fall, as soon as the ice got strong enough to hold, the fall sledging of supplies began. I was out in the field for about a month, sledging about five hundred miles, but after one two-week trip came in with two heels, two big toes, and ball of one foot frost-bitten, which was damnably annoying, as it laid me up a month. Cause, inexperience. Was all right by the December moon, when I sledged some two hundred and twenty-five miles in ten days, taking provisions toward Cape Columbia. In the January moon I went with four Eskimos to a large glacier about one hundred miles from us, in the interior of the country. We went after deer, but didn't get any. However, hares were so thick you'd fall over them, and one day we struck a herd of a few millions, and annexed sixty. Not bad for one rifle and one shotgun with twenty shells. We cached them in an igloo till the next day, when we would come after them with the dogs and sledges.

"Now about this time of the year cold was no name for it, for on the bed platform of my igloo in the mountain one night it was minus 17 degrees Fahrenheit, with two two-burner, four-inch wick stoves going, and you can guess what it was like outside—nearly minus 50 degrees. Well, the next day we went after them, I mean the hares, with the sledges and dogs, but on the way back, though we had only six miles to go, a terrific wind with a blinding drift came up, so we could not see ten yards. The Eskimos and I after fighting for a couple of hours to find our igloo gave up and sought shelter behind our sledges. They had forgotten our snow knives and could not build an igloo, and for twenty-four hours we were hung up there. I didn't care do as they did, lie down and let the snow cover me up and go to sleep, for fear I'd freeze, so I had an unpleasant time until the wind died down enough for us to find our way back to our igloo, not half a mile away, which we did some twenty-four hours afterward. The way we then proceeded to pile in the grub would have made you sit up and take notice. We each ate a ten-pound hare, tea, pemmican, and biscuit. Luckily we came through uninjured, though I froze the ends of four or more fingers. We killed eighty-three hares this trip, average weight nine to ten pounds. In the February moon two Eskimos and I went hunting to Clement Markham Inlet for an eight-day trip, but saw nothing.

"I left the boat for the northern trip February 19th. There was enough twilight to see to travel eight hours a day by, though the sun did not come back till March 6th, the last time I saw it in the fall being October 8th. I left Cape Columbia in command of the advanced supporting party on February 28th, with the thermometer at minus 50 degrees. At that temperature whisky froze stiff, alcohol so cold you can drop a match in it and it will not light, your nose freezes every ten minutes unless you warm it up, and the ends of your fingers by this time are all excoriated from being repeatedly frost-bitten, etc.

"I went with the captain, who, with three men, was the trail picker. Three marches out I dumped off the load of all my party, and we headed for the land according to orders, some twenty-five miles distant in an air line. The Commander was to leave March 1st, and was to give me instructions on meeting the returning party what to bring back. Marvin also was to come back with me. A heavy wind from the east had gotten in the game the second day out, and faulted the trail, blowing the outside ice away to the west of the inside ice. The result was I missed Peary on my way to the land. After a good deal of lost time the original trail was finally found, and after doubling back some four miles in an unsuccessful attempt to overhaul him I lit out for Columbia because if I went any further after him I'd be unable to make land the same day and so lose valuable time. The march was a 'heller,' about eighteen hours long, with no time to eat; the sea ice had drifted from ten to fifteen miles west of where I had left the land ice, and the total distance we covered was not far from forty miles, fully one-half of which I ran.

"The next day a heavy wind prevented our starting, as we couldn't see the trail. This wind was only in evidence about five miles out to sea, so Marvin, who had been sent back as soon as the Commander had found I'd gone by, managed to reach Columbia late that day. The next day, March 5th, after being held up by a wind for five hours, we got under way, but where the sea ice and the land ice meet there was a stretch of open water about one hundred yards wide, extending in either direction as far as the eye could reach. Being shy both of airships, boats, and submarines, and as it was a bit too cold for swimming, there was nothing to do but wait for it to freeze over or be jammed together. This took place six days later. These six days were the longest and most hellish I ever want to see. It isn't the physical side of the game which is bad; it's the mental strain. We knew how vital it was to get out to Peary with our loads and with a lot of alcohol. The tins of fuel he had with him went to the bad, or threatened to, the second day out, and without hot tea twice a day, with these temperatures, I doubt if man could live. I know I couldn't. Besides, the Eskimos were losing their 'sand,' wanted to put for the boat, said we'd all die out at sea, etc., and we were afraid of a wholesale desertion.

"On the morning of the sixth day the lead closed, and two Eskimos, both afflicted with cold feet, came to land and said Peary had been held up four days by open water four marches out. We trail made by the captain and me eleven days before, over which the Commander had gone. A storm and the darkness forced us to halt got under way at once, and following their trail, found the original at the first encampment. Here one of my Eskimos went temporarily 'bughouse,' and, stripped to the waist, began running around outside, looking for trouble. We managed to get his clothes on after a while, and prevented him from getting frost-bitten. That day we made a forced march of twelve hours or more, and got to the third encampment.

"The next day we marched about eighteen hours and slept at the fifth encampment. It was very cold, minus 53 degrees, and I froze my left heel, where I had done it last fall. The husky who was bughouse the night before thawed it out on his stomach. At the fourth encampment we got a note from the Commander saying he had left that camp the previous morning, March 11th, after waiting six days. It said: 'It is vital that you overtake and give us fuel.'

"We were now only one march behind him. Marvin called for a volunteer to go ahead and tell the Commander we were behind. The best man, named Sigloo, who afterward went to the Pole with Peary, responded, and after four hours' sleep went on. That was going some. After forty miles or so he went with only five gallons of alcohol, dumping off his loads. The rest of us were dead tired after the march the day before, and so were the dogs. The result was we merely held our own and did not gain on the flying leader. A good rest, and the next day we decided to catch him or 'croak,' and we did without trouble, as he waited. I guess the finish of that Marathon race of four and a half days to catch the main party, which had a head start of more than forty miles, when the Commander came out to shake me by the hand, was the best day of my life.

"MacMillan, my roommate, went back from here with a badly frozen heel; the doctor, too. I went on five more marches to about 85 degrees 23 minutes, or about one hundred and thirty-six knots from the land, when I was sent back in command of the second supporting party. On reaching the shore, in spite of two cripples, I went a hundred miles west to lay down a cache, in the eventuality of the Commander being driven to the west. Then I headed for the ship, fair heel-and-toe walking every bit of the way, covering about eight hundred miles.

"I stayed on board seven days, when the remnants of the ill-fated third supporting party came in. As a rule the sledges come in at full speed, but these came in at a funeral gait, and Marvin nowhere to be seen. The first words of his two Eskimos were enough: 'Marvin gone—young ice.' The poor fellow was dead. The shock was pretty fierce, you bet. He was a dandy man, a fine leader, and devilish sandy. They came in Saturday at midnight.

"Now, MacMillan and Marvin were to have gone to the most northern point of Greenland to lay down a line of supplies in case the Commander hit that coast like he did last time. Well, Marvin being gone, I took his place, and after hurrying preparations, MacMillan, as cool, nervy, sandy and strong as they make 'em, and I left the 'Roosevelt' in thirty-six hours and reached Cape Morris Jesup, past Lockwood's furthest of 83 degrees 24 minutes, with ease. Here we stayed two weeks, 'Mac' going out to 84 degrees 15 minutes to sound, and I making tidal observations, according to orders. Here we lived high, killing forty-seven musk oxen in four hunts, and dogs and men had sirloin and tenderloin all the time. As none of us had had any fresh meat in three months, it was more than good. I got mixed up in one herd of sixteen, and took some good photos of them. Then we killed them all by gun. I beat all records, Duffy's included, when I got within ten feet of a big bull, held at bay by two dogs, to take his photo, and he charged the dogs, which happened to be on a line between us. I only hit the high spots for a hundred yards or so.

"Coming back we made what I believe is a world's record in sledge traveling. The last two days or so we were all more or less snow blind. Rested up one week, then went off on a hunting trip. Killed four musk oxen, 100 miles away, and brought back a calf on the sledge alive to the boat, only to have it die the next day. When we got down to Eskimo land we put in about four days walrus hunting. In all, about seventy-two were secured. Some very exciting scenes occurred. Once a bull walrus, when we had engaged a herd of fifty, came up alongside of me, got his tusks on the gunwale of the boat so close to me that, to hit him with my rifle, I had to let her go off at port arms, as, if I fired it from my shoulder, the muzzle would have been beyond his head. It was exciting, all right, to have his great, ugly face right alongside of me, when it would have been easier to smash him with my fist than gun.

"On another occasion a big bull dived and put a large hole in the bottom, which, owing to its being double, we couldn't repair, and one man had to be kept baling. The walrus came up again, and I hit him in the head, wounding him badly but not killing him. He stayed down twenty minutes, and while we were all looking for him, smash! rip! bang! he came up under the stern, nearly knocked the bo's'un overboard, put a hole you could put both fists through just above the water line, dived, came up just fifteen yards off, gave his fierce battle cry of 'Huk! Huk! Huk!' and charged us. I got my artillery in action, and sunk him for keeps before he could do any more. When we reached the 'Roosevelt' we were half full of water. He was a scrapper, and don't you forget it.

"The worst jar I ever had was when 'Mac' was shot. The bullet smashed through two partitions, missed one man's head by two feet, passed two feet over the mate, who was lying on his side on the partition, two feet over my head on the other side, and smashed poor 'Mac' all to hell. I heard the report in my sleep. Poor 'Mac,' saying: 'My God, he has got me,' jumped out of bed, too. I saw him hanging on to one arm while blood was everywhere. Quoth he: 'Gee! this is worse than being wakened by an alarm clock.' Maybe he isn't sandy. He is nearly well now, thank God."

The shooting here referred to came about in the following way: Peary had ordered one of the crew to clean a rifle that had been used in the walrus hunting a week before. MacMillan was asleep at the time in his bunk on the port side of the ship, two rooms removed from that in which the gun was being cleaned. He slept on his right side with his left arm thrown over his head.

In ejecting a loaded shell from the rifle the man cleaning it accidentally exploded the shell. The bullet passed through the pine partition a few inches over the head of the man who was sleeping in the next room, went on through the room and the further partition and struck MacMillan's left forearm, where it lay thrown across his face. It tore the flesh from the arm to the wrist, which it penetrated; thence it passed through his right shoulder and then through the finger of his left hand, which was clasping the shoulder.

When Dr. Goodsell examined MacMillan's wound he found that extraordinary luck had shielded the Worcester Academy professor. Not a bone was broken and no arteries were severed.

"Your letters, clipping, and rifle received from the 'Jeanie' August 23d. Many thanks. They were great. Also whaler's mail left by Adams, of the 'Morning Star,' two days later. It was bully of you to think of getting so much up to me, especially Mickleson and Amundsen, also letters from my friends."

The "Jeanie" here spoken of was the relief ship sent north for Cook, also to bring back the young sportsman, Whitney.

"I did most of the photograph work. The big camera was great, especially the finder, which, in taking photos of musk ox, etc., enables you to keep an eye on the brute, so as to be ready to make a quick getaway when he charges. A few yards start gained in this way is very useful in avoiding being caught in close contact with his horns.

"I broke through young ice several times, but got out all right. It wasn't very cold when I went in.

"Peary has been just great. This expedition from start to finish is a picnic compared to what sufferings most Arctic expeditions go through. We went in parlor cars, thanks to the Commander who has worked the Arctic ice problem out and down to a science. Instead of the inactivity of previous expeditions in the winter, we were all out, most of us going 500 to 600 miles. Thirty years ago a man venturing on an extended journey of several hundred miles would have been committing suicide. Nares, the leader of the English expedition of 1875-6, says that men can't face a wind in a temperature of minus 30 degrees, but we did that, and a darn sight lower, in the wind. He also says, 'Only for life or death must a man go out in the fearful cold of March.' We went out all winter, and the English didn't start from the boat till April 2d.

"Just one example of the advantage of dog power instead of man power. Beaumont, a man of indomitable energy, of the English expedition, went to his furthest on the Greenland coast at thirty marches, which Mac and I covered in spite of two short ones on account of smashed sledges. He and his men were dead at the end, but we were going at a canter.

"Greely, speaking of Lockwood and Brainard's work, says about as follows concerning an attempt to beat their mark furthest north, obtained on the Greenland coast, 'that only perfect ice conditions, indomitable energy of leader and men, would enable their record to be smashed.' They took a whole season to do it. We did it, coming back from the northern expedition with ridiculous ease.

Just a picnic from start to finish. This is not blowing my horn, but simply to state a few facts that will speak for themselves.

"These performances were due to the great system Peary has developed, to his breaking us in the best way so that when we started north in February Dr. 'Mac' and I, who had never been in the Arctic before, had stacked up against conditions many other expeditions would never dare face, and had sledged enough to make us veterans. Result, confidence in ourselves and equipment, and, what's more, as to the conditions likely to be met with.

"Another point, in a country where the English found no game they died of scurvy. Where Greely, Brainard and Lockwood, fine men as they were, could obtain no game, we, through the Eskimos, never were in want of fresh meat, and, unlike what you will find in most books, I don't imagine you will find in my diary or in those of the others, which are fairly voluminous, any evidence that I was conducting a clinic or a continual squeal on the cold.

"I can tell you this member of the class of 1908 has been up against some queer conditions, and I have learned many things since I saw you last. Possibly the queerest, but not the most uncomfortable, was when my Eskimo and I had run out of fuel after being hung up at Cape Fashaw Martin for four days by heavy winds. We had to beat in the teeth of a howling gale and drifts so bad the dogs could hardly be induced to face them, which nipped and froze our faces for twenty-five miles, when it was so cold we had to run practically the whole way to keep warm, but I could appreciate the humorous side of it.

"One thing is sure, this Arctic shows, as you have often told me when up against it good, and you are here a good deal of the time, there is nothing like going at everything with a grin and good-naturedly, like the Eskimos; and no matter how scared, as when I had an angry Eskimo, whom I had thrown, point his rifle at me and look as though he meant business, or when crossing ice which bends beneath you and the thermometer in the minus fifties, so if you break through, c'est fine—no matter how worried or put out, to keep that grin that won't come off there, and don't show a sign of fear, as the Eskimos are none too sandy anyhow, and it's up to you to furnish the ginger, steam, and sand to keep them jollied and care free no matter how you feel. GEORGE BORUP."

Of equal interest and of value in giving another and different phase of the northern experience is that of Professor MacMillan, as told on the deck of the "Roosevelt" to newspaper men while lying at Battle Harbor, Newfoundland. From the lips of this quiet-spoken, unemotional man from Massachusetts came tales the like of which are rarely told. He stood in the center of a group of correspondents on the grease-caked forward deck and as simply as he would recite the taking of a hazard or the toll of mallards in a shooting blind he told of finding relics of men who had given up their lives in pursuit of the aurora's end, and he read selections from the records dead men left behind them in the ice wilderness twenty-five years ago. The correspondents halted in their note-taking and tangled their memoranda because of the spell of his words.

"Hardships!" he said, in answer to a question, "why, yes, there were some; but they were forgotten each night after we had turned into snug igloos. The excitement of the whole thing far outweighed the dangers, and all in all, I don't believe you will find a man on the ship who realizes to-day that what we considered just a bully good time was really an event so important that you fellows chase us away up here to get the news of it. If they start to give us any demonstration in New York, we won't know how to take it. Of that I am certain."

The man who stood with his fur-clad head leaning against the mast and his hands jammed into his pockets found the correspondents importunate. They wanted all he had to tell. He shrugged his shoulders good-naturedly and began to speak of remarkable adventures in the light of commonplaces.

"I had to turn back at 85 degrees because I had frozen one of my feet pretty badly." Others had said that MacMillan kept up for days with his frozen foot before Peary himself ordered him back. "You see, we all wore grass between our deerskin socks and the soles of our kauiks or boots. Should that grass slip out and allow the soles of the feet to touch the boot insole itself the feet would surely freeze in cold weather. That's what happened to me. I had my foot frozen on March 15th, when the thermometer was down to 58 degrees below zero.

"So Peary ordered me dragged back to the ship on a sledge and left with me the command that when I got to the 'Roosevelt' I should go with Marvin on a geodetic survey and tidal measurement expedition to Cape Morris K. Jesup in North Greenland. But I had to take Borup instead of Marvin, because before we started the Eskimos had come to me to tell of Marvin's death. They hung their heads in the telling and pointed downward, repeating, 'Young ice, young ice.' We understood.

"One day before we left the 'Roosevelt' for Greenland Borup and I tried a little stunt. There was a ribbon of open water near the ship and we stripped and plunged in. It was on April 17th, I remember, and the thermometer stood at 29 degrees above. When we got out we found that the ice wasn't as cold at the water and we ran up and down on the ice sheet near the ship for about five minutes while the huskies yelled with laughter. They thought we were off our dot, first because we had taken a bath at all and then because of the manner of our taking it.

"On April 19th we left the ship for the trip across Grant Land and North Greenland to Cape Morris K. Jesup. We had six sledges and forty-eight dogs with four Eskimos who helped drive. We took provisions according to Peary's order to put in caches along the Greenland coast in case he might be carried thither on his return trip as he had been on his return from the 87 degrees 6 minutes mark in 1906."

Cape Morris K. Jesup, it is well to say, is the most northerly and nearly the most easterly point in that region, it being in the north of an island known as Peary Land, and the best place to leave an easterly food cache for the explorers, in case they were rapidly carried to the east, as in the former expedition. MacMillan continues:

"On April 23d we crossed Robeson Channel and we reached Hand Bay, in Hall Land, the next day. In four marches we made the distance that the Lockwood and Brainard expedition took twelve days to cover. We reached Peary's cairn at Cape Washington which he had erected in 1900 at 83 degrees 30 minutes, on May 4th, and we got to Cape Morris K. Jesup two days later. We had been following the route of the Lockwood-Brainard party up as far as DeLong fiord and one day we found directly in our path a linen cuff with the name 'Lockwood' pencilled on the face of it. It had been there ever since Lockwood himself had passed that way.

"It was on May 8th that Karko and Wee-Shah-Ok-Sie, two of the 'Roosevelt's' Eskimos, hurried up to us with a message from Peary."

MacMillan went to his bunk and returned with a worn and soiled sheet of paper bearing the "Roosevelt" letterhead. It read:

"APRIL 28, 1909.

"MY DEAR MACMILLAN:

"Arrived on board yesterday. Northern trip entirely satisfactory. There is no need of Greenland depots. Captain Bartlett came aboard the 24th. Concentrate all your energies on tidal observations and line soundings north from Cape Morris Jesup. Use intended supplies for me for this purpose.

"COMMANDER R. E. PEARY."

"You can imagine how happy that letter made me," MacMillan continued, "although it left so much unsaid. How successful had Peary's northern trip been? Did he mean that he had reached the

Pole? We hardly dared to believe it, although we had both left him with conditions favorable for the achievement.

"We returned from Cape Morris K. Jesup to the ship as quickly as we could after completing our observations.

"Oh, by the way, I haven't told you what I found at Fort Conger, have I?" ejaculated MacMillan.

The correspondents shook their heads.

"Well, you may find it interesting," MacMillan remarked as a prelude to his tale.

This did not belong to the expedition above described, but to one made in November, 1908, when the "Roosevelt" was in winter quarters at Fort Sheridan. He and Borup had started south on a hunting expedition. When ninety miles from the ship, in latitude 81 degrees 44 minutes, they had come on the base of the Greely expedition. Fort Conger it was then and is still called. Here it was that the expedition had established a base after being landed from the steamer "Proteus" in 1881, and it was this last bulwark of safety that Greely and his men abandoned in 1883 after vainly waiting for the return of the "Proteus." The relief ship had been crushed in the ice, and the consequent tragedy of slow starvation at Cape Sabine, the point reached by them in their retreat south, is common in the annals of Arctic exploration. The particulars of the Greely horror will be given in a later chapter.

The two hunters came upon the old stronghold of the Greely expedition in the middle of the Arctic night some time in January. The storehouse, with its twenty-seven years of snow blanketing, still stood as it had been left the day that the sorely stricken men of the "Proteus" had forsaken it to turn southward—just a monument to the lure of the northland, there alone in the mystery of a dead world.

MacMillan and Borup entered the place after cutting through the snowbanks blocking the door. They made a light and then began to examine the relics of men some of whom had afterwards died in the misery of Cape Sabine's shores, while others escaped death only by a mere hairbreadth.

One thing they found was an empty trunk with the name David L. Brainard on the cover. This MacMillan dragged out of the hut and used to protect himself while taking observations.

Then in carefully written pages they found General Greely's report of the food caches he had made throughout the vicinity of Lady Franklin Sound. It was all very methodically and carefully entered, an ironical testimony to the fruitlessness of man's precautions in the desolate ice waste.

In a chest they found General Greeley's dress uniform, brass buttons and gilt epaulets untarnished and the navy cloth unfretted by moths, the coat being in so good a state of preservation that he wore it. The dress uniforms that other men had carried north with them in their vanity reposed in other chests. There were also cuff links, scarf pins and the whatnots of a man's toilet.

Over in one corner was a school text-book, evidently a boy's book, which had seen much use. In a boyish hand on one flyleaf were written some words, and as McMillan now held the page open the correspondents copied:

"Lieutenant Fred Kislingbury.

"To my dear father from his affectionate son: May God be with you and return you safely to us.

"Harry Kislingbury."

Lieutenant Fred Kislingbury was one of the seventeen men who slowly starved to death at Cape Sabine. His body lay there under a cairn of rocks and the snow for many years. More recently it was brought home to his native city of Rochester, N. Y.

On an opposite leaf were the names of several students, evidently at Assumption College, Sandwich, Ontario, and the address presumably of Harry Kislingbury, which was Fort Custer, Montana.

Another of the dead lieutenant's books lay near by. It was a hymnal of temperance songs and in the flyleaf was the inscription:

"To Lieutenant Frederick Kislingbury, from his old friend and well wisher, the author, George W. Clarke, Detroit, Mich., May 18, 1881."

Between the pages of a magazine of the date of 1881 were developed plates that had belonged to George W. Rice, the official photographer of the Greely party. On the floor was a fugitive sheet of paper closely written. It was the dope sheet on all the best performances of the trotting horses in America in 1880.

MacMillan brought out from a bearskin wallet another folded sheet of foolscap and spread it on top of one of the sledges.

"This may interest you also," he said, and the correspondents craned their necks. There was a part of a humorous speech that a member of the party had prepared, possibly to enliven some holiday feast that was celebrated before the pinch of famine came—just two paragraphs and the formal opening, "Mr. Toastmaster."

"There are some fair friends somewhere, who doubtless would be pleased to be about our festal board to-night," were the words on the foolscap, "but the somewhat inclement weather probably has prevented their attending. I'm afraid the gentlemen assembled here to-night will have more than the usual post-prandial difficulty in returning to their homes, for the aurora borealis is confusing at best."

Borup picked up in the hut an ocarina, one of those wooden wind instruments that look like a sprouted sweet potato. The latitude of Fort Conger was cut into the wood.

There was much food in the hut, food which the Greely party had been forced to leave behind on the despairing march to the south. Hominy, coffee, tea, canned potatoes, canned rhubarb, bacon which Observer Ernest, long now in the New York Weather Bureau, had piled with his own hands, so he said; hard bread and sugar

—all these stores which had been denied to the twenty-five desperate men who wintered at Cape Sabine in 1883.

McMillan and Borup ate some of the food and took other parts with them when they left. It was as sweet and clean as the day it was placed there.

Other relics of former exploring expeditions these two from the "Roosevelt" found during the course of their long hunting trips. On Littleton Island, in frozen Smith Sound, they came across the remains of the frame house that Commander Hall, of the ship "Polaris," had erected at Thank God Harbor on his expedition of 1871. The Arctic winds had strewn most of the timbers over half the island, and nothing but some of the foundation posts remained. Near by were some brass fittings stamped "U. S. S. 'Polaris,' Washington Navy Yard, 1871."

Still another record of past incursions into the frozen silence fell to the hands of the "Roosevelt's" men. One day they came to the hut of an Eskimo, who called himself Jacob Schunah, away down a hundred miles and more south of the "Roosevelt," at Cape Sheridan. Asking for food, McMillan was surprised to have whale meat served on a real china plate. He turned the plate over when he had finished his meal and on the bottom was the single word "Gjoa," the name of the ship in which Roald Amundsen discovered a northwest passage to the Pacific in 1903.

"I offered the woman a cup in exchange for the plate, and she jumped at the chance swiftly, lest I change my mind. When she got the cup she laughed at me, thinking she had bested me in the bargain, but I would have been willing to give a hundred cups for that one bit of china.

"During our expeditions about Cape Sheridan we came upon the winter camp of the British party which went in search of the Pole in 1876 under Admiral Sir George Nares.

"We found the beach literally covered with empty coal bags. Several tons of coal and a great quantity of firewood was piled against the cliff, crockery and cartridges were scattered about, indicating a hasty departure. The cartridges were still good after thirty-three years, but I imagine they would have done little execution. They did not fit our guns, so we were unable to test them.

"While the party was quartered here they used a small push-cart to carry their wood and water from the hills. This cart was taken away, but the tracks of its wheels, though made many years ago, were as plain as if made yesterday. I made some photographs which show how well they have been preserved."

Professor McMillan in every case took to the ship all that was practical of the relics to be turned over to the Peary Arctic Club.

We may close with the following telegrams, which tell their own story. Taft evidently is not especially eager to annex the North Pole.

"William H. Taft, President of the United States: Have honor place North Pole your disposal.   "R. E. PEARY, U. S. N."

"Commander R. E. Peary: Thanks for your interesting and generous offer. I do not know exactly what I could do with it. I congratulate you sincerely on having achieved, after the greatest effort, the object of your trip, and I sincerely hope that your observations will contribute substantially to scientific knowledge. You have added luster to the name 'American.'
                                                    "WILLIAM H. TAFT."

CHAPTER V

Early Life and Experiences of Dr. Frederick A. Cook

ABOUT the year 1849 there came to America from Hamburg, Germany, as one of the Teutonic emigrants to this favored land, a physician who bore the name of Theodore Albert Koch. Landing in New York, he quickly made his way into the interior, having decided to locate himself in the frontier settlements and make his way upward with the growth of the country. Pushing forward over a region then thinly inhabited, he in time reached a village named Calicoon, now a station on the Erie Railroad, in Sullivan County, New York. Here he concluded to settle down, as one of the pioneer physicians of that wilderness-like region.

Calicoon is near the border-line of northwest Pennsylvania, a hundred and thirty-eight miles from New York City, and was then decidedly in the backwoods. At the date named the nearest point which the traveler could reach, either by boat or train, was Newburg, thirty miles away. Landing from the Hudson River boat, the newcomer to America traversed the woods, with two or three others, until he reached the selected place. Here he built a log cabin and entered upon his career as a country doctor. Ten miles further in the wilderness was the home of a family which had reached America ten years earlier, and in this family Dr. Koch found his future wife, Miss Magdelena Long. Their marriage took place three years after his arrival, and the log cabin was replaced by an ampler and more comfortable house.

The immigrant physician gathered a little property, comprising about fifteen acres of land, in the midst of which stood the family homestead. It still stands, dwelt in by one of his sons, being among the oldest houses in that part of the State. Here he thrived in a modest way, and here was born to him a family of four children, three sons and a daughter, the one with whom we are especially concerned, Frederick Albert Cook, being born in the Calicoon homestead on June 10, 1864. He therefore passed his forty-fifth birthday in June, 1909, somewhere in the frozen north, on his return from his great discovery of the North Pole. The name of Koch became Americanized into its present form of Cook during the Civil War, before the birth of the future explorer, in the following manner: His father joined the medical corps of the army, and through the mistake of a government clerk his name was entered on the medical roll as Cook. By this name he was afterwards known, though the other branches of the family hold to the original name.

Until he was six years of age young Cook's life was an easy one, and the family perhaps as prosperous and happy as any in that section of the State. The early death of the father did not reduce the family to poverty. The efforts of the mother to keep her small household together, and the products of their little farm, enabled them to live in some degree of comfort, the elder son, then twelve years of age, being a help to his mother in his care of the fatherless flock. Life in the Cook home went on with little change until 1878, when Frederick was fourteen years old.

During this period the frugal mother not only managed to provide for her small family, but prudently saw that their schooling was not neglected. About the time of his father's death, when he was nearly six years old, young Frederick was sent to school in the primitive schoolhouse at Hortonville, a short distance from Calicoon. His brothers went there also, though not for a long time during the year, the period of tuition in the old district schoolhouse lasting only four months annually. In those days, as soon as the farming season began, the school closed its doors. The boys could not be spared from work on the farm. But the youngster was ardent as a student and managed to make very satisfactory progress, standing, as we are told, always at the head of his class, and doubtless winning the warm encomiums of his teacher by his diligence and intelligence. It is said that he was especially interested in geographical studies and locations, and that as he grew older he gathered every book on this subject which he could obtain and studied their contents closely, never tiring of his pursuits in this direction. If this was the case it becomes apparent that the favorite inclinations of the man were already stirring in the soul of the boy, and a prophet might have predicted that this youthful geographer was destined to make a mark for himself in geographical research. It may be said, however, that he disclaims any such inclinations.

Yet the winning of an education was uphill work for him and his brothers, as anyone will know who is familiar with the school methods of that day, at least those of the frontier regions. The fine schoolhouses, the numerous books, the trained teachers, the detailed and well-arranged courses of study of the present day had not then come into existence, and the methods used were often crude and primitive in the extreme. Books were few, school accommodations miserably contracted, and teachers frequently ignorant and unfit to develop the minds of the young. Of system there was none, while discipline consisted in the frequent use of the birch, applied with or without cause, and so indiscriminately that the pupil who escaped at least one whipping a day felt that he had missed his just deserts. For the boys—and girls, too, for that matter—were apt to take pains to deserve the whippings by which the teacher sought to stimulate their budding intellects.

It must, of course, be admitted that all schools—even all frontier country schools—were not of this description, and it is quite possible that the little Hortonville district school was of a higher type. At any rate, young Cook seems to have obtained there the rudiments of an education and developed a thirst for mental advancement that stood him in good stead in his later years.

It was not only in his love for geographical study that the career of the man was outlined in the boy. A quiet, reticent, studious lad, he loved to get apart by himself and to explore alone solitary places. Adventure seemed to be the spice of his young life. At every opportunity he would go into the woods, or up the mountain sides—sometimes alone, sometimes is company with his brothers—always seeking some new and unknown place. Here, after losing himself in the wildwood as completely as possible, he would endeavor, and usually with success, to find his way back by observing the direction of the sun, and perhaps by studying other natural indications, such as the moss on trees and the various methods he had become familiar with by reading books of travel.

We are told that Daniel Boone, the greatest of American pioneer explorers, had similar habits when a boy, leaving home and living the life of an Indian in the deep forest, subsisting on game shot by himself and cooked by his camp-fire. While not up to this standard, young Frederick Cook is said to have manifested some of the same inclinations, those native to the born hunter and adventurer. What dreams came to him while thus tracing his way in Indian fashion through the forest, we are unable to say. Apparently he was giving way involuntarily to instincts native to him. An explorer in grain, the coming career of the man was prefigured in the favorite enjoyments of the boy, and while wandering thus alone far from human habitation, making his way homeward as the bird makes its way to its nest, or the bee to its hive, he may in fancy have been journeying in uninhabited wilds, over polar ice-fields, or up the slopes of great mountains, doing in waking vision what he was destined to do in reality in his later life.

Much the same as any other boy and in the same manner as his brothers, "Freddie" Cook, as he was then familiarly termed by all who knew him, worked about the small fifteen-acre farm that had been left to his family by the boy's father. Until he was fourteen years old young Cook lived the same kind of life day after day. He would depend upon no one where he felt that his own efforts would result in his obtaining what he sought.

So much was this the case that young Cook would not ride on a "store bought" sled when his companions went out for sport on the inclines covered with snow. Repeatedly, according to William L. Cook, his brother, the present-day conqueror of the Arctic, went off into the woods back of his home with an axe and cut down young trees. After he had carted them into the open country, where the homestead was situated, he went patiently to the labor of fashioning them into a "bunker." When he had finished, he had a sled of such quality that there was none in the country to equal it. He was in those days by no means a person of exceptional physical development. But what he lacked in strength was made up in courage that was backed by a wonderful amount of determination.

"I remember well how Fred and I engaged in boys' quarrels, and even in punching matches," says William Cook.

Yet all does not seem to have gone well with the family at Calicoon. Misfortune appears to have descended upon them and they were obliged to leave the homestead and seek a place elsewhere, where life would be easier. The oldest son, then a grown man, seems to have remained at the old home, but the mother, with her younger children, sought a new home in Port Jervis, in the adjoining Orange County.

"We were pretty nearly down and out," said William Cook, expressively, "when we went finally to our new home in Port Jervis." Those few words indicate a severe struggle against poverty.

Yet Frederick did not give up his school studies. He was now fourteen years of age, and did what work he could find to do before and after school hours, but, with steady determination to win an education, he succeeded in keeping up his studies at the Port Jervis high school during the two years that he lived there, standing high in his classes throughout. In 1880 a new move was made, this time to Brooklyn, New York, where the family lived until the death of

EARLY LIFE AND EXPERIENCES OF DR. COOK 89

the mother, shortly before her distinguished son made his dash for the Pole.

Let us now go forward to a later period in the boyhood life of our hero. It was evidently necessary for Mrs. Cook's sons to do their utmost for the support of the family, and Frederick and William both obtained employment in the produce house of George W. Ihrig, Fulton Market, New York. Here they became engaged in the sale of vegetables, working hard for small salaries. But Frederick, the younger of the two, had no thought of abandoning his efforts to gain an education. He had always been a silent, reflective, studious lad, apparently regarding a book as his best companion, and a youth of that disposition could not content himself to give up his studies. He soon learned that the high schools held evening sessions, for the benefit of those who could not attend during the day, and he lost no time in entering one of these, the Boys' High School of Brooklyn, or some similar institution.

Thus engaged, working hard at Fulton Market all day and studying hard and earnestly every evening, ambition awoke in his young soul and he grew eager to complete his education by a college course. To do so, it would be necessary to earn more money than was to be had from his market stand, and he looked around for some more profitable occupation.

What course of study he should pursue in college also occupied his mind, and he was not long in deciding upon medicine as the best choice of a profession. It was one that was in a sense hereditary in the family. His father had been a doctor, and so had been his grandfather, and the profession may have reached farther back. Thus it was that he decided upon the study of medicine and chose the Medical School of Columbia College as the best place to obtain the necessary instruction.

Two methods of making the necessary money successively presented themselves to the young student, and in both of these he engaged. He became interested in printing, and with some money he had saved bought a small hand-press and began the work of printing visiting cards for his friends and neighbors. There are doubtless some still living in Brooklyn and Williamsburg who will remember the young man who, back in the eighties, printed cards for them to be used in their social calls.

So closely did the young man apply himself to this work that very soon he found himself able to earn more money as a printer than he could hope for in Fulton Market, so he decided to give his time over entirely to the new business, and did so for almost a year before disposing of it. He finally sold it that he might invest his saved earnings and the capital realized by the sale of his printing business in a new field of industry.

As he looked about for a promising investment young Cook saw an opportunity to purchase a small milk route. He thought there were possibilities of a young man succeeding in this business if he applied himself. He purchased the route and the business quickly brought returns that permitted him to enter upon the college course desired.

Not much time, however, was free to him. It was necessary for the young collegian to begin work at one o'clock in the morning. He delivered his milk to his customers between that time and seven o'clock. Then he hurried to his Brooklyn home, and with his books under his arm reported for study at Columbia at nine o'clock. He remained in school until four o'clock in the afternoon. Between that time and one o'clock in the morning he slept. Lack of sleep was made up on Saturdays and Sundays, when there was no school. But there was work on those days as well as others. As may be seen, the opportunities for study outside the college were few, but whatever spare moments the young man had he spent in studying.

As time went on young Cook's close attention to his business brought such success that he found the work growing too much for him in connection with his college duties, and he invited his brother William to share the business with him on a partnership basis.

This accomplished, he continued his studies. But the demands of his business upon his time were such that it took him six years to complete his course at Columbia, he being a member of the class that graduated in 1890. He was then in his twenty-fifth year.

His business at that time was sufficiently profitable to justify him in seeking to make a home for himself, and in 1890, the year of his graduation, he married Miss Libbie Forbes, of Brooklyn. But, as fortune willed, this early married life, doubtless a happy one, was very brief, the young wife dying within a year after the wedding. As there were no children, the husband was free to accept any line of work that might open to him. His brother was conducting the milk business and he had not yet succeeded in building up a practice as a physician, so that he naturally looked around for some more promising employment.

At that time Lieutenant Robert E. Peary was making preparations for a polar expedition to north Greenland, and, about six months after he left college, the new-fledged doctor saw a newspaper statement that a surgeon was needed for the Arctic voyage. He wrote to Lieutenant Peary, offering himself as an applicant for this position, and for two months patiently awaited an answer. He had almost given up hope of receiving one when a telegram from Peary reached him, asking him to come to Philadelphia. An interview was held, the applicant proved satisfactory, and young Dr. Cook was engaged as surgeon in the North Greenland Arctic expedition.

As he tells us, he applied for this position simply to give him something to do, and not from any proclivity for Arctic work, in which he had previously taken no special interest. But the love of adventure must have been latent in him, for it became a passion with him after this expedition, and since that time there have been few years in which he has not been engaged in explorations.

A few words more must serve to complete our record of Dr. Cook's private life, it being with his career as an explorer that we are especially concerned. Between his various exploring trips he established himself as a physician in the Williamsburg section of Brooklyn, where his energy and ability won him a fair measure of success in his practice. In 1902, after his return from Greenland, he married again, his second wife being Mrs. Marion F. H. Hunt, the widow of a well-known and wealthy Philadelphia physician and surgeon. Mrs. Cook had at the time of her second marriage a child named Ruth, and it is stated that her acquaintance with Dr. Cook began in his being called in to prescribe for some sickness of the child. His family now includes a second daughter, Helen, who was four years old at the time of his great exploit.

His life after this period was one of intermittent practice as a physician and voyages to the Arctic and Antarctic seas, with two adventurous efforts at mountain climbing in Alaska. The details of these will be given later, and it need only be said here that his 1907 expedition to the north polar region was undertaken with no public knowledge that it was intended as other than a hunting excursion, he going as surgeon on an Arctic trip in search of big game conducted by John R. Bradley, a New York capitalist.

It has been stated that no one, not even his wife, knew that he had any thought at the time of making a dash for the Pole, but this statement is largely conjectural and probably has no foundation in fact. The preparations made by Mr. Bradley for the expedition indicated that something more than ordinary hunting was in view and certainly suggested that the North Pole was the big game at which Cook was aiming. Though this was not widely known in 1907, it certainly was in 1908, when Mr. Bradley returned, leaving his surgeon in the Arctic. That Cook had left Etah to cross Ellesmere Land was then well known, and that he had an attempt to reach the Pole in view had become a matter of common speculation. The details of this notable expedition will be given in a later chapter.

CHAPTER VI

Cook in the Antarctic and in Alaska

WHILE for years strenuous efforts were being made to break through the circle of mystery surrounding the North Pole, and place that unknown region in the category of the known, the study of the Antarctic realm remained long neglected. The most brilliant period in Antarctic research was that extending from 1838 to 1843, when three great national expeditions, under the command of Admiral D'Urville for France, Sir James Ross for England, and Captain Wilkes for the United States, sought that distant region. Captain Wilkes gave America pre-eminence in the results, by discovering a continental stretch of land, extending over many parallels of longitude. Though his results have been discredited and the importance of his discovery allowed to sink out of sight, recent research, especially that of Lieutenant Shackleton, has confirmed his statements, and Wilkes' Land has won its true place in Antarctic geography. Sir James Ross discovered active volcanoes in South Victoria Land, 12,000 feet in height, but a great wall of ice prevented him from reaching them.

For many years after this period the Antarctic region was practically deserted by explorers, and it was not until the final decade of the nineteenth century that active attention was again directed towards it. This is of special importance to us here, from the fact that Dr. Cook, fresh from his expedition to North Greenland with Lieutenant Peary, was one of the first of recent geographers to direct attention to the South. As he had aided in exploring the North, he burned with the desire to plunge into the secrets of the far South, and in 1894 proposed an expedition in that direction. He hoped that the experience gained by him in the art of resisting the extremities of Arctic temperature and in the use of sledges and Eskimo dogs, might enable him to reach a high southern latitude. Peary gave the highest testimonials to Cook's hardihood, boldness and trustworthiness in his report of the expedition of 1891-92, and the young aspirant for polar honors came into the field with an excellent record.

It may be said here that Dr. Cook had caught the Arctic fever strongly, and manifested the infection in various ways. Instead of settling down to the practice of his profession he lost no time in making his way to Greenland again, first going on a cruise northward in 1893, as commander of the yacht "Leta," and then, in 1894, organizing a voyage north in a small steamer named the "Miranda." This was intended simply as a summer trip, but the "Miranda" had a serious time in the realm of ice, her career ending by a journey to the bottom of the sea, to which watery goal the adventurers escaped accompanying her.

Leaving New York on July 7, 1894, with a party of enthusiastic young men, the first trouble of the party came shortly after leaving the harbor of St. John's, Newfoundland. They were but a day out when they found themselves in the midst of a long procession of icebergs, of all shapes and sizes. Beautiful, many of them, one large mass looked like a vast cathedral in ruins, with a stately, glittering tower rising above its huge bulk. Beautiful—but perilous; dangers in dozens lay hidden in those gleaming ice wonders.

Fog fell the next day, thick and dense, and then the peril developed. Without warning a great white mass loomed out of the fog before them, and before the engines could be reversed the ship struck it full and square. The iron prow buried itself fully seven feet in the face of the berg, the shock bringing a heap of crumbling fragments down upon the forward deck. Was the "Miranda" wounded unto death? This could not be told until the reversed engines drew her from the ice. Fortunately, she had struck a

COOK IN THE ANTARCTIC AND IN ALASKA

projecting portion of the berg above the water-line and the ship's bottom was safe. The hole torn in her bows was above the danger line and the adventurers breathed freely once more.

It became necessary, however, to return to St. John's and repair the ship, after which, on July 28th, her nose was turned northward again, the first sight of the Greenland coast being caught on August 3d. On August 7th they entered a snug little harbor where lay the Eskimo settlement of Sukker Toppen (Sugar Loaf), which was presided over by a Danish governor.

This was their farthest north. They visited the Eskimo, climbed a glacier, gathered specimens of various kinds, had some minor adventures, and then took ship again, hoisted anchor, and steamed for the harbor's mouth, headed north. Suddenly there came a tremendous crash and a frightful sound of ripping timber. The ship had struck with fearful force on some hidden reefs, which tore through her bottom as though it had been of paper. Only that the wound was in the ballast tank, the roof of which acted as a false bottom, the vessel would have gone to the ocean depths at once.

As it was, they got her to the shore again, and sent out scouts in search of relief, a Yankee fishing vessel, the "Rigel," being found, whose captain agreed to leave his work on the halibut grounds and tow the "Miranda" south. All but the captain and his crew were forced to crowd into very close quarters into the little craft, and off she went, towed by the "Miranda." On the second day out rough weather developed, and at midnight three shrieks from the steamer's whistle gave signal of distress. The rusty top of the ballast tank had given way; the water was oozing through; to keep her afloat was hopeless; and at day dawn her captain and crew were taken off and the towing rope thrown off. Away went the hapless "Miranda," her lights burning, her engines at work, soon vanishing in the mist and fog, to find a grave somewhere in the ocean depths. With her went all the worldly effects of the woe-begone explorers, their outfits, guns, ammunition, stores, collections, everything but the few necessaries they had brought back with them on board the schooner.

They got to port safely, dodging the ice-bergs and landing seventeen days later at Sydney, C. B., whence the wrecked party made its way back to New York. The only permanent result of this expedition was the Arctic Club, which was organized by the explorers on their way home, and has since been enlarged until it now numbers in its membership nearly all the Arctic explorers in America and many in Europe. At a later date, in 1903, Dr. Cook, Henry C. Walsh, the historian of the "Miranda" expedition, and others organized the Explorers' Club, of which the first president was General Greely, the second Dr. Cook, and the third Commander Peary.

In the year of this unlucky excursion, Dr. Cook proposed, as we have said, a more serious undertaking, a voyage to the Antarctic region, which, after long neglect, was once more attracting attention. While Cook was seeking to interest the public in this ambitious project, a Norwegian whaler, the "Antarctic," reached Cape Adare, in Victoria Land, at about 72 degrees south latitude, and on its return an interesting account of the voyage was published by C. E. Borchgrevinck, a young Norwegian, who was on the vessel and gave entertaining details of what he had seen. His account excited so much attention that a proposition was made to send him south again, at the head of a small party of scientists, the purpose being to land and seek a route inland by aid of the ski-runners of his country.

But before anything could be materialized in this direction an expedition was organized in Belgium, which in 1897 sailed southward in the "Belgica," under the command of Lieutenant de Gerlache. This expedition was sent out at the expense of the Belgian government and private subscribers, it being the only polar venture from that quarter. The "Belgica," formerly a whaler, was remodelled on the lines of Dr. Nansen's "Fram," being thus admirably fitted to bear the ice crushes which she was destined to endure. To the expense of the refitting and equipment the Belgian govern-

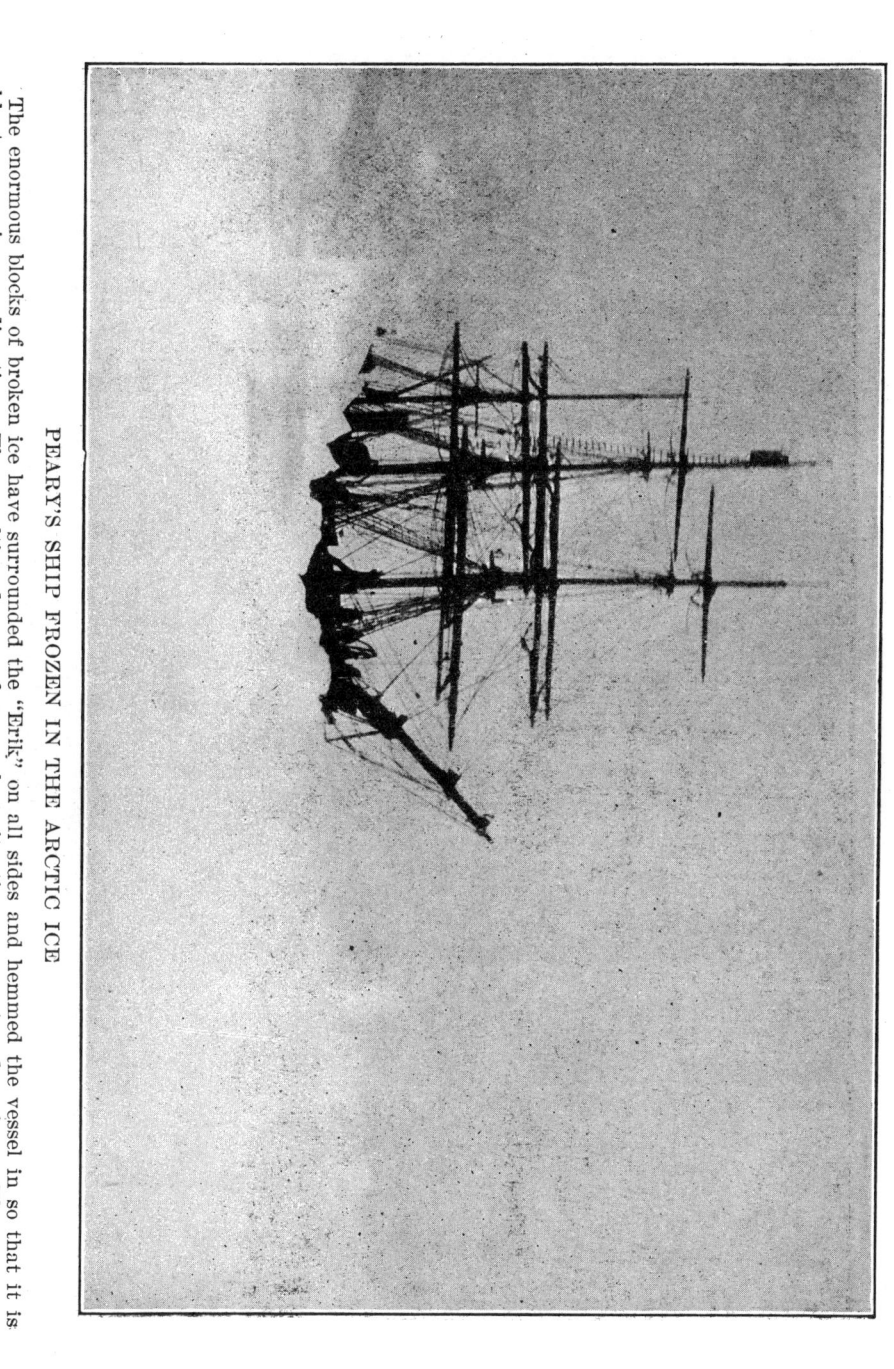

PEARY'S SHIP FROZEN IN THE ARCTIC ICE

The enormous blocks of broken ice have surrounded the "Erik" on all sides and hemmed the vessel in so that it is unable to move in any direction. The resulting dangers from such a situation are great and various. The vessel so beset may drift for months with the ice pack, and if the ice field is small the crushing and grinding of other floes may hurl great masses of ice around the vessel threatening to overwhelm her. When broken up by tidal or other action the pack may release the vessel for a time, only to come together again and crush her in its deadly clutch.

ONE OF PEARY'S DOG SLEDGES

A train of Eskimo dogs with the Arctic sledges in common use, and their driver and helpers, is here shown in the foreground, with two of Peary's Arctic vessels appearing moored to the ice floe. It was with these outfits that the intrepid explorer made marvelous speed over the frozen surface of the Polar ice on his journey to and from the Pole.

CHARGING AN ICEBERG

BREAKING THROUGH THE YOUNG ICE ON AN OPEN LEAD

MATT HENSON

Peary's faithful personal attendant, the only colored man who has ever been to the North Pole.

PROFESSOR ROSS G. MARVIN

The only man on Peary's Expedition whose life was lost. Marvin broke through thin ice and was drowned.

ment contributed $50,000. A captive balloon, intended to facilitate observations and surveys, was part of the equipment, and carrier pigeons were taken, one of these bringing back word from the "Belgica" in January, 1898.

In addition to the captain and crew, the "Belgica" bore a scientific corps, consisting of George Lecointe, of Belgium, astronomer and magnetician; Emile Danco, of Belgium, magnetician; Emile Racovitza, of Rumania, zoologist and botanist; Henryk Arctowski, of Russia, geologist; Autek Dobrovolski, of Russia, laboratory assistant, and Frederick A. Cook, of the United States, surgeon, anthropologist and photographer. The connection of the latter with the expedition came about in the following manner, as stated by himself:

"Two days before the 'Belgica' left Europe I received this cable: 'Could you join us at Montevideo?' Signed 'Gerlache.' To this I answered 'Yes.' It was followed by: 'Meet us at Rio, end of September.'

"I had only a few days to prepare myself and my outfit, but I was determined to go, and so it came about that in September I found myself on the way to meet my companions on the unfriendly bosom of the Atlantic, seasick and miserable from rough weather and tropic heat."

It was his record as surgeon on Peary's vessel that gained him this opportunity to join an Antarctic expedition. It had its defects, for the language of the scientific corps was French, of which he spoke not a word, and which he never succeeded in mastering. But time brought him into companionship with them, and especially with Raold Amundsen, mate of the "Belgica," and destined to win fame later by his conquest of the Northwest Passage.

Dr. Cook joined the expedition at Rio de Janeiro in October, 1897, gratified to become a member of the first Antarctic expedition fitted out with modern appliances and with a vessel built expressly for the work before it, and the first of any kind which had been sent to explore the southern realm of ice for over fifty years. The ship passed on to Montevideo and Punta Arenas, and thence westward through the Strait of Magellan and the Beagle Canal to Ush'ina, where the last coal was taken on. The expedition left civilization behind early in January, 1898.

The soundings made south of the Shetland Islands showed an unexpected depth of from 3,000 to 4,000 feet, while the greatest depth attained was 13,251 feet. For the greater part of the way the ocean bed seemed to be a plateau, over which the "Belgica" drifted to and fro, and where soundings showed the depth in places to be only about fourteen hundred feet. Just before reaching the Shetland Islands one of the sailors was lost overboard in a storm.

Passing out into the Pacific, the "Belgica" turned south and soon sighted Alexander Island and also Adelaide Island, which was found to be much larger than was supposed. Continuing to the south, the ship entered the pack ice, reaching 70 degrees of south latitude, and penetrating ninety miles into the floe, into which it was frozen in March, 1898. The party remained in the floe thirteen months, during a greater part of which time the ice was swept by terrific storms.

The Antarctic night came on in May and the "Belgica" was in darkness for seventy days. During that time every member of the party suffered from anæmia, due to the excessive humidity, the unceasing night, the lack of fresh food and continuous storms. It was at this time that Professor Danco, the magnetician, died, a loss which was greatly deplored by his scientific associates.

Dr. Cook ascribes great value to the meteorological observations made at this time. The chart of magnetic variations made indicated that the magnetic pole was probably two hundred miles east of the location made out by Sir James Ross in his expedition of 1839 to 1843. Cook found that the aspect of the ice field in the Antarctic differed considerably from that with which he was familiar in the Arctic region. The pack is somewhat heavier and the "pans" considerably smaller. The vessel was subjected to a severe crushing in the pack, in which only her stout frame saved her from destruction, and drifted about two thousand miles.

With the approach of summer the ice field began to open, but they remained frozen in during nearly the whole southern summer. Not until March, 1899, did they succeed in making their way out. They were obliged to cut a canal a mile in length through ice five feet thick. Every man, from commander to cook, worked at the saws, and dynamite was used to break up the blocks of ice and free the "Belgica."

The most important results of the expedition were a complete series of magnetic and meteorological observations, extended through a whole year within the Antarctic circle and the making of the first profile of the ocean's bed to the south of Cape Horn. A valuable collection of the fauna and flora of the Antarctic region was also obtained. About two hundred miles of new coast were discovered, and an ocean highway was found thirty miles broad, perfectly free for navigation during the summer months, passing from Bransfield Strait two hundred miles southwesterly through an unknown region to the Pacific. This highway was named from the ship, Belgica Strait. To the eastward of it was discovered a high continuous country, connecting with the land charted as Graham Land. This was named Danco Land, in honor of Professor Danco, the deceased member of the party.

Dr. Cook's assistance on this expedition was of great value, not only as a physician, but as a photographer and scientist, though his services as an anthropologist ceased after Terra del Fuego was left. During the long months of involuntary seclusion he was the life of the party, cheering up his companions time after time when their courage failed.

Returning to civilization in 1899 Dr. Cook settled down for a time to the practice of his profession, but the Arctic fever had taken hold of him too strongly to permit him to lose any opportunity to seek the seas of ice. In 1901 he sought the northern waters again as surgeon of the Peary auxiliary expedition on the "Eric," which took up new supplies and equipment for the indefatigable explorer.

A second short period of home life followed his return from this expedition, but his restless spirit would not let him remain long in civilized lands. There were new tracks of discovery to follow, new heights to climb, and while his route now did not lie towards the Pole, it tempted him to a field no less icy and little less difficult than that of polar travel, the severe and dangerous work of mountain climbing. Mount McKinley, in Alaska, looked upon as the highest peak in America, lured him to its conquest and he set out in 1903 to assail its frozen heights. The story of his feat, as told by him, is one full of adventurous interest and forms an important part of the record of Dr. Cook's career.

If it be asked where Mount McKinley is situated, it can only be answered by some brief consideration of the lofty mountain ranges of Alaska. Mount St. Elias, the summit of which was reached by the Duke of the Abruzzi not many years ago, long held precedence in height among the known mountains of this region. This was due to its nearness to the coast of the Alaskan Gulf and its towering elevation, its summit being visible for many miles at sea. This had given it a reputation as a great mountain landmark from early Russian times. In the range of which it forms part there are five or more peaks of over 16,000 feet in height, one of them surpassing Mount St. Elias. This is Mount Logan, which has an elevation of over 19,000 feet.

In the country to the west of the St. Elias range lies the Alaska range, extending northeasterly from the neighborhood of Cook Inlet on the south to the headwaters of the Tanana River on the north, a length of about two hundred and fifty miles. Far inland in this range rises the gigantic bulk of Mount McKinley, visible from the coast only in weather of unusual clearness. It has long been known under Indian and Russian names signifying "big mountain," the first white man to approach within a hundred miles of it being a gold prospector named W. A. Dickey, in 1895, who gave it its present name of Mount McKinley.

Attention being called by him to its great height, several efforts were made to approach it, the first to reach its base being two explorers, Alfred H. Brooks and D. L. Raeburn, in 1902. The growing conception of its vast mass and great altitude, estimated at over twenty thousand feet, gave inspiration to Dr. Cook, then looking about for "other worlds to conquer," and in 1903 he set out at the head of an expedition towards these seemingly loftiest of American peaks. Following the Susetna River inland from Cook Inlet and then taking the route followed by Brooks and Raeburn, the party reached the northern base of the mountain. Two attempts were made to scale its mighty mass and an altitude of 11,000 feet was attained. The season being then too far advanced for further effort, the explorers returned to their starting point, Tyonek, on Cook Inlet.

Observations made at this time convinced Dr. Cook that the mountain could be best approached by a power boat up the Chulitna River, a branch of the Susetna, leading to the region of the great glaciers descending from the southern and eastern sides of the mountain. By packing over some of these glaciers supplies might be taken to a point near the mountain's base fitted for an attempt to reach the summit.

In 1906 Cook returned, eager to complete the enterprise of scaling the mountain, now accompanied by Professor Herschel O. Parker, Belmore H. Browne, an experienced Alaskan explorer; R. W. Porter, of Arctic experience, and a number of able packers and assistants. It was no light task that lay before this party of enthusiastic mountaineers, as they were to find. Glacial streams of ice-cold water traverse this country in various directions, navigation of them being difficult and crossing often dangerous.

This way led from Cook Inlet up the Yentna River, with the idea that a pack train might be taken through a pass at its head and the northern base of the mountain thus be reached. But the very rapid current of the stream made navigation difficult, and the pack train, which was sent overland, had a swampy and otherwise troublesome country to traverse. The crossings of the stream, where deep enough to require swimming, were so perilous that several of the men had very narrow escapes. Ice cold and often running like a mill race, only the strongest swimmer could sustain himself for more than a brief interval in these waters. After the two parties joined at the head of navigation they traveled together up the stream until the mouth of a deep canyon near the headwaters of the Yentna was reached. Dr. Cook and three members of the party sought to explore the gorge on horseback, but soon found the walls becoming vertical, while the water rushed through with such force as to make progress impossible. Desperate chances were taken in swimming the horse across several frightful side channels, but in the end the party was obliged to return.

It was now decided to cross a width of unexplored country to the Chulitna, a branch of the Susetna River, and follow this up to one of the great glaciers at the foot of the mountain. The work was one of great difficulty, the route being in cases almost impassable; but after some very hard work the Chulitna was reached.

Here the problem of fording the river proved most serious. After wading through a half mile of ice-cold water they had to give up the attempt and encamp on a sand bar. By good fortune they found that a gold-mining prospector had located on the river side near this point, and a boat was obtained, by the aid of which the men and packs reached the other side. The horses, now unladen, swam across. Many prospectors had already reached this locality and some of them had made a trail over a mountain pass about two thousand feet high. This was followed over swamps and other obstacles until a great glacier descending from the cliffs at the base of Mount McKinley was reached.

The foot of the mountain was still about twenty miles away,

the path to it blocked by glaciers, over the surface of which it must be approached. To learn the chances of ascent a mountain's peak was here climbed and careful observations made of the distant mass. From the point of outlook the southern face and the eastern and western ridges of the mountain could be clearly seen.

As for the southern face, this was far from promising, it consisting of a series of great cliffs above which the mountain was heavily snow-bound. The eastern and western ridges were also largely covered with snow, and each seemed broken by cliffs rising like great walls. Ascent from this direction seemed hopeless, and the only chance of finding a feasible route appeared to be one over steep glaciers and snow fields between the snow-clad sides of Mount McKinley and the neighboring Mount Foraker to the western or northwestern ridge of the mountain. This had previously been observed and seemed not without promise.

It was finally decided, however, that success by this route was so improbable that it was not advisable to try to climb the mountain by any route leading from the south. The best thing to do seemed to abandon the project for that season and try the north side of the mountain in another season, following the easy path of approach offered by the Yukon and Tanana rivers, thence following a branch of the latter, the Kantishna, which approached the mountain on its northern side. The project was therefore abandoned for the time being, the party, with a few exceptions, returning to the coast, whence Professor Parker took ship for home on August 8th.

Dr. Cook, however, decided in doing some more exploring before the close of the season, and returned with Mr. Browne and some others of the party. This proved a fortunate return, since it led to an interesting result of which the world was soon after informed, Dr. Cook announcing that the summit of Mount McKinley had been reached. We may condense the explorer's report of how this was done.

In their return toward the mountain the party was divided,

two members of it going in one direction and two in another to collect natural history specimens, while Mr. Porter with a third section of the expedition undertook to explore the region south of Mount McKinley and make a map of it. Dr. Cook, taking with him two companions, Barrille and Dokkin, set out to explore the system of rivers and glaciers east of the mountain and examine the northern side for a possible route for future ascent.

They succeeded this time in ascending the Susetna and Chulitna rivers by boat, and followed a branch of the latter to the first of the glaciers they had recently visited. Here they put there boat in safe harbor and established a base camp. To the east, a few miles away, were the bold uplands and low woodlands of the river valleys; to the west the foot-hills of the range which Mr. Porter was then prospecting; to the northwest, forty miles away, McKinley lifted its soaring peak far above the clouds. Dr. Cook, in ascending the Chulitna, had again become hopeful of a possible ascent of the mountain from this quarter, and as the weather had changed from its rainy and disheartening recent state to clear skies and a dry and brisk air, he felt encouraged to make the attempt.

He did not think of reaching the top. The approaching winter was already sending its pioneer snows and freezing chill to the upper regions, and fast rendering them unassailable. But he hoped to be able to ascend the glaciers for some distance and get a reasonable idea of future prospects and possibilities. He and his companions were obliged to make the attempt in light marching order. They had with them no guides or porters and no elaborate equipment. They were there to blaze the way for later explorers and set out with the idea of quick marches and light weights and of minor results. They proposed to carry shoulder packs of fifty pounds each, these containig all their needs for a ten days' mountain journey. In preparing for this biscuits were baked and then dried and hardened by a slow fire, so that there would be no moisture in them to freeze. The other food substances taken were pemmican, sugar and tea. Wood alcohol was taken for fuel. The food and fuel consumption allowed for was thirty-four ounces daily for each man, and this allowance proved so liberal that their supplies lasted for nearly thirteen days.

In addition they took a silk tent, a sleeping-bag for each man, rubber floor-cloth, axes, a photographic camera, and a small assortment of domestic and scientific implements. Dressed in heavy woolens, they took no extra clothing except stockings. As it proved, they underestimated the Arctic chill they would have to endure, and only that their sleeping-bags had been made in sections and could be used as ponchos, they would not have been able to endure the severe cold of even the middle height.

Thus equipped, the party set out on the morning of September 8th, from an altitude of one thousand feet, on a bright, clear day, with temperature near freezing. Trails lay before them, first one made by moose and bear, then a blazed trail made by gold prospectors, and farther on an old caribou track that yielded excellent travel. At the end of the second day they crossed a bend in the glacier and camped on a mossy point about fifteen miles from the mountain they sought.

Here they lost one of their party. Dokkin was a new member of the expedition and became so frightened by the crevasses in the glaciers that he refused to go any farther, saying that he would not trust his life to the security of his footing, Cook and Barrille were older hands at the work and did not hesitate to jump crevasses. However, as they did not then intend to climb more than about twelve thousand feet, and from this point outline a route for a climb the next year, they felt that Dokkin was not needed and sent him back with instructions to plant emergency caches on the return route.

On the next day their journey was resumed, the snow here being hard and offering a splendid surface for a rapid march. Yet it added an element of danger by bridging crevasses in a treacherous manner. As the sun set that day, from the height they had reached they were amazed to see before them no fewer than twelve conical peaks in an air line, all nearly twelve thousand feet high, the last of them a pinnacle in the huge northern barrier ridge of Mount McKinley.

Ptarmigan—a hardy variety of grouse—were here abundant, and Barrille succeeded in shooting some of them, but to cook them with their sparse fire proved far from easy and they had much difficulty to get them into eatable condition. At the end of the following day they pitched their camp at a height of eight thousand feet. All so far had gone well. In three days they had advanced over thirty-five miles of the foot-hills of the mountain, and reached what seemed a good position for an attack upon its heights. Every point and surrounding landmark was carefully charted as they went and their route clearly defined.

The fourth day dawned and the march was resumed, the snow improving in condition as they advanced, though the crevasse gaps became wider. But what chiefly troubled them now were the avalanches, which became perilously close and numerous. Yet there was no safer route to follow and they went on. The close of that day brought them to the level they had laid out as the extent of their present climb, and to a region of biting gusts, to escape which they felt it necessary to build a snow-house—a sort of Eskimo igloo. Here they were comfortably housed for the night, though the temperature outside was below zero and the muffled roar of falling avalanches reached their ears during the night. Eating their evening meal of pemmican, biscuit and tea, and creeping into their warm sleeping-bags, they passed a warm restful night in their igloo, safe from the Arctic weather that raged without.

When they emerged from their close beds the next morning and ventured abroad, they were gratified to find that the clouds had fled and there was an unobstructed view of the mountains and glaciers which they had climbed to this point to study. Completing their general observation, they examined the mountain before them for possible lines of ascent. There seemed several promising ones, leading over narrow glaciers and ice-sheeted ridges, both to the east and the west, but every such possible route was crossed somewhere by an avalanche track. This great downpour of snow and rock could not be risked, and no chance of progress remained unless they should follow the cornice of the northeastern arête upon which they were encamped.

This route seemed a hopeless one. In following it they would have to trust themselves to a ridge of crusted snow, with a sheer drop of four thousand feet on each side, and in the distance they could see a huge rock blocking the path, its vertical sides rising one thousand feet. Beyond it were other ice-clad cliffs, and farther still appeared a steep arête, which led to a glacier on the northern face, and into a valley between two lofty peaks. These formed a double summit to the mountain.

The locality seen could be reached only in one way. A path must be picked around the great rock. But if they could succeed in doing this, it seemed to Dr. Cook advisable to try for the top. They had food and fuel enough for the purpose, but the season was so far advanced as to make the attempt desperate. At any rate it was safe enough to venture somewhat farther, and adjusting their necksacks and life-line they set out boldly on their dangerous mission.

To their gratification they found that a narrow cornice led around the great rock, and they tramped doubtfully onward, now through narrow gorges between steep pinnacles, now over dangerous snow bridges. All day long they continued the difficult work of step-cutting, making little in height, but in the end passing the frowning barrier. Before them now was a steep, snow-covered ridge, a hard climb, but a vast relief from what they had just passed through.

Night found them at a considerable height up this icy slope, and with no shelter point anywhere in sight. The slope was one of nearly sixty degrees, but the snow was firm and the danger from avalanches very small. There was no alternative but to trust themselves to it, by digging a shallow ditch or cave into the icy mountain side and there spending the night. To prevent themselves from rolling out during sleep, with a fall of some thousands of feet below them, they drove their axes securely into the ice, and wrapped themselves and all their belongings into a bundle, which they lashed to the axes. Here, not daring to move for fear of disturbing the snow and bringing it in a shower upon them, they spent a long and stormy night, with the roar of avalanches on both sides for a lullaby, anxiety robbing their eyes of slumber.

Daybreak after that awful night was gladly welcomed. During the hours of the night they had made up their minds, if they ever saw the morning break again, to hasten at all possible speed down from that inferno. But the coming of the sun had a reassuring effect and they quickly changed their plans. Not to go back, but to go on, was now their determination. On crawling out of their bed of terror and looking about them in the frosty air, they saw that all the barriers to the ascent had been left behind them. Above them were slopes that seemed easy and unbroken. The way was apparently open and they hopefully took up the trail again. But as they climbed, the task before them grew steadily larger. Crest after crest had to be crossed, and when at length they reached what they thought to be the top of the mountain, it proved to be only a spur, with many like it beyond.

The cold increased steadily and their exhaustion, mostly due to their loss of sleep the night before, grew extreme. Soon after noon they passed from the ridge they had followed to the surface of a glacier, and here they were obliged to halt, being too fatigued to proceed. It was just past noon, but a long rest had become necessary. The snow proved easy to build with and a snow-house was soon completed. Crawling into this, they indulged in the luxury of sleep until the stars of the following night faded before the dawn of a new day.

This was the sixth day of their climb. Observation gave the height they had reached at 16,300 feet. The effect of the lofty altitude here became severely felt, and after toiling up 2,000 feet along easy slopes, they pitched their tent in the early afternoon for another rest. Observations from this point showed them that there were two main peaks, about two miles apart, with lower ranges between them. The one to the east was the highest and towards this they turned their steps on the following morning.

The final climb of the two explorers was one that needed their utmost resolution. The temperature was 16 degrees below zero, and the wind bitingly cold. The lofty elevation seriously affected their strength and caused their hearts to labor to keep up the circulation. The chill crept into their very bones, the only alleviation to it being hot tea. But at that elevation it was difficult to melt snow and the water boiled at so low a temperature that the tea was weak and not very hot.

But, taking their sleeping-bags and a light emergency ration, and carrying a flag, once more, with grim determination, they faced upward on their final climb, over the feathery snow-field that clothed those high altitudes. Much of their route lay in the shadow of rock pinnacles, and here the chill was piercingly severe; but in the sunshine they felt a distinct sensation of warmth.

Progress was very slow. At every hundred steps they had to halt and lean on their axe-handles to rest. Gasping for breath, they dragged themselves onward. When near the summit they fell exhausted and gasping on the snow. The final stages of the climb were almost beyond their powers, and the relief was great when climbing came to an end and they stood on the summit of the heaven-soaring peak. With clasped hands and looks of gladness they stood in silence. They had not breath enough to shout or even to speak, and they could only express their feelings by their eyes. It was the 16th of September, 1906. The altitude they had reached, as indicated by their aneroid barometer, was 20,391 feet.

From where they stood the world seemed stretched before them. Miles and leagues they gazed, over mountain peaks, on the plain below with its silver-threading rivers, out upon the distant Pacific and Bering Sea. Here Dr. Cook took his final photograph, one of Barrille standing on McKinley's broad peak, with the American flag lashed to his axe.

A record of their achievement and a small flag were placed in a metallic tube and this put into a protruded nook a short distance below the summit. There it remains for those to find who follow Cook and Barrille to the summit. This done, their steps were turned downward and what had been almost impossible difficulty became comparative ease. Yet it took them four days to reach their base camp and breathe the lower air once more. Here their boat awaited them and their return to the realms of civilization was quickly achieved, the bold explorer being greeted with an enthusiasm which was a foretaste of the supreme reception which has since been accorded him.

CHAPTER VII

Bradley's Account of the Cook Expedition

NEVER did any great human expedition set out more modestly or with less blare of trumpets and rattle of drums than that which was headed by Frederick A. Cook and John R. Bradley, and which left Gloucester for the polar regions in the summer of 1907. There was nothing from which the general public could judge that anything more was intended than a fair-weather excursion to the Arctic seas, with a Rooseveltian inclination to make havoc among the big game of those icy waters. If Dr. Cook had it in mind at that time to make a dash for the Pole, he kept it from public notice, and among the polar expeditions chronicled for that year nothing was said of this, the most momentous of them all. Yet there were some who had reason to be better informed, for Dr. Cook had sought aid elsewhere for a polar trip before Mr. Bradley became his patron.

Mr. Bradley, an explorer and big game hunter, said nothing of any ulterior purpose. He was, to all appearance, only concerned with the shooting of walrus and polar bears. Yet, as now appears, the great expedition was already mapped out in the minds of these co-conspirators, as one may judge from the supplies taken with them on their ship. These went vastly beyond the requirements of a hunting excursion and covered every essential needed in a search for the Pole.

Everything about the expedition was kept so quiet that even the captain of the ship that bore them north did not know its purpose, though he shrewdly suspected that something more than a shooting and fishing trip was in prospect, from the variety and character of the supplies.

Mr. Bradley has given a detailed account of his connection with the expedition and his reasons for taking part in it. A member of the Explorers' Club, of which Dr. Cook for one term was president, their acquaintance had ripened into friendship. Himself fond of travel and discovery, Mr. Bradley was familiar with Cook's record on the "Belgica" and his ascent of Mt. McKinley, and looked upon him as a well-seasoned explorer, full of resources, courage on critical occasions, confidence in his own powers, yet with the saving grace of caution and circumspection in emergencies. He was impressed by him as a reliable man, in no sense a dreamer, but one with the spirit of a practical scientist and one preferring to do things before speaking of them.

Bradley had been a hunter in the temperate and torrid zones and had a desire to add to his experiences some acquaintance with hunting in the frigid zone, where the polar bear offered the kind of fighting game he sought for. He had it in view to write a book to be entitled, "Hunting Big Game from the Arctic to the Equator," and the Arctic section of it needed to be completed. In December, 1906, on his return from a hunting trip to Asia, he said to Dr. Cook: "My next will be the Arctic." In the spring of 1907 he decided to go that year and invited Dr. Cook to accompany him as his guest, he to shoot bear and walrus and Cook to photograph the Eskimos. Nothing was said then about exploration, polar or otherwise, though it was not long before that came up as a possible outcome of the trip.

The plan made, the obtaining of a suitable vessel came next. Ships built for Arctic work were to be had at St. John's, Newfoundland, sealers that lay idle during the summer, and Bartlett tried at first to obtain one of these. But as none of the owners would hire unless he would consent to be under the command of a captain, he decided to buy one for himself and thus have a vessel which would be under his own control.

A vessel suitable for the purpose was found at Gloucester, Massachusetts, a fishing schooner of 111 tons, named the "George

Lufkin." This he purchased and thoroughly overhauled and refitted, braced it fore and aft, put in new sails and new rigging, sheathed it with steel plates on bow and stern, put in gasoline engine and tanks, and renamed it the "John R. Bradley." The schooner was in a measure rebuilt and made stanch enough for the Baffin's Bay trip. Cabins were put in for himself, his guest and the officers, the equipment resembling that of a private yacht. A large supply of gasoline was provided, the vessel provisioned for two years in case of shipwreck, and everything done that experience suggested for shooting and navigation in the Arctic region.

He had Captain Robert Bartlett, in command of Peary's ship, the "Roosevelt," go with him to Gloucester and see his vessel. Bartlett was impressed with its fitness and pronounced it as safe a ship as ever left for the Arctic.

These details are incidental to what followed, the broadening of their plan into a polar expedition. This came about in the following manner: The preparations being complete, one day, about four weeks from the date fixed for sailing, Cook and Bradley lunched together at the Holland House, New York, and during their talk about the trip Cook remarked, in his quiet manner:

"Why not try for the Pole?"

"Not I," replied Bradley in surprise. "Would you like to try for it?"

"There is nothing that I would rather do; it is the ambition of my life."

The proposition thus incidentally made had very likely been in Dr. Cook's mind in accepting his friend's invitation, and he had simply awaited a proper opportunity to present it. In his opinion $8,000 to $10,000 more than had already been spent would furnish the necessary equipment. Their conversation ended in Bradley's remarking:

"We'll fit out this expedition for the Pole, and say nothing to anybody about it."

As Bradley has since stated, they wished to keep it out of the newspapers, and also to prevent Peary getting wind of it, hastening to Etah and buying up all the dogs. Bradley wished to do some hunting on the way up and did not care to be hurried.

The equipment necessary to carry out Dr. Cook's plans was added to that already on the vessel, everything being made as light and compact as possible so as to reduce weight. Thus the fifteen-pound stoves used by Greely in his trip north were replaced by three-pound aluminum stoves, and everything else was cut down to the lowest limit of weight. Yet nothing which Dr. Cook's experience told him would be necessary in such a trip was omitted, camp equipments, tools, provisions, sled material, etc. It was decided between them that if they found the Eskimos in poor health, the dogs scarce, or other conditions unfavorable at Etah, they would give up the polar project, call it a hunting trip, and come quietly home again after their summer's sport. But if conditions should prove favorable the dash for the Pole would be made.

It must not, however, be taken from the above that the whole expense of this expedition fell upon Mr. Bradley. Dr. Cook has stated since his return that its total cost was about $50,000, of which he contributed $20,000, Mr. Bradley supplying the remainder. Mr. Bradley has told the story of the trip with such brisk conciseness that we shall now let him speak for himself. He says in continuation of his account of the expedition:

"I engaged as captain Captain Bartlett's nephew, Moses Bartlett, who had been first officer on the "Roosevelt." The mate was Mike Wise, and we had a first-class sailor in a young Irish boy named Kirby—as tough as nails was he.

"We left Gloucester, made a good trip without hurrying too much, and got into Melville Bay. It took us seven days to cross Melville Bay, which is one hundred and seventy miles wide. We got into the ice three times, nearly lost the ship, but finally got out safe. We did not take Captain Bartlett into our confidence in

BRADLEY'S ACCOUNT OF THE COOK EXPEDITION 115

the matter of our destination. He was curious and interested at times.

" 'Got enough pemmican here to feed a tribe of Eskimos,' remarked he one day.

" 'Oh, yes,' I answered. 'Might need it in case we are shipwrecked.'

" 'Quite some hickory wood aboard,' he remarked later.

" 'Quite so,' I answered. 'We may need it to build houses with when we get crushed in the ice.'

" 'Well,' he answered after a moment's thought, 'if I didn't know you were going on a fishing trip I would say you were going to find the Pole.'

"Well, we arrived and everything seemed to be adapted for the attempt which Dr. Cook had in mind. We went thirty-five miles above Etah at first and Dr. Cook went ashore. He returned to the vessel and reported that he considered the conditions ideal for his purpose. Now let me show you how he reasoned and let us see whether or not this was the harum-scarum dash of a man for the Pole in a straw hat?

"First, he made a census of the natives at the point where he landed and found that there were 240 of them, as compared with 250, according to the last record, which made a decrease of only ten in twenty years. The little colony was in the pink of condition; the young men were strong and healthy. The Eskimos had had a good winter, for it was on August 28, 1907, that we landed. They had plenty to eat. Game was abundant, musk oxen, walrus and other animals were everywhere in evidence, and there were large numbers of fish. We found that there was little ice in Kennedy Channel, that the traveling over the land was good and that weather conditions were perfect."

Mr. Bradley diversified their trip with some shooting, going for duck, seal, walrus, bear and every other kind of northern game, and various trips were made about the vicinity. One morning after this, while they were breakfasting on board the schooner, Cook said:

"I'm going to stay."

"All right; you're past twenty-one. Think it over before you finally decide."

Cook needed no further thought; his mind was made up.

There could not have been a combination of circumstances better adapted to his purposes. He saw the chance and he took it, and he had the nerve and the will to avail himself of his opportunities. Let us take up again Mr. Bradley's narrative:

"On our way up we had encroached a good deal on the stock of five thousand gallons of gasoline with which we had started, and we were taking on ballast. As we were running a little light, I came on deck and said to Bartlett: 'Captain, get all the men ready and send all the natives aboard ashore. Prepare to unload as soon as possible, for we are to put Dr. Cook and his supplies ashore for the winter.'

" 'Is this a polar expedition?' he asked.

" 'It is,' I answered.

" 'I knew it! I knew it!' he exclaimed. 'Never was there a ship fitted out as this one is which was not intended for the Pole. Expect me to stay all winter?'

" 'Not if we can help it,' said I. 'I wouldn't stay here myself. It is not necessary to stay here on account of Dr. Cook. We have a house on board for him.'

" 'Glad to hear you say that,' was the captain's answer. 'I wouldn't stay here for anybody on earth.'

"We lost no time. The supplies were loaded into dories, which were towed ashore by my motor boat, which was in reality a strong whale-boat twenty-seven feet long, with powerful engines. Dr. Cook managed the motor boat, for he is fond of running engines. We landed supplies at a rapid rate for a while, and then the ice began to drift in, and the captain said that he did not care much about staying about that neighborhood, as we stood a chance of losing the vessel or staying that way all winter. He asked if it made any difference if he landed the supplies in not precisely that place. I told him to do as he liked about that, and he strung the stuff up and down the coast for about five miles, and we had a lively time doing it.

" 'That will be all right,' said the Captain. 'We are putting it on land ice and Dr. Cook can have the Eskimos gather it together.' Meanwhile he had sent a lookout aloft to keep an eye on the ice, which was beginning to drift in from both directions. It took thirteen hours to land the supplies, including forty tons of coal, which shows that we had something of a polar expedition to look after. The coal alone would have lasted him for ten years, for both he and his assistant could hardly have used three tons of it a year.

"Three years' supplies were left with Dr. Cook. That does not convey much of an idea perhaps, but if I had the inventory of it at hand it would astonish those persons who speak of this expedition as a haphazard affair with nothing but the nerve of Dr. Cook to back it. There were tons of pemmican and that kind of material, sugar, tea, coffee, canned goods, dried meats, quantities of hickory for sled building, hardware, iron, steel, copper, cooking utensils of all kinds, 150 feet of stove pipe, ten thousand boxes of matches, bales of biscuits, one hundred and twenty thousand cans of food, 150 gallons of alcohol, barrels of rice and flour, guns for trading, knives, beads and trinkets of all kinds and boxes of instruments for observation.

"Cook was a master at handling the Eskimos. He knew their capabilities and their sensibilities. At his suggestion we carried as part of our stores a barrel of gum drops and these passed as currency among the natives at Annootok. They would work more for a handful of gum drops than they would have done for so much silver, for they do not know the meaning of money.

"Our expedition had the latest devices for minimizing weight and at the same time increasing efficiency. For instance, I knew of an expedition several years ago which carried five or six brass stoves weighing from sixteen to eighteen pounds each, to be used with kerosene or oil for making tea. Our stoves were made of aluminum, their weight was three pounds each and they did precisely the same work. We got rid of twelve or fifteen pounds on each stove, and without impairing our efficiency disposed of as much unnecessary weight as a dog can pull and had so much more for food. We proposed to make our tea only once a day and to keep it at an even temperature by carrying it in a patented heat-preserving bottle.

"Dr. Cook is one of the ablest men with all kinds of appliances I ever met. He has wonderful mechanical skill and for twenty years he has been taking observations of the kind necessary to find out if a man were really at the North Pole. He is a trained scientist and an explorer of experience. I am no scientist—but a hunter of big game. With his experience in the Arctic and the Antarctic, I think that Dr. Cook knew very well what he was doing. I have seen him taking the observation for the day on board the yacht both alone and with either the commander or the mate. He had a sextant of aluminum which was an especially fine instrument, and was so much admired by Captain Bartlett that he said that if he were not a strictly moral man he would have stolen it long ago. The sextant was used in taking the observations of the "Bradley" all the way and much of the time it was handled by Dr. Cook himself. He also had eight or ten of the best compasses that money could buy, an artificial horizon, as well as various meteorological instruments. It seems to me that Dr. Cook was eminently qualified by long experience for the task of reaching the North Pole, and I think that scientists will agree that he was sufficiently versed in the knowledge necessary for him to tell whether or not he had arrived.

"Dr. Cook has been breaking precedents in this trip to the Pole. His methods violated all the old traditions. He went at a different season; he did not leave a ship frozen in the ice in the old, regular way. Also, he was taking a course which no explorer ever took before, in keeping away from the eastern drift of the ice from the Bering Strait. He profited by other men's mistakes. He made his dash to the Pole from the west, relying on the drift of the ice to carry him to the eastward. Now, that seems to have worked all right.

"In his outfit was a canvas boat, one which was easily collapsed, and it occupied some of the space and weight which might have been used for food, but it was worth it. Now, according to the books, when your Arctic explorer gets a great lane of water in the ice or a lead he sits down by the side of it for a while and keeps hoping until it closes up. Sometimes two or three days pass before his hope comes out. Dr. Cook was able to go across these places in his canvas boat. The boat could be used for a tent at night and was handy when not in commission for use as a tarpaulin cover.

"It was the idea of Dr. Cook that the people he left behind him on the land should cover his retreat. That left him about three hundred and fifty miles to traverse from March 17th to April 21st, the date of his discovery, or thirty days according to my calculation. This is an average of only ten miles a day. The sleds which he had were exceptionally good, for he made them himself, and the dogs he obtained from the Eskimos were in the finest condition. They were fat, strong and full of life; in fact, according to all I can hear, better dogs were never seen. At that, of course, there were some which would weaken and have to be killed, these being fed to their mates. With a little good luck here and there the dogs could easily beat ten miles a day, and some days go far beyond it. Mr. Peary in some of his books speaks of going as high as thirty and forty miles a day. One can go on dog sleds over reasonably good land ice at the rate of sixty miles a day.

"Before Dr. Cook left me he said he would do another thing that no other explorer had done, and that was to come back from the farthest north on foot, whether he was successful or not, and to reach the Danish trading post of Upernavik, where he knew that in time a vessel must arrive. All this had been carefully mapped out two years ago.

"He made his way back slowly. He lived in Ellesmere Land.

He used the meat which he had left in caches, the oxen and the hares and so forth, which had been killed on his way up. He subsisted at times on what he could find. It was only this spring that he was able to get over into the neighborhood of Etah, where there were caches.

"Now he comes at last to Cape York. He knows that the Danish government sends a ship there to look after its colony and to take calico and merchandise to trade for ivory of the narwhal, eiderdown and blubber. He knows that he can eventually meet that ship. So I suggested to him that he keep stowed away about his clothing in sealskin bags 100 pounds in English gold with which to pay his passage to Copenhagen, and from there to the United States. This he did as he said he would. So, when everything had been arranged and I felt that nothing could go wrong, I resented it a little when I was asked to contribute to a relief expedition which I felt sure that Dr. Cook did not want and felt sure that I did not.

" 'But how is he going to get home?' Mr. Bridgman has asked.

" 'The natives,' I replied, 'have gone across that ice for thousands, perhaps millions, of years. I do not see why Dr. Cook cannot.'

" 'Well,' Mr. Bridgman said, 'he might. He certainly has the nerve.'

"He did. And now for the last objection. How could he induce the natives to go with him to the North Pole and risk their lives? How does anybody induce the Eskimos to do anything? Here was as fully equipped an expedition as ever went to the frozen seas, excepting neither Peary, Dr. Nansen or the Duke of the Abruzzi. It was quietly prepared, that was the only difference. It was peculiarly fitted out with things which were dear to the heart of the Eskimos, and Dr. Cook had enough of them to be liberal. An Eskimo will go anywhere for a gun. One will work all day for a biscuit. How about a box of matches occasionally? I had shipped 10,000 boxes of them. A biscuit, a cracker, a bit of tobacco—anything like that would bring an Eskimo to your feet.

"These Eskimos are much like monkeys. At Etah when we were unloading the supplies for Dr. Cook, an Eskimo was sitting in the stern of the whale-boat and Dr. Cook was looking after the engine. The Eskimo was holding a conversation with the cook, who presently turned to me and said the Eskimo wanted to know if I could get him an engine like the one in the boat. When he was asked with what he would run it he said there was plenty of water in the ocean which he could use. He imagined the gasoline used was water from the ocean.

"They are crazy for trinkets. An Eskimo woman would rather have a mirror than anything else. But they are reliable people and will do anything for you. Captain Amundsen, who discovered the Magnetic Pole, said to me he considered the Eskimos the most reliable people he ever met. He said that one winter in the Arctic an Eskimo came along with a team of dogs and a bow and arrow. He said he was a Hudson Bay Eskimo.

"He told Amundsen of two ships wintering there, and he asked this native if he would take some letters down to them—remember, this was some hundreds of miles down the ice—and for this Amundsen promised him a rifle, a cheap one, worth a few dollars.

"He taught the native how to use the rifle. The native started off and on his return shot off one of his fingers. He was advised not to make the trip back to Amundsen, but he replied that he had promised to return, and he did. And this over hundreds of miles on the ice.

"Mr. Peary used to promise every Eskimo who went with him a gun when the party got back. Those guns cost him about $2.50 each, I should say. The native used to pick them to pieces and come to us to find out how they worked. There were twenty-five guns prepared just for the purpose of rewarding the faithful Eskimos. But beyond all this there is a personal element that must be considered, for the Eskimos are very fond of Dr. Cook. They remembered him when he came with Peary; they recalled his other expeditions. When they saw him coming ashore they ran up and down the shore for joy, waving their hands and shouting their welcomes.

"He can speak their language, and they know that he is a square and honest man. He could get them to go with him anywhere, no matter what extremes of temperature they might have to endure. And then there is the question whether or not the Eskimo considers that he risks his life wandering up to the North Pole. His ancestors have been doing that kind of thing for many generations, and, after all, our brother of the North does not care so much for a few degrees of cold. I am deeply interested in this matter, and when there is talk of Dr. Cook not being properly equipped I feel like just rising up and showing that he did not start for the North Pole in a straw hat."

CHAPTER VIII

Robert E. Peary, the Indomitable Polar Explorer

TO briefly summarize for the reader the earlier events of Commander Peary's life, before taking up the story of the great achievements which have brought him into the limelight of public approbation, we give the following concise account of his early history and of his services in the employment of the government before he began his famous explorations:

Robert Edwin Peary is a Pennsylvanian by birth, having been born at Chester Springs, near Altoona, in the western section of that State, on May 6, 1856. Descended from a family of hardy Maine lumbermen, his immediate ancestors were Charles Peary and Mary (Willey) Peary. His father had migrated to Pennsylvania and became engaged in the lumber business there, but died in 1858, when his son was two years old. We next hear of the family in Portland, Maine, to which they had removed and where the boy's early life was spent and his primary education obtained. Having prepared for a higher education, he entered Bowdoin College, and graduated there with second honors in 1877. Throughout his college career the study that most fully interested his attention was the subject of Arctic exploration, which from early life had held a peculiar fascination for him, and was the subject of his most earnest reading.

On leaving college he adopted the profession of civil engineer, for which he had fitted himself in his college career, his first employment being as a land surveyor at Fryeburg, Maine. In 1879 he became engaged upon the Coast and Geodetic Survey at Washington, remaining in this field of duty until 1881.

In the latter year the young surveyor passed the Navy Department examination for the admission of civil engineers, and was commissioned an engineer in the naval service, October 26, 1881. He has since remained a civil engineer in the navy, having advanced from the rank of lieutenant to his present rank of commander.

In this service Lieutenant Peary built a pier at Key West, Florida, in 1881. This the contractors had abandoned, as impossible to be built for the appropriation, but the young engineer completed it at a cost well within the sum appropriated. He subsequently became sub-chief of the Inter-Oceanic Canal Survey in Nicaragua, Central America, and in 1886 he was made engineer-in-chief of this important survey, in connection with which he invented some important apparatus. In 1888 he was sent to superintend the building of the new dry-dock at the League Island Navy Yard in Philadelphia.

Previous to this he had taken the first step toward the realization of his boyhood dream, that of adventure and research in the polar region. Greenland was as yet the utmost goal of his ambition, and in 1886 he applied for leave of absence from his naval duties to visit this realm of his ardent hopes.

His application was granted, and in July of that year he went north on the first of his many expeditions. It is interesting to be able to state that on this occasion he took with him Matthew Henson, the faithful mulatto servant who has been with him on every expedition since and has formed one of his chosen companions on his dashes for the Pole. Henson was a Philadelphia boy who had made his way to Nicaragua, where Peary engaged him and has kept him as his personal attendant ever since. It was not Lieutenant Peary's purpose on this expedition to seek the Pole, but to explore the interior of ice-clad Greenland, in which no white man had gone inward beyond the lowlands bordering the coast. It was an excursion not without its fruits. Starting from Disco Bay, near the seventieth degree of latitude, he penetrated many miles into the interior, and discovered that Greenland was an elevated island, the elevation, however, consisting of a mountain height of eternal ice, the depth of which no one knew. For all that could be told this icy elevation might cover an interior hill country or a low land like that of the coastal plain. The result of this expedition was to acquaint him with the state of affairs in the interior, information which served him in good stead in his crossing of Northern Greenland in 1892. In this field he was a pioneer, Nansen's crossing of Southern Greenland not being achieved until several years later.

It was after this expedition that Peary's marriage took place, his bride being Miss Josephine Diebitsch, of Portland, Maine, whom he had known and loved since boyhood. As events proved, she was a born mate for an Arctic explorer, as she showed in their later careers.

The disaster and suffering which characterized the termination of the "Polaris" and Greely expeditions did not tend to recommend Arctic exploration as a national enterprise to the Government of the United States. But a vast amount of highly valuable information had been obtained, not only by these expeditions, but also by the expedition sent out by the British Government under the command of Sir George Nares. And, in addition to the information, a further knowledge had been gained, the knowledge that the same spirit of indomitable pluck, the same tireless energy, and the same loyalty and devotion to duty dominated both branches of the great English-speaking race. These facts stirred up the adventurous to further efforts.

The discoveries along the north coast of Greenland opened up the very interesting question whether that land did not extend right up to the Pole itself. As far as any one had penetrated to the north of the coast, land was still to be seen farther on; it was an open question whether this great ice-covered country was an island, with its northern shores swept by the polar ice-floes, or whether it extended to the dimensions of a continent in the polar region.

The problem appealed strongly to two explorers whose names, by reason of their exploits during recent years, have become familiar. They are Nansen and Peary. The former, by his dash for the Pole, during which he surpassed all previous records of the "farthest north," had dwarfed his Greenland performances; the latter, by his journey of 1,300 miles over the ice-crowned interior of Greenland, went far to prove the insular character of the country.

Lieutenant Peary, failing to obtain government supplies for a scheme of an overland journey to the northern coast of Greenland, devised by him in 1891, was supported in it by the Philadelphia Academy of Natural Sciences. The expedition was necessarily small, but that did not affect its utility. It was, moreover, unique, by the inclusion of Lieutenant Peary's wife as one of its members; the account which she has given of her sojourn in high latitudes is one of the most interesting of books on the Arctic regions.

The party left New York on June 6, 1891, on board the steamer "Kite," for Whale Sound, on the northwest coast of Greenland, the party including several prominent members of the Philadelphia Academy. The voyage was satisfactory in every way until June 24th, when an unfortunate accident befell the leader.

The "Kite" had encountered some ice which was heavy enough to check her progress, and, to get through it, the captain had to ram his ship. This necessitated a constant change from going ahead to going astern, and, as there was a good deal of loose ice floating about, the rudder frequently came into collision with it when the vessel was backing. Lieutenant Peary, who was on deck during one of these manœuvres, went over to the wheelhouse to see how the rudder was bearing the strain. As he stood behind the wheelhouse, the rudder struck a heavy piece of ice and was forcibly jerked over, the tiller, as it swung, catching him by the leg and pinning him against the wall of the house. There was no escape from the position, and the pressure of the tiller gradually increased until the bone of the leg snapped.

Dr. Cook, who formed one of the party, immediately set the limb; but the sufferer refused to return home in the return voyage of the ship, and when, a few days later, the "Kite" reached McCormick Bay, he was carried ashore strapped to a plank.

The material for a comfortably sized house was part of the outfit of the expedition, and this was in course of erection the day that Lieutenant Peary was landed. For the accommodation of himself and wife, a tent was put up behind the half-completed house, and, as a high wind arose, the remainder of the party returned on board the "Kite."

As the hours passed away the wind became stronger. The tent swayed to and fro, and Mrs. Peary, as she sat beside her invalid and sleeping husband, realized what it was to be lonely and helpless. She and her husband were the only people on shore for miles; her husband was unable to move, and she was without even a revolver with which to defend herself. What, she asked herself, would be the result if a bear came into the tent? She could not make the people on board the "Kite" hear, and she was without a weapon. Though throughout the stay in the north Mrs. Peary proved herself not only to be a woman of strong nerve and self-reliance, but also an excellent shot with either gun, rifle, or revolver, yet it was as much as she could stand when her anxious ears caught the sound of heavy breathing outside the tent.

For a time she sat still, fearing to disturb her husband, until the continuance of the sound compelled her to look out. A school of white whales were playing close inshore, and it was the noise of their blowing, softened by the wind, which had so disturbed her. But so self-possessed was she over it that her husband did not know till long afterwards the anxiety she had experienced during the first night she spent on the Greenland shore.

The following day rapid progress was made with the house, and some of the party stayed on shore for the night, so that there was always some one within call of the invalid's tent until the house was completed and he was removed into it. By that time the "Kite" had started home again, and the little party of seven were left to make all their arrangements for the winter.

They had determined to rely entirely upon their own exertions for the supply of meat for the winter and also to obtain their fur clothing on the spot, killing the animals necessary for the material and engaging some of the local Eskimos to make up the suits. Deer would give both meat and fur, and as there was every prospect of the neighborhood affording these in plenty, as soon as the house was up and the stores packed, the majority started away in search of game.

The place where they had erected their camp was a verdure-covered slope lying between the sea and the high range of bluff hills which towered about one thousand feet over them. In the spring the ground here was covered with grass and flowers, the bay in front was full of seal, walrus, whales, and other marine animals, anl along the hills behind experience showed that land game was present in abundance. The Etah Eskimos, the most northerly people in existence, lived along the shores of the bay and neighboring inlets, and, as soon as the camp was settled, they were kept busily employed in the making of fur garments, proving themselves docile and peaceful. It was often difficult for the members of the expedition to realize that the site of their camp, with the abundance of food to be had, was only from fifty to eighty miles distant from the spots where the castaways of the "Polaris" suffered so acutely and the members of the Greely expedition slowly starved, many of them to death. For more than a year the little party of seven lived in good health, without a suggestion of scurvy making its appearance and with only one fatality, this being accidental.

The first hunting expedition was in search of deer, and everybody took part in it except the crippled leader and his wife. For two or three days the hunters were away, for they were fortunate in discovering a herd of deer which they followed until all were

Photo by Pictorial News Co., New York.

THE REUNITED PEARY FAMILY ON BOARD "THE ROOSEVELT."

Commander Peary's first thought after his successful expedition to the North Pole was to rejoin his family as quickly as possible. Although intensely fond of family life, the exacting demands of the career to which he had set himself had kept him away from sight or communication with his loved ones most of his married life. On returning from the North Pole he announced that he would in future remain at home to enjoy the companionship of his wife and children which fate had denied him for so many years. The members of this interesting group reading from left to right are: Miss Marie Peary, the explorer's daughter, who was born within the Arctic Circle; Commander Peary, Robert E. Peary, Jr., and Mrs. Peary.

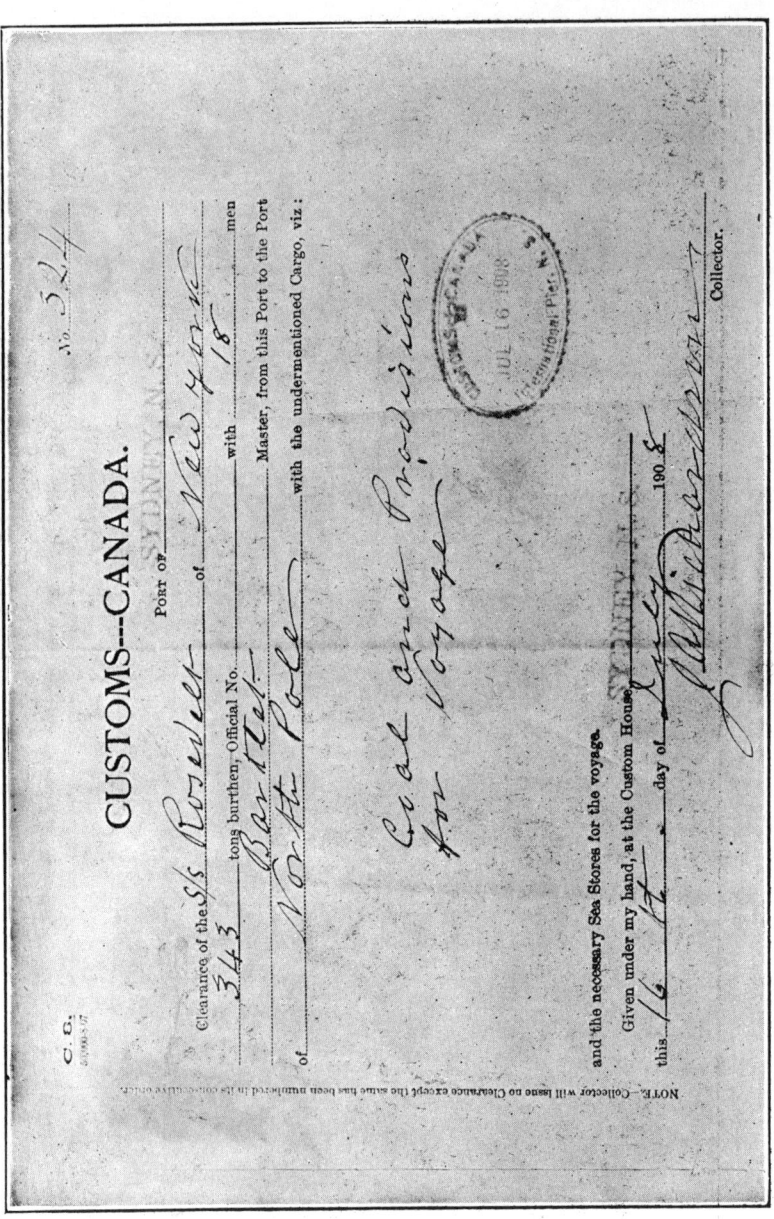

Photo by Pictorial News Co.

CLEARANCE PAPERS OF "THE ROOSEVELT" TO THE NORTH POLE

Although "The Roosevelt" was listed as a yacht, and therefore did not require them to take out the customary clearance papers in leaving a port, the Collector of Customs at Sydney, Nova Scotia, with a sense of humor made out this paper officially authorizing the vessel to proceed to the North Pole. This unique paper was a valued treasure in the ship's archives.

Copyright, 1909, by George Grantham Bain.
COMMANDER ROBERT E. PEARY AND CAPTAIN BARTLETT OF "THE ROOSEVELT"

This unconventional photograph, taken upon the arrival of "The Roosevelt" from her victorious expedition in search of the North Pole, shows the Commander and his right-hand man wreathed in smiles of satisfaction at the successful conclusion of their perilous mission. Captain Bartlett, a Canadian by birth, was selected by Peary to lead the supporting party, which came nearer to the Pole than any of the others except his own.

McMillan. Borup. Gushue. Henson.

LEADING MEN OF PEARY'S PARTY ON THE SLEDGE WHICH REACHED THE NORTH POLE

Some of Commander Peary's principal assistants in his great dash for the North Pole are here shown dressed in Arctic costume, seated upon the sledge which carried the Commander over the long sledge journey, and with which he reached the North Pole. The names of the quartette reading from left to right are Professor McMillan, George Borup, Gushue, mate of "The Roosevelt," and Matt Henson. The latter, who has been Peary's personal attendant for many years, and an expert sledge maker and driver, holds in his hand the long whip with which the Eskimo dogs were lashed to their best speed.

bagged. With as many as they could convey of these the hunters set out for the camp. Their approach was duly signalled, and upon hearing that they were returning laden, Lieutenant Peary, for the first time, hobbled out of the house on crutches. As they came up he rested on one leg and his crutches, while he photographed them and their trophies, after which the double occasion was celebrated by a banquet in which venison played an important part.

The deer skins were very important additions to the stock of material from which the winter clothing was to be made, but other kinds of skins were needed, especially of the marine animals, as well as some native tailors to fashion them into coats, hoods, mittens, and all the other articles of Arctic wear. A boat party was therefore despatched along the shores of Inglefield Gulf to spy out the localities where walrus was to be found, and to induce some of the natives of a village, seen from the "Kite," to come over to the camp and sew the new garments.

The party was successful in both instances, for a number of walrus were seen and an Eskimo family came back by the boat. The "huskies," as the explorers familiarly named these people, consisted of a man, his wife, and two little children, and they moved to the camp with all their belongings. The dress of these northern natives, which the explorers found it advisable to copy in most particulars, consisted of tunics and short breeches with sealskin boots reaching above their knees. The costume of both sexes was very similar, the only practical difference being in the tunic or jumper, that of the woman having the hood longer and deeper for the accommodation of her infant. They had broad, good-natured faces, not especially handsome nor intelligent in appearance, and distinctly dirty.

In fact, the use of water, other than for drinking, did not appear to be known to them, and it was very much a question whether they had ever tried the experiment of a wash. Mrs. Peary was once tempted to give one of the little ones a bath, and she records how intensely amazed it was at being put into the water, although it was more than two years old. Surviving the shock, however, it manifested its pleasure by lustily kicking and splashing. Perhaps later it enjoyed a well-merited honor amongst its own people as the only one of the tribe who ever passed through the extraordinary ordeal of soap and water.

In consequence of their innocence of water as a cleansing medium, the "huskies" had two distinguishing characteristics not entirely pleasing to more civilized people. They carried around with them a distinctly impressive aroma, and also thriving colonies of what are politely termed parasites.

In the matter of clothes they carry their wardrobes on their backs. Fur garments do not wear out very rapidly, and, when a "husky" is full grown, the suit of clothes, made in honor of the event, remains in constant wear until one of two things happens. If the man kills a bear, he has a costume made of the skin and discards the ordinary sealskin suit for it. If he does not kill a bear, he wears the sealskin suit until it no longer keeps him warm, when he gets another. In their snow-houses during the winter and storms, if the temperature is too warm for them in their thick clothing, they take the clothing off; being a primitive people, their manners are as simple as their minds.

The first arrivals at the Peary camp were, however, very useful people. There being no trees in this far northern region, and wood, consequently, being one of their most valued treasures, they were for some time unable to comprehend how the timber to build the house had been acquired. When they saw a fire made in the stove of refuse bits of wood they were still more amazed. Never before had they seen so much fire all at once, and the man, growing curious, kept on feeling the stove to see what the effect would be. When it was hot enough to burn his hand he developed a wholesome respect for it, and afterwards preferred to look at the uncanny object from a distance.

The problem of how the sewing was to be done was rather a

difficult one to the white people for a time. To allow the furs to be taken into the Eskimo tent was to invite the introduction of an insect population of which it would be impossible to get rid later. On the other hand, to allow the "huskies" to enter the house too frequently was equally dangerous from the sanitary point of view. A compromise was effected, by the Eskimo woman doing the sewing near the door of the house with some one always keeping an eye on her. Later on, when it was found that little danger of the spread of insects existed if reasonable care were taken, the workers sat inside the house. They were fairly deft in handling the needle, and the suits they made for the party were all excellent and serviceable. These were made on the native pattern, and the later experience of Lieutenant Peary and his comrade Astrup in their journey over the great ice-cap proved that the native pattern was the best for Arctic wear.

The woman being set to work, a boat expedition in search of walrus was organized, with her husband as guide, Lieutenant Peary and his wife also going. They had not proceeded very many miles up Inglefield Gulf before a light breeze when they saw, on a floating piece of ice, a dozen or so of the animals huddled together apparently asleep. Sailing gently towards them, every one with a rifle ready, a sudden puff of wind sent the boat ahead quicker and farther than was intended, and it struck the ice. The walrus, never having seen a sailing boat before, looked round at it without paying any more attention than if it had been another piece of ice. But the sight of so many valuable creatures within reach of his harpoon was too much for the Eskimo, and he buried the weapon into the nearest.

At once the attitude of the walrus changed. The wounded member of the tribe tried to escape, bellowing in its pain, and the rest slid off the ice into the water and surrounded the boat. Others from neighboring ice patches charged rapidly on to the scene, and the situation of the boat and its occupants was dangerous in the extreme. The poor Eskimo, his face showing the terror he felt, crouched down in the boat, evidently expecting to be annihilated by the furious animals that surged round. As they came up to the boat, they tried to get their powerful tusks over the gunwales, and, had one succeeded in doing so, there would have been little hope of any one escaping. Yet to keep the angry crowd off was no easy matter.

They swarmed all around, and not less than two hundred and fifty were estimated to be engaged in the attack. Lieutenant Peary, with his injured leg, sat in the stern of the boat, firing at them, and the other white men also kept up a fusillade, Mrs. Peary giving evidence of her strong nerve and courage by sitting beside her husband and loading the weapons as soon as they were emptied. The walrus came on in numbers to the attack, but when fired at all those nearest to the boat leaped out of the water, and then plunged out of sight. There was always the danger of one of the huge creatures rising under the boat, and so capsizing it; but the occupants had no time to think of this. Directly one batch jumped and disappeared, another hastened forward to meet the volley of bullets, and be in turn succeeded by another batch.

The boat was meanwhile gradually approaching the shore, and as the water became more shallow the walrus exhibited less desire to come to close quarters, until, at last, the adventurers found that they had beaten off the last of the swarm. The main body had retreated far up the gulf, only a few remaining near. Several of those which had been shot, however, were floating on the surface of the water, and it was decided to go back and secure them, even at the risk of another attack. Already some of them were sinking, and many must have gone down while the fight was in progress. There was a necessity for haste if any of the slain were to be secured, and with rifles loaded and ready for a fresh attack, the boat was headed towards the floating carcases.

The operation of securing them was performed without any interruption from the survivors, and a run was then made for the shore, where the Eskimo said a lot of sealskins were "cached." This is the term used in the Arctic regions to denote the local method of storing food or possessions. A space is hollowed out in the ground, which, even in the summer time, is frozen hard a few feet below the surface. The articles to be stored having been placed in the space, it is covered over with stones, and the "cache" is completed. Throughout the winter the contents become frozen into a solid mass, which, protected by the stones or other covering, does not thaw out during the short summer, and so remains in a good state of preservation for an almost indefinite period.

Occasionally the "cache" fails to preserve the articles of food entirely in that state which by the European is termed "fresh"; but as they rarely have recourse to "cached" provisions, it does not matter very much. The Eskimo, who constantly preserves his winter supplies in this manner, has, happily for himself, easier notions about the state and quality of his food. This was brought home to the party very forcibly. They had visited several "caches," and obtained enough seal-skin for their purpose, and, having enjoyed some refreshment, were considering their return. The Eskimo, Ikwa, then told them that, as all the flesh at the camp was recently killed, he and his family did not like it. There was, he said, a fine seal cached in the neighborhood, which would form a delicious store for him and his family, and if the leader allowed him to move it to the boat, and convey it to the encampment, he would be prepared to yield some of it to the members of the party for their own special enjoyment. The seal was a beauty, he said, and just in the very pink of condition. The necessary permission having been given, Ikwa hurried away for his treasure.

Shortly after, the members of the party noticed a strange penetrating odor in the air which they at first attributed to the flayed walrus. It steadily increased, until they were unable to tolerate it, and started out to seek the cause. As they emerged from under the shelter of the jutting rock where they had been resting, they descried the little Eskimo staggering towards them under the burden of a seal almost as large as himself. The creature had been "cached" about two years, and was in such a state that gentles fell from it at every step the man took, and, as Mrs. Peary recorded in her diary, both the sight and the scent of it overpowered the white people. But to Ikwa it was just in good condition for eating, and he was especially indignant when he was made to relinquish it. His clothes, however, would not part with the odor, and for many days the members of the expedition had reason to remember that Eskimo like their game high.

As the time passed, and winter approached, every one was kept busy preparing for the long dark night, and for the journey over the ice-cap which was to be undertaken directly spring began. Several families of Eskimos were now residing near the encampment, the women mostly engaged in making winter fur garments for the members of the expedition, and the men in hunting. As dogs were required for the sledging expedition, constant bartering went on between the Eskimos and the white men, and the latter undertook occasional journeys to localities where other members of the tribe were encamped.

A great deal of very interesting information was thus derived about the natives, who were, so far as known, the most northerly living people in the world. Mrs. Peary, as the first white woman they had ever seen, was a particular object of attention. As their custom is for men and women to dress very much alike, they could not quite understand Mrs. Peary's costume, and when the first arrivals saw her and Lieutenant Peary together, they looked from one to the other, and ultimately had to ask which of the two was the white woman.

The tribe did not number three hundred in all; they held no communication with the Eskimo farther south, and, except for the occasional visit of a sealer or a whaler, knew nothing of the outer world. None had ever seen a tree growing, nor had they ever penetrated over the ridge of land which lay back from the coast, and over which glimpses were caught of the great ice-cap. The latter, they said, was where the Eskimo went when they died, and if any man attempted to go so far the spirits would get hold of him and keep him there. They consequently warned Lieutenant Peary against venturing. There was no seal up there; no bear; no deer; only ice and snow and spirits, so what reason had a man for going?

Their belongings were extremely simple. A kayak, a sledge, one or two dogs, a tent made of walrus-hide or seal-skin, some weapons, and a stone lamp, comprised, with the clothes they wore, their property. Wood was the most valuable article they knew, because they could use it for so many purposes, and had so little of it. The possession of knives and needles was greatly desired; but scissors did not appeal to them, since what they could not cut with a knife they could bite with their close even teeth. Money had neither a suggestion nor a use with them; trade, if carried on at all, was merely the bartering of one article for another.

The animals they liked best were dogs and seals; the former being their beast of burden and constant companion, the latter the provider of food, raiment, covering and light. Every seal killed belonged to the man who killed it, but the rules of the tribe required that all large animals should be shared among the members in the neighborhood; the skin of a bear, however, remaining in the possession of the man who secured it. But so unsophisticated and easy-going are these contented people that individual property scarcely exists with them; every one is ready and willing to share what he has with another if need be. The articles borrowed, however, are always returned, or made good if broken or lost. The boys are taught how to hunt, how to manage the kayak and sledge, and how to make and use the weapons of the chase, while the girls are taught how to sew the fur garments, and keep the stone lamp burning with blubber moss, so as to prepare the drinking water and the frizzled seal flesh they eat. This constitutes their education, and beyond this their chief desire is to live as happily as they can, which, according to those who have been amongst them, they manage to do merrily and well.

During the visits paid to the different encampments by Lieutenant Peary and his wife, about a score of dogs were obtained, a number which would be sufficient to carry out the work of the ensuing spring. They were usually obtained in exchange for needles and knives, but the purpose for which they were needed always formed a subject of wonder to the unambitious "huskies."

By the time that a return was made to the house—Redcliff, as the explorers named it—the season was well advanced towards winter. The roof and sides were covered with walrus hide, and moss, gathered in the early autumn, was stuffed into any crevice through which the cold wind might find a way. The drifting snow soon piled up round the walls and over the roof, and the extra covering added to the warmth and comfort of those within. Fur clothing was now worn generally, and the little party, keeping in good health and spirits, managed to pass the gloomy period of winter with little to mar their contentment.

Christmas they celebrated in proper form by having a sumptuous dinner, the menu of which, preserved by Mrs. Peary, is worthy of being quoted, as showing what can be done in a place where shops are unknown and darkness reigns at midday. The feast consisted of salmon, rabbit pie and green peas, venison with cranberry sauce, corn and tomatoes, plum-pudding and brandy sauce, apricot pie, pears, sweets, nuts, raisins and coffee: a very creditable repast to be put on the table of an Arctic residence.

When every one had satisfied the demands of appetite, the table was cleared, and then respread for the benefit of the "huskies," who were brought in to gain their first experience of Christmas fare. A somewhat different assortment was prepared for the visitors, the dishes consisting of milk punch, venison stew, cranberry tart, biscuits, sweets, raisins and coffee. This was certainly a variation to their ordinary food of seal or walrus flesh and water, and they showed their appreciation of it by leaving no crumbs and sticking to their seats until, at half-past ten, they were gently told that it was time to go home. Then they left, but the next day they came again, and were perhaps not the first who, having enjoyed a hearty Christmas dinner, felt disposed to complain that Christmas can only come once a year.

CHAPTER IX

Peary Crosses Greenland

IT is at present our task to tell the story of Lieutenant Peary's first memorable exploit, that in which he crossed the frozen interior of North Greenland from the west to the east coast, reaching land never before seen by man, and adding greatly to our knowledge of the geography of the Arctic region. While he did not reach the northernmost extremity of Greenland, he found abundant evidence to prove that this lay little north of the point achieved, a fact which was proved in subsequent expeditions.

We are still concerned with the voyage of the "Kite," in which Peary met with the unfortunate accident described in the last chapter. While his broken leg limited his activity, it did not diminish his enterprise, his companions, Gibson, Astrup, Dr. Cook and others being sent out by him on various excursions, food-getting and exploring.

The long winter wore slowly away and by February Lieutenant Peary was able to use his wounded leg effectively, he setting out with Dr. Cook and Mr. Astrup on the 14th to witness the first appearance of the sun, which was due by the almanac on the morning of the 15th. The venture proved a severe trial to his new strength, for scarcely had they reached the top of the bluffs when they were assailed by a ferocious storm of wind, rain and snow, which continued for forty-eight hours, almost blew down the house in which the winter had been passed, and buried the exploring party so deeply under the snow drifts that they extricated themselves with difficulty.

In the succeeding weeks an exploration was made of Inglefield Gulf, more than two hundred and fifty miles of distance being covered and many enormous glaciers discovered. This work was done by Peary and his devoted wife, attended by a native driver. It occupied a week, during which a storm compelled them to spend one night in an Eskimo igloo, housing with the natives—an experience the reverse of agreeable.

On their return, the final preparations were made for the inland ice journey which Lieutenant Peary had long held in view. In 1886 he had gone a hundred miles inland from Disco Bay, in central Greenland. Now he proposed to cross the island from side to side in its northern region, if possible, as Nansen a few years before had crossed it in the south. On the last day of April the work of transporting provisions and other supplies to the summit of the ice field began, the ground being so steep and broken that the whole outfit had to be transported up the long and difficult slope on the shoulders of the men of the party and of the Eskimos of the settlement.

Three days later, on May 3, 1892, the time to start arrived. At eight o'clock in the morning Henson, Peary's faithful attendant, set out for the ice-foot with a large dog-sled. The stalwart mulatto had become an experienced whip, but the wolf-like dogs, fresh from a long rest and in the highest spirit, gave him all he could do to keep them in order, their pulling being diversified with intervals of snarling and fighting.

The starting point was reached at three on the following morning, after a weary climb up the sloping side of the rugged gorge. Peary followed Henson, after bidding an affectionate farewell to his wife, in which they both realized the fact that it might be a final one, since no one knew what perils the ice wilderness held.

At the top of the gorge Dr. Cook, Gibson and Astrup, who had been carrying stores to the upper ice, were found slumbering in their sleeping-bags, but quickly rose to aid in the work of packing the sledges, an important task which occupied two full days. At length all was ready, the dogs, twenty in all, were harnessed, and the party got under way, Peary leading, followed by Gibson, Astrup and Cook, each with a team. Henson had frozen his heel during the past winter, and it grew so painful after a mile's walk over the ice, that he was sent back as unfit to proceed.

Almost at the start misfortune came upon them. On May 8th the wind blew so violently from the interior, hurling frozen particles of snow with great force into the faces of the party, that they were obliged to halt and build igloos of snow in which to shelter themselves from the blizzard. After twenty-four hours of this confinement Peary and Gibson left their igloo to seek their companions, who were encamped farther on, and found them so deeply buried that only the extremity of their upright sledges appeared above the drifts. The snow had made Cook and Astrup prisoners in their igloo and it took hours to extricate the buried sledges.

This done, another and worse trouble awaited the explorers. The dogs had broken loose, had chewed up their harness and devoured every accessible particle of food, and their recapture was a matter of no small difficulty. Almost as wild and savage as wolves, patience and dexterity were necessary to subdue the untamed animals. The usual method of doing this was to coax them within reach by the display of food, seize them, and bury their heads in the snow. With skill in handling the brutes this might be done with the infliction of a bite or two, though before they could all be subdued some had to be lassoed and nearly choken to death.

As will appear from what has been said, the explorers had no pleasure excursion before them. Only three days out and all this already passed through! The prospect was startling. As for the igloos, they took so much time to build and were so cold and generally disagreeable when built that during the remainder of the expedition they were dispensed with, sleeping-bags replacing them.

It was May 14th before the uphill course was completed and the true inland ice was reached. From this time forward progress was easier, the slope of the ice being easy and gradual. But other troubles had come, four of the dogs having died of a disease to which these animals were subject. Also the travelers had been obliged to abandon four of the eight sledges with which they set out, these having proved unserviceable.

On the 21st of May, at a point on the edge of the great Humboldt glacier, one hundred and thirty miles from Redcliff House, the place of starting, a halt was made and the question of what was still to come was considered. It was evident, as Peary said, that they had before them no holiday jaunt. He had decided that he could not safely take more than one companion, and as the others had now gained a foretaste of what they would have to endure, he called upon them to volunteer for this duty. Dr. Cook was the first to respond, followed eagerly by Astrup and Gibson, each being so anxious to proceed that Peary was obliged to choose between them. He selected Astrup as the best fitted for the work, and kept three of the sledges and thirteen of the dogs for his own use. Gibson and Cook were sent back with the remainder, the latter being put in charge of the Redcliff House station until his chief should return.

The course now lay directly northeast, Peary striding forward in advance, his attention being given closely to the work of keeping the true direction, while Astrup followed in charge of the dogs and sledges. This order of march was kept throughout the journey. As the days went on, the dogs grew more manageable, buckling down to their work with good will and following their leader obediently, Astrup encouraging and urging them occasionally with voice and whip. Peary's task was the more arduous of the two. To keep the right direction in that limitless white wilderness, without landmark of any kind, as level and unbroken as the trackless ocean, was no light labor, every faculty being kept on the strain to prevent a loss of direction. Constant references to compass, charts and other means of determining position were necessary and the strain at times was very great.

One purpose was to avoid the Peterman Basin, a fiord setting inward from the west coast. In this Peary failed, his route trending too much to the northward and a detour of ten miles became necessary on the seventh day's march to avoid a series of crevasses and inequalities, the presence of which proved that a gorge was at hand. This gorge or fiord was reached on the last day of May, a clear, pleasant and summerlike one, the mercury standing at 77 degrees at midday. Here the explorers encamped for thirty-six hours, taking advantage of the sunny warmth to give their clothes a thorough drying, and enjoying the luxury of a snow bath in the mild air.

So far their route had been a comparatively easy one, but as it proved they had got considerably off of the right track and on the 8th of June a period of difficulties began. In the days that followed many crevasses and ice hillocks broke the hitherto smooth surface and they soon found themselves on the edge of a glacial depression, with steep cliffs and icy slopes visible beyond. At this depressing interval a severe storm broke upon them, driving them to shelter for two days. Their camp now consisted of an excavation in the snow, they gaining further protection from the wind by banking their sledges and spreading a tarpaulin to windward.

The storm abating, they were obliged to turn on their tracks, heading southward and enduring two days of difficult and wearisome climbing before the surface level was again reached. This lay more than six thousand feet above the sea. In the days that followed new troubles were encountered, including bewildering fogs which for many hours rendered progress impossible. In addition, Nalgaksuk, the best of their dogs, sprained his foot and showed such signs of the fatal dog disease that they were obliged to kill him. The large sledge had also suffered from the strain of the long journey and a whole day was lost in repairing it and in readjusting the loads, everything that could be spared being thrown away.

When they started again the sun was shining brightly, but the heat had grown so severe that all their outer clothing had to be laid aside, while the snow grew so soft and sticky under the solar rays as greatly to impede their speed. All this affected their spirits, and Astrup, hitherto bright and cheery, and showing his genial disposition by merry singing, as he walked, grew glum and silent, his compressed lips showing the strain as he aided his team in drawing the heavy sleds up the steep slopes.

On the 26th of July the eighty-second parallel of latitude was reached, and now a cheering indication appeared. The coast, seen in occasional glimpses, had invariably lain to the northwest, but now it suddenly was seen to the northeast, trending gradually eastwardly, and finally bending to the southeast. Several glaciers also were passed, all moving in a northeasterly direction. Here were evidences that the island was nearly crossed and that the Atlantic could not be far distant.

At length, on July 1st, the travelers saw land lying due east, lofty in elevation and free from ice and snow, and through a depression in the ridge they discovered indications of the near vicinity of the ocean waters that washed Greenland's eastern coast. They were apparently in the vicinity of a lofty headland which they fancied faced the open sea. At the foot of its inner slope, as they went forward, was seen a bare, stony reach. They had left the glacial mass of interior Greenland behind them, and had excellent reason to believe that the Atlantic lay beyond that mountain ridge.

Eager to satisfy himself, Peary now left Astrup in camp and set out alone over the broken land in front towards a depression which opened through the highlands in front. It seemed but a few miles away and he felt sure that he could quickly traverse it and return. But as he went forward the hills seemed constantly as far away. Each elevation he climbed only revealed another eminence behind it, and this continued wearisomely. The heat, the steady climb, the repeated disappointments, seriously depressed his spirits, while the sharp edges of the broken stones cut through his shoes and made walking a torture.

Yet he was not without hopeful glimpses. A merry twitter gladdened his ear and a little snow-bunting flew overhead. And the desolately barren ground was soon broken by a little patch covered luxuriantly with grass. Close inspection also showed traces of musk oxen—hairs and other indications, and finally a bleached skeleton, the bones of which were broken as if by gnawing wolves. Flowers, also, were soon seen, purple, white and yellow Arctic poppies, while the snow-buntings now fluttered about in numbers.

The hopeful explorer could not but feel that what he sought must be near at hand, but his expected five miles had extended to fifteen and the looked-for sea waves still remained unseen. He could go no farther. His cut and lacerated feet and the distance that lay behind him admonished him to return. He reached camp after a heart-breaking struggle and found Astrup anxiously awaiting him and prepared to serve him with all three of the deferred meals of the day in one. For twenty-four hours he had been wandering and came back worn in body, though far from sick at heart.

Sleep revived him in body and soul, and, leaving the sledges he and Astrup set out with the dogs over the same path, taking with them rations for five days. Everything now looked hopeful. The scent of the land so excited the animals that they could barely be held in leash. The melted ice formed ponds in the glacier front which broke through the soft snow banks that held them and tumbled in cascades down the steep slope, forming a river at its foot. But the march over the stony ground grew distressing to men and dogs alike, and at length, completely worn out, they lay down for a few hours of much needed rest.

The march had not long been resumed when, as they were picking their way down a steep incline, two significant black spots were seen in the distance. Were they boulders or musk-oxen? A second look told the tale. They moved! They were alive! Here was fresh meat to replace the pemmican which for two months had formed their chief diet. Cautiously creeping forward, Peary came within gunshot without alarming the animals, and succeeded in bringing them down, a bull and a cow, and also a yearling calf which appeared behind the larger animals.

Where were their aches and pains now? Lost or forgotten. The animals were rapidly skinned, the sirloins and other choice morsels cut out, and one of the carcases was shouldered and thrown to the dogs. With howls of delight the pack rushed upon the raw, bloody flesh and fell to with such ravenous appetites that in a short time nothing was left but a heap of bones. Meanwhile Peary and Astrup prepared a savory supper of musk-ox steak, which they ate with a relish which the most sumptuous meal of civilization would not have awakened.

After this hearty repast a few hours' rest for men and dogs alike became a necessary relaxation. Setting out again in the best of spirits, the summit of the high land was at length reached, and they found themselves on a small plateau, the edge of which descended in a cliff four thousand feet sheer down to the sea. Before them was seen a great bay stretching far to the east and northeast. The extremity of Greenland in this direction had been reached! The Atlantic lay before them, bathing the eastern shores of the land they had crossed!

It was the 4th of July, 1892, and as the only way they could celebrate the natal day of American independence, they named the harbor before them Independence Bay. A great glacier which curved round it and formed its shores, they called Academy glacier, in honor of the Philadelphia Academy of Natural Sciences, which had financed the expedition. A cairn was built of stones and in it a record was placed by Lieutenant Peary, while the gold-fringed silken banner presented by the Academy, which the explorer had brought with him, was raised upon the cairn, the first banner of any nation to float over the eastern shores of Greenland north of the seventy-sixth parallel of latitude.

The remainder of our story may soon be told. On July 5th

the return march began, and it is an interesting fact that on the same day the "Kite" left St. John's, Newfoundland, on a relief expedition to bring back the exploring party, the relief party being under the command of Professor Angelo Heilprin, of the Philadelphia Academy of Natural Sciences.

Peary and Astrup crossed Greenland on their return trip with no serious misadventure, their total journey being 1,300 miles in length.

As they neared their goal all superfluous baggage was cast aside, the remainder being loaded on one sled, drawn by five dogs, all that remained alive. As they neared the coast they saw a number of dark objects two miles off, seven or eight in number. On they came, dogs and men, in a dead run down the slope, and in a few minutes more the explorers found themselves among Professor Heilprin's party, eagerly shaking hands and exchanging joyous greetings and warm congratulations.

The expedition above described was not the only one made by Lieutenant Peary for the exploration of North Greenland. He had heard the "Call of the Wild," and was no sooner back in the United States than he set himself energetically to the work of collecting funds for another voyage northward, to complete the tale of the discoveries he had made. Most of this he earned himself, $13,000 of it lecturing. He spoke one hundred and sixty-eight times in ninety-six days. He also earned money by letters to the New York *Sun*, and from the proceeds of a book written by Mrs. Peary, and finally finished his equipment by exhibiting his vessel, the "Falcon," at various ports, charging a small price for admission.

In June, 1893, the expedition sailed, Mrs. Peary again being a member of the party. Many men desired to go with him and much too large a party was taken. As a result, dissensions arose and nearly all of them returned home at the end of the first year, when a relief ship sought the exploring party in the north. Its coming was necessary, for the "Falcon" had gone to the ocean's bottom on her return voyage, with all on board, leaving the exploring party marooned on Greenland's icy shores.

An interesting incident of the first winter was the birth of a daughter to Mrs. Peary, the first white child ever born in the far North. "Anighito," the Eskimos called her, the "Snow Baby," and the little Greenlander—Marie is her American name—was in excellent health when her mother brought her home in the relief ship. Mrs. Peary's return was necessary, for her husband found himself heavily handicapped, his means being now exhausted. It was the chosen task of his devoted wife to raise the money necessary to send a ship for him in the following year. He had no thought of returning himself until his task was accomplished. He was sternly bent on going poleward over the great ice.

The sailing of the relief ship left Peary almost alone in the North. Only two men remained with him, Matt Henson, his faithful servant, and Hugh J. Lee. The summer of 1894 was spent in preparations for the crossing of the Greenland ice-cap, several caches of provisions being made at successive distances inland, chiefly composed of pemmican and alcohol, the two absolute essentials to a successful Arctic sledge journey. The caches were marked by upright poles in the usual way, and when the spring of 1895 came round the time for the great journey was at hand. The greater part of a year had been employed in providing what seemed the assured means of success in the coming journey. The explorer little dreamed of the misfortune that awaited him, the dismay into which he would be thrown.

In April, 1895, the journey began, half a dozen Eskimos being joined to the party of three, while the equipage consisted of six sledges and sixty dogs. They ascended as before to the ice-cap, Lee in the lead, followed by Henson, the Eskimos, and the sledges, Peary bringing up the rear. They were none too well provided with supplies and fuel, but were full of hope in view of the fact that they had made such plentiful provision on the route.

Misfortune awaited them, deep and desperate. The caches had disappeared! The storms of winter had overthrown or buried their signal poles and only a hopeless stretch of white desolation was to be seen. Under those trackless snows lay buried forever three-quarters of a ton of pemmican and all the alcohol fuel. The situation was terribly disheartening. All their search ended in the finding of only one of the caches, and that the least valuable of the whole. What was to be done? To yield to fate and turn back? No! The resolute explorer was not to be defeated so easily. Sending back the Eskimos, he went sturdily onward with his two companions, though he knew that it was to meet with possible, even probable, death by starvation. Of such stuff are heroes made.

Three of the sledges and forty-two of the dogs were taken with them. The cold was intense, for they were now on the Greenland ice-cap, about six or seven thousand feet above sea-level, and facing a constant current of biting wind that blew downward from the still higher regions of interior Greenland. With it came a blinding flood of snow, now only ankle deep, now blotting out their view of the sky.

Lee fell ill, leaving all the work to Peary and Henson and delaying the march. At times they had to drag him on the sledges. The dogs fought like wolves and one went mad. One sledge after another had to be abandoned, and when all the walrus meat was devoured, they had to kill dogs and feed them to the pack. At length the divide of central Greenland was passed and the slope began to trend downward towards the Atlantic. It was necessary to reach the coast, and that as quickly as possible, to obtain food for their remaining dogs. Finally they pitched their camp on the crest of the ice-cap, overlooking Independence Bay, five hundred miles from their starting point.

Their situation was now desperate. They had supplies still for themselves, but if food was not found not a dog in the pack would get even half-way home again, and they would have to drag the sledges themselves for some five hundred miles on twenty days' rations.

Leaving Lee behind to care for the dogs, Peary and Henson set out to make their way down the sharp ice slope to the land, which lay at a level nearly a mile lower and many miles distant. It was midnight when they started, though the sun was shining as though it were midday. Down they went, snow beginning to fall as they advanced and snow-covered crevasses giving way under their feet. They saved themselves from sinking into them by throwing themselves flat on their faces whenever they felt the snow give way under their feet.

When the bare rocks at length were reached it was still worse, for the sharp stones cut through their shoes, wounding their feet so badly that they were glad to get back to the ice and snow. Worn out with the effort, they threw themselves down for an hour or two of sleep. Then, waking, they struggled on as before until, after twenty-five miles of fruitless wandering, they were forced to return empty-handed to the camp. The experience was much like that which Peary had gone through in the same vicinity three years before. It took them ten hours to reach the camp, where they had only a tale of bad news for the waiting Lee.

Retreat was suicidal. They must go forward and seek food. The next day the three of them, with their nine remaining dogs, made their way down the ice-slope until checked by a severe storm of wind and snow, which kept up for two days. When it was over Peary and Henson set out again, once more leaving Lee behind, the dogs going with them and dragging a sledge with four days' half rations. For twelve hours they pressed on without seeing a trace of animal life.

For several miles onward they went and Peary, who was in the lead, eagerly called to Matt to leave the dogs and bring a gun. He had found a fresh hare track and followed the white creature to its lair. Matt, though an excellent shot, was so unnerved that he fired twice without hitting the fluffy, squatting animal. The third shot brought it down, and the half famished men devoured the hare to the last morsel. It was their first full meal for nearly forty days.

Then they lay and slept on the snow, without covering except that of the snow-flakes which fell upon them. Refreshed by food and slumber, the next morning they set out again, and soon, at the entrance to a small valley, found the track of a hoof, but so faint that it might have been made six months before. But further on they saw a calf's track that was evidently of late making. With new hope, they fastened the dogs to a rock, muzzling them with thongs so that they could neither bark nor chew themselves loose, and then hurried down the valley, rifles in hand.

The tracks grew more numerous as they went on. They reached a place where the animals had fed the day before, digging away the snow to get at the frozen grass and moss beneath. Yet no living thing was visible. The valley was swept with the field glass, but only the drear snow appeared. At last, after long hunting, on a little terrace at the crest of the white ridge, they saw a group of black dots. The herd was found! The men were saved!

Creeping slowly upon the wild creatures, they went on until near enough to count the herd, twenty-two in all. One old bull was standing guard and two others locking horns. The cows and calves were lying down. Lurking behind a boulder, the hunters glared upon this welcome game, ravenous but unnerved. After a short interval to regain their nerve they rushed and dashed upon the herd, rifle in hand. The old bull gave the alarm, snorting and stamping. In a moment the whole herd was afoot, facing these strange foes with lowered fronts. Fearful that they would take to flight, the hungry men could have shouted for joy to find their prey awaiting the onset. At fifty yards off Peary's rifle spoke. The bullet went true; the big bull fell. Again and again they fired and had killed half a dozen of the animals before the others took to flight. Then, like savages, as Peary tells us, they glutted themselves with warm, raw flesh.

There was food for all, for dogs and men, but the loss of their caches had limited the possible extension of the journey, and the explorer was obliged to turn upon his trail, leaving further discovery for future years. Sad was the backward march, with the feeling that nothing had been gained beyond what he had accomplished three years before. They threw away everything that would impede their march, even to their very tent, and their nautical almanac, except the three leaves containing the calculations they still required.

On over the endless snow they went with steadily decreasing dogs until but one sledge and two dogs were left. For five days they lived on a few biscuits and a little tea. Then they killed one of the dogs, dividing its meat between themselves and the one that remained. At length the last morsel of food was eaten and the home camp was still twenty miles away.

What troubled them now was the terrible fear that the Eskimos they had left might have played false, looted the camp, and left them to starvation. Fortunately they proved faithful, and when the three gaunt, wasted men arrived, with their single emaciated dog, food and rest awaited them; they were saved.

For days they lay and rested, scarcely able to move, sickened by the food they ate, bleeding at the nose, their legs swollen to twice the natural size. The dog, like themselves, ate and slept, hiding the food he could not eat, as if going back to the wild habits of his kind. There they remained until the arrival of the relief party which Mrs. Peary had succeeded in sending. Such is the story of the great polar explorer's most critical adventure, the one in which he came nearest to meeting the fate of so many of those who had gone before him to the frozen North.

CHAPTER X

Peary's Farthest North of 1905-6

COMMANDER PEARY'S three expeditions of which we have written, those of 1886, 1891-92 and 1893-95, had to do with the exploration of Greenland, not with that search for the North Pole to which so many of his later years were devoted. He went north again in 1896 and 1897, this time for still another purpose. In 1894 he had discovered near Cape York a large mass of meteoric iron, from which the Eskimos for many years had chipped off fragments for knives and spear-tips. There were two smaller masses which were easily removed, but to bring the larger one to civilized lands proved a task almost beyond the means that could be employed in that northern region.

The huge bulk, twelve feet long by eight feet wide, and weighing about one hundred tons, was no light thing to lift out of its ancient resting place in the ground, transport it for some distance to the coast, and place it in the hold of a ship for transportation southward. The first year's effort proved a failure. The huge meteorite was brought down to the natural rock-pier where the ship lay ready to take it on board. But the winter was at hand, the ice-floes came drifting into the bay, and the "Hope" had to cut loose and glide away.

The next year (1897) the "Hope" returned and made fast opposite the great iron mass, which was finally loaded on the ship by the aid of a bridge of stout timbers leading from the rock to the ship's deck. There were critical moments when it seemed as if it would topple over and sink to the sea bottom. But the arts of man overcame the resistances of nature and the huge bulk was finally lowered into the ship's hold and wedged so tightly that no pitching of the ship would loosen it. This was a necessary precaution, for the "Hope," on her return, passed through a series of frightful gales, none of which moved the great mass from its resting place. The prize thus wrested from its native lair now lies at the service of science in the vestibule of the Museum of Natural History in New York City.

Hitherto the discovery of the Pole had in no instance been Peary's main object, but in 1898 he went north with that alone in view, prepared to stay for years if a long sojourn would aid him in his ambitious effort. He did stay till 1902, and it is the events of these years in the Arctic ice that we must here briefly recount.

On July 7, 1898, he left Sydney, Cape Breton, in the ship "Windward," prepared to storm the Pole or do all of which man was capable in the attempt. Etah, the first goal of all recent polar voyagers, was duly reached, and the "Windward" was pushed northward from there into Princess Marie Bay, where the ice stopped her course and the first winter came upon the adventurers.

Winter, however, did not check the indefatigable explorer. On the 20th of December he left the ship to attempt a sledge journey to Fort Conger, Greely's former winter quarters. The results were serious. Their supplies gave out at Cape Desfosse, and they groped their way over broken and snow-covered ice in the winter midnight across Lady Franklin Bay, stumbling into Conger on January 8, 1899.

The worst result of the journey was the freezing of Peary's feet, they being so badly frosted that Dr. Dedrick, the surgeon of the expedition, had to amputate seven of his toes. This was roughly performed, with unsuitable instruments, at Fort Conger, and the invalid lay there helpless for six weeks. Then he had to be dragged back to the ship, two hundred and fifty miles away, strapped on a sledge, through a temperature ranging from -53 to 65 degrees Fahrenheit. The journey was one of intense suffering to the invalid, and after the "Windward" was reached and proper surgical instruments obtained the operation had to be completed, a necessity that involved another six weeks of illness.

This accident put an end to any attempt upon the Pole in 1899, but by April 19th Peary was on his feet again, sledging to Fort Conger, killing and caching for future use twenty-five musk oxen and making important explorations, in one of which he crossed the ice-cap of Ellesmere Land, reaching an elevation of more than four thousand feet and looking down on the snow-free western coast of that large island—the one which Dr. Cook crossed in the start of his polar trip. An ice-free fiord was seen about fifty miles to the northwest and beyond that more distant land.

A second winter passed and the year 1900 came. Fort Conger was sought again, being reached on March 28th. It was the purpose of the explorer now to follow the northwest coast of Greenland and settle the question definitely of the northern upreach of that great island. For all that was then definitely known it might stretch upward to continental dimensions or offer a pathway to the Pole. In this expedition Peary was notably successful. On May 8th the cairn left by Lockwood eighteen years before was reached, and another march led the adventurer around Cape Washington, which he had feared to be the northern point of Greenland.

On rounding it he was gratified to see another splendid headland beyond, with two large glaciers debouching near it. He knew now that the discovery of Greenland's northernmost cape was left for him. Continuing the journey for several marches more, in which they reeled off noble distances, the party reached a magnificent cape in the same latitude as Cape Washington. This was named after one of the principal patrons of the expedition, Cape Morris K. Jesup.

The next two marches lay in a southeasterly direction, and here, on May 22, 1900, Peary erected a cairn at what appeared to be the most northeasterly point of the American half of the world.

He was satisfied that he had determined conclusively the insular character of Greenland, and reached the point at which its coast trended southerly toward Independence Bay, discovered by him in 1892.

So far he had not been able to make the dash northward over the polar ice so long contemplated by him, and two more winters passed before he felt that the time had arrived. He made a start from Fort Conger on April 5, 1901, but on reaching Lincoln Sea, as the ocean north of Greenland is called, he gave up the attempt on the Pole as hopeless for that year, neither men nor dogs being in condition to venture upon such a journey. He therefore reluctantly turned back, reaching the "Windward" at Payer Harbor on May 6th. Here the rest of the year was spent. Much had been done and important discoveries made. The lay of the farthest north land had been definitely traced and charted from the eastern side of Greenland to the western side of Ellesmere Land. The attack upon the Pole was laid aside for the work of the coming year.

One difficulty in the venture before them lay in the fact that the "Windward" was harbored so far to the south. Two hundred miles had to be traversed before Fort Conger was reached, and a considerable distance farther before they came to Crozier Island, where Robeson Channel opens out into Lincoln Sea and the polar pack is reached. This journey occupied the explorers a full month, from March 6 to April 6, 1902, during which they had gone over four hundred miles of arduous travel, in a temperature ranging from —35 to —57 degrees Fahrenheit, to reach their true starting point, in the vicinity of the one used by Peary in his later polar voyages.

On the morning of April 7th the small party of adventurers climbed down the island shore and over the ice-foot to the polar pack, and the dash for the Pole began. It was a small party that set out on this journey of peril, consisting of two Americans, a white and a black, Peary and Henson, with eight or ten Eskimos and sixty dogs. They had large supplies of food for the men and eighty tons of meat for the dogs, forming an ample supply. The Eskimos were sent back, one by one, as the stores taken on their sledges were exhausted, until the white and black Americans, with a reduced number of dogs and sledges, were left to make the last stage of their journey alone.

It was an ugly road over which they had to travel, the roughness of the ice being made doubly difficult by gales of wind and spaces of open water. Such a lead—as these water spaces were called—was encountered on the 13th, but the next day it closed sufficiently for them to rush the sledges across. Beyond the lead they came upon a series of high ice ridges, followed by another series of rugged old floes, the whole so obstructive to rapid travel that it took them sixteen hours to advance two or three miles.

On the next day the same trouble was encountered, fragments of heavy old floes, drifting eastward, frequently forcing them to halt until the cakes of floating ice massed together sufficiently to offer a path for the sledges. Day after day this continued, the leader of the expedition slowly losing hope in view of the obstructions constantly confronting him. By the 21st he felt obliged to give up the fight. Only he and Henson then remained, and it was impossible for so small a party to make farther headway. On the night of this day of steady struggle he wrote these words of deep discouragement in his journal:

"The game is off. My dream of sixteen years is ended. It cleared during the night and we got under way this morning. Deep snow. Two small old floes. Then came another region of rubble and deep snow. A survey from the top of a pinnacle showed this extending north, east and west as far as could be seen. The two old floes over which we have just come are the only ones in sight. It is impracticable and I gave the order to camp. I have made the best fight I knew. I believe it has been a good one. But I cannot accomplish the impossible."

Such are the words of a valiant soldier who finds the task before him too great for human power to overcome. To go on was but to sacrifice their lives. The polar monarch had his outposts far advanced to repulse the bold navigator who was seeking to unfold his long hidden mystery, and the feeble force that assailed them was far too weak to break through their serried ranks. Nothing remained but retreat and acknowledgment of defeat.

As they rested that night in their camp—a night in which the sun scarcely set—they heard the ice to the north moving and grinding with a noise like that of surf beating heavily on a rocky shore. It was the slogan of defiance of the ice king's battalions. The next day they took observations of the sun and found the latitude to be 84 degrees 17 minutes 27 seconds, the highest so far reached in that part of the Arctic Sea. Some few photographs were taken, the dogs were given a double ration, a few hours of sleep were taken, and then, with heavy hearts, they turned back upon their track.

On their homeward path rose obstructions of another sort. Where open water had crossed their outward road they were now confronted with a huge pressure ridge of ice, estimated to be from seventy-five to one hundred feet high. A new road had to be made around this, but soon their old path was struck again, and on they floundered through snow, ice and storm until April 29th, when the shores of Crozier Island rose before them and their journey over the polar pack was at an end. Four more marches took them to Fort Conger. Here they stopped to dry their clothes, repair their sledges and give their dogs the rest they sadly needed, and then set out on their final march for Payer Harbor, which they reached on May 17th.

With this the four years of hard labor and strenuous effort ended. It ended in defeat, but not wholly defeat. Though the problem of the Pole remained unsolved, though Peary's "farthest north" lay two degrees south of those of Nansen and Abruzzi, he had accomplished much in the way of giving the world new geographical knowledge. He had especially proved the insular character of Greenland and traversed its northern coast practically as far as Independence Bay, thus completing the circuit of the island with the exception of a small portion of its eastern coast, which has since then been traversed.

The ship he had left no longer awaited him, but on August 5th a new "Windward" steamed into the harbor, a relief ship sent northward by the Arctic Club. And to his delight and comfort, on its deck appeared Mrs. Peary and her little daughter, the "snow-baby" of nine years before. Hastily getting on board all that he had to take back, he crossed the sound to the Greenland side and there landed at their home the Eskimos who had faithfully stood by him throughout these four long years of labor and adventure. One other duty remained, to provide them and their dogs with food for the coming winter. This was done by the killing of sufficient walrus for the purpose, and then the "Windward" turned her prow southward, reaching the outpost of civilization at Sydney, N. B., on September 17, 1902, after an absence of four and a quarter years.

It might be supposed that Commander Peary—a rank he had now attained—would have been ready to desist from Arctic exploration after his sixteen years of almost continuous effort in the Arctic wilds. But what he had done only whetted his appetite for what remained to be done. The Pole was not yet reached and he could not rest content until that goal of his life's struggle was attained. He had not even reached the latitude gained in the Siberian seas, and he could not rest until America had matched Europe in northward progress. He was scarcely home from his four years in the Arctic before he began to lay plans and make preparations for another journey to the north, supported as before by the Peary, Arctic Club.

A new ship was built for him, the first American ship ever expressly constructed for Arctic work, one in a measure laid down on the lines of Nansen's "Fram," and strengthened in every way available against the crushing force of the floating ice. The "Roosevelt" it was called, a name significant of effort, energy and success.

It is not necessary to describe this vessel here; that has been done in a former chapter, for the "Roosevelt" was the good ship that carried Peary to triumph in 1909, as already told. We have here to narrate the events of its pioneer voyage, that of 1905-06.

Leaving New York on the 16th of July, 1905, completely equipped in every particular for a long siege in the sea of ice, the "Roosevelt" headed north with the Stars and Stripes floating at her peak and made her way to Sydney, N. B., where every inch of emptiness in her hold was filled with coal. Reaching the Greenland in due time a new work was begun, that of taking on Eskimos and their dogs. Etah reached, the coal that had been used was replenished from the "Eric," an auxiliary ship, and on August 17th the "Roosevelt" put out into the icy waters of Smith Sound, having on board half a hundred Eskimos—men, women and children and all their earthly goods—and over two hundred Eskimo dogs.

On this occasion there was no intention to seek a wintering place at Payer Harbor, as before, but to push upward to the most northerly point possible to reach. It was proposed to make this harbor a sub-base, and put there a large supply of food-stuffs, but it was so packed with ice that no ship could enter, and the proposed depot of supplies was made farther north. The fight with the ice that took place in their further voyage is too much like that to be found described in Arctic navigation in general to need telling here. It must suffice to say that the sturdy ship fought her way mile by mile northward, now finding open water for a hasty dash, now environed with ice until escape seemed impossible. Through Kennedy Channel, Kane Sea and Robeson Channel the gallant contest continued, until the end of the latter channel was nearly reached and the Polar Sea approached. Here a terrible crush tried the strength of the "Roosevelt" to the utmost and seriously injured her rudder and steering apparatus, but she was pushed onward still to the mouth of Robeson Channel and into the waters of Lincoln Sea, farther north than any ship had ever been in that quarter of the

Arctic area. Here, steaming at full speed through the heavy floes, they "fairly hurled the 'Roosevelt' into a shallow nook on the face of the ice-foot under the point of Cape Sheridan, just as the polar pack closed in compactly against the shore."

It was an exposed position, but no effort they could make was able to carry the ship farther, and her destruction here seemed imminent when, on the evening of September 16th, a heavy floe came sweeping round the cape and pressed against the vessel with terrific force. For the moment all seemed at an end. The ribs and bracing of the "Roosevelt" cracked like volleys of musketry. The main deck bulged upwards several inches and the masts and rigging shook as if in a violent gale. Then, with a mighty tremor, the ship jumped upward over the interior ice and the great floe moved onward, groaning and crumbling, leaving the ship stranded but safe.

To avoid danger of a new crush that might grind the ship to powder, the supplies and equipment and a large quantity of the coal were hastily landed and a camp made on shore for the winter now close at hand. A season of hunting followed, successful hunting, as it proved. A large number of Arctic hares were first obtained. Then a hunt for musk oxen proved very successful, and by the 1st of November about two hundred and fifty of these fine food animals had been secured. The party revelled in fresh meat. Another interesting animal was met with, a species of Arctic reindeer which Peary had discovered in 1902, a magnificent, snow-white animal, with splendid, branching antlers. Of these more than fifty were secured. Yet one serious misfortune came upon them. The whale meat which had been depended upon for dog food proved poisonous and about eighty of these animals died before the cause of their death was discovered. The remainder of the whale meat was now thrown away, and to save the rest of the dogs it became necessary to find game to carry them through the winter.

This was done by prospecting the Lake Hazen region to the south, in which many animals were found. During the winter the

Copyright 1908 by Harris & Ewing.

COMMANDER ROBERT EDWIN PEARY

Photographed just before his departure on the world-famous expedition, which has just been brought to a successful conclusion.

MISS MARIE PEARY, "THE SNOW BABY"

Daughter of the Great Discoverer, born within the Arctic Circle, and farther north than any other white child.

Photo by Underwood & Underwood, New York.

PEARY'S ESKIMO GUIDES

An Eskimo family photographed on Peary's ship. No Eskimo man will travel without his entire family. It was said that Dr. Cook was accompanied by two men who had formerly been with Peary.

Photo by Underwood & Underwood, New York. AN ESKIMO SETTLEMENT

Etah, Greenland. The most northerly village on earth. It was from near Etah that Dr. Cook made his dash for the Pole and past which Peary sailed. These Eskimo huts are made of skins and are covered with snow and ice in winter. They are about twelve feet in diameter at the bottom.

dogs and most of the Eskimos lived in this region, subsisting upon the country, and in every full moon season sending sledge-loads of meat to the ship, taking back tea, sugar, biscuit and oil. The winter proved one of unusual mildness, adding to the ease of this hunting life and the comfort of those remaining in the camp.

On February 7th the last of the field parties came in, and on rounding up the dogs it was found that there were one hundred and twenty left, enough for twenty teams of six dogs each. The time was near at hand for the beginning of the polar dash, and preparations for it were set in train, parties being sent west to Cape Hecla, the proposed starting point, with advance loads of supplies. From the summit of Hecla, 1,600 feet high, a telescope showed the disagreeable prospect of many leads of open water, sure to give trouble to the expedition now at hand.

By the 23d the total exploring party, with their sledges and dogs, were collected at Cape Hecla, ready to start northward as soon as all their apparatus was in condition. The leader proposed an advance in four divisions, Captain Bartlett, commander of the "Roosevelt," leading the first, and Commander Peary the last. The route was to be divided into sections of about fifty miles each, each section to be under the charge of a white man and a few Eskimos with dogs and sledges. Each party was to continually traverse its section back and forth, thus steadily carrying forward supplies and forming caches for the aid of the party of advance when the time of retreat should arrive. A well devised plan, but the chances of polar travel were to render it of no avail.

In advance of all was to go a pioneer party, with very light sledge-loads, to pick out a route and break a trail for the heavier sledges that followed.

This seemed an ideal organization of the party, and would have been such on a solid surface, but on drifting ice it was in constant peril of disruption. It might well have enabled Peary to reach the Pole and return in safety in that unusually open season but for the delay caused by a big lead and the misadventure of a six-day's gale, which rendered all their careful preparations of no avail and in the end brought the leading party into a position of the most critical danger.

On February 28th the first party set out, following the ice to Cape Moss, about twenty miles west of Cape Hecla. From this point the northward journey began, the separate divisions following each other on successive days. Trouble with leads and moving ice was soon encountered, while the ice between the leads was often so rough that much of the trail had to be cut with pickaxes, progress in consequence being slow.

At eighty miles from land the ice surface grew much better, but the leads came oftener and were wider. The worst of them was met at 84 degrees 38 minutes north latitude, where Peary came upon all of the advance parties, those led by Bartlett, Henson and Clark, huddled together on the margin of a big and impassable lead, stretching so far to the east and west that they were unable to go round it at the ends.

The situation was an ugly one. Bartlett and Clark were sent back for more supplies, while Peary and Henson waited for an opportunity to cross the water lane. At this time three of the supply parties, those of Marvin, Wolf and Ryan, were bound outward from land on their second trip as food carriers.

For six long days the impatient voyagers waited beside the great lead, now two miles wide. Then young ice crossed the interval and they ventured across with half loads, the ice bending under the weight. The opposite side reached, Henson and his party at once hastened forward, Peary waiting for a day to make a cache and leave instructions for the supporting parties when they should arrive.

When the Commander next set out the weather was so thick that he had much ado in following Henson's path, but finally reached him, after three days' marches, at latitude 85 degrees 12 minutes, camped in a dense fog. A gale succeeded, snow flurries accompanying it, and increased steadily in violence, blowing without intermission for six days. When it ceased an observation of the sun showed that the drifting ice had borne them seventy miles to the eastward. All their well-laid plans of supporting parties were destroyed and twelve priceless dogs had been lost. Nothing remained for them but a dash forward, with possible aid, possible obstruction, from the conditions of wind, water and ice.

There was no time to be lost. Henson was at once dispatched on the forward path and two Eskimos were sent back on the trail, to meet any supporting parties that might have crossed the lead and bring up the cache left beside the open water. In twenty-four hours they came back. They had not been able to get half way to the cache, open water and shattered ice cutting off the way. It was evident that the plan of support was irretrievably damaged and nothing remained to do except to dash forward as fast and far as possible.

We may quote Peary's own account of what followed the march from Storm Camp, as he called their resting place after the gale:

"At Storm Camp we abandoned everything not absolutely necessary and bent every energy to setting a record pace. In the legacy of retrievable damage which the storm had left us was one small codicil—such snow as the wind had not torn from the face of the floe was beaten and banked hard, and the snow which had fallen had been hammered into the areas of rough ice and the shattered edges of the big floes so that they gave us little trouble. North of Storm Camp we had no occasion for snowshoes or pickaxes.

"The first march of ten hours in the lead with the compass, sometimes on a dog trot, the sledges following in Indian file with drivers running beside or behind, placed us thirty miles to the good; my Eskimos said forty. Four hours out on the second march I overtook Henson in his third camp, beside a lead which was closed. When I arrived he hitched up and followed behind my hurrying party. I had with me now seven men and six teams, with less than half a load for each.

"As we advanced the character of the ice improved, the floes becoming much larger and rafters infrequent, but the cracks and narow leads increased and were nearly all active. These cracks were uniformly at right angles to our course, and the ice on the northern side was moving more rapidly eastward than that on the southern.

"As dogs gave out, unable to keep the pace, they were fed to the others. April 20th we came into a region of open leads, leading nearly north and south, and the ice motion became more pronounced. Hurrying on between these, a forced march was made. Then we slept a few hours, and, starting again soon after midnight, pushed on till noon of the 21st.

"My observation then gave 87 degrees 6 minutes. So far as history records, this is the nearest approach to the Pole ever made by human beings.

"I thanked God with as good a grace as possible for what I had been able to accomplish, though it was but an empty bauble compared with the splendid jewel for which I was straining my life. But, looking at my remaining dogs and the nearly empty sledges, and bearing in mind the moving ice and the unknown quantity of the big lead between us and the nearest land, I felt that I had cut the margin as narrow as could be reasonably expected.

"My flags were flung out from the top of the highest pinnacle near us, and a hundred feet or so beyond I left a bottle containing a brief record and a piece of the silk flag which six years before I had carried round the northern end of Greenland."

Such is the dramatic story of Peary's "Farthest North" of 1905-06.

The return journey must be much more briefly told, though it was one replete with perils and hardships. Their carefully planned line of supplies cut off, and the food brought with them so reduced in quantity that he had not dared to advance a mile further, they were in serious danger of starvation before they could reach the ship again. Their journey back was thus a race for life, and one made in the face of an unremitting blizzard, through which "none but an Eskimo could have kept the trail."

The blizzard past, a region of broken ice and huge pressure ridges was encountered, in which their pickaxes were constantly in use. Slow and exhausting was their progress, and when the ridges were passed a greater danger yet confronted them. There ran the big lead, a band of black water extending in both directions to the limit of vision. It had delayed their outward march; it was to delay more perilously their return march.

Efforts to cross it with their sledges and the light remaining loads of food were tried in vain. In one place they tried to cross on half-frozen rubble-ice, but finding that it was parting under their feet they hurried back in alarm. Then for five dismal days they remained marooned on a piece of old floe ice, drifting steadily to the east, while the lead continued to widen. Commander Peary tells what followed so graphically and well that we must borrow again from his own narrative:

"On the fifth day two Eskimos whom I had sent reconnoitering to the east reported young ice a few miles distant which might support us on snowshoes across the lead, now over two miles wide. No time was lost in hurrying to the place when it was evident that it was our chance or never. Each man tied on his snowshoes with utmost care and we began the crossing in widely extended line. Each man was intent upon his snowshoes which could not be lifted from the ice, while the slightest unsteadiness or stumbling would have meant his finish. The thin film crusting the black water bent and yielded beneath us, sending undulations in every direction. I do not care for another similar experience.

"Across those intermediate miles we walked in silence. It was with an inexpressible relief that I skipped on the firm ice on the other side with a number of my party still on the ice. As we left the lead a widening lane of black water cut the frail bridge upon which we had crossed into two parts.

"During the remainder of this march and the next week we cut our way slowly through such a hell of shattered ice as I hope never to see again, a conglomeration of fragments in size from a paving-stone to the dome of the Capitol, rounded by the terrific grinding they had received between the jams of the big lead."

During these five days of dismal waiting beside the waters of their Styx, as Peary christened this sullen river in the ice, they had to kill the few dogs that remained for food and break up their sledges for fuel to cook them with. It was as well, for they could not have taken them across that frail bridge of ice.

On they went, as fast as their feet could carry them. Finally the white peaks of Greenland became faintly visible in the distance and their hearts leaped with hope. On the 12th of May they dragged themselves ashore at Cape Neumeyer. They were not far from starvation, but knew from old experience that there was hope of food at this point. In an hour they had found and killed four hares. "And how delicious they were!" Peary exclaims.

Just before reaching land they had passed sledge tracks leading eastward, followed by the stumbling footsteps of four men. Two Eskimos were sent on the trail, and returned with Clark and two Eskimos, feeble and on the point of starvation. They had been rescued just in time.

There is little more to tell. The hares they continued to find served them as food, and soon they reached Robeson Channel, the crossing of which brought them in a short time back to the "Roosevelt." Sending scouts to call in the parties still out, preparations were made to break out for the voyage south as soon as possible. Meanwhile a journey was made to the western shores of Grant Land and here another discovery was made, that of snow-clad summits in the far northwest, indicating land in that direction. A hitherto unknown island apparently lay there, marked on recent maps as Crocker Land.

With all their efforts, it was near the end of August before the

"Roosevelt" was got into open water in Robeson Channel, and September 16th when Etah was reached. Their broken rudder gave them trouble throughout, and it was November 23d when the crippled "Roosevelt" steamed into Sydney Harbor and the news of Peary's farthest north was telegraphed south and became the leading topic of the civilized world.

CHAPTER XI

Europe Gives Honor to Dr. Cook

SEPTEMBER 4, 1909, will long be a memorable day to the inhabitants of Copenhagen, Denmark. Brief interviews and laconic wireless telegrams had announced that Dr. Cook would land that day, and the eyes of the world were turned toward Denmark, impatient for news of the great discovery and the man who had made it.

Preparations on a regal scale had been going on since the receipt of the news. The steamer "Hans Egede," on which the intrepid explorer was returning from the frozen North, had passed Cape Skagen, the northern extremity of Denmark, on the 3d, and was due at her dock the next morning. An enterprising correspondent secured an interview with Dr. Cook on board ship, and even greater interest was aroused by the statement of the returning explorer that he would submit evidence which would prove beyond a doubt that he had attained the goal sought for so many years at such a fearful cost in lives, suffering and money. Further brief statements of conditions at and near the Pole whetted the appetites of the waiting scientists. Copenhagen was filled with visitors and draped with flags and bunting in honor of the occasion, and all the carriages in the city had been engaged to take the crowds down to the pier to meet the incoming hero.

At 9.30 o'clock on the morning of the 4th Dr. Cook landed from the "Hans Egede" amid a scene of indescribable enthusiasm, in which the King of Denmark, the Queen, princes, scientific men of world-wide reputation, the American Minister, scores of Americans and thousands of Danes took part. As a preliminary to the reception by the people, Crown Prince Christian of Denmark, the American Minister, Maurice Egan, the Danish Minister of Commerce and various committees boarded the "Hans Egede" before docking and welcomed the explorer in the name of the nation and the city.

A weather-beaten figure, clad in rusty black canvas clothes and shod with moccasins, greeted them, and it was a little difficult for a moment to reconcile the keen-eyed, shaggy-haired man before them with the scientist whose skill and indomitable courage had led him, as they believed, to the top of the world.

A naval launch brought the explorer ashore, accompanied by Crown Prince Christian, Commander Hovgaard, of the king's yacht, and Captain Johan Hansen, Minister of Commerce. They landed with their guest at the water steps in front of the Meteorological Institute. On ascending the steps Dr. Cook was literally mobbed by the enthusiastic crowd, and if it had not been for the sturdy phalanx of Americans who constituted his bodyguard he would have had the clothes torn from his back. Speaking from the balcony of the Meteorological Office, where he was conveyed for safety's sake, Dr. Cook said:

"I have had a hard time coming here. I cannot say how glad I am at the opportunity of landing in Denmark. I thank you."

He was then taken in a motor car to the American Legation, where he reported himself to Minister Egan. On his way to the Hotel Phœnix, Dr. Cook received a magnificent ovation from an enormous multitude which blocked his progress. He could scarcely reach the hotel and remarked jokingly: "All obstacles encountered on the way to the Pole were scarcely as formidable as these of admirers."

At the hotel he received cables from his wife in Maine and messages of congratulation from Belgian, French, Scottish and German geographical associations. A few hours made a vast difference in Dr. Cook's appearance. His room at the hotel, where he was the guest of the Danish Geographical Society, was littered with ready-made suits of clothing, new patent leather boots, hats, etc., which were tried on while a hairdresser was cutting his tangled hair. None recognized in the well-groomed, dapper new gentleman, who soon issued from the apartments, the travel-stained, weather-beaten individual who arrived a few hours previously.

After lunching with Minister Egan at the American Legation, the explorer was received in private audience by King Frederick of Denmark, the Queen and her three daughters, Princesses Ingeborg, Thyra and Dagmar, being present. Dr. Cook was presented by Maurice Egan, the American Minister, and was received most cordially by King Frederick, who asked him many questions and drew from him a long account of his expedition. The audience lasted for half an hour.

Returning to his hotel, he received a battalion of correspondents, who subjected him for another hour to a merciless cross-examination, demanding explanations of all the criticisms that had been leveled against his claims.

These questions Dr. Cook answered with the best temper, frankly and fully. Whatever was thought of Dr. Cook elsewhere, he impressed all who talked with him there as a modest, frank and able man. Scandinavian explorers—and Scandinavia is the home of many Arctic pioneers—were the first to indorse Dr. Cook's claims to the discovery of the Pole and his methods of getting to the goal. Their opinions were based primarily on personal knowledge of Dr. Cook's character and former achievements. Only after consulting them confidentially and receiving the fullest pronouncement of their belief in the genuineness of his feat did the Danish government give its official seal, by this reception, to Dr. Cook's good faith.

In the evening the first public banquet to Dr. Cook was given in the magnificent municipal building. Four hundred persons, many of them ladies, attended, while thousands congregated in the streets in a drenching rainstorm to catch sight of the explorer when he entered.

The menu was an example of enterprise, with a lithograph of the Crown Prince greeting Dr. Cook and a map of the Arctic Circle giving Dr. Cook's route and a fac-simile of his autograph, with the date, which was a reproduction of a souvenir he gave Miss Egan.

The speeches teemed with compliments to Dr. Cook. The Mayor of Copenhagen remarked that the name of Cook was a second time enrolled among the great explorers. Minister Egan briefly proposed a toast to the King of Denmark, and the corporation president, in proposing a toast to the President of the United States, spoke of the pride that must be felt by the nation which could boast that it was her son who first planted the flag where no human being had ever before set foot.

The Minister of Commerce, in proposing the health of Dr. Cook, paid a warm tribute to "his noble deed." He thanked him for spending a little time in Denmark, and said that the privations of the explorer were appreciated most by the men of Denmark there present, whose names are written with honor on the ice rock of Denmark's northern colony.

When the Minister raised his glass to "Our Noble Guest" there were nine hurrahs. He was followed by Commodore Hovgaard, who spoke from the standpoint of an expert explorer and warmly commended Cook's methods.

Dr. Cook replied in a few words, modestly saying:

"I thank you very much for the warm and eloquent words, but I am unable to express myself properly. It was a rather hard day for me, but I never enjoyed a day better. The Danes have taken no active part in polar explorations, but they have been of much importance as silent partners in almost all Arctic expeditions in recent years. The most important factor in my expedition was the Eskimo and the dog world, and I cannot be too thankful to the Danes for their care of the Eskimos, and now they also have instituted a mission at Cape York. Had I not met with the right Eskimos and the right dogs and the right provisions I could never have reached the Pole. I owe much to the Danish nation for my success."

Such was Dr. Cook's first day on shore. Royalty, scientists and people of all degrees of life vied with each other to do him honor, while the rest of the world eagerly read the news flashed over the cables. Eminent scientists in Copenhagen were given a chance to examine Dr. Cook's diary and to a man were satisfied that his claim of having reached the Pole was true. After having received this report and satisfied himself that Dr. Cook was to be believed, King Frederick instructed the court chamberlain to summon the explorer to dine with him on the evening of the day after his arrival.

The dinner at the royal castle at Charlottenlund was the scene of the greatest enthusiasm. The king and every member of the royal family, even the smallest children, assembled. Dr. Maurice F. Egan, American Minister; Rev. Dr. Daae, of Chicago, and several other guests completed the party. The dinner passed off quietly, as is customary on Sunday in the Danish royal household, but after the dinner there was a regular rush around Dr. Cook, who began a succinct recital of his adventures. The graphic depiction gained much support from the calmness and candor of the speaker. One after another of the royal personages plied him with questions which marked their intelligent appreciation of the conditions in Arctic seas, and then waited eagerly while the explorer answered, always without hesitation.

During these days the men of science from every part of Europe poured into Copenhagen and sought an interview with Dr. Cook, while in every capital and city the discovery formed the chief subject of discussion. Crowned heads bowed to the dauntless explorer and telegraphed their congratulations. Geographical societies in many cities acknowledged his triumph over the obstacles which had defied the world for centuries and acclaimed him as the victor. Throughout the civilized countries of the earth the returned explorer was the man of the hour.

Dr. Cook had imagined that he would be able to get back to New York quietly and have a chance to revise his scientific records and put them into shape to lay before the geographical societies and the world at large, little anticipating the ovation awaiting him. On one occasion during the first few days after his arrival he managed to escape the interviewers and ask a few questions on his own account.

"What was the remarkable play, the 'Merry Widow,' of which he had heard from the Danes in Greenland? What was Taft's majority?" and similar questions. To many this seemed amusing, but to a man cut off entirely from the world for two years, news of any kind was like food to the starving.

The King of Denmark, acting on carefully considered advice from experts, continued to distinguish Dr. Cook with such honors as never before had been given to a private person. All the Danish newspapers, after a brief period of skepticism, accepted him wholly. There had been some doubt of his claims before his arrival, but one of the strongest factors in the universal confidence with which he was received was the simplicity and earnestness of his manner, his engaging personality and the absolute freedom and candor with which he answered all questions. Instead of avoiding the men of his own profession—exploration—he spent every possible moment with them discussing eagerly observations, ice-floes and drifts, dogs and supplies, and they accepted him with whole-hearted trustfulness.

One of the most dramatic incidents of Dr. Cook's first days in Copenhagen was the remarkable trial of the explorer before a jury of fifty representatives of the world's press at the Phœnix Hotel. Of this interview one correspondent said:

"Dr. Cook had just returned from a reception by Princess Marie at Bernstoff Castle through a crowd of surging, cheering people.

He had been received by the King, feted at the American Legation, and treated with the homage given to a warrior returning from his conquests, and now there was something pathetic in the fact that he was called on to prove his claim as the greatest explorer the world has ever known.

"I could almost fancy the shades of Cabot, Franklin and Andrée standing with folded arms behind the little man as he spoke quietly in his curious American drawl tinged by years in the Arctic with a Scandinavian accent. We seemed to be making history, and behind the greatness of it there was something grotesque.

"Here was a man whose greatness will live as long as the world lasts arraigned like a prisoner in the dock, charged with discovering the North Pole. For an hour he was submitted to a searching cross-examination and sat there answering questions with a map of the Arctic regions spread before him, tracing the adventurous journey with his forefinger from his last glimpse of land to the great ice desert.

"He smiled indulgently now and again as if he pitied our incredulity, but never once did he decline to answer questions, and they were put to him baldly and directly. It was a trial of veracity. Dr. Cook, with his back to the wall, was fighting to convince a world of unbelievers. The picture will ever remain with me out of to-day's record of a little, sturdy man with dreamy gray blue eyes that seemed to vision the desolate days, what had been a trim, fair mustache stubbling his upper lip and a firm, strong chin, now shorn of beard.

"A very ordinary catalogue of a man's features, but that is the most remarkable thing about him. He is just a man of the type you see every day. If there is anything persistent in his individuality it is those haunting eyes, the eyes of a man who has looked for an empty horizon. He turned this way and that, replying like a witness giving evidence before a royal commission.

"He belongs to the supermen of to-day, the Shackletons, the

Bleriots and the men who are carrying on the great traditions not of nations but of all mankind. I felt, I think all felt, that the verdict of the Copenhagen jury was quite unanimous as to the discovery of the Pole."

The early morning and the late evening seemed the only times in which Dr. Cook could attend to his correspondence. A mountainous pile of letters, telegrams and cablegrams descended upon him every day—kings, princes, potentates, scientists and men of letters in all parts joined in congratulating and paying tribute to him, but he received with the greatest gratification of all a characteristic reply from the President of the United States to his message announcing the discovery of the North Pole. The text of these messages is as follows.

"COPENHAGEN, September 4.
"*President, the White House, Washington.*
"I have the honor to report to the Chief Magistrate of the United States that I have returned, having reached the North Pole.
"FREDERICK A. COOK."

"BEVERLY, Mass., September 4.
"*Frederick A. Cook, Copenhagen.*
"Your dispatch received. Your report that you have reached the North Pole calls for my heartiest congratulations and stirs the pride of all Americans that this feat, which has so long baffled the world, has been accomplished by the intelligent energy and wonderful endurance of a fellow-countryman.
"WILLIAM H. TAFT."

It seemed that every honor in the gift of the Danish people had been laid at the feet of the hero of the hour, but one—in the view of the scientific world perhaps the greatest—was reserved to the last days of the explorer's stay in Denmark. This climax came when the University of Copenhagen, a world-famous institution of learning, decided, after long and careful examination of the claims made by Dr. Cook, and consultation with the greatest authorities on the subject, to confer upon him the honorary degree of "Doctor of Science." The occasion of September 9, 1909, was one never to be forgotten by a witness. In the presence of the Crown Prince of Denmark and many other people of high rank, the honorary degree of doctor of science was conferred upon Dr. Cook in the handsome hall of the university. The floor and gallery were packed. The ceremony was of the simplest kind. No academic pomp was present, and there was no sign of academic robes.

At one o'clock the Crown Prince and Princess, accompanied by Prince and Princess George of Greece, all in morning dress, entered and took seats on the dais opposite the rector of the university's tribunal and the professors. Dr. Cook, in evening dress, sat at the other side beneath the tribunal.

The rector ascended the tribunal and in a short address thanked the Crown Prince for attending the ceremony. He then gave a brief sketch of the rise and development of polar exploration, mentioning the best known names, and said that the distinction of this degree ought to be conferred on Dr. Cook not only for his achievements in science and exploration, but as a natural expression of the university's esteem for a man who one way and another through great personal achievement had "given us something that makes us look up to the doer as a man of thought and action, a true *homo sapiens.*"

"Such a man," continued the rector, "is Dr. Cook. Soon after we received the news of his achievement we learned that another well known explorer had solved the same problem; but this can in no way lower Dr. Cook's personal value or our own admiration for his deeds. We are glad that it was an American who succeeded in linking closer the old ties between the two countries."

Addressing Dr. Cook personally, the rector added: "Whether your scientific research will rank very highly or not the faculty gives you this degree in recognition of your great achievements in exploration and the qualities you have shown therein."

Descending from the throne, Rector Magnificus Torp handed to Dr. Cook a diploma in a red case and motioned him to ascend the throne. As Dr. Cook complied the audience broke into handclapping that was prolonged for fully a minute and a half. Dr. Cook looked pleased and a trifle shy; but when the clapping ceased he glanced almost sternly around the hall and said with a sharp, staccato manner and in a clear voice:

"I accept this degree with due appreciation of the honor done me. By it you have stamped my journey to the Pole. All my records of observations and papers of every kind are to be examined forthwith by a proper tribunal. When that has been done they will be sent here for you to see and examine first. I ask you only to wait until then. I do not want you to examine mere fragments, but want you to examine it all.

"Since unfortunate rumors have been circulated, I will, at my own expense, send a ship for the Eskimos who were with me. They will be taken to New York and examined there by Rasmussen, whom I regard as the greatest authority on Eskimo and the Eskimo language."

This speech was greeted with fresh applause. After the explorer had descended from the tribunal the members of the royal family left the hall, each stopping to shake hands with Dr. Cook and congratulating him warmly.

A scene of great enthusiasm followed as Dr. Cook left the hall. An enormous crowd had gathered to wait for him, as they were unable to gain admittance to the hall to witness the ceremony. On his appearance they cheered him wildly and great numbers followed his motor car to the hotel.

Another great triumph came to Dr. Cook on the occasion of the reception and lecture under the auspices of the Royal Geographical Society of Denmark, which was held in Odd Fellows Hall, as the chamber of the Geographical Society was altogether too small for the purpose. The affair was one of the most brilliant in the scientific history of the Scandinavian State.

Many of the royal family were present, and there were representatives of the army, navy and all learned bodies. The Crown Prince pinned the gold medal of the Geographical Society on Dr. Cook's breast, and afterward Dr. Cook went to the balcony and witnessed a torchlight procession of Danish students dressed in historic costumes.

This was the last great event of Dr. Cook's stay in Copenhagen. He had accepted invitations to go to Brussels and to Paris to deliver lectures and was considering a similar plan for London, when the news came of Peary's achievement and soon afterward his denunciations of Dr. Cook began to pour in. Shocked and hurt by these charges and anxious to defend himself, the accused explorer decided to sail at once for New York.

On Saturday, September 11th, he left Copenhagen on his way to New York and his home and family in Brooklyn. Up to the last minute the Danish people continued to express their entire confidence in Dr. Cook and absolute belief in his story in spite of any doubts cast upon it by his rival, and the last words in his ears were expressions of the greatest friendship and good will.

CHAPTER XII

Receptions of Cook and Peary on American Soil

THE announcement had no sooner been made that Dr. Cook would leave Denmark on September 11th for New York than great preparations were begun to give him a rousing reception home. Many people, his neighbors in Brooklyn, friends of early days, his comrades in the Explorers' Club and the Arctic Club, as well as thousands of New Yorkers who felt merely a general interest and entertained a patriotic enthusiasm to welcome the returning victor, at once began to lay plans to make his homecoming a memorable occasion.

Although great interest prevailed not only in New York, but over the whole country, the enthusiasm was greatest of all in Dr. Cook's home city of Brooklyn. Eminent citizens, military and civil organizations, friends and neighbors, and the people at large of the city determined to show the country and the world that the returning explorer belonged to them and that they proposed to assert the fact.

The Citizens' Committee, appointed by President Byrd S. Coler, of the Borough of Brooklyn, held a meeting and decided on the program for the reception. In the meanwhile New York had not been idle. The Arctic Club, of which Dr. Cook is a member, chartered the excursion steamer "Grand Republic" to take more than twelve hundred people down the bay to Quarantine that they might secure the first glimpse of the explorer and take him home to Brooklyn.

Invitations to banquets and receptions of all kinds, sent by wireless, nearly overwhelmed the discoverer. Mrs. Cook naturally claimed her right as his wife to greet her husband before all others, and those in charge of the arrangements acceded to the request readily and graciously. It was arranged that a tug should be secured to transfer Dr. Cook from the "Oscar II" to the "Grand Republic," and that Mrs. Cook, her children, Dr. Cook's two brothers and a few members of the Executive Committee should be the only passengers on this vessel.

Meanwhile the "Oscar II" was rapidly approaching, and at about three o'clock in the afternoon of Monday, the 20th, she anchored off Fire Island, bringing her eminent passengers practically in sight of home. He was on deck almost constantly, and as sunset approached he watched the brilliant panorama, and conversed with newspapermen with a brief hail in reply to their greetings through a megaphone.

"I feel anxious to get ashore," he said to those who were grouped about him on the deck. "It seems about ten years since I left, instead of only two and a half, but I dread the ordeal of landing tomorrow. I would much prefer landing quickly and quietly without a repetition of the scenes at Copenhagen. I hope that I shall be left in peace with my family by tomorrow night at least."

The first tugs, bearing the advance guard of newspapermen from New York, reached the "Oscar II" that night, but no one was allowed aboard the vessel except Anthony Fiala, the Arctic explorer, who was a friend of Doctor Cook. He swung himself up from a tug, held a brief conversation with the explorer and departed.

To those on the "Oscar II" the night seemed a long and anxious one. With New York but a few miles away and anticipation of the great events of the morrow to keep them awake, it proved an uneasy night for the passengers. The "Oscar II" lay at anchor off Fire Island until shortly after midnight, when she weighed anchor and proceeded to quarantine. There she anchored to await the inspection of the health officer at 6 o'clock. At sunrise the ship was dressed with flags and preparations were made to receive the explorer's wife and children and the Reception Committee of city officers and friends of Dr. Cook on the "Grand Republic."

From five o'clock in the morning the explorer paced the deck watching every vessel which approached to see whether it bore his wife. One moment he thought he saw her and waved his hat. Then he dashed down to the waist of the ship, where a temporary companionway had been rigged to permit him to descend to the tug bearing his wife. It was a false alarm, and the explorer returned to pace the deck and wait.

At last the right tug was dimly outlined in the mist, and Dr. Cook was down the ladder before it came alongside. The sea was running at a good rate, and as the tug threw her line aboard her beam crashed into the companionway and forced the explorer to beat a hasty retreat. Then he ran down once more, leaped across the intervening stretch of water to the tug, dashed up to the hurricane deck, where his wife was waving the Stars and Stripes, and folded her in his arms. He held her thus without a single word being uttered.

Then he broke the silence.

"Where are the children?" he said.

His wife did not reply, but led him to them a few steps away. He kissed his elder daughter, then seized the younger one in his arms and raised her to his shoulder. At this the spectators broke into cheers.

"Bravo, Cook." "Welcome home." "We're proud of you," ran out across the water. Then the song "For He's a Jolly Good Fellow," was sung by Doctor Cook's fellow passengers on the "Oscar II" as the tug left the ship's side.

Doctor Cook was transferred quickly to the Grand Republic, which was lying a quarter of a mile away. Cinematographs and cameras were turned on him from every point of vantage as he passed through a guard of honor of the Forty-seventh Regiment to receive the greeting of the Reception Committee.

As he was greeted by them, a wreath of roses was placed about his neck by Miss Ida A. Lehman, a daughter of one of his old Brooklyn friends, who had been delegated to decorate the explorer in accordance with the custom followed at his welcome at Copenhagen. As Miss Lehman threw the garland about his neck she said:

"You hero of the North, come to us, your friends, associates and business acquaintances of your neighborhood, Bushwick. Your record with us was one of honor, character and conscience and your word the synonym of truth. We believed you from the far North and are here to proclaim you a 'gentleman of Bushwick.'"

Doctor Cook wore the garland during the reception ceremonies, although he did not look particularly comfortable with it.

Borough President Coler welcomed the explorer on behalf of Brooklyn. He said:

"I regret that we have not a Mayor as big as our town to receive you. You are not only a great explorer, but a thorough American gentleman, and Mrs. Cook is a thorough American lady."

Captain Bradley S. Osbon, secretary of the Arctic Club of America, spoke for that association, and read a letter from its president, Rear Admiral Schley, who regretted his inability to be present. In this letter Admiral Schley said:

"I hope you will carry to Doctor Cook my congratulations and abiding faith in the great achievement he has accomplished."

In reply to these greetings Doctor Cook made a short speech, in which he said:

"To a returning explorer there can be no greater pleasure than the appreciation of his own people. Your numbers and cheers make a demonstration that makes me very happy and should fire the pride of all the world. I would have preferred to return first to American shores, but this pleasure was denied me. Instead I came to Denmark and the result has come to you by wire.

"I was a stranger in a strange land, but the Danes with one voice rose up with enthusiasm and they have guaranteed to all other nations our conquest of the Pole.

"You have come forward in numbers with a voice of appreciation still more forcible. I can only say that I accept this honor with a due appreciation of its importance. I heartily thank you."

In the front rank of those greeting Doctor Cook as the speech-making ended was his sister, Mrs. Joseph Y. Murphy, of Toms River, N. J. The explorer took her in his arms and hugged and kissed her regardless of the cameras trained upon them. Then he saluted his niece, Miss Lillian Murphy, and shook hands with Joseph Murphy, his brother-in-law.

It was a disheveled discoverer that finally returned to his cabin, where he remained during the rest of the voyage up and down the North River. The "Grand Republic" steamed up the North River amid a shrieking of whistles of all sorts of craft from the Battery to the foot of West 130th street, where a short stop was made. The vessel continued as far as Spuyten Duyvil and then moved downwards to the foot of South Fifth street, Brooklyn. It was half an hour too early for the Brooklyn reception, so another turn around the river was made, while the band played "Auld Lang Syne" and "Home, Sweet Home."

Brooklyn's reception had all the elements of a riot except violence. From the moment the explorer, flanked by militiamen and police, fought his way into an automobile at the pier, until he left the Bushwick Club at night for the Waldorf-Astoria, in Manhattan, the surging crowds often got out of control of the police.

As the Grand Republic reached her dock the whistle of every

craft was tied down and for five minutes the brass bands were drowned. Doctor Cook, surrounded by eight militiamen, came up the gangway. The police threw a cordon around the party and pushed them through to the automobile to which Mrs. Cook and the children had preceded. A huge motor truck with a brass band pulled out ahead and Cook's automobile followed. More than 500 other automobiles, every one aflutter with bunting, fell into line and the two-mile procession moved to the Bushwick Club.

It was just noon and thousands of school children lined the streets, shouting one word in chorus, "Cook!" Trolley traffic was paralyzed, business was suspended; there was only one person of importance in Brooklyn—Cook. Along the five miles of avenues through which the explorer passed mounted police were continually fighting a way for his automobile.

Every street near the Bushwick Club was choked. First one section of the crowd would charge toward the club, and by the time the police had it under control again another wedge had shoved forward. There was a full hour's tussle before Cook's automobile came in sight.

His friends, headed by John R. Bradley, surrounded the machine, while the crowd whooped and whistled. Doctor Cook bowed and went into the house, but the mass of humanity cried, "Speech!" "Speech!" If the explorer had chosen to make one he could not have been heard. He stepped onto the balcony and bowed.

After an hour's rest, in which Dr. and Mrs. Cook were entertained at luncheon, the public reception began. The crowd filed through the billiard room, where the guest of honor stood, a wreath of flowers about his shoulders, and passed out the back door. Policemen stationed every few feet hurried the crush along. Doctor Cook bowed smilingly, occasionally breaking the rule, against the protests of the committee, and grasping the hand of some old friend.

After three hours it was decided not to tax him further, although not a quarter of those waiting their turn outside had been admitted. The doors of the club house were closed and a thoroughly tired and rather frayed citizen took off his classic garlands and sat down to his first meal on his native soil in two and a half years.

In an interval of the dinner Dr. Cook went out on one of the balconies of the club house, with the flags and streamers that swung from the gables of the building to the boxed bay trees on the sidewalk flapping in his face, and a handful of friends and relatives around him as he looked down on the crowd that eddied out across the street, stretched a block in each direction along Bushwick avenue and blocked the throat of Hart street as far as the Japanese lanterns along the parkings lighted the way.

When he came to the rail of the balcony there was a blowing of horns and a banging of tin pans that sounded like an election night and a Coney Island Mardi Gras rolled into one.

Directly below him were the 500 members of the United Singers of Brooklyn, who had come to serenade him, and in and around the club house, which is a little way from Dr. Cook's home, were jammed his neighbors and the other people who had squirmed through the police lines to welcome him home.

For a while he stood there bowing and smiling that smile that seems to have become more a matter of habit than a sign of pleasure, and then he opened his mouth to speak. The hubbub kept going with even more vigor than before. Then he smiled a real smile as he realized that it was a hopeless task to try to talk to that crowd.

A second attempt was no more successful, but by the time a third was made the efforts of the club members, who were waving their arms for silence and uttering sounds which were calculated to still the noise of the over-enthusiastic, succeeded in producing an appreciable lull in the immediate vicinity of the club house, and Dr. Cook spoke as follows:

"Ladies and gentlemen, I thank you for the honor, the music and the welcome!"

That was all there was to it, but an oration couldn't have drawn out a lustier response. The people, who had stood there for from three to six hours to catch a glimpse of this man who says that he has stood at the ninetieth parallel of north latitude, set up a tumult that made their previous efforts sound like the whispering of a lot of children. That was the only chance they got to see him, except the momentary flash as he was whisked away in his automobile.

When the balcony scene was finished Dr. Cook went back to the room on the fourth floor of the club house, where he was having dinner with his neighbors. They sat at a U-shaped table, with Dr. and Mrs. Cook at the apex, and the flags and bunting around the room left little doubts as to the nationality of the explorer. The interruption in the dinner had been caused by the arrival of the Brooklyn singers, who had come to give him some of the melody that they gave to the public at Madison Square Garden last winter.

All the Brooklyn saengervereins met at Arion Hall early in the evening and marched behind a band to the Bushwick Club. Arthur Clausen, the director, climbed to an uncertain footing on one of the iron railings and the 500 lusty German-American voices apprised Dr. Cook of their presence with Beethoven's "The Lord's Day." It was when this first number was finished that Dr. Cook came to the balcony and thanked them.

After that he went back to finish his dinner. Louis Berger, president of the Bushwick Club, and Samuel S. Whitehouse sat near him, and the rest of the guests were the committee that had been selected to receive him and their wives. When it was over Dr. Cook read a speech, written on the paper of the "Oscar II." This is what he said:

"You have shown me that it is good to go to the Pole. In re-

RECEPTIONS OF COOK AND PEARY 187

turning it was a delight to receive the cheers of other nations. But there is no human ecstasy so great as that which comes from the hearts of one's own people.

"If I talked for an hour I could not adequately express a suitable appreciation of this momentous welcome. To feel this cordiality for one moment is to dispel all the discomforts of the Arctic quest."

A few minutes later he went down to the big room of the clubhouse and stood at the angle of a narrow roped-off lane. Then the United Singers were allowed to file past him, but he refrained from shaking any hands except those of the most insistent.

"Just salute Dr. Cook and pass on!" was what the members of the club were shouting. Sometimes only one would sing out this chorus and at other times there would be as many as ten directing the movements of those who were being received.

Dr. Cook by this time was showing the effects of the day of excitement. Every now and then he passed his hands over his face and rubbed his eyes and then returned again to the task of smiling. One man out of ten refused to be satisfied with a bow and stood stockstill in front of the explorer until he took his hands from behind his back and turned over the right one to the mercies of the zealous admirer.

It was a few minutes after 9.30 that the committee allowed the explorer to telephone to some of the friends who had sent him messages, and then they announced very ostentatiously that Dr. Cook was going to be allowed to rest for a while. At the same time an automobile horn sounded at the side entrance of the clubhouse and those who were wise jumped around to this door in time to see him bundled into an automobile with his wife and Secretary Weber, of the club.

The machine, attended by motorcycle policemen, hurried Dr. Cook to the Waldorf-Astoria, where Mrs. Cook had engaged rooms for the explorer, herself and the children some days before.

On arriving here, Dr. Cook, tired out by his strenuous day, denied himself to all callers and retired to his apartments.

Such were the events of Dr. Cook's first day on his native soil. It was one which, while doubtless a source of intense gratification to him, must have taxed his powers of endurance to the utmost. It was but a foretaste of what was to come. In the days that followed the enthusiasm of the people and their eagerness to see and greet him remained unsated, and when he began his round of lectures the people of the other great cities turned out in similar multitudes to welcome the man who had come to them from the mysterious realm of the North Pole.

Meanwhile, Dr. Cook's rival for polar honors, Commander Peary, was making his way with exasperating slowness from the far North to his native land, the people of which were ready to accord him as enthusiastic a reception as they had given his predecessor, if the opportunity were granted them.

As it proved, Commander Peary's welcome to his native land presented very different features. The people were not given the opportunity they had enjoyed in the case of Dr. Cook. Had Commander Peary similarly landed in New York he would undoubtedly have been received with an ovation equally great and enthusiastic. In the smaller places at which he did touch the people turned out en masse, and their ardent welcome must have been very gratifying to the veteran explorer, who was returning victorious from his life-long quest. Hearty greetings came at Battle Harbor, Labrador, reaching him in that desolate spot through a party of newspaper men, who, growing tired of waiting for him at Sydney, Nova Scotia, chartered a steamer and made the four-hundred-mile run to Battle Harbor to bid him welcome and get the news of his journey to the Pole at first hand. It was a novel experience for the correspondents, who found the voyage not altogether an agreeable excursion. Even after they had arrived at Battle Harbor their troubles were not over.

With the waves high and a choppy sea, the problem of landing the scribes was a really dangerous one. Captain Dickson got away first in his gig, rowed by a quartet of husky sailormen. As soon as he was clear of the ship the order was given to lower the port surfboat, and immediately followed a wild scramble by photographers and correspondents for the honor of being in the first boatload. When the boat found the water a dozen men were clinging to the seats and more piled in when it was brought to the companion ladders. With the boatswain, William Goodwin, steering, the four oars struck the water and the tiny craft was headed for the entrance of the harbor. After half an hour's pull, the heavily loaded boat reached the lee of the ledge of rocks which forms a natural breakwater to the tiny harbor of Battle Harbor. During that half hour one photographer's hat went by the board and another, that of a correspondent, would have followed had it not been attached to him with half a fathom of cable.

All were thoroughly glad and as thoroughly wet when they rounded the entrance and beheld the Roosevelt lying at anchor. Beside her was the tug D. H. Thomas and the Associated Press scribes. There were lusty cheers, and an instant later sixteen able-bodied newspaper workers were scrambling over the Roosevelt's sides and the attack on the vessel was begun.

If there was any one on the Roosevelt who was not quizzed until he wished himself back safely at the Pole, it was not the fault of the scribes and camera men. The wireless operator, Gordon Spracklin, was rounded out of his beehive and half a dozen cameras fired in unison.

Then came the inquisition of the commander. This was in two instalments, and when the smoke cleared away late in the afternoon the party of "visiting press men," as the captain called them, was taken back to the Tyrian in a sea less turbulent than that which had greeted them on their arrival. After lying at anchor all night to avoid the dangers of navigating the unlighted

Belle Isle Strait in the dark, the Tyrian was headed south on her 400 odd miles of return to Sydney.

On September 18 Peary in the Roosevelt set out for Sydney, having given orders to time the ship to arrive there about eleven in the morning of Tuesday, September 21.

In the meanwhile, however, the inhabitants of Sydney and the crowds of visitors grew more and more impatient at the delay day by day. But their impatience was as nothing to that of Mrs. Peary and her two children. Every one in the town took a close and almost proprietary interest in them, since several times before they had seen Mrs. Peary waiting there for her husband to come down out of the North.

On the twentieth great excitement prevailed in Sydney. Peary was expected to land that day. Reports that the Roosevelt was on the bar aroused the citizens at seven o'clock in the morning, and from that time the whole city was on edge for Peary's arrival. On both sides of the harbor there was little to be seen but a mass of bunting, and crowds of people thronged the waterfront anxiously awaiting the news that the Roosevelt had been sighted off the entrance. Many times the rumor spread, but always there came the same answer from the Low-point signal station: "Nothing to be seen of the Roosevelt yet."

Just as impatience had reached its height a cable message came announcing that the awaited ship had come to anchor off St. Paul's Island, a point 70 miles distant, and that the vessel would not reach Sydney until 9 o'clock on the following morning.

The Roosevelt remained at anchor till 8.30 o'clock that night, and only then began working her way slowly down the Cape Breton coast. Later on, Sydney realized that it had only itself to blame. For it then recalled the fact that Peary had promised the citizens that he would arrive there on Tuesday. It was now apparent that the Roosevelt had purposely been halted off St. Paul's Island, to remain there until such time as would bring her into Sydney on the promised hour on Tuesday morning.

On that morning, however, all disappointments were forgotten and the city turned out with renewed zeal. Commander Peary received a taste of the greeting that awaited him while still far from Sydney. A flotilla of craft, ranging from palatial yachts to small buzzing motor boats, came out to escort him, each displaying every bit of bunting that it owned. All the while whistles were screeching in a deafening din. Out of this fleet shot a launch, and Mr. Kehl, the American Consul at Sydney, climbed on board to welcome the explorer.

Next a press tug ran alongside and correspondents came on. Then a tug chartered by the Italian Consul and filled with his fellow countrymen came near. The launch of a photographer was caught in the water washing between the tugs and capsized, but the photographer was dragged out by the heels.

More of the welcoming flotilla came by. Peary, standing on the deck, doffed his cap to every salute. The harbor mouth was entered and a vista of green grass was opened up.

"Gee," said one of the Roosevelt's crew, "wouldn't I love to get out in that grass and wallow."

Then the town of Sydney came into view, the place fairly smothered in waving flags and its waterfront black with waiting throngs. These held their peace until the Roosevelt was well within range of their voices, and then they lifted these to the utmost. And all about was a tossing sea of flags, English and American waving side by side.

The Roosevelt herself was gayly decked with bunting, and from her mizzen gaff rippled the Stars and Stripes with the words "North Pole" inscribed on a field of white cut diagonally across its folds. Beside the commander, proud in his achievement after 23 years of nearly constant effort, stood his wife and daughter and little son. Mrs. Peary, for the first time in the many times she had come to greet her husband homebound from the frozen North, had gone to greet him victorious at sea. She and her children and Colonel Borup, father of one of Peary's companions, had gone forth as the guests of John Ross on his steam yacht Sheelah. That meeting of husband and wife who had been "married twenty-three years but lived only three" was touching in the highest degree. This was the real welcome toward which the conqueror of the Pole had looked. Then the Roosevelt resumed its way toward the waiting throngs at Sydney, preceded by the Sheelah to signal that the Arctic heroes would soon be there.

When the Roosevelt touched the wharf Mayor Richardson leaped aboard to extend the welcome of the city. Soon afterward Mrs. Peary and her daughter were helped over the gangplank, Commander Peary and the Mayor following. A bevy of girls surrounded the explorer and presented a massive emblem, a mound of white flowers surmounted by the American flag, emblematic of the conquered Pole.

Commander Peary, the Mayor and the United States Consul forced their way through the throng to a richly decorated carriage which had been held in waiting, running the gauntlet as they did so of a battery of snapping cameras. As the carriage started for the drive to the Sydney Hotel the vehicle and its occupants were pelted with a storm of flowers, while cheer after cheer broke from the surrounding multitude. The carriage made its slow way to a point in front of the hotel veranda, where it came to a halt, and Mayor Richardson delivered to Peary a short address of welcome.

As the explorer rose to reply another burst of cheers came from the throng and continued for several minutes. But at last the tumult sunk so that the voice of the speaker could be heard. The Commander said that he was no stranger to Sydney; that all of his expeditions to the Pole had started there and ended there.

"And now, thank God," said the explorer fervently, "I have brought back the Pole."

Photograph, Underwood & Underwood, N. Y.

ESKIMOS BRINGING FURS TO TRADE

This photograph, taken at Etah, from which point the discoverers made their celebrated dashes for the Pole, shows natives coming to Peary's vessel with skins to trade with the crew for such useful or gaudy articles as attracted their fancy.

Photograph, Underwood & Underwood, N. Y.

SCENE AT ETAH, THE MOST NORTHERLY ESKIMO SETTLEMENT

This photograph shows the method of drying meat out of the reach of dogs and polar bears, so that it can be carried on a long journey without deterioration. It was at this point that Dr. Cook was landed from the schooner, "J. R. Bradley," to make his dash for the Pole, and from the same neighborhood Peary disappeared into the unknown. In the foreground is seen one of the Arctic sledges such as are commonly used by travelers in the most northern regions.

SALOMON AUGUSTE ANDREE

The ill-fated Arctic explorer who set sail in his balloon in 1897 to reach the North Pole and **never was heard from again**.

WALTER WELLMAN

Who sailed from Spitzbergen in his **airship** August 23, 1909, to reach the North Pole and **broke down** after going thirty-two miles.

THE WELLMAN AIRSHIP EXPEDITION

Hauling ashore the cases containing Walter Wellman's airship, with which he made an unsuccessful attempt to fly to the North Pole.

ANDREE'S BALLOON

In which he started to go to the North Pole and which bore him to his death.

The crowd pressed to the carriage to shake the explorer's hand. The police formed a line on one side of the carriage, and for nearly two hours the hand-shaking went ont. It had been planned to have a banquet that evening in honor of the hero of the North, but the Commander let it be known that he would much prefer to spend the evening with his family. This pleasure was regretfully foregone by the Reception Committee.

Peary's journey from Sydney to Portland, Maine, where he had in view a long rest, was one continual ovation. Leaving Sydney on Wednesday, the 22d, he arrived in Portland at eight o'clock at night. All the way across the State the welcome grew steadily more enthusiastic.

When Commander Peary arrived in Portland, his home city, he received an enthusiastic welcome by a large part of the population. He was met on the station platform by Mayor Leighton, of Portland, and Mayor Hamilton, of South Portland, who, with the Reception Committee in carriages, escorted him to the auditorium, a spacious hall, where he had a notable public reception.

Four companies of militia and a large procession of citizens, all carrying red fire, marched behind the carriages. The streets from the station to the auditorium were lined with people. Thousands cheered the explorer as he passed by and later shook his hand. A banquet, with Commander Peary and several distinguished guests as speakers, followed the reception.

Such was Peary's welcome home, for his place on Eagle Island is only fifteen miles from Portland, and he proposed to take an extended rest there before showing himself in the great cities. If whole-hearted enthusiasm and admiration for the indomitable courage which had set the crown of success on his almost life-long efforts could bring him pleasure, he had it in full measure that day, for his countrymen had indeed given him a royal greeting.

CHAPTER XIII

The Controversy Between Cook and Peary

IT is indeed a regrettable thing that the glory of such an achievement as the conquest of the North Pole by two Americans should be tarnished by a controversy between them.

When the news came that Dr. Cook had discovered the North Pole there was felt, unquestionably, considerable sympathy for Commander Peary. The latter had made several unsuccessful attempts and there was a general recognition of the fact that he deserved to win in the end.

But little time was given the world to indulge this tender feeling. Hardly had Peary's announcement of his success been made when the following message came by wireless from him at Indian Harbor, Labrador, to the Associated Press in New York:

"I have nailed the Stars and Stripes to the North Pole. This is authoritative and correct. Cook's story should not be taken too seriously. The two Eskimos who accompanied him say he went no distance north and not out of sight of land. Other members of the tribe corroborate their story.

(Signed) "PEARY."

And on the same day he wired Mrs. Peary:

"Good morning. Delayed by gale. Don't let Cook story worry you. Have him nailed.

(Signed) "BERT."

The controversy was launched full size and the inhabitants of the civilized world divided themselves into two camps of Cook adherents and Peary adherents. It was the all-absorbing topic of the day and a war of words raged everywhere.

The attitude assumed by Peary that he alone was capable of reaching the Pole and the denouncing of Cook as a pretender could not fail to alienate much of the sympathy felt for him in his great disappointment. Such messages as the following to the New York *Herald:* "Cook has simply handed the public a gold brick. He has not been at the Pole April 21, 1908, or any other time. The above statement is made advisedly and at the proper time will be backed by proof," could not fail to create a feeling of regret.

Immediately upon receipt of that despatch the *Herald* sent a message to Mr. Peary stating that his accusation would be published and asking him to wire the evidence on which it was based, stating that the unsupported charge was liable to excite a public sentiment adverse to himself. It seemed that "the proper time" to furnish proof of the assertion that Dr. Cook was untruthful and in effect a swindler was when the accusation was made.

Mr. Peary replied that the despatch was not intended for publication and if he so intended it he would have modified the "gold brick" expression to something more elegant but not less forcible or significant.

More remarkable even than the discovery of the North Pole by two rival Americans, after intrepid and adventurous explorers had sought it in vain for centuries, was the astonishing fact that the news of the achievement—first by Dr. Cook and then by Commander Peary—should be given to the world within the span of five days. Naturally, the question presented itself, Was it a mere coincidence that these similar messages should have come out of the land of eternal snow and ice almost simultaneously? Did Dr. Cook know that Commander Peary, formerly his friend, but later his rival, had reached the North Pole? Did Peary divine that Cook had been there? And in consequence, did they both hasten homeward, each desperately eager to be the first to tell the news?

With only a limited knowledge of the Arctic region, it was not difficult to conceive of the possibilities of "faking" the discovery of the North Pole, but it was not easy to credit that any man would attempt this sort of thing, hoping to escape exposure. That Dr. Cook had devoted himself to exploration, that he had become an earnest pole hunter, that he had actually invaded the Arctic region, exposing himself to all its dangers and risking his very life—these things were immediately accepted by the public.

That Dr. Cook and Commander Peary should have opposing views as to the most practical means of making the trip to the end of the earth's axis did not prove that Cook was an impostor. That he should have proceeded with only two Eskimo companions while Peary's party numbered forty white men and Eskimos did not prove it. That they had different routes and chose different seasons of the year for the final dash over the ice did not prove it. They both agreed that the Pole could be reached only by means of Eskimos, their dogs and sledges. Men of science and others interested in the controversy gave up guessing and decided to wait for the actual proof from both men. What would the records show? Perhaps by them it would be possible to determine how the honor of reaching the North Pole should be divided. Until these had been examined, Dr. Cook stood pre-eminent as the discoverer.

As for Peary, he deserved the nation's congratulations for his persistence and his determination that he would find the North Pole. There was not a man in America, however proud he was of Dr. Cook, that would not have been glad to have had Peary as the North Pole's discoverer after his twenty-three years' effort. He had devoted his life to the work, not merely of reaching the Pole, but of showing the world the way. As with every man who has a single purpose, Commander Peary's became part of his life.

When, after he had achieved his supreme triumph, he heard of Cook's claim to have been at the Pole earlier, it was undoubtedly a severe shock to him. But if he had stopped to reflect that his own

THE CONTROVERSY BETWEEN COOK AND PEARY   197

achievement was not only independent of Dr. Cook's, but in ignorance of it, he might have felt that he lost nothing because the other man had done a similar feat. For it was parallel rather than prior. In that northern desert even time itself is frozen. That he had finally reached the Pole was an accepted fact, and that his observations are thorough and accurate no one doubted. So fixed was he in his position that even his rival, Dr. Cook, could prove his own claims only through Peary's data.

To return to the controversy, the fact developed soon after it started that Peary had begun his attack on Cook before setting out on his own expedition in May, 1908. The New York *Times,* which had taken the Peary side of the dispute for polar honors, stated that before his departure from New York, Commander Peary left with the editor of the *Times* a letter expressing his views on the secrecy with which Dr. Cook had prepared his expedition. Commander Peary pointed out in this letter the evident intention of Dr. Cook to forestall him in obtaining the services of Eskimos and dogs assembled to await Peary at Etah, these Eskimos having been trained by Peary for protracted Arctic sledge work.

The etiquette of polar exploration is a closed book to the general public, and it must be admitted that the feeling prevailed that Dr. Cook had achieved his object and as first on the spot had a right to the natural facilities of the country. Throughout America and Europe the impression grew that Peary considered the North Pole as his own ground and that no one else should attempt to reach it.

Dr. Cook, under the storm of denunciation poured upon him by Commander Peary, maintained throughout an extremely dignified attitude, which earned for him anew the plaudits of the world.

He was in Denmark when the first messages came from Peary denying his claim to having reached the Pole. At that time he entered a simple denial of the charges and reiterated his statements previously made as to his success. On board his steamer when leaving New York, however, he made fuller statements of his position in the controversy. In a signed statement he said:

"Commander Peary has as yet given to the world no proof of his own case. My claim has been fully recognized by Denmark and by the King of Sweden; the President of the United States of America has wired me his confidence; my claim has been accepted by the International Bureau of Polar Research at Brussels; most of the geographical societies of Europe have sent me congratulations, which mean faith and acceptance for the present, and almost every explorer of note has come forward with warm and friendly approval.

"A specific record of my journey is accessible to all, and every one who reads can decide for himself. When Peary publishes a similar report, then our cases are parallel. Why should Peary be allowed to make himself a self-appointed dictator of my affairs? In justice to himself, in justice to the world and to guard the honor of national prestige, he should be compelled to prove his own case; he should publish at once a preliminary narrative, to be compared with mine, and let fair-minded people ponder over the matter, while the final records by which our case may eventually be proved are being prepared.

"I know Peary, the explorer. As such he is a hero in Arctic annals, and deserves the credit of a long and hard record. To Peary, the explorer, I am still willing to tip my hat, but Peary's unfounded accusations have disclosed another side to his character, which will never be forgotten.

"When Peary wired that he had nailed the Stars and Stripes to the Pole, I immediately sent congratulations. I then believed, as I do now, that his work over a new route far east of my line of travel was a new conquest of great importance, and of course, that his position at the Pole would supplement my work with valuable data. There is room enough and honor enough for two American flags at the Pole."

Just before leaving the ship at Quarantine Dr. Cook issued another statement over his signature which took up the different aspects of the controversy at greater length. He said:

"After one of the most delightful trips of my life across the Atlantic I am indeed glad once more to see the shores of my native land. I have come from the Pole. I have brought my story and data with me. The public has already a tangible and a specific record of that trip. In a very short time the narrative, with all the observations, will be published and placed before the world for examination.

"It is as easy for you as for me to understand why I cannot, on the impulse of the moment, read off a manuscript which covers the work of two years. As said upon several occasions, all the charges, accusations and expressions of disbelief are based upon entire ignorance of the supplementary data which I possess. No one who has spoken or written on the subject in opposition to my claim knows of the facts with which such work of exploration is measured. All of the criticisms have been based upon obvious errors in the reproduction of my first despatch or upon the discussions of petty side issues presented by unfair critics.

"The expedition was private. It was started out without the usual public bombast. John R. Bradley furnished the money and I shaped the destiny of the venture. For the time being it concerned us only, but the results were so important that on returning I at once placed before the public a report containing the main outline of the work.

"I have not come home to enter into arguments with one man or with fifty men, but I am here to present a clear record of a piece of work over which I have the right to display a certain amount of pride. When scientists study the detailed observations and the narrative in its consecutive order I am certain that, in due course of events, all will be compelled to admit the truth of my statement.

"I am perfectly willing to abide by the final verdict of this record by competent judges. That must be the last word in the discussion, and that alone can satisfy me and the public.

"Furthermore, not only will my report be before you in black and white, but I will also bring to America human witnesses to prove that I have been to the Pole.

"FREDERICK A. COOK."

While Dr. Cook declined to be driven to a hasty laying of his proof before the world, before he was in full readiness to do so, and reiterated his intention to stand by his promise to present it first to the scientists of Copenhagen; stating, however, that he would immediately afterward offer it to the geographical societies of the world, in order that their decision might be given simultaneously; Commander Peary was similarly deliberate in making public his proposed annihilation of Cook's claim of discovery.

He finally sent his statement to the Peary Arctic Club, which was equally deliberate in offering it to the public. When at length, on October 12, 1909, the officials of the association answered the impatient demands of the public and gave Peary's detailed statement to the press, it was read with avidity, but created no fresh sensation. It had been taken for granted from his many utterances as to the complete character of his evidence, that he had new and significant proofs of the position he had taken and maintained. Yet when the statement was read there was scarcely an iota of evidence offered beyond that he had already given to the world. It proved to be a formal extension of the wireless message he had sent from Indian Harbor on his first reaching there, to the effect that the two Eskimos who accompanied Cook had said that they had gone little distance north and not out of sight of land, and that other members of their tribe had corroborated their story.

This statement, seemingly based upon what he had been able to obtain from two Eskimo boys whom Cook said he had pledged to silence—an assertion in which Whitney had corroborated him—was a distinct disappointment to those who had eagerly awaited it. It was merely a reiteration of what they had heard six weeks before, and it is not surprising that it fell flat on the public ear. The case was left largely where it had been before.

What Dr. Cook said when he read it was in effect what the general public thought and said:

"It is the same old story," was his comment. "I have replied to the points raised a dozen times. The map published by Commander Peary in itself indicates that the Eskimos have respected their promise made to me that they would not give any information to Peary or his men.

"The Eskimos were instructed not to tell Mr. Peary or any of his party of our trip over the polar sea. They were told to say we had been far North.

"They have kept their word. Mr. Whitney has said that during the cross-examination conducted by Commander Peary and others of his expedition the Eskimos did not understand the questions put to them or the map which was laid before them. Their replies to the questions put have been twisted to suit a perverted interest.

"I will not enter into any argument about the matter, but I will bring the Eskimos to New York at my own expense, and they will prove, as did Mr. Whitney, all that I have claimed.

"The Eskimos," he continued, "are only too willing to say something that they think will please their questioners."

The explorer was not at all perturbed by the accusations. A confident smile played over his bronzed face when they were shown to him. "I fully expected to see something of the kind," he said. "The document looks formidable over so many signatures, and will probably appear so to the public. There is, however, nothing in it. It is based upon the distorted and evasive replies of persons who were told not to give any details."

What would be the ultimate result of the whole matter no one was prepared to say. That would depend on nothing that Commander Peary could say, since he had evidently said his utmost at the start, but on the decison of science upon Dr. Cook's evidence when presented and his record for veracity. Dr. Cook's claim that he climbed Mount McKinley in Alaska, had been publicly questioned and denied by persons who were said to have been with him on this occasion, and both friends and enemies began to investigate the accuracy of his report in this matter. It was generally felt that the proving or disproving of the Mount McKinley story would have great weight in deciding Dr. Cook's credit. Those interested in the discussion—and this included most of the thinking people of the world—sank back into a waiting attitude, convinced that the truth was sure to come out and the position of the two rival explorers to be finally determined to the satisfaction of all.

CHAPTER XIV

Interesting Scientific Work in the Arctic

THE scientific methods used by a polar explorer in determining his position are practically the same as those employed by a navigator in ascertaining his location at sea. The instruments are the same in design, but necessarily vary slightly in construction on account of the rough usage and extremely low temperatures to which they are subjected.

The most important of these instruments is the sextant, a lightweight, portable instrument for measuring the altitudes of the heavenly bodies, the sun, moon and stars, above the horizon, or their angular distance as seen in the sky. This instrument consists of a small telescope and a series of mirrors, by means of which the angle between the heavenly body selected and the horizon may be read on a graduated scale in the form of an arc attached to the instrument.

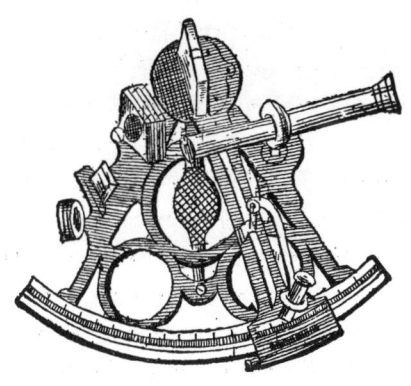

SEXTANT.

Instrument by Queen & Co., Philadelphia.

On shipboard the material used in the sextant is brass or bronze, but for ice traveling in late years aluminum has been employed.

Other necessary instruments are chronometers, or large watches, with compensating balance wheels, constructed for extreme accuracy in timekeeping, every known device being employed to insure absolute uniformity of running. They are set to the exact time of a standard meridian (such as that of Greenwich, England), several being carried, of which the exact rate of gain or loss in each is known. By comparison of these with each other the observer is able to tell the precise moment of taking his observation.

Particular care must be taken in the selection of the chronometers. These instruments are subject to errors in timekeeping under the most favorable conditions of handling and temperature. It is inevitable, during the hard knocks of a sledge journey in a temperature low enough to congeal the oil with which they are lubricated, that they cannot be considered the instruments of precision they are under better conditions.

As their use is principally in determining the longitude, errors in this direction are of little moment near the Pole. At the Pole, where all meridians converge, one longitude is the same as another, and every altitude is a "meridian altitude," which does not require a chronometer for its solution.

An artificial horizon completes the list of indispensable instruments. The greatest difficulty in astronomical work in the Arctic lies in getting a suitable horizon. The mariner in the open sea in clear weather has little difficulty in measuring the angle between any heavenly body and the actual visible sea horizon. On shore or surrounded by a sea of ice in various forms there is no such thing as a level, unbroken horizon, so that it becomes necessary to resort to an artificial horizon of some sort.

The usual method is to use a basin of mercury, which, when sheltered from the wind by a glass cover, forms a perfectly smooth horizon surface in which the heavenly bodies are brilliantly reflected. It is then necessary only to measure with a sextant the angle between the body in the heavens and its reflection in the artificial horizon to determine its actual elevation

INTERESTING SCIENTIFIC WORK IN THE ARCTIC

above the true horizon. It must be remembered, however, that mercury freezes at about forty degrees Fahrenheit below zero, and has accordingly a very limited field of usefulness in the Arctic. For this reason and on account of its weight some other form of artificial horizon is necessary.

Other liquids besides mercury have been used, as have also glass mirrors made horizontal by means of screw legs and spirit levels. These last require great care in adjusting, and there is always more or less error attending their use. With the above instruments one can determine his position with sufficient accuracy whenever the sun, moon or any of the principal stars are visible, but, having done so, it is a matter of no small difficulty to ascertain what is the proper direction in which to travel to be sure of always going north.

The compass, to which we are accustomed to look for guidance, does not, as is well known, point to the geographical pole, but to a region some distance south of it, called the magnetic pole. This has been located to the northwestward of Hudson Bay, and at any place between that and the true pole the compass needle will point toward that pole. If to one side of the magnetic pole, it will point more or less east or west, as the case may be.

In preparing for a sledge journey in the Arctic it has been found advisable to have a special chest for instruments, usually secured to the front of the sledges. This should contain a sextant, an artificial horizon of a non-freezing type, one or two chronometers and the tables of logarithms and astronomical data of the sun, moon and stars, necessary in working out observations.

It is advisable that a pocket chronometer be carried on the person, in order that it may get the warmth of the body and be spared the jolting of the sledge.

Other instruments may be carried for the collection of scientific information, but the above are all that is necessary for locating one's position. They should be made as light as possible and secured in a watertight box, so that, although the sledge may be completely upset or immersed in water, no damage can come to the instruments.

A chart of some sort is desirable, but, as in polar journeys it covers a field entirely unsurveyed, it may be composed of a blank sheet of paper, with a dot in the centre representing the pole.

The drawbacks to determining one's position in the Arctic do not lie in the computations, but in the great difficulty of securing

ARTIFICIAL HORIZON.
Instrument by Queen & Co., Philadelphia.

accurate observations. The lenses and mirrors of the instruments are covered with frost from the warmth of the body or the breath, the lubricating oil freezes in the joints, the silver backing of the mirrors cracks and granulates in the cold, and the artificial horizons freeze if liquid, and refuse to stay horizonal if solid.

Should there be fog or the heavens be overcast, no observations are possible. During the six months of summer daylight the stars are not visible, although the brighest planets might be seen in especially favorable circumstances. The pole star, even if visible in winter, is of no practical utility. After the observation is taken certain corrections must be applied to the observed altitude to convert it to the true altitude. Of these the correction for refraction is the most important.

The irregular appearance of the disc of the sun near the horizon when rising or setting is well known. In the Arctic the sun is always close to the horizon, and its rays in traversing the atmosphere are strongly refracted. This, if not allowed for, is sufficient to cause an error of from two to thirty-six miles, but as its amount is known and tabulated for ordinary conditions such errors are not very likely to occur.

As the pole is approached the observations become very simple. At the pole the altitude of any heavenly body—the sun for instance—is the same as its declination or distance north of the equator as given in the astronomical tables. An explorer, then, approaching the pole, needs only to take an observation of the sun at noon, and after correcting the observed altitudes for errors of instruments, refraction, etc., to compare his correct altitude with the declination given in the tables. The difference between the declination and the altitude is the distance he is from the pole. As he draws nearer to the pole it becomes of continually lessening importance that his observation be taken exactly at noon, and when at the pole it may be taken at any time and will be the same as the given declination at that time.

It thus becomes a very simple matter to determine one's position at the pole. As one's distance from the pole increases the computation requires slightly more time, but still remains very simple. The following method can be employed at any time, but various other methods are equally available:

The time of the observation is taken by the pocket chronometer, and by a comparison with the other chronometers the exact time of Greenwich is determined. To this is applied the longitude (approximate) and the difference between watch time and sun time (equation of time), which gives the time as shown by the sun; that is, its angle from the meridian at the observation. With this "hour angle" and the declination and approximate altitude, the sun's altitude is computed by a simple formula of trigonometry.

The altitude of the sun thus obtained is then compared with the observed altitude after correction, and the difference is the distance in miles the observer is from the assured position given by the latitude and longitude used in the computation.

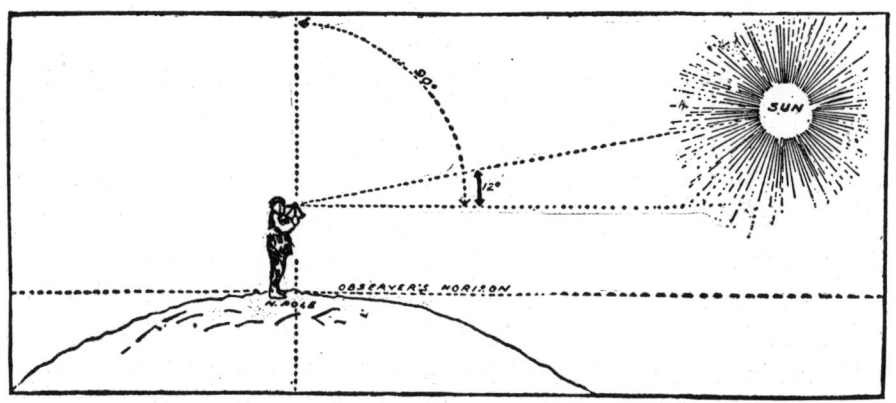

Method of determining the position of the North Pole with a sextant.

His direction from the assumed position is toward or away from the sun, according to whether his observed altitude is greater or less than the altitude obtained by computation. By marking on the chart the assumed position in the latitude and longitude used and drawing a line through this point in the direction of the sun's bearing (the direction which would be indicated by the shadow of an upright staff), the correct position can be found by measuring off on this line, away from the assumed position, a distance equal to the difference between the observed and the calculated altitudes.

In view of the many questions raised as to the accuracy of Dr.

Cook's and Commander Peary's statements as to having reached the North Pole, we may properly quote here the views of a few eminent scientists on the subject. Dr. Wright of the famous Lick Observatory in California, has said:

"The only instrument needed is a sextant. With three observations taken the same day Dr. Cook could have determined his position with a possible error of less than ten seconds of arc. This would be, roughly, a thousand feet, and Dr. Cook says positively that the pole was somewhere within a circle of 500 feet radius within which he himself was standing.

"As these observations could be faked by any one with a fair knowledge of astronomy, the discovery rests on Doctor Cook's veracity alone. For my part, I do not think him a man who would fake his observations, and from what I have read, I believe he made the journey.

"At the North Pole the sextant would read 0 degrees minus the declination of the sun for April 21, with a correction for refraction. It would be a matter of little difficulty to fake three readings that would indicate the discovery of the pole. So that until some one else finds Doctor Cook's flag and brass tube at the pole, the matter rests with his veracity alone."

Prof. George Davidson, of the University of California, a writer of note on astronomical subjects, has said that with a proper outfit of instruments Doctor Cook could have determined the position of the pole within a possible error of a mile, provided that he had a clear ice horizon for his observation. This possible error of a mile would mean an error equal to one-thirty-second part of the disc of the sun as viewed with the sextant.

"If Doctor Cook's observations are sufficiently numerous," said Professor Davidson, "any imperfections in them can be used by astronomers to determine the general credibility."

Professor S. Alfred Mitchell, of Columbia University, said:

"In the sledge trip to the Pole, a distance about equalling that from Washington to Boston, no heavy instruments could be carried, and especially so in the final dash like that accomplished by only Cook and two Eskimos. The ordinary navigator's sextant would be too heavy and bulky, and would have to be replaced by a less cumbersome instrument. Peary ordinarily carried a small sextant, a so-called pocket sextant. The ship's chronometer in its square case would give way to a good pocket timepiece, though two or three small chronometers might be carried.

"The sea captain observes the altitude of the sun by bringing it in contact with the horizon where sea and sky meet. But in the frozen north there is no such horizon, the ice floes are thrown up into hummocks and hills, and an altitude of the sun above the visible horizon would lead to inaccurate results. On land exploration, an artificial horizon is made by pouring mercury into a little shallow tray. But mercury freezes at 40 degrees below zero. A blackened glass plate made horizontal by means of spirit levels was used by Cook and well answered the purpose.

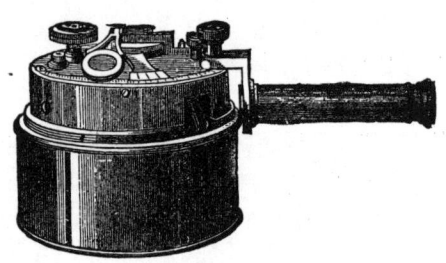

POCKET SEXTANT.
Instrument by Queen & Co., Philadelphia.

"In a polar dash, the latitude is the important information desired. Longitude, i. e., the difference between local and Greenwich time, is difficult to obtain and inaccurate. Consequently, latitude must be determined by methods which will not involve an accurate knowledge of the time. The sun's greatest altitude during the twenty-four hours would give the time of local noon, and latitude from such an observation could be readily determined; and twelve hours later at midnight the sun's altitude would be least, and latitude could again be determined. When the greatest and least altitudes were the same, or in other words, when the sun did not change in altitude at all (except for its change in declination in the sky), then was the latitude 90 degrees, and the North Pole was reached. It is readily seen that the small instruments, the difficulty of determining horizon, and the bitter cold combine to make the observations of no great accuracy. Under such conditions it is questionable whether the position of the Pole could be determined within ten miles!"

Dr. Bernachi, physicist of the "Discovery" Antarctic expedition, had this to say in regard to determining the location of the Pole:

"At the poles of the earth, which are, mathematically speaking, 'singular points,' the definitions of meridians of North and South, etc, break down. Here in this latitude we speak of the zenith directly above our heads, and we are acquainted with the Pole star (Polaris), so called because it almost coincides with the Pole (celestial). There the celestial pole and zenith coincide, and any number of circles may be drawn through the two points, which have now become one. The horizon and celestial Equator coalesce, and the only direction on the earth's surface is due south (or north at the South Pole)—east and west have vanished. A single step of the observer will, however, remedy the confusion—zenith and Pole will separate and his meridian will again become determinate.

"At the North Pole the sun is visible above the horizon for six months—namely, from March 21st to September 22d, the dates of the vernal and autumnal equinox respectively, or when the sun

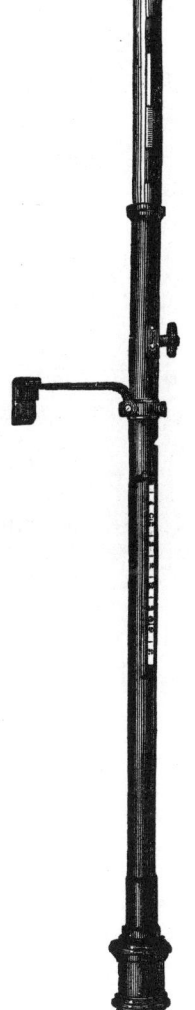

BAROMETER.
Instrument by Queen & Co., Philadelphia.

crosses the celestial Equator coming north and going south. Supposing Dr. Cook had reached the North Pole on March 21, he would see the sun gradually rise in the south and move right round his horizon, in sight the whole time, and return again to the south point. It would not rise or fall with regard to the meridian, as the sun does in these latitudes, but would very gradually rise along its whole course in the form of a spiral, and this change in altitude would be equal to the change in the declination of the sun.

"This gradual change in altitude goes on in the same spiral manner until June 21, the date of the summer solstice, when the sun has reached its farthest point north, and its maximum altitude is about 23½ degrees. It then gradually falls in the same manner toward the horizon, disappearing on September 22 and remaining out of sight until the following March. The stars would then be visible—that is, all the stars between the Pole and the Equator, and these stars would neither rise nor set, but would describe great circles around the observer, remaining practically at the same altitude.

"The stars, indeed, would be the most satisfactory and accurate guides in determining the latitude when the Pole had been reached, more especially the Pole-star itself, which would be in the zenith and free from the uncertainties due to refraction, etc. Unfortunately, only the sun is available in the summer, and unless the explorer reaches the Pole near midsummer, when its altitude is well above the horizon, at other times it is distorted and affected by refraction, and errors of observation are unavoidable. The compass, of course, is still of use, but the north-seeking end, instead of pointing north, would point south in the direction of the North Magnetic Pole, which is situated in North America, and some degrees to the south of the North Pole.

"Traveling toward the North Pole, and when within reach of his goal, an explorer should exercise the minutest care in his astronomical observations, and greatly multiply them. The best instrument under such conditions is perhaps a small theodolite, as used by Captain Scott in the Antarctic. This instrument is steadier than a small sextant, which has to be held in the hand, and probably more accurate.

"The readings of altitude of the sun should be checked, if possible, by another member of the party, and carefully noted in the traveler's field book or diary, with a record of the temperature at the time and the barometric pressure, so that corrections may be applied for these two influences. The altitudes should be roughly worked out on the spot to indicate how closely he was approaching to the Pole. Having reached what he believed to be the position of the Pole, he should be careful to take a very large number of different altitudes over a period of hours, or even days, and the mean of these observations would undoubtedly give him a fairly accurate result.

"These original notebooks, absolutely unaltered, and the testimony of his fellow-travelers, are practically the only evidence he could produce of having reached the Pole. If he possessed a camera, it might be of some value,

POCKET COMPASS.
Instrument by Queen & Co., Philadelphia.

if he were on perfectly level sea-ice, to take a photograph of the sun showing the horizon line below. The phenomena at the South Pole would be identical, excepting that the sun would be always in the north, and all lines would lead north, and the dates of the sun's visibility would be reversed—namely from September 22d to March 21st; the maximum altitude of the sun being reached on December 22d. The south-seeking end of the compass would point north in the direction of the South Magnetic Pole."

While not indispensable to an explorer, there are several other instruments of great value to him and records of which are of the utmost importance to science. Among these may be noted the Aneroid Barometer, an instrument used for determining the pressure of the atmosphere. If the pressure at sea level is known, this instrument will give a fairly accurate reading of the altitude at which the observer is standing, on the well-known principle that the pressure of the atmosphere grows less in exact proportion as the altitude increases.

The thermometer, giving the temperature of the air, is naturally of great interest and value to the explorer. Several are usually carried, both on account of the risk of accident and because of the great variation in temperature to which they may be subjected. The ordinary mercury in glass thermometer is useless in extremely low temperatures, from the fact that mercury freezes at a temperature of 37.8 degrees Fahrenheit below zero. Consequently it is necessary to use what are known as spirit thermometers, or instruments in which a fluid having a lower freezing point than mercury is employed. This fluid may be alcohol or a liquid called toluene, known to science as methyl benzene. This fluid is recommended and adopted by the International Bureau of Weights and Measures as giving more accurate results than alcohol.

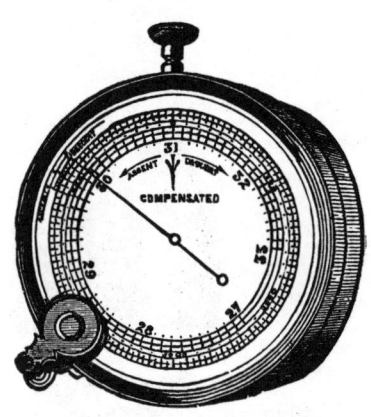

ANEROID BAROMETER.
Instrument by Queen & Co., Philadelphia.

If the observer wishes to obtain an automatic record of either the highest or lowest temperature to which the instrument has been exposed, he may use what are known as Maximum or Minimum Thermometers. These are simply thermometers containing a device which remains fixed either at the highest or lowest temperature recorded. In the Arctics naturally a set of the latter instruments relieve the explorer, as the reading may be taken at any time for the lowest or highest point reached since the last setting of the instrument.

Continuous recording thermometers, which give an hourly record in ink upon a paper cylinder, are far too delicate for the rough handling of a sledging trip, and consequently are not carried.

A full equipment of scientific instruments might also include a wind gauge or Anemometer and deep-sea sounding instruments.

The Anemometer consists of a small fan, upon which the wind acts. The revolutions of this fan are recorded by a series of dials, which indicate the velocity of the wind in feet per minute.

For deep-sea sounding, a sounding machine is used which automatically records the pressure of the water, and from this the depth may be ascertained, as the two are in exact proportion.

ANEMOMETER.

Instrument by Queen & Co., Philadelphia.

The well-known compass completes the explorer's outfit of instruments, but, as has been explained, it is of little use in the high latitudes near the North Pole, because it points, not to the actual North Pole, but to the Magnetic North Pole, a point far distant.

CHAPTER XV

Animals of the Arctic Region

AS one might readily suppose, there are not very many species of animals fitted by nature to contend with the rigors of the Arctic climate. Verdure is very scarce north of the Arctic Circle, and on this account many of the animal inhabitants must live by preying on each other, and in winter most of them fair badly.

The largest and most formidable animal found in the Arctic Circle is the well-known polar bear. Nature would seem to have been particularly careful in fitting the bear for the life he has to lead, if we may judge from his organization. Owing to the scarcity of food on land he must be equipped to find and capture it either on the ice floes or in the water. As his principal diet consists of fish, seal and walrus, it is apparent that very different methods must be employed for securing food than in the case of his cousins, the bears of the north temperate zone. The polar bear is provided with a very heavy coat of white fur, which not only protects him from the cold on land and in the water—but makes him almost invisible against a background of snow and ice. He is able to dive and swim with the greatest facility, thus being able to capture game in the water with ease. For ice travel the soles of the bear's feet are thickly covered with hair to give him a firm grip on the ice and protect him from the cold. Further than this, the feet are very large, in some cases eighteen inches long, and act as paddles in the water. It is a remarkable fact that polar bears are known to have been able to capture fish by their superior speed in the water. Another useful trait possessed by the bear is an extremely keen sense of smell, which enables him to track his prey and detect the scent of the seal about the small breathing holes they break in the ice.

The strength of the bear is very great and the paws, armed with strong claws, are such powerful weapons that the huge walrus often falls a victim to this formidable animal.

The manner in which the bear attacks his victim is very singular. Creeping cautiously up to the walrus as it lies sleeping on the shore, the agile beast leaps suddenly on its back and begins to rain a shower of mighty blows upon its head. The terrified walrus, finding that it cannot shake off its foe, at once makes for the sea, knowing that if it can but dive under the water the bear must soon release its hold and rise to the surface to breathe. It is not often, however, that the walrus succeeds in this, for the strokes of the claw-tipped paws are so heavy that his skull is generally crushed in.

Another well-known animal of this region is the reindeer—indeed, so important a part does it play in the social economy of the Laplanders that more has been written of its habits than of any other species of deer. It is found distributed through the Arctic regions of Europe, Asia and America. In Spitzbergen, Finland and Lapland it attains the largest size, being inferior in strength and stature in parts of Norway and Sweden. In Iceland it has been introduced and thrives, and the domesticated reindeer of Lapland has recently been introduced in Alaska and Labrador.

The caribou is the name by which the wild form is known in the New World, in which it extends through Greenland, Canada and Newfoundland. The horns of the American variety differ from the horns of those of the Old World so much that it is difficult to recognize their origin; nevertheless the attempts which have been made to establish a specific difference between the two forms have not found much favor with naturalists generally.

This animal, with a characteristic deer-like form, is powerfully built, with short legs and heavy neck. The feet have the outside horny shell or false hoofs well developed, while the fissure between the median toes is so much extended upward and the ligaments which bind them together are so loose that their hoofs spread out considerably when pressed upon the ground and thus the surface for support upon the yielding snow, their most frequent foothold, is much increased. When the legs are raised in rapid action, these hoofs make a sharp snap at the moment they come together.

The reindeer, from the nature of the country it inhabits, is compelled to lead a migratory life, in which the natives of Lapland, who have to depend entirely for subsistence on the animal, have to participate. Troops of them during the winter months reside in the woods, feeding upon the lichens that hang from the boughs of the trees, as well as on those that grow on the ground beneath. In the spring they go to the mountains in order to escape the swarms of stinging gnats and gad-flies which attack them in the lowlands. It is interesting to state that Commander Peary, a few years ago, found a variety of this interesting animal in Grant Land—the northern part of Ellesmere Land—snow-white in color, and occurring in fairly large numbers.

A singular animal of the desolate northern region is the musk-ox. It is now confined to the Arctic regions of North America, though it was once circum-polar in its range, and in Pleistocene times existed over all Europe and in America as far south as Kentucky.

In size it resembles a small domestic ox. The body is covered with long brownish hair with a warm undercoat of wool, very thick and tufted on the neck and shoulders and elsewhere long and flowing, so that it hangs down almost to the feet. The legs are short and strong and the hoofs of unequal size and shape, the outer being much broader than the inner one. The horns are broad at the base, covering the forehead and crown, much as do those of the cape buffalo, then curving downward between the eye and the ear, and then bending upward and backward. The chief peculiarity of these animals is, however, the faint odor of musk which belongs to them.

It does not come from any particular gland but seems a general emanation.

In habits the musk-ox is gregarious, moving in herds of twenty or thirty in search of food, which consists of moss, lichens, herbage and the twigs of small trees which grow in parts of their country.

In winter they migrate south from the most northern and exposed places, to localities where food is more abundant, and where they are constantly hunted by the Eskimos for food and skins. Fur traders and explorers have killed a great many in addition, so that now their numbers are much diminished.

By all odds the most useful animal of the Arctic is the Arctic dog. The Eskimos use dogs exclusively to draw their sledges, as being the most hardy and easily handled draught animal within their reach. It is not necessary to shelter them, as they very cleverly bury themselves in the snow when getting ready to sleep. They will eat any kind of meat or fish and can make great speed over the ice. For these reasons they are of incalculable value to polar explorers. These big, powerful, heavily furred dogs are so like wolves that it is not difficult to believe that they are first cousins of the Arctic wolves. In fact many Eskimo dogs are more closely related to their wolfish neighbors and often there does not seem to be a hair's difference between dog and wolf.

The Eskimos hitch them up in teams to their sledges, the number of dogs varying with the load to be drawn. No reins are used, but the dogs are guided either by a lead dog which is clever enough to follow a trail or by word of mouth backed up by the long stinging whip.

An animal of little use to mankind, except for its fur, is the Arctic fox, otherwise known as the blue fox. In summer this animal is of a brownish color, but in winter the fur turns pure white with a bluish under-fur.

This species lives upon birds, which it is able to run down on the ground, upon young seals, and upon whatever offal it is able to steal from the Eskimos. In winter the foxes are often seen in great numbers about the carcass of a whale or some other animal and are apt to be much daubed with grease. In appearance the Arctic fox resembles his cousins often seen in the Temperate Zones.

The polar hare closely resembles the domestic variety, save that its fur is pure white. It feeds chiefly on the scanty Arctic vegetation in the form of lichens, moss and the bark of small stunted trees.

These are the prominent land animals of the Arctic Zone, but there are various species which live chiefly or altogether in the water.

First and largest of these is the whale, the greatest of all mammals. The variety which we shall treat of here is that known as the Greenland or Right Whale. Its total length is from fifty to seventy feet and the weight is about seventy tons. Of this weight about thirty is in oil, the valuable whale oil of commerce. The Eskimos use the oil for light and heat throughout the winter, and before the discovery of petroleum, it formed the chief lighting agent of civilization.

The structure of the whale is like that of a gigantic fish, with fish-like fins and tail. The head occupies about one-third of the total length and contains rows of fine teeth which are useful to it in obtaining its food, which consists chiefly of the small ocean animal life. The whale opens its mouth as it rushes through the water and takes in a great quantity of water containing those minute forms. The jaws are then closed and the water squeezed out through the teeth which retain the living food. An important peculiarity of the whale is that, when it wishes to sink to the bottom or below the surface of the water, it has the power of reducing its bulk so materially by means of its muscles, that without exertion it can go down as far as desired. The whales are much hunted for their oil and for the substance known as whale-bone, which is taken from their jaws.

A curious feature of the whale is the blow-holes, two in number, situated, nearly on the crown of the head. Through these the animal partly breathes and when beneath the surface, the act of respiration causes them to throw up a considerable quantity of water. At other times they emit only columns of vapor which are visible at a great distance. The sound produced by the animal on these occasions is called blowing; it resembles the discharge of a cannon and often directs the whaler to his prey.

Of late years, constant hunting with harpoon guns and explosive shells has thinned out the whales to such an extent that it is no longer profitable to fit out expeditions to search for them.

Another variety of whale found only in Arctic waters of the extreme north, is the White Whale. Its length is only about twelve feet.

An interesting member of the group of mammals is the narwhal or sea unicorn. It belongs to the family of the dolphin and is distinguished by the tusk which springs from its upper jaw, a long spiral tapering horn of ivory, frequently eight or ten feet in length.

The Eskimos and Greenlanders give the narwhal a high place among their ocean treasures. The long ivory tusk serves them for spear heads, the flesh is considered excellent eating, both fresh and cured, and its oil, though not abundant, is of good quality. They travel in great herds and we hear of thousands being seen swimming together in regular order.

The appearance of the narwhal is peculiar—the back is gray in color, mottled with black, the sides and belly paling downwards to white and equally spotted with gray or a darker tint. They have half round or half moon blow-holes which appear on the outside to be single. Occasionally they utter a gurgling noise. They swim with great swiftness and are very active creatures. In length, they measure as a rule about twelve to fifteen feet, although some of twenty feet in length have been found.

The Europeans and Americans catch the narwhal. for the sake of its tusk, while Eskimos eat its flesh cooked and dried, its skin and fat raw, burn its oil, make twine from its tendons, and bladders from its gullet, which they use in catching fish.

Of all the species which inhabit the Arctic region, civilization places the highest value upon the seal. This animal, like those just named, belong to the group called mammals and is peculiarly adapted by nature for life in this dreary region of snow and ice and water.

In many respects it resembles a fish in structure, having the same tapering body and being provided with fin-like flippers. There is no tail, but the two hind flippers are placed close together and in the water they act like a tail. The front flippers are not used in the water, being folded close to the body, and seem to be useful only on land or ice, as legs to move about on. They are not very effective and at best the motion is a clumsy waddle. However, the seal can and does spend much time out of the water, as it is equipped with lungs and breathes air like an animal. It is therefore classed by some among the amphibious animals, though not correctly so.

There are several varieties of seals, but the only one of value for its fur is the fur-seal of the polar seas. The movements of the fur-seals are much more agile, both in the water and on land, than those of the common seal. They are also much bolder in their resistance to an enemy and much larger than the German or dog-fish variety.

The fur of this seal is so fine and has become so popular that all nations have taken measures to protect them. Laws have been passed forbidding the killing of young male and all female seals. Six or seven year old males provide us with all the skins we use.

It is an interesting fact that, in spite of their stupid looks, seals may be trained to perform intricate tricks; and it is no uncommon sight to see troops of them performing in shows with great cleverness.

An animal not unlike the seal in many ways is the walrus. So far as looks are concerned, scarcely a more uninviting fellow can be conceived than this animal, which the Greenlanders and Eskimos call "Awuk," from its peculiar guttural cry.

This ungainly creature, though so unsightly in features, is in reality quiet and inoffensive, unless attacked or roused in love-time, when woe betide those who measure his strength, especially if he reach his native watery element. Some travelers represent him as distrustful, ferocious and suspicious. They are very seldom met with singly, but often found in herds from a dozen to several hundreds, as Captain Cook, the great explorer, long ago observed. They crowd up from the water on to the rocks or ice one after the other, grunting and bellowing. The first arrived is no sooner composed in sleeping trim, than a second comes prodding and poking with its blunt tusks, forcing room for itself, while the first is urged farther from the water; the second in turn is similarly treated by the third; and so on, until numbers will lie packed close, heads and tails resting against and on each other, in the most convenient and friendly manner possible. There they sleep and snore to their hearts' content, but nevertheless keep sentinels on guard in a singular fashion. Some one would seem to disturb another; then this fellow would raise his head listessly, give a grunt and a poke to his nearest companion, who would rouse up a few minutes, also grunt, and pass the watchword to his neighbor, and so on through the herd, this disturbance always keeping some few on the alert. Danger announced, they scuttle pell-mell and topsy-turvy into the water.

However, the walrus is as decidedly lord and ruler of the Polar waters as the bear is of the Polar lands. Its head has not the regular oval of the seal; but, on the contrary, the skull slants abruptly to the eyes, while the upper portion of the face has quite a square form. The muzzle is less protruding than the seal's, while the cheek and lips are completely concealed by the heavy quill-like bristles. Its most remarkable feature, however, consists in the two large teeth, or tusks, which project in a bold curve from the upper jaw, and are nearly two feet in length. They are of beautiful white bone, almost equal to ivory. and dentists use the material in the manufacture of artificial teeth.

The figure of the walrus is more noticeable for strength than grace, though in its outline there is a something suggestive of a bulky horse—and hence our seamen sometimes call it the seahorse. Its length varies from twelve to fifteen feet in different individuals, and from eight to ten feet in circumference; its head is comparatively small, and its somewhat short limbs may be described as intermediate between fins and legs. Like the whale family, its body is wrapped round with a layer of oily fat; while its skin, an inch thick, is covered with close hair.

In localities where the walrus have long been the object of man's pursuit they have grown vengeful and wary; in less frequented regions they lie on the ice in unsuspecting security, and do not suffer the approach of the hunters to disturb them. They do not willingly attack man; but, when forced to fight, conduct themselves with wonderful coolness and courage—dash in serried array against the boats, and with their massive tusks endeavor to capsize them. They display a truly heroic devotion to their young, and will perish in their defence.

The walrus is partial, like some higher animals, to the sound of its own voice, and will recline on the ice for hours listening to its continuous bellow.

[Copyright, 1909, by Underwood & Underwood.]
DR. COOK'S TRIUMPHANT ARRIVAL IN NEW YORK

The great discover with his family on board the tug and alongside the steamer Grand Republic which was thronged with 2,000 friends and neighbors to greet him. Dr. Cook in the center of the picture with hat in hand is acknowledging the cheers of the enthusiastic crowd while his wife and daughter are waving American flags beside him.

Photo by Paul Thompson, New York.

THE ENTHUSIASTIC RECEPTION OF DR. FREDERICK A. COOK

Upon landing from the Steamer "Grand Republic," which was chartered by several thousand of his friends to take him from the transatlantic liner, "Oscar II," upon his arrival in New York, Dr. Cook was surrounded by a dense crowd of admirers. A wreath of flowers was thrown over his shoulders, a bouquet thrown into his hand, and he was conducted to the Bushwick Club, Brooklyn, where a cordial reception was given him.

Photo by Paul Thompson, New York.

TRIUMPHAL ARCH ERECTED IN HONOR OF DR. COOK

Enthusiastic friends and citizens of Brooklyn built this arch of welcome opposite the great explorer's home in Bushwick Avenue in anticipation of his return from Europe. The automobile which conveyed the discoverer to his home is seen passing under the arch, and a cordon of police, assisted by the Forty-seventh Regiment, formed an escort of honor which accompanied him from the landing place to his residence.

SLIDING TO DEATH IN A CREVASSE

DIFFICULT SLEDGING AMONG THE HUMMOCKS

CHAPTER XVI

Terrors and Mysteries of the Polar Regions

THE search for the Poles, the daring venture into the realm of eternal ice, has long been looked upon as the acme of romantic adventure. Terrors surround it and marvels loom up in its frozen depths; terrors which have only slowly been dispelled; marvels which had held men's minds captive for ages and are only now being replaced by new-found facts.

Hardihood and indomitable courage must be the possession of those who dare the perils of this long mysterious realm, and it is only by the exercise of these qualities that it has, step by step, been added to the world of the known, the last great exploits in this field, which have gone far to unlock the secrets of the vast white world, being those of Peary, Cook and Shackleton.

Full of pluck and daring are all the records of Polar exploration, and, in addition to that attraction, there is something else about the subject which fascinates and holds the imagination. There has long been a mystery about the cold, white, silent region; the mystery of an unsolved problem, the mystery which clings to the few spots on the world's surface where the foot of adventurous man has never trodden. Everywhere else man has gone; everywhere else men have subdued Nature and wrested her close-kept secrets from her; everywhere save the Poles, and almost as we write man has conquered one of these and closely approached the other. The mystery of the past is becoming a mystery no more.

It is no modern idea, this search for the North Pole. King Alfred the Great is credited with having sent expeditions towards it, and long before his day men had sailed as far as they could to the North, far enough for them to return with vivid tales of marvel and adventure. The earliest of whom there is any record is an ancient Greek mariner, Pytheas, who sailed north until he came to an island which he named the Land of Thule. This may have been the Shetlands; it may have been Iceland; but wherever it was, this ancient mariner found it far from agreeable, in spite of the fact that the sun did not set while he was there. This prolonged daylight caused him much uneasiness, and he hastened farther to the north, with the hope of finding better conditions, but the farther he went the more curious and extraordinary he found the region to be. The sun, which had at first refused to set, now refused to rise, and he found himself in perpetual darkness instead of perpetual day. More than that, he tells how he came to a great dark wall rising up out of the sea, beyond which he could discern nothing, while at the same time something seized and held his ship motionless on the water, so that the winds could not move it and the anchor would not sink. He was quite convinced in his own mind to what place he had come; the wall in front of him was the parapet which ran round the edge of the world to prevent people from falling over, and, like a wise man, he hastened home, where he told his friends that he had penetrated to the limits of the earth.

What the Arctic regions were then, they are to-day; but we, with a greater knowledge, are able to understand what was incomprehensible to the ancient Greek navigator. At the limit of the ice two phenomena are met with which explain the fanciful legend of Pytheas. As summer gives place to the cold of autumn, and as winter gives way to the mild temperature of spring, there comes down upon the water a dense mass of fog, to which the name "frost-smoke" is given. It would appear, as it rolled along the surface of the ocean, a veritable wall to one accustomed to the clear atmosphere of the Mediterranean, and a thin sheet of ice might give the meaning to the "something" which he encountered. As for the succession of perpetual day and perpetual night, these are ordinary phenomena of the polar circle.

Later navigators, curious to learn whether the story of Pytheas were true or not, followed his course. Some of them went on until they were caught in the rigors of the Arctic winter and perished in the crashing ice-floes. Occasionally some came home again, after having reached far enough to see the great icebergs, floating with all their stately majesty in the blue waters and towering as high as mountains, their summits a mass of glittering pinnacles and their sides scored and grooved with cavities and caverns. Some of them saw the animals which live in that cold, barren region; the great white bear, with its coat of thick shaggy fur, its long ungainly figure and heavy swaying neck; the walrus, with its gleaming tusks hanging down from its upper jaws; the seals, with their great round eyes staring at the unknown intruders; above all, the huge whales, spouting and floundering in the sea, coming to the surface with a snort which sent the spray flying high in the air, and disappearing again with a splash that was like a crashing billow. Little wonder that those who returned from seeing such sights and hearing such strange sounds should tell wonderful stories about the weird creatures inhabiting the place.

The sounds must have been as terrifying and mystifying as the sights, for in the clear, intense atmosphere of the winter months in the Arctic region, noise travels over almost incredible distances. When Parry was on Melville's Island, he speaks of hearing the voices of men who were talking not less than a mile away. In the depth of winter, when the great cold has its icy grip on everything, the silence is unbroken along the shores of the Polar Sea; but when the frost sets in, and again when the winter gives way to spring, there is abundance of noise. As the frost comes down along the coast, rocks are split asunder with a noise of big guns, and the sound goes booming away across the frozen tracts, startling the slouching bear in his lonely haunts, and causing him to give vent to his hoarse, barking roar in answer. The ice, just forming into sheets, creaks and cracks as the rising or falling tide strains it along the shore; fragments, falling loose upon it, skid across the surface with the ringing sound which travels so far. In the spring the melting ice-floes groan as they break asunder; with a mighty crash the unbalanced bergs fall over, churning the water into foam with their plunge, and bears and foxes and all the other Arctic animals call and bark to one another as they awaken from their winter sleep. Just as these incidents occur to-day, so did they occur a thousand years ago; and if to modern ears they sound weird and awe-inspiring, what must they have been to the men who succeeded Pytheas?

Nor does this exhaust the marvel of this bleak and fascinating region. In the long winter nights the aurora borealis glares and blazes in the sky, "roaring and flashing about a ship enough to frighten a fellow," as an old quartermaster, who was with Sir F. L. McClintock in his search for Sir John Franklin, used to tell the midshipmen. In the prolonged sunset and sunrise the sky is ablaze with color, and, when the sun has gone, the rarefied atmosphere produces many curious astronomical figures. As explorers penetrate farther into the great ice-bound region they encounter fresh peculiarities. The moon, which shines continuously during the three weeks of its course, frequently appears surrounded by belts and bands of light, in which mock moons are visible. Long after the sun has disappeared a mock sun will often shine in the sky, and in the twilight, when shadows are no longer cast, men and dogs are liable to walk over cliffs and fall down crevices in the ice through being unable to distinguish them. Penetrating farther into the ice world, they learn that throughout the winter the ice heaves and crashes upon itself, making an incessant uproar as it groans and creaks. The experience of Nansen and the "Fram" emphasized this, but in the earlier days of Polar research silence was presumed to reign in the vicinity of the Arctic basin.

General Greely adds his testimony to the above in the following graphic statement:

"If one would gain an adequate idea of the true aspects of such voyaging he must turn to the original journals, penned in the great White North by brave men whose 'purpose held to sail beyond the sunset.' In those volumes will be found tales of ships beset not only months, but years, of ice packs and ice fields of extent, thickness and mass so enormous that description conveys no idea; of boat journeys where constant watchfulness alone prevented instant death by drifting bergs or commingling ice floes; of land marches when exhausted humanity staggered along, leaving traces of blood on snow or rock; of sledge journeys over chaotic masses of ice, when humble heroes straining at the drag ropes struggled on because the failure of one compromised the safety of all; of solitude and monotony, terrible in the weeks of constant polar sunlight, but unsettling the reason in the months of continuous Arctic darkness; of silence awful at times, but made yet more startling by astounding phenomena that appeal noiselessly to the eye; of darkness so continuous and intense that the disturbed mind is driven to wonder whether the ordinary course of nature will bring back the sun or whether the world has been cast out of its orbit in the planetary universe into new conditions; of cold so intense that any exposure is followed by instant freezing; of monotonous surroundings that threaten with time to unbalance the reason; of deprivations wasting the body and so impairing the mind; of failure in all things, not only in food, fuel and clothing and shelter—for Arctic service foreshadows such contingencies—but the bitter failure of plans and aspirations, which brings almost inevitably despair in its train."

The Arctic regions are not solely scenes of terror or awe-inspiring marvels, they have their visions of beauty and picturesque grandeur as well. The supernal charm of the aurora, already spoken of, is not confined to the Arctic seas, but here it offers its grandest displays, and glows in beauty until the very vales of Paradise seem opened. Many striking accounts of its varying beauty have been penned, from which we extract one by Dr. Hayes.

As he describes an auroral scene, witnessed by him, the darkness was so profound as to be oppressive. Suddenly, from the rear of the black cloud which obscured the horizon, flashed a bright ray; but before one could say "Behold!" the "jaws of darkness did devour it up." Presently an arch of many colors fixed itself across the sky, like a bridge for the armies of the Unseen, and the aurora gradually developed. The space within the arch was filled by the black cloud; but its borders brightened steadily, though the rays discharged from it were exceedingly capricious—now glaring like a vast conflagration, now beaming like the glow of a summer morn. More and more intense grew the light, until from irregular bursts it matured into an almost uniform sheet of radiance.

Towards the end of the display its character changed. The heavenly dome was all aflame. Lurid fires flung their awful portents across it, before which the stars grew pale, and seemed to recede farther and farther from the earth. The color of the light was chiefly red, but every hue had its turn, and sometimes two or three were mingled; blue and yellow streamers shot across the terrible glare, or, starting side by side from the wide expanse of the radiant arch, melted into each other, and flung a strange shade of emerald over the illuminated landscape. Again this green subdues and overcomes the red; then azure and orange blend in rapid flight; subtle rays of violet pierce through "a broad flush of yellow," and the combined streams issue in innumerable tongues of white flame, which mount towards the zenith.

It may well be credited that the play of these orange and red and violet and emerald lights upon the surrounding objects produced the most marvelous effects. "The weird forms of countless icebergs," says Hayes, "singly and in clusters, loomed above the sea, and around their summits the strange gleam shone as the fires of Vesuvius over the doomed temples of Campania. Upon the mountain-tops, along the white surface of the frozen waters, upon the lofty cliffs, the light glowed, and grew dim, and glowed again, as if the air were filled with charnel meteors, pulsating with wild inconstancy over some vast illimitable city of the dead."

As a contrast to the glow and splendor of the foregoing picture, we may place one of the Arctic night, when its deep-blue skies are no longer illuminated by electric coruscations.

All authorities agree in speaking of the severe ordeal to which the Arctic night exposes the European explorers. Physically, the experience is endurable; though there can be no doubt that its influence is to some extent unwholesome, and that the withdrawal of light acts upon the human frame as it does upon vegetation. But to civilized man's moral and intellectual faculties it is a bitter trial. To that new world which it unfolds to the senses they do not harmoniously adapt themselves. A discord and a difference exist between man and nature. He feels, for the first time, how salutary and delightful are those changes of morn, and noon, and night which refresh more temperate regions; what strength, and joy, and renovating energy there are in the alternation of sunrise and sunset, day and night. How he longs to see again the warm glow of morning reddening the eastern skies, lighting up the tops of the hills, and gradually wakening into life the quiet valley, the flowery plain, and the crystal stream! How he longs for the golden noon, with its genial sunshine, and the soft murmuring sounds which bear testimony to nature's happiness! How he longs for the purple glories of the sunset, when the great orb of day sinks serenely and majestically below the horizon, and the earth kindles in the reflection of its departing pomp! How he yearns for those healthful influences of dawn which brace him up for his daily labor; how he misses the tranquillizing power of twilight, which soothes and encourages to rest! From day to day he finds himself possessed by a single desire; on his lips and in his heart is Goethe's well-known prayer: "Light! light! more light!" He wearies of the continual gloom; it becomes to him a burden and a terror; he feels as if it had laid hold upon him with an icy grasp, and would no more let him go.

On the other hand, it may be conceded that the Arctic night has its interesting and fascinating aspects for the cultivated mind, when it can shake off the weight and oppression of the prolonged silence and almost continual darkness. It has, as we have seen, its glorious auroral phenomena, flooding land and sea with a many-colored radiance, which may well recall "the consecration and the poet's dream," for only in "poet's dream" could anything so strangely beautiful have been imagined. Then there is a charm in the keen, cold light of the stars, in the eery lustre which falls upon the hills and icebergs, in the flashing whiteness of the snow-shrouded mountain-peaks and majestic glaciers.

"Nature," says Dr. Hayes, "is here exposed on a gigantic scale;" that is, man stands so completely face to face with it, that he feels himself dwarfed in its presence, and recognizes for the first time the grandeur of its proportions. Out of the glassy sea rise the dark fronts of lofty clips, flinging their shadows over the desert of frozen waters. Mountain-summits, which foot of man has never profaned, seem to pierce the very heavens, and lift to the stars their virgin snows. In huge and massive floods the glaciers roll their burden of the innumerable ages into the sea. "The very air, disdaining the gentle softness of other climes, bodies forth," says Hayes, " a loftier majesty, and seems to fill the universe with a boundless transparency; and the stars pierce it sharply, and the moon fills it with a cold refulgence. There is neither warmth nor coloring underneath this ethereal robe of night. No broad window opens in the east, no gold and crimson curtain falls in the west, upon a world clothed in blue, and green, and purple, melting into one harmonious whole, a tinted cloak of graceful loveliness. Under the shadow of the eternal night, Nature needs no drapery and requires no adornment. The glassy sea, the tall cliff, the lofty mountain, the majestic glacier, do not blend one with the other. Each stands forth alone, clothed only with Solitude. Sable priestess of the Arctic winter, she has wrapped the world in a winding-sheet, and thrown her web and woof over the very face of Nature."

CHAPTER XVII

The Search for the Northwest Passage

ARCTIC exploration has had a double purpose, one commercial, the other geographical. The first consisted in efforts to find an available water route north of America or of Europe and Asia, by which the long journey around the southern capes of America and Africa might be avoided and easy intercourse between the East and the West be attained. These long-sought-for channels were known as the Northwest and the Northeast Passages. They have been discovered only in our own days, and their hoped-for commercial utility has proved an illusion, through the almost insuperable difficulties which they present.

The second consisted in efforts to reach the North Pole, and, as supplementary to this supreme triumph, to gain a general idea of the geography of the polar regions. Such were the purposes of Cook and Peary in their recent exploits. Both the objects named have led to adventurous voyages, and many important results have been attained, while the romantic and perilous incidents involved have been innumerable.

It may be said here that the earliest voyages of modern navigators in this direction had no definite purposes. What they did was the work of chance. Yet as they resulted in the discovery and settlement of Greenland—the ice-clad island which forms the American gateway to the Pole—some brief mention of them seems here in place.

The voyagers here referred to were the hardy and daring Norsemen, the Viking adventurers who for so many years kept

Europe in dread and turmoil. Direct descendants of these bold navigators are Nansen, one of the leaders in polar research; Amundsen, the first to sail through the Northwest Passage, and Andrée, who daringly ventured in a balloon into the unknown North. These men are of the type of the Vikings of old, who in their single-masted, many-oared galleys dared the storms of the Atlantic, sailing without compass or chart many leagues into the trackless seas.

In the year 860 Noddoddr, one of these reckless mariners, ventured so far from land that he was caught in a gale and blown on the shores of an island in the northern seas, which, from its frozen aspect, he named Iceland. This discovery, more than a thousand years ago, was the first made by European navigators in the Arctic waters. The next came in 876, when a second Viking sailor, driven far beyond Iceland by a storm, saw in the distance the coast of an unknown land, on which, however, he did not land.

Though this discovery was reported to his countrymen, more than a century elapsed before an expedition was made to the unknown land thus seen. Then, about the year 981, Eric the Red, outlawed in Iceland for the then very ordinary offense of killing one of his foes, took to the seas and sailed west in search of this untrodden shore. He reached it in due time, discovered a country still more ice-clad than Iceland, but named it Greenland as an inducement to his countrymen to settle there. The settlement made by Eric existed for some five centuries, and was the basis of the first discovery of America. The continent was first seen in 985 by a vessel blown out of its course by a gale, and in 1000 it was visited by Leif, son of Eric the Red, at a place named by him Vineland (wine-land), but no permanent settlement was made.

This discovery of Greenland is of much interest, since the Danish settlements in that island have been very useful as the basis of modern explorations. The early Norse settlement was abandoned about the period of the discovery of America by Columbus, it being decimated by the "black plague" and troubled by marauders. But about a century later the island was revisited by Captain John Davis and was claimed by Denmark. The present Danish settlements were founded in 1721, the most northern station (72 degrees 48 minutes north latitude), being Upernavik, a name of frequent occurrence in the stories of Arctic voyages, as a useful starting point into the unknown.

The earliest purpose in view in the prosecution of polar voyages was the commercial one, the discovery of an easy passage through or around the American continent by which commerce with India might be facilitated. The lack of knowledge of the width of the continent led to hopes that a water channel might be found across it to the Pacific, and various rivers were ascended with this end in view, such as the Chickahominy by Captain John Smith and the Hudson by Captain Henry Hudson. Hopes also of finding a practicable passage around the continent on the north were early entertained, and these led to the first Arctic expeditions, those of Frobisher, Davis and others.

England was early in this field, the pioneer expeditions starting from that land. The earliest on record was an expedition said to have been sent out in 1527 by Henry VIII of England for "discoverie even to the North Pole, two faire ships well manned and victualled, having in them divers cunning men to seek strange regions." Its success was small, one of the two ships sent being lost north of Newfoundland, while the other returned to England.

The next expedition that calls for attention was that under Sir Hugh Willoughby, who sailed from England in 1553, "'for the discovery of regions, dominions, islands, and places unknown." He set sail with three vessels, the largest being of 160 tons. These crossed the North Sea in company, sighting the coast of Norway about the middle of July. In September they were parted by a storm, two of the ships reaching the coast of Russian Lapland, where it was determined to pass the winter. Here Sir Hugh and all his companions perished, probably from scurvy. The third ship, under Richard Chancellor, reached the mouth of the Dwina, in the White Sea, and entered the harbor of Archangel. Here the mariners were well treated by the Russians and returned to England in the following summer. Thus ended the first northeast expedition. Its chief result was to open commercial relations between England and Russia.

The first expedition with any notable results was that of Sir Martin Frobisher in 1576 to the northwest. He tells us, in the quaint diction of his day, that, "being persuaded of a new and nearer passage to Cataya (Cathay) than by Capo d'buona Speranza, which the Portugalles yeerly use, began first with himselfe to devise, and then with his friendes to conferre, and layde a playne platte unto them, that that voyage was not only possible by the northwest, but also, as he coulde prove, easie to be performed." It was "the only thing left undone in the world whereby a notable mind might be made famous and fortunate."

Sailing from Deptford with three small barks, he explored the coast of Greenland, discovered the strait now known by his name, and found on its shores a black mineral in which was visible a yellow substance resembling gold. This unlucky find put an end to the main purpose of the expedition, the ships returning to England with some of the illusory substance, which, on examination by London goldsmiths, was pronounced to be gold. The announcement raised high enthusiasm in the country, and a new and large expedition was fitted out and despatched in 1577, returning with an abundance of the black earth. In 1578 it went again and this time brought back a great cargo of the deceptive material. With this the story ends; we hear no more of Arctic gold. The stuff was doubtless tested and found to be what is designated as "fools' gold," but no mention was made of the result, and the record came to a sudden end.

The historian of Frobisher's expedition gave many details of their experience with the Eskimos, and presents us with a graphic description of these people, one well worth repeating. "They are," he says, "of the color of a ripe olive. They are men very active and nimble. They are a strong people and very warlike, for, in our sight, upon the tops of the hills, they would often muster themselves after the manner of a skirmish, trace their ground very nimbly, and manage their bows and darts with great dexterity. They go clad in coats made of the skins of beasts, as of seals, deer, bears, foxes, and hares. They have also some garments of feathers, being made of the cases of fowls, firmly sewed and compacted together. In summer they use to wear the hair side of their coats outward, and sometimes go naked for too much heat; and in winter, as by signs they have declared, they were four of five fold upon their bodies, with the hair for warmth turned inward. These people are by nature very subtle and sharp-witted, ready to conceive our meaning by signs, and to make answer well to be understood again; and if they have not seen the thing whereof you ask them, they will wink and cover their eyes with their hand, as who would say, it hath been hid from their sight. If they understand you not whereof you asked them, they will stop their ears. They will teach us the name of each thing in their language which we desire to learn, and are apt to learn anything of us. They delight in music above measure, and will keep time and stroke to any tune you shall sing, both with their voice, head, hand, and foot, and will sing the same tune aptly after you. They will row with our oars in our boats, and keep a true stroke with our mariners, and seem to take great delight therein."

Frobisher was quickly followed by another notable navigator, John Davis, who made three voyages between 1585 and 1587 in search of a northwest passage, discovering the strait which bears his name and advancing as far as the 72d degree of north latitude. His remark that he found himself "in a great sea free from ice, neither was there any ice toward the north, but a sea free, large, and very salt and blue, and of unsearchable depth," added nothing to the discovery of the passage beyond the renewed conviction of that day that the way toward the north was without impediment.

As the discoverer, or pioneer, of the Baffin's Bay route Davis occupies a place of renown among Arctic navigators. On his final voyage he reached the latitude of 72 degrees north, two hundred and fifty miles farther north than any explorer before him had attained, and discovered a little cape which he named Sanderson Hope. It is in the vicinity of the present Danish colony of Upernavik. Confident that he had found the long-sought passage to Cathay (China), he fancied that an open route in that direction lay before him. But he was soon undeceived, finding himself surrounded by huge icebergs, to escape which needed all his skill and seamanship. For three days he sought an outlet, but the great bay was everywhere covered with thick ice, and he was forced to put back, reaching England with his battered and leaking ship on the 15th of September, 1587.

One more expedition was sent out in the sixteenth century, this being a Dutch enterprise under William Barentz, who sailed north in the European seas, reaching a much higher latitude than that gained by Davis. In his first voyage, in 1594, he attained the latitude of 77 degrees 21 minutes, near Cape Nassau, Nova Zembla, and in 1596 reached the higher latitude of 79 degrees 49 minutes, off North Spitzbergen, in the region now known as Barentz Sea.

We have next to deal with an English explorer, but one best known for his exploits in the Dutch service, the famous Henry Hudson. His reputation, indeed, rests mainly upon his discovery of Hudson River and New York Bay, but he also ranks high among Arctic navigators, making in all four voyages to the icy seas, and sailing due north, northeast and northwest. He was the first whose direct purpose was the discovery of the North Pole, and he made a record of high latitude that was not surpassed during the two centuries following.

His first voyage was made in 1607, under the direction of the Muscovy Company; and the order he received was straightforward and simple in the extreme: "Go direct to the North Pole." And this order he attempted to carry out in a small decked boat, with a crew of ten men and a boy! He steered due north along the shores of Spitzbergen, until he reached latitude 80 degrees 23 minutes; and then, for want of provisions, and owing to the approach of winter, was forced to return. When we consider the perilous character of the navigation of these northern seas, we cannot but marvel as we record that Hudson's little barque arrived safely in the Thames, on the 15th of September.

In the following year he sailed again, but took a northeasterly direction towards Nova Zembla. His ship was somewhat larger, and his crew numbered fourteen men. But he ascended no higher than 75 degrees, and returned to England in August.

His third voyage, in 1609, was made in the Dutch service and led to unintended results. At first he made for the northeast, but being baffled by the ice-drifts, he sailed west, and touched the American coast in the neighborhood of New York Bay. He discovered the noble river which still bears his name and on whose banks the Dutch afterwards established a colony. Among their descendants long flourished strange legends of Hudson and his men. "It was affirmed," says Washington Irving, "that the great Hendrik Hudson, the first discoverer of the river and country, kept a kind of vigil there every twenty years, with his crew of the 'Half-Moon'; being permitted in this way to revisit the scenes of his enterprise, and keep a guardian eye upon the river and the great city called by his name."

In 1610 he made his fourth and last voyage, in a vessel of fifty-eight tons, stored and provisioned for six months. Frobisher Strait was gained on the 1st of June. Then came a desperate struggle against floating ice and contrary winds; but Hudson kept perseveringly to the westward, passed through the strait now known by his name, reached the extreme point of Labrador, which he called Cape Wolstenholm, and discovered an island-group to the northwest, the southern headland of which he named Cape Dudley Digges. Here a vast sea broadened before his astonished gaze; and the restless waters for the first time rolled and seethed under an English keel.

Into this great bay or sea, Hudson Bay, as it is now known, he sailed for several hundred miles; and winter coming on, he encamped his crew upon Southampton Island, and hauled his ship aground. The hardships he and his men endured were terrible, for they were ill-fitted to contend with an Arctic winter, and had neither sufficient provisions nor stores. Hudson bore the trial uncomplainingly, sustained by a noble enthusiasm; but his followers grew discontented, and then mutinous, and on Hudson's attempting to resume the enterprise at the return of spring, they seized upon him, his son, and several sick sailors, and threw them into an open boat, in which they had previously stowed a fowling-piece, some gunpowder and shot, a small quantity of meal, and an iron pot (June 21, 1611). The castaways were voluntarily joined by John King, the carpenter, who refused to take part in and bear the shame of mutiny, remaining faithful to his captain to the last.

To the last it proved, for Hudson and his companions were never more heard of. They perished miserably in that inland sea or on its barren shores. The ringleader in the mutiny and five of his companions were slain in an encounter with the natives on an island near Cape Digges. Of the remainder, some died of starvation, the survivors managing to carry the ship back to the British Isles. Thus ended in disaster one of the most promising of the early expeditions.

The tidings of the great stretch of open water discovered by Hudson deeply impressed the imagination of the adventurers of his time. It seemed to them that here was the route to Asia which had been so diligently sought. It was not long before others followed in his track, the first being Captain Button in 1612, who reached and named Nelson River, at the spot where the Hudson Bay Company founded its first post. He also discovered the Mansfield Islands, in latitude 65 degrees. Two years later a voyage was made by William Baffin and in 1616 one by William Baffin and Robert Bylot, which resulted in the discovery of Whale Sound, Smith Sound, Jones Sound, Lancaster Sound, and Baffin Bay. These were notable additions to the chart of the Arctic World, which British enterprise was gradually defining and filling up; but by Baffin's contemporaries they were discredited. As Mr. Markham observes, the memory of a bold and scientific navigator had to wait many weary years for that full justice which comes at last. It was two centuries before another vessel forced her way into the "North Water" of Baffin Bay, and the great pilot's discoveries were almost forgotten. On maps published as late as 1818, may be seen a circular dotted line to the west of Greenland, with this legend, —"Baffin's Bay, according to the relation of William Baffin in 1616, *but not now believed.*"

The all-important discovery made by Baffin was that of the great channel leading out of his bay in a northerly direction, and opening upon the vast and still unknown region which stretches towards the Pole. He named it after Sir Thomas Smith, the governor, we may almost say the creator, of the East India Company; and a man of great sagacity, liberality, and enterprise. Of this sound Baffin says: "It runneth to the north of 78 degrees, and is admirable in one respect, because in it is the greatest variation of the compass of any part of the world known; for, by divers good observations, I found it to be above five points, or 66 degrees, varied to the westward, so that northeast by east is true north, and so of the rest. Also this sound seemeth to be good for the killing of whales, it being the greatest and largest in all this bay." It is now regarded as affording the only practicable route to the Polar Sea.

Several other voyages, of no great importance, took place

during the remainder of the seventeenth century, but for a century after 1631, when Captain Thomas James made a voyage chiefly notable for its misadventures, the search was abandoned. It was in the service of Russia that it was resumed in 1741, when Vitus Bering, or Behring, a Dane, explored the coast of Kamchatka for the Russian government and sailed into the strait since known by his name. Several other Russian expeditions brought up the work to the opening of the nineteenth century, and two British expeditions worthy of mention took place.

The first was that under Captain J. C. Phipps, sent out by George III, at the instance of the Royal Society of the Admiralty, in 1773, toward the regions north of Spitzbergen. In his "Journal of a Voyage to the North Pole," the captain entered the sea "during a summer affording the fullest examination; but the wall of ice between latitudes 80 and 81 degrees showed for more than twenty degrees not the smallest appearance of any opening." The highest latitude reached was 80 degrees 48 minutes. In this expedition Horatio Nelson, then a boy of fifteen years of age, took part, and exhibited a bravery and cool courage prophetic of his subsequent career.

The other was the famous one of Captain Cook, who was sent to make discoveries in the Pacific and to return to England, if possible, by way of Bering Strait, making a northeast passage. His ships were totally unfit for this purpose, and after exploring the strait and reaching Ivy Cape, he was driven back by the ice and forced to return by the southern route.

It is well here to speak of another expedition, not that it had any special importance, but from the fact that it was the first authentic American attempt and was backed by Benjamin Franklin. Here is a letter from Franklin concerning it:

"PHILADELPHIA, February 28, 1753.

. . . "I believe I have not before told you that I have provided a subscription here of £1500 to fit out a vessel in search of a northwest passage. She sails in a few days, and is called the 'Argo,' commanded by Mr. Swaine, who was in the last expedition in the 'California,' and author of a Journal of that voyage in two volumes. We think the attempt laudable, whatever may be the success. If she fails, 'magnis tamen excidit ausis.' With great esteem,

"BENJ. FRANKLIN.

"MR. CADWALADER COLDEN, N. Y."

Of this voyage the *Pennsylvania Gazette,* "printed for Benjamin Franklin, postmaster, and D. Hall," November 15, 1753, says:

"Sunday last arrived here the schooner 'Argo,' Captain Charles Swaine, who sailed from this port last spring, on the discovery of a northwest passage. She fell in with ice off Cape Farewell; left the eastern ice and fell in with the western ice, in latitude 58 degrees, and cruised to the northward to latitude 63 degrees, to clear it, but could not; it then extending to the eastward. On her return to the southward, she met with two Danish ships bound to Ball River and Disco, up Davis Straits, who had been in the ice fourteen days off Farewell, and had then stood to westward and assured the commander that the ice was fast to the shore all above Hudson's Straits to the distance of forty degrees out: and that there had not been such a severe winter as the last these twenty-four years that they had used that trade; they had been nine weeks from Copenhagen. The 'Argo,' finding she could not get round the ice, pressed through it and got into the strait's mouth the 26th of June, and made the Island Resolution, but was forced out by vast quantities of driving ice, and got into a clear sea the first of July. On the 14th, cruising the ice for an opening to get in again, she met four sail of Hudson's Bay ships endeavoring to get in, and continued with them till the 19th, when they parted in thick weather, in latitude 62½ degrees, which weather continued until the 7th of August. The Hudson Bay men supposed themselves 40 leagues from the western land.

"The 'Argo' ran down the ice from 63 degrees to 57 degrees 30 minutes, and after repeated attempts to enter the straits in vain, as the season for discovery on the western side of the Bay was over, she went on the Labrador coast, and discovered it perfectly from 56 to 55 degrees, finding no less than six inlets, to the heads of all of which they went, and of which we hear they have made a very good chart, and have a better account of the country, its soil, produce, etc., than has hitherto been published.

"The captain says it is much like Norway, and that there is no communication with Hudson's Bay through Labrador where one has heretofore imagined, a high ridge of mountains running north and south, about fifty leagues within the coast."

Not satisfied with the results of this attempt, Captain Swaine again sailed in the "Argo" the following spring, and the *Pennsylvania Journal and Weekly Advertiser* of Thursday, October 24, 1754, published in Philadelphia, says:

"On Sunday last arrived here the schooner 'Argo,' Captain Swaine, who was fitted out in the spring on the discovery of a northwest passage, but having three of his men killed on the Labrador coast, returned without success."

CHAPTER XVIII

The Ross and Parry Polar Voyages

INTO the seas containing the goal sought by Peary and Cook in the early years of the twentieth century expeditions, led by daring navigators, pushed in the early nineteenth, the first of these being Captain Scovesby, a successful and adventurous whaler. It was in a whaling voyage that he made his famous northward trip. While lying-to for whales, in 1806, in the seas east of Greenland, the idea entered his mind to make a bold dash toward the Polar Sea, which he believed lay open to the north.

With a boldness and energy rarely equaled he pushed his ship far through the pack ice, succeeding in the end in clearing this formidable barrier and entering "a great openness or sea of water," in which he reached the latitude of 81 degrees 30 minutes, the highest as yet attained. He added largely to our knowledge of the east coast of Greenland and of the phenomena of the Arctic region.

The next to follow was Captain John Ross, in 1818, with two vessels, the "Isabella" and the "Alexander," the latter commanded by Lieutenant William Parry, the man with whom we are here principally concerned. With Captain Ross sailed as a midshipman his nephew, James Ross, also of fame in polar annals. Both these men ended their careers as admirals in the British navy, under the titles of Sir John Ross and Sir James Ross.

This expedition followed the usual Baffin Bay route and in latitude 75 degrees 54 minutes met with a village of Eskimos who had never before seen white men. They curiously queried: "Who are you? Whence came you? Is it from the sun or the moon?"

To these Ross gave the name of Arctic Highlanders, a designation since then often used. He was the first to discover cliffs covered with seeming red snow; this is now known to be due to the growth in the snow of a minute red lichen. At the farthest point which he reached, Ross was too far south to discern more than the outline of the land near Smith Sound; but he named the bold headlands which guard the entrance to this famous channel after his two ships, Cape Isabella and Cape Alexander.

Descending the west side of the bay, he found the waters clear of ice, and extremely deep. The land was high, and the range of mountains, in general, free from snow. A noble inlet, fifty miles wide, with cliffs on both sides, now offered itself to view, and the ships entered it on the 29th of August. But they had scarcely accomplished thirty miles when Ross, to the surprise and vexation of his officers, declared that he saw land stretching across the inlet at a distance of eight leagues, and ordered the ships to tack about and return. To this imaginary land he gave the name of Croker Mountains. Parry, on the other hand, was of opinion that this great inlet, now recognized as the Lancaster Sound of Baffin, was no land-locked bay, but a strait opening out to the westward; and on the return of the two ships to England he openly declared this opinion. The English public supported the energetic Parry; and, after a vigorous wordy warfare, the government resolved to place him in charge of the "Hecla" bomb-ship and the "Griper" gun-brig, with which he sailed for the north on the 5th of May, 1819.

On the 15th of June Parry came in sight of Cape Farewell, and sailed on up Davis Strait and Baffin Bay as far as 73 degrees north latitude, where he found himself hemmed in by masses of ice. On the 25th, however, a way opened up, and Parry pushed forward, boldly and energetically, until he reached Lancaster Sound. Here he was on the ground made familiar by the expedition of the preceding year, and was soon to determine whether Ross' supposed mountains had any real existence. "It is more easy to imagine than describe," says Parry, "the almost breathless anxiety which

THE ROSS AND PARRY POLAR VOYAGES

was now visible in every countenance, while, as the breeze increased to a fresh gale, we ran quickly up the sound."

As they advanced, the "Croker Mountains" disappeared into thin air, and Parry proceeded as far as the mouth of a great inlet, which he named Barrow Strait. Entering this, he sailed onward to Prince Regent Inlet, which, with various capes, bays and islands, he named and surveyed. On approaching the magnetic (not the actual) north pole, he found his compasses rendered almost useless by the "dip" or "variation" of the needle. Great was then the excitement on board the two ships; the excitement increased to enthusiasm when, on September 4th, after crossing the meridian of 113 degrees west longitude, Parry announced to his men that they had earned the government grant of £5,000. This was offered to the navigator who should penetrate to the meridian of 110 degrees west, within the Arctic Circle.

Two weeks later, they were beset by the ice, and in the Hecla and Griper Bay, on Melville Island, Parry resolved to pass the winter. In the following year, the thaw did not set in until July, and it was August before Parry released his ships. Then he started for home, and on arriving in England, about the middle of November, 1820, was received with a hearty welcome.

His success led to his appointment to the command of another expedition in 1821. His ships, the "Hecla" and "Fury," were equipped with every appliance that scientific ingenuity could suggest or unlimited resources provide. They sailed from the Nore on the 8th of May; they returned to the Shetland Isles on the 10th of October, 1823. In the interval—seven-and-twenty months—Parry and Lyon (his lieutenant) discovered the Duke of York Bay, numerous inlets on the northeast coast of the American mainland, Winter Island, the islands of Annatook and Ooght, Hecla and Fury Strait, Melville Peninsula, and Cockburn Island. A glance at the map will show the reader how far to the westward these discoveries carried the boundary of the known region.

While encamped on Winter Island, the English were visited by a party of Eskimos, whose settlement they visited in turn. There they found a group of five snow-huts, with canoes, sledges, dogs, and above sixty men, women and children, as regularly and to all appearance as permanently fixed as if they had occupied the same spot the whole winter. The astonishment with which the English surveyed the exterior aspects of this little village was not diminished by their admission into the interior of the huts composing it. Each was constructed entirely of snow and ice. After creeping through two low passages, having each its arched doorway, the strangers found themselves in a small circular apartment, of which the roof formed a perfect arched dome. From this central apartment three doorways, also arched, and of larger dimensions than the outward ones, opened into as many inhabited apartments, one on each side, and the third opposite the entrance. Here the women were seated on their beds, against the wall, each having her little fire-place or lamp, with all her domestic utensils, about her. The children quickly crept behind their mothers; the dogs slunk into the corners in dismay.

The construction of the inhabited part of the hut was similar to that of the outer apartment, being a dome, formed by separate blocks of snow laid with great regularity and no small ingenuity, each being cut into the shape requisite to build up a substantial arch, from seven to eight feet high in the center, and with no other support than this principle of building supplies. Sufficient light was admitted by a circular window of ice, neatly fitted into the roof of each apartment.

In 1824 Parry went north again in connection with a series of expeditions sent out by the British government. He was to explore Prince Regent Inlet, and the others were to investigate the northern lands of the continent, with the purpose of obtaining a knowledge of their configuration. One of the latter was under the command of the afterwards famous Sir John Franklin.

Parry, with his ships, the "Hecla" and "Fury," soon reached Lancaster Sound, the goal of his former voyage. But here the ice imprisoned his vessels and he was forced to spend the winter at Port Bowen. With the spring came new misadventures. Vast masses of ice pressed upon the "Fury," driving her ashore and crushing her so that she became useless. Parry, therefore, was obliged to remove her men and stores to the "Hecla" and set sail for England, being in no condition for a further advance.

In 1827 the indefatigable Parry started with an expedition for the north shore of Spitzbergen. It was characterized by his daring attempt to cross the pack-ice in light boats and sledges; the former being used in the water-ways and pools, the latter in traveling over the frozen plains. Nothing but the strongest enthusiasm could have rendered this enterprise possible. It was the first attempt of the kind, though later experience proved that it was the only available one. When the explorers arrived at a gap in the ice, they launched their boats and embarked. On reaching the opposite side they landed, and by sheer force hauled up the boats; a laborious process, occupying much time, and making such demands on the men's strength that only eight miles were accomplished in five days. They could not travel except by night, on account of the glare of the snow, which threatened them with blindness. Breakfasting soon after sunset, they labored for some hours; then made their chief meal; and towards sunrise halted, lighted their pipes, wrapped themselves up in their furs, and laid down to rest.

The reader must not suppose that the ice-fields of the Polar regions are as smooth and level as the frozen surface of an English river. They are intersected by "lanes" or "leads" of water, and broken up by rugged hummocks of ice, which can be crossed only with extreme difficulty. In spite of every obstacle, Parry pressed on, ambitious to reach the eighty-third parallel of latitude. But at last he became aware of the startling circumstance that, faster than he moved forward, the ice was carrying him backward; in other words, it was slowly drifting southward beneath his feet, and bearing him and his party along with it. To struggle against an adverse Nature was hopeless. In latitude 82 degrees 45 minutes he gave up the struggle; for, though they had traveled nearly three hundred miles over the rugged ice and through frozen water, they had advanced no more than one hundred and seventy-two miles from the "Hecla." Parry's trouble in this instance has been experienced by other polar navigators since his time, the ice of the polar seas being in almost continual motion. But he had won the honor of making the highest point north yet reached, and which was not equalled until fifty years afterwards. With this success the gallant Parry closed his polar record.

Parry's successful voyage was quickly followed by one commanded by Captain Ross, his 1818 associate, who went north again in 1829. Steam navigation had now been introduced and this voyage was made in a steamship, the "Victory," the first of her kind to navigate the Arctic seas. The "Victory" made her way into Prince Regent Inlet; found the wreck of the "Fury" on the 12th of August; and on the 15th reached Parry's farthest point. Thence she accomplished three hundred miles along a previously unexplored coast; and on the 7th of October went into winter quarters in what is now called Felix Harbor. There Ross was held fast by the ice for eleven months. In September, 1830, he once more got under way, but, after sailing for about three miles, was again caught in the pack-ice, and shut up until August, 1831. On this occasion the "Victory" accomplished *four* miles, and on the 27th of September was imprisoned for another winter; having thus achieved exactly seven miles in two years.

In 1831, James Ross, who had again accompanied his uncle, made a sledge excursion to the westward, and crowned himself with glory by reaching and fixing the magnetic north pole in latitude 70 degrees 5 minutes 17 seconds north, and longitude 96 degrees 46 minutes 45 seconds west. This is the point at which the

THE ROSS AND PARRY POLAR VOYAGES 251

magnet points vertically downward, indicating that it marks the extremity of the earth's magnetic axis. Why it does not coincide with the geographical pole no one knows, but its discovery was in its way as important as that of the latter in 1909.

The long imprisonment in the ice had by this time seriously affected the health of the crew; and as there was no chance of releasing the ship, Ross determined to abandon her, and effect his escape from the polar solitudes in boats and sledges. He made first for the wreck of Parry's ship, the "Fury," in order to avail himself of what remained of her stores and materials; and after a terrible journey reached it, but so spent and broken down that farther progress was impossible. Here he wintered; the whole party undergoing the most fearful sufferings, and several dying. With the first warm days of the summer of 1833 their hopes revived. They resumed their perilous adventure; and on the 15th of August gained the open sea, and took to their boats. At midnight they passed Edwin Bay and next morning reached the farthest point to which they had advanced in the preceding year. Finding an open "waterlane," they kept to the northward, and in the evening were tossing off the northeastern point of the American continent. On the 17th great was their joy to see before them the ample expanse of Barrow Strait; and with a favorable wind they now steered to the south, passing Cape York and Admiralty Inlet, and on the 25th reaching the eastern shore of Navy Board Inlet.

At four o'clock on the following morning the lookout man announced that a ship was in sight; but as the breeze was blowing freshly, she bore away under all sail, leaving them behind. Fortunately a dead calm succeeded, and by dint of hard rowing our explorers approached so near that their signals were descried, when the ship heaved to and lowered a boat, which made directly towards them. The mate in command asked them if they were in distress, and offered assistance, adding that he belonged to the "Isabella," of Hull, once commanded by Captain Ross, but then by Captain

Humphreys. He was with difficulty convinced that his former commander stood before him,—declaring that it was all a mistake, for he had certainly been dead two years. When finally satisfied, he hastened back to his ship with the glad tidings, and immediately her yards were manned, and three ringing cheers greeted the captain and his party.

As soon as possible Captain Humphreys steered for England, and on the 12th of October reached Stromness in Orkney. The intelligence of the rescue so happily accomplished quickly spread thence throughout the kingdom; and Captain Ross and his companions were received as men who had risen from the grave. On his landing at Hull he was welcomed by enthusiastic crowds, like a general fresh from the field of victory. He fully deserved the reception thus accorded to him.

CHAPTER XIX

The First Franklin Expedition

JOHN FRANKLIN, the afterwards famous Sir John Franklin, was born at Spilsby, in Lincolnshire, England, in 1786, one of a family of ten. His father intended him for the clergy, but as the boy grew older his disposition seemed to unfit him decidedly for this profession. He was a restless lad, with the spirit of the rover born in him, and manifested early in life a strong predilection for the sea, Admiral Nelson being the idol of his heart, while he read with avidity all the books he could obtain dealing with sea life and adventure. Living not far from the coast, the scent of salt water filled his nostrils, and the sight of the open sea was familiar to his eyes.

These influences and the romantic yarns spun to him by any old sailor he chanced upon exerted over him the spell which was to mould his later life. The long stretch of moving water, which rolled between him and the sky-line, was the home of all that was wonderful and glorious; the ships which sailed over it were, to his enthusiastic mind, floating homes of mystery, adventure and beauty. Beyond the sea lay the lands where the coco-palms grew, where Indians hunted and fought, and where roamed mighty beasts of strange and fantastic shapes. Over the sea, also, lay the realms of ice and snow, of which more marvelous tales were told than of the golden islands of the Southern Seas. As a result a great yearning came upon him. The life on shore, in peaceful, steady-going Lincolnshire, was too dreary and hopeless; nowhere could he be happy save on that boundless ocean, with room to breathe, and surrounded by all the glamour of romance.

The elder Franklin probably looked upon all this as a boyish whim, and wisely fancied that the best way to cure it would be to let the ardent lad have a taste of a sailor's life, thinking that the rough fare and hard work which it involved would cure him of his desire and make him welcome the quiet career proposed for him. He therefore arranged for him to make a voyage in a trading vessel to Lisbon and back. His scheme had not the desired result. The boy came back fuller of the desire to be a sailor than before. As a consequence his father obtained a place for him in the Royal Navy, and he had the happiness to serve under his supreme hero Nelson, at the battle of Copenhagen. He also served under Nelson with distinction in the battle of Trafalgar, and was present at the battle of New Orleans in 1815, where he received a slight wound.

Franklin's first Arctic experience came in 1818, when he had reached the rank of lieutenant and was second in command of an expedition sent out to find a way through Bering Straits. Two vessels formed the expedition—the "Dorothea," 370 tons, under Captain Buchan, and the "Trent," 250 tons, under Lieutenant Franklin, the latter carrying a crew of ten officers and twenty-eight men. Their instructions were to sail due north, from a point between Greenland and Spitzbergen, making their way, if possible, through Bering Straits. The ships, which would to-day rank only as small coasting craft, were soon imprisoned in the ice and so severely crushed that as soon as the winter passed and escape was possible they were turned towards home. The practical results of the expedition were valueless, and only one circumstance in connection with it saved it from being a failure. This was the introduction of Franklin to that sphere of work which, during the remainder of his life, he was so brilliantly to adorn.

In the following year (1819) Franklin left Gravesend in a merchant ship of the Hudson Bay Company, his purpose being to explore the northern coast of America in co-operation with Parry, who, as already stated, was despatched to Lancaster Sound. The outcome of Parry's voyage we have told; that of Franklin's journey may be briefly stated. At that time the whole northern coast of the continent had been explored at two points only, the mouth of the Coppermine and Mackenzie Rivers, and it was desired to gain a wider knowledge of this unknown region.

With Dr. Richardson as naturalist, Midshipman Hood and Back, and a few men from the Orkneys, Franklin reached his starting point, York Factory, on Hudson Bay, August 13, 1819. Thence, by a journey of seven hundred miles, the party reached Fort Cumberland, wintering the first year on the Saskatchewan. Another year was passed in the wilderness of northern Canada and a second winter weathered through in "the barren grounds." In the following summer it was proposed to descend the Coppermine to the Arctic Sea, and a journey marked by terrible suffering and hardship began.

Fort Enterprise, the camp occupied during their second winter, stood on a gentle ascent, at the base of which slept the frozen current of Waiter River. Here the explorers employed themselves in killing reindeer, and in preparing with their fat and flesh that dried, salted and pounded comestible called pemmican. About one hundred and eighty animals were killed. But even this number did not furnish an adequate supply for Franklin's party; and as the expected stores of tobacco, ammunition and blankets did not arrive, Mr. Back, with some Indian and Canadian attendants, returned to Chipewyan for them. Having obtained them, he once more rejoined the party at Fort Enterprise—after an absence of five months and a journey of 1,104 miles, "in snowshoes, and with no other covering at night in the woods than a blanket and deerskin."

It was the middle of June, 1821, before the ice broke up in the Coppermine River. Then Franklin began his journey, passing down the stream in light birch-canoes, and occasionally pausing to hunt the reindeer, musk-oxen and wolves which frequented its banks. Having reached the mouth of the river, the twenty adventurers now composing the expedition launched their barks upon the Polar

Sea, which they found almost tideless, and comparatively free from ice.

The extreme westward point at which, after many perilous experiences, Franklin arrived, was situated in latitude 68 degrees 30 minutes, and he appropriately named it Point Turnagain. Between this headland on the east and Cape Barrow on the west, a deep gulf opens inland as far south as the Arctic Circle. It was found to be studded with numerous islands, and indented with sounds affording excellent harbors, all of them supplied with small rivers of fresh water, abounding with salmon, trout and other fish. The survey of George IV's Coronation Gulf—to adopt Franklin's barbarous nomenclature—being completed, the explorers prepared to return to Fort Enterprise. The overland part of the journey was attended with the most terrible hardships. They suffered from the combined afflictions of cold, hunger and fatigue. They were so reduced in bodily strength that it was with difficulty they could drag along their languid limbs; and when at last within forty miles of their winter asylum, they found themselves at their last ration. No food, no shelter and the severity of an Arctic winter pressing upon them! Mr. Back, with three of the stoutest Canadians, gallantly started forward to seek assistance; and were followed in a few days by Franklin and seven of the party—leaving the weakest, under the care of Dr. Richardson and Mr. Hood, to proceed at leisure. Four of Franklin's companions, however, soon gave up the attempt from absolute physical incapacity. One of these—Michel, an Iroquois—returned to Dr. Richardson; the others were never again heard of. Franklin pushed forward, living on berries and a lichen called *tripe-de-roche,* and reached the hut; but it was without an inhabitant, without stores and blocked up by snow. Here he and his three companions lingered for seventeen days, with no other food than the bones and skin of the deer which had been killed the preceding winter, boiled down into a kind of soup. On October 29th Dr. Richardson and John Hepburn, one of the seamen, made their appearance.

A FIGHT WITH A POLAR BEAR

A DANGEROUS WALRUS HUNT

FUR SEALS FIGHTING OVER A CAPTURED FEMALE

Like the whale the seals are mammals and live in the cold waters of the North around Alaska and Labrador.

ESKIMO ATTACKING A POLAR BEAR

The Polar or White Bear is a native of the Arctic regions. It feeds on seals, fish and walrus, dives and swims with ease. It is the favorite game of the Eskimo, who eats its flesh and wears its skin.

GRAMPUS OR SWORDFISH ATTACKING A NARWHAL

This ferocious animal congregates in herds to hunt members of its own family. We see them here attacking Narwhals, which the Greenlanders give a high place among their ocean treasures.

THE FIRST FRANKLIN EXPEDITION

Dr. Richardson had a tragic tale to unfold. He stated that for the first two days after Franklin's departure his party had nothing to eat. On the third day Michel arrived with a hare and partridge, which afforded each a small morsel. The fourth day they fasted. On the 11th Michel offered them some flesh, which he declared to be part of a wolf; but they afterwards had good reason to suspect it was the flesh of one of the unfortunate men who had left Franklin to return to Richardson. They noticed that Michel daily grew more furtive and insolent, and were convinced that he had a supply of meat for his own use. On the 20th, while Hepburn was felling wood, he heard the report of a gun, and, turning quickly round, saw Michel dart into the tent. Mr. Hood was found dead; a ball had penetrated the back of his skull: there could not be the shadow of a doubt that Michel had fired it. He now grew more suspicious and impatient of control than ever; and as he was stronger than any other of the party, and well-armed, they arrived at the conviction that their safety depended upon his death. "I determined," said Dr. Richardson, "as I was thoroughly convinced of the necessity of such a dreadful act, to take the whole responsibility upon myself; and immediately upon Michel's coming up I put an end to his life by shooting him through the head."

They occupied six days in traveling twenty-four miles, existing on lichens and pieces of Mr. Hood's skin cloak. On the evening of the 29th they came in sight of the fort, and at first felt inexpressible pleasure on seeing the smoke issue from the chimney. But the absence of any footprints in the snow filled their hearts with sad forebodings, which were fully realized when they entered the hut and saw the wretchedness that reigned there.

The exploring party was now reduced to four—Franklin, Richardson, Hepburn and an Indian; and that these could long survive seemed impossible, from their absolute weakness and lack of food. Happily, on the 7th of November three Indians arrived, whom Mr. Back had despatched from Chipewyan with supplies;

and they tended the sufferers carefully until all were strong enough to return to the English settlement. And in this way was accomplished a journey of 5,500 miles; mostly over a bleak and barren country and under an inclement sky, with terrible cost of physical and mental suffering and with much loss of life, but with results which greatly enlarged the boundaries of geographical knowledge.

In a second land expedition, made in conjunction with Parry's voyage of 1824, Franklin discarded the Mackenzie and traced the coast line through 37 degrees of longitude to near the one hundred and fiftieth meridian. The English government, appreciating the services of one who, through great danger and suffering, had carried these expeditions over nine thousand miles, and added to the charts twelve hundred miles of the northern coast line, knighted him in 1829. He also received the honorary degree of D.C.L. from the University of Oxford, was awarded the great gold medal from the French Geographical Society, and was elected a member of the Academy of Sciences, Paris.

As governor of Tasmania, 1836-43, he accomplished much for the advancement of the colony,—among other benefits founding the Royal Society of Tasmania at Hobart Town, the meetings of which were held in the Government-house, and the papers printed at his expense. By a singular coincidence, among the Antarctic expeditions visiting the colony he had occasion to welcome the "Erebus" and "Terror," the ships which he was afterwards to command in the final and fatal expedition of his life.

CHAPTER XX

The Terrible Fate of the Sir John Franklin Expedition

THE records of polar expeditions are full of tales of disaster, suffering and death, at times sudden, at times drawn out through the long and slow agony of starvation. While the later explorers, such as Nansen, Peary, Cook and others experienced the pangs of hunger in only a minor degree, some of those of earlier date passed through long-drawn sufferings of the most terrible description. We may instance the cases of the Greely and DeLong expeditions, and above all that of Sir John Franklin, the mystery surrounding which enveloped it in a romantic interest, which was greatly added to by the results of the many relief expeditions sent out and the years that passed before the fearful fate of the unfortunates became known. In the romance of polar research—the romance of terror—the tale of Sir John Franklin's final expedition stands first, and a detailed account of it comes here in order.

On Franklin's return to England from his governorship of Van Diemen's Land, in 1844, he found the Admiralty exercised on the subject of a new Arctic expedition, proposed by the Royal Society at the instance of Sir John Barrow. He claimed the command, and was appointed. On this occasion the first lord of the admiralty said to Sir Edward Parry, of former Arctic fame, "I see that Franklin is sixty years of age; ought we to permit him to go out?" to which Parry replied, "He is the ablest man I know, and if you do not send him he will certainly die of despair."

Franklin himself said, when asked, "Can you not repose on the laurels won in such good service for your country," "My lord, I am but fifty-nine." "He appeared," says La Roquette, "as jealous of a few months of his age, when it was a question of exposure to great danger, or of executing a work of difficulty or suffering, as a woman would be of being thought older than the parish register showed."

The prestige of Arctic service, and of his brilliant experience in that field, brought around him a crowd of volunteers for the new expedition, which set out under the best auspices and with ardent hopes of a brilliant and successful voyage. Franklin's experience had previously been along the northern coast line of the American continent. Now he proposed to traverse the islanded seas bordering that coast, with the purpose of discovering that famed Northwest Passage which so many navigators of the past centuries had sought in vain. Daring mariners had fought their way far through the channels and passages of that region, and there was reason to hope that Franklin, with his superior equipment, and his use of the charts made by former voyagers from Frobisher down, would succeed where so many had failed.

The ships chosen were the 370-ton screw steamer "Erebus" and the 340-ton "Terror," vessels which had already made a record in the Antarctic region and whose good fortune, it was trusted, would follow them into the Arctic. These were the vessels which had borne Sir James Ross and his party in his memorable Antarctic exploration of 1839-43, when he reached the seventy-eighth degree of south latitude and discovered an ice-bound region of continental extent, which he named Victoria Land and traced its coast for seven hundred miles. These vessels, the "Erebus" under Sir John Franklin and the "Terror" under Captain Crozier, both carefully refitted and provisioned for three years, sailed from the Thames in the spring of 1845.

The officers and men were one hundred and thirty-four in number, a transport ship accompanied the expedition to carry stores to Disco, Greenland. The "Erebus" and "Terror" were fitted with every appliance then considered essential to success, though much of the provisions taken proved later to be of a quality detrimental to the success of the expedition. Such was the party and the equipment which started out with the warmest anticipations of a glorious and fortunate voyage, only to plunge into the depths of that terrible sea of ice from which no man of the party was ever to return.

On the 8th of June they left the Orkneys, steering for the extreme point of Greenland known as Cape Farewell; where, indeed, the adventurer does, as it were, bid farewell to the security and liberty of the civilized world. A month later they lay at anchor in the middle of a group of rocky islets on the east side of Baffin Bay. Yet another fortnight, and we may see them with the mind's eye, as some whalers saw them, gallantly struggling with the ice which impeded their progress across the Bay of Baffin to Lancaster Sound. Seven officers manned a boat and dragged her across the ice to visit the whalers. They went on board the "Prince of Wales" of Hull. "All well," they reported, and expressed the blithest, cheeriest confidence in the success of their enterprise. After a hearty hand-grasp, they said good-bye and returned to their ships. On the same evening (July 26th) the ice broke up, the westward route lay open, and the Arctic expedition plowed the waves for Lancaster Sound. Thereafter a cloud descended upon it; it passed into the heart of the grim solitudes of the Polar World, and men heard of it no more. When two years had elapsed without any tidings of the expedition reaching England, the public mind grew seriously alarmed. Expectation deepened into anxiety; anxiety darkened into fear. When the winter of 1848 passed away, and still no tidings came, it was felt that further inaction would be intolerable. Hitherto the great object had been the discovery of the Northwest Passage; now the thoughts of men were all directed to a search after Franklin and his companions. Strangely enough, Providence had so ordered it that in the search after these "martyrs of Science" the former object was attained.

An expedition in search of the missing heroes was despatched under Sir James Ross; and another under Sir John Richardson: both added to the stores of geographical knowledge, but nothing more. These had worked from the eastward; Captains Moore and Kellett worked from the westward, entering Bering Strait, and actually reaching, by their boats, the mouth of Mackenzie River. In the spring of 1849, the British Government offered a reward of £20,000 to any private explorers, of any nation, who should discover and succor the wanderers; and Lady Franklin, out of her own resources, organized several relieving parties. So it happened that, in 1850, no fewer than twelve vessels, led by Ross, Rae, McClure, Osborne, Collinson, Penny, Austin, Ommaney, Forsyth and De Haven, besides boat and sledge companies, plunged deep into the far northern wilderness to trace the footprints of the lost.

The Admiralty orders to Franklin had been, to pass through Lancaster Sound into Barrow Strait; thence to Cape Walker; and from Cape Walker, by such course as he might find convenient, to Bering Strait. The general opinion was, that he had got to the west of Melville Island, and then been caught by the ice among the numerous islands lying in that part of the Arctic Sea. And it was supposed that he would be engaged in an effort to cross the ice, and reach either one of the Hudson Bay settlements, or some whaling-station.

In August of the year named the first traces of the missing party were found. These consisted of scraps of rope and canvas, a long-handled rake, the ground plan of a tent, etc., found by Captain Penny on Beechey Island. In conjunction with Lieutenant De Haven, of the American Grinnell expedition, he now undertook a careful search in the vicinity of Wellington Channel, with the result that they found a carefully built pyramidal cairn. It was constructed of meat-cans which were filled with gravel and sand and arranged to taper upwards from the base to the summit, where was fixed the remnant of a broken boarding-pike. But no record could be found; nothing to connect it with Sir John Franklin. Presently, as they looked along the northern slope of the island, other strange objects caught their eye. Another rush of eager, breathless beings, and all stood in silence before three graves. Some of them were unable to refrain from tears as they muttered the words inscribed upon the rude tablets, "EREBUS AND TERROR."

During the succeeding years various other expeditions were sent out, but nothing of importance was found until the expedition of Captain McClintock of 1857-59. McClintock had served under Sir James Ross in his Franklin search expedition of 1848-49, and in later attempts, in which he performed remarkable feats in sledge traveling. In 1857 he was chosen to command the expedition sent out by Lady Franklin for a final effort to obtain tidings of the lost navigator. In the winter of 1858-59 he and his officers made extensive sledge journeys, and in May, 1859, found at Point Victory, on King William's Island, a record of Franklin's death and the remains of the last survivor of his party. For his success he was knighted and received various honors and rewards.

The finding of this paper and the expedition itself were the result of the last of Lady Franklin's various efforts to discover the fate of her husband. To this object she had dedicated all her available means, and, aided by sympathizing friends, had purchased and fitted out the "Fox," in which McClintock sailed. The paper was found by Lieutenant Hobson, enclosed in a tin cylinder, in a cairn twelve miles from Cape Herschel, and, with a large number of relics obtained at this and other points, it was deposited in the Museum of the United Service Institution, Whitehall Yard. The discovery of this paper first definitely made known the fate of the party,—an issue generally apprehended in England from the time of Rae's discoveries in 1854, for the relics which in that year he had brought from the Eskimos were articles of personal property of the officers, including Sir John Franklin's own star of the Order of Merit.

We may briefly refer to two other search expeditions headed

by Americans. One of these was headed by Captain C. F. Hall, who reached King William's Land in 1866 and obtained from the Eskimos of that region a variety of interesting relics of the Franklin party. He also learned from them that their people had been, at one time, alongside of "the ships," and had seen the great Eshemutta (Franklin). "This Eshemutta was an old man with broad shoulders, gray hair, full face, and bald head. He was always wearing something over his eyes,"—"spectacles," as they described them. "He was quite lame and sick when they last saw him. He was always very kind, wanted them to eat constantly, very cheerful and laughing; everybody liked him, Innuits and all on the ship; they on the ship would always do what he said. The ship was crushed by the ice. While it was sinking, the men worked for their lives, but before they could get much out from the vessel she sank. For this reason Aglook (Captain Crozier) died of starvation, for he could not get provisions to carry with him on his land journey."

Hall returned to King William's Land in 1869, and on this occasion also obtained a considerable number of relics of the Franklin party from the natives, saying that such relics were "possessed by natives all over the Arctic regions from Powel's Bay to Mackenzie River."

The final search expedition was made by Lieutenant Frederick Schwatka, of the American Army, who obtained leave of absence in 1878 to command a Franklin search expedition in the Arctic Ocean. King William's Land was reached and searched, the principal result being the discovery and burial of the skeletons of various members of the Franklin party. Many relics were found, but the papers of which the Eskimos had spoken, and which were believed to contain the more important records of the party, had disappeared. Eskimos had taken them from the cairn in which they were deposited and, being deemed of no value, had suffered them to be destroyed.

One important find made by Schwatka was the remains of a skeleton near which was found a silver medal bearing the words,

"Awarded to John Irving, Midsummer, 1830. Second Mathematical Prize." This identified the remains as being those of Lieutenant Irving, of the "Terror." As this was the only case of possible identification, the remains were carefully gathered and conveyed to New York, whence they were forwarded to Edinburgh, Irving's native town. Here they were given a public funeral on January 7, 1881.

Coming now to what we know of the voyage of the last party and what we can reasonably conjecture by piecing out the information obtained and weaving it into a consecutive narrative, we may present the following account as probably representing the general facts:

When the "Erebus" and "Terror" parted company, on July 4, 1845, with the despatch-boat that had accompanied them, they shaped their course through Baffin's Bay towards Lancaster Sound. Continuing their way, they passed Cape Warrender and ultimately reached Beechey Island at the entrance of the then unexplored waters of Wellington Channel. They passed through the channel, taking such observations as were necessary as they went, until they had progressed one hundred and fifty miles. Further advance being stopped by the ice, they passed into another unexplored channel between Cornwallis Island and Bathurst Island which led them into Barrow's Strait, nearly one hundred miles west of the entrance to Wellington Channel.

The ice was now forming thickly around them, and attention was directed to discovering a comfortable haven where they could remain while the winter ice closed in around them. A suitable harbor was found on the northeasterly side of Beechey Island and the ships were made snug. All the spars that could be sent down were lowered on to the decks, and the rigging and sails stowed away below before the ice surrounded them, so that when the floes began to pack and lifted the hulls of the vessels, there should be no "top-hamper" to list them over. On the frozen shore huts were built for the accommodation of shore parties, and, as the ice spread around and the snow fell, the men found exercise and amusement in heaping it up against the sides of the vessels as an extra protection against the cold, a thick mass of frozen snow. But where there were fires always going to maintain the temperature of the cabins, the danger of an outbreak of fire had to be zealously guarded against. With all the ship's pumps rendered useless by the frost, and the water frozen solid all around, a conflagration on board a vessel in the Arctic seas is one of the grimmest of terrors. The safeguard is the maintenance, in the ice near the vessel's side, of a "fire hole," that is, a small space kept open by constant attention down to the level of unfrozen water.

During the long winter months there was plenty of time to estimate the progress they had made, and there must have been considerable satisfaction on all sides at what they had accomplished. They had circumnavigated Cornwallis Island and had reached to within 250 miles of the western end of the passage.

New Year's Day was saddened by the death of one of their comrades, and the silent ice-fields witnessed another impressive sight when the crews of both vessels slowly marched ashore to the grave dug in the frozen soil of Beechey Island. The body, wrapped in a Union Jack, was borne by the deceased man's messmates, the members of his watch headed by their officers following, and after them the remainder of the officers and crew. The bells of each ship tolled as the *cortège* passed over the ice, the crunching of the crisp snow under foot being the only other sound till the grave was reached. There the solemn and impressive service of a sailor's funeral was said, the mingled voices as they repeated the responses passing as a great hum through the still, cold air. A momentary silence followed as the flag-swathed figure was lowered into the grave, and then a quick rattle of firearms as the last salute was paid echoed far and wide among the icebergs.

Twice more was that scene repeated before the ships cleared

from the ice, and one of the first signs discovered by the searchers after Franklin were the three headstones raised on that lonely isle to the memory of W. Braine, John Hartwell, and John Torrington, who died while the ships were wintering in the cold season of 1845-6.

By July the ice had broken up and the voyage was resumed and passed without any exceptional incident, up to the middle of September, 1846, when they were again caught by the ice, but 150 miles nearer their destination than the year before. Only a hundred miles more to be sailed over and they would be conquerors—but that hundred miles was too firmly blocked with ice-floes for them ever to sail over.

The winter of 1846-7 was passed off the most extreme northerly point of King William's Land. The ice was particularly heavy, and hemmed the vessels in completely, the surface being too rugged and uneven to permit of traveling in the immediate vicinity even of hunting parties. This was the more unfortunate because the provisions were growing scant, and supplies brought in by hunters would have been of great assistance. At the time of starting, the vessels had been provisioned for three years. Two had now passed, so that only a twelvemonth's stock of food remained in the holds. It might take them all the next summer to work through the remaining hundred miles of the passage, and that would leave them another winter to face, unless they should find open water when they reached the end. But, on the other hand, they might not be able to get through in the time, or the passage might not be navigable. Either possibility was full of very grave anxiety for those in command, for it was a terrible prospect of being left, with one hundred and thirty men to feed, in the midst of the frozen sea, "a hundred miles from everywhere."

The anxiety felt was shown by the despatch, as early as May, or two months before the first flush of summer was due, of a specially selected party of quick travelers to push forward over the ice and spy out the prospects ahead. Lieutenant Graham Gore, of the "Erebus," commanded the party, which consisted of Charles des Voeux, ship's mate, and six seamen. They carried only enough stores to last them on their journey, and each one had to contribute his share to the labor of hauling the hand-sledges over the jagged ridges of broken ice. Skirting along the coast of King William's Land, they arrived at a point from the top of which they were able to discern the mainland coast trending away to the horizon, with a sea of ice in front.

To commemorate the fact the little party built a cairn upon the summit of the point, which they named Point Victory, and enclosed in a tin canister they deposited, under the cairn, a record of their trip and its result. Twelve years later this record was found, and by it the honor due to Franklin for the discovery of the passage was confirmed. But the manner of its finding must be told later on.

The record left by them stated that all the crews were then well and Sir John Franklin in command. They returned to find that he was sick unto death, their gallant leader dying shortly after, on June 11, 1847. Death served him well in one particular, it saved him from the terrible experience of those he left behind.

Captain Crozier, of the "Terror," assumed command, but it was as the leader of an almost hopeless enterprise. The ice did not break up, as was hoped, and the two vessels, with their inadequate supplies, were held fast for another winter,—the winter of 1847-8, —during which no fewer than nine officers and fifteen men died. On the 22d of April, the survivors came to the resolution of abandoning the doomed ships; and, one hundred and five in number, and led by Captains Crozier and Fitzjames, they started for Great Fish River. The great quantity of articles left at the point of departure is a significant evidence of their enfeebled condition. We can only conjecture the events of their journey. From this spot to a point about half-way between Point Victory and Point Herschel nothing important concerning them has been discovered; and the skeletons and relics found were all deeply embedded in snow. At the halfway point just spoken of, however, Lieutenant Hobson, in his search, caught sight of a piece of wood projecting from the snow; and on digging round it exhumed a boat, standing on a very heavy sledge. Within it were two skeletons: one, lying in the bottom of the stern-sheets, and covered with a quantity of clothing; the other, half-erect in the bows, as if the poor fellow had crept there to look out, and in that position had yielded to the slumber which knows no waking. A couple of guns, loaded and ready cocked, stood close at hand, apparently prepared for use against wild animals. Around this boat was found another accumulation of cast-off articles; and McClintock conjectured that the party who had dragged the sledge thus far were *returning to the ships,* having discovered themselves unequal to the terrors of the journey they had undertaken. This is possible; but we can hardly doubt that the stronger portion of the crews pushed forward with another boat, and that some reached Montreal Island and ascended Great Fish River. The record left by them in the cairn which Lieutenant Gore had erected tells their story to this point, ending with, "Start to-morrow, April 26th, for Back's Fish River."

In 1854, Dr. Rae, in his overland expedition, fell in with some Eskimos who spoke of having seen forty men dragging a boat near the Fish River, under the leadership of a tall, stout, middle-aged man; a description fairly agreeing with the appearance of Captain Fitzjames. Sherard Osborn is of opinion, therefore, that the strongest of the survivors, under Fitzjames, pushed on to perish in the dreary wildernesses of the Hudson Bay territory (for relics have been found on the Fish River, fifty miles above Montreal Island); and that the weak, if ever they reached the ships again, did so only in time to see them wrecked by the breaking up of the ice in the autumn of 1848. We know from the Eskimos that one ship sank; and that the other, on board of which was one dead person, "a tall, large-boned man," was driven ashore. These wrecks, however, could not have occurred on the coast between Capes Victory and Herschel; for in that case the natives would assuredly have appropriated the relics discovered by McClintock and Hobson. We come, therefore, to McClintock's conclusion, that the wrecked ship went ashore somewhere within the region frequented by the Fish River Eskimos; and that in the years 1857-58 the ice had probably swept her away again, and finally destroyed her.

Let the reader remember, as a commentary on the vanity of human wishes, that the point at which the "Erebus" and "Terror" were caught in the ice in 1846, was but ninety miles from the point reached by Dease and Simpson in their boats in 1838-39. So that had Franklin and his followers but accomplished those ninety miles of open water, they would have won the prize for which they had dared and endured so much, and have returned home to enjoy the well-earned applause of their countrymen. But Providence had decreed otherwise. "They were to discover," says the historian of their labors, "the great highway between the Pacific and Atlantic. It was given them to win for their country a discovery for which she had risked her sons and lavishly spent her wealth through many centuries; but they were to die in accomplishing their last great earthly task; and, still more strange, but for the energy and devotion of the wife of their chief and leader, it would in all probability never have been known that they were indeed the first discoverers of the Northwest Passage."

We have not completed our story. Closely connected with it is another record of adventure, that of the solution of the problem of the Northwest Passage by the actual fact of passing through it. As this was accomplished by one of the searchers for the Franklin relics, the relation of it properly fits in with the story of the search. The feat was performed by Captain Robert McClure, partly on shipboard and partly by sledging, in 1853. His voyage was one of leading importance, in view of its result, and merits description here.

The "Investigator," McClure's ship, had sailed in 1850 with several others for the Bering Strait entrance to the Polar Sea. Here they parted company to work over different areas, the "Investigator" sailing along the waters bathing the northern coast of the continent. She was soon in front of the ice pack, which stretched with an unbroken form from east to west, all that could be seen in the distance being a great herd of walrus huddled together on the ice like a flock of sheep. Open water was found, however, between the ice and the land, and the ship was pushed into this lead, McClure keeping well in towards the shore on the lookout for natives. At Cape Bathurst, near the Mackenzie River, a region which Franklin had explored in his land trip of many years before, a large tribe was observed, and at once a boat party put off from the ship.

As they approached the shore, thirty tents and nine winter-houses were seen. Immediately the boats were run ashore a tremendous stir was caused in the village, the men running to and fro and then charging down a steep slope to where the boats were aground on the beach. As they drew near it was seen that each man carried a drawn knife in his hand, as well as bows and arrows, and their warlike intentions were still more clearly shown when the fitted arrows to the bows and began to aim at the white men. The interpreter Miertsching, clad in native costume, advanced from the explorers towards the angry Eskimo, holding his hands above his head in the position which expresses peace amongst these primitive people.

When told that no harm would be done them they were persuaded to lay aside their bows and arrows, but would not relinquish their knives until the whites had put down their rifles. Amity was reached when one of the rifles was given to the chief to carry, the Eskimos now offering their knives to the safe keeping of the visitors. It was a hunting village that had been reached, containing more than three hundred men, women, and children. They told the whites that the ice beyond the open passage was the realm of the white bear, which roamed there in numbers and of which they were in great fear, telling several tales of its ferocity.

Upon the interpreter explaining how the white men's rifles could kill the bears, the chief at once invited him to come and live with them, offering as inducements his own daughter, a pleasant-looking girl of about fifteen, a fully furnished tent, and all the other necessary possessions of a well-to-do Eskimo. Failing in that, they invited the explorers to a feast of roast whale and venison, salmon, blubber, and other delicacies; but instead of taking these, the explorers presented them with a number of gifts, and left them on the best of terms.

A few days later another small band was encountered farther along the coast, one of whom was wearing a brass button in his ear. The button was off a sailor's jacket, and upon being asked how he obtained it, the man replied it had been taken from a white man who had been killed by the tribe. He was asked for further particulars, in case the unfortunate might turn out to be one of Franklin's men. The Eskimo replied that it might have been done a year ago or when he was a child, but the huts the white men had built were still standing. The explorers at once persuaded him to take them to the spot, but on arrival they found the huts so weather-worn and overgrown with moss that more than a generation must have passed since they were built.

Winter was now setting in, and as there was no suitable harbor at hand, Captain McClure determined to pass the season amongst the ice-floes. His decision was largely due to the fact that as the ice was forming around them, a great mass of old ice, over six miles in length and drifting at the rate of two miles an hour, came upon them. Its enormous weight crushed everything out of its way, and the ship could only manœuvre sufficiently to graze it with her starboard bow. Fortunately on the other side of her there was only freshly formed and comparatively thin ice, otherwise she would have been hopelessly crushed at once. As it was, the gradual drifting past of the mass was disconcerting, and it was decided to make fast to it. A great mass which they ascertained extended downwards for forty-eight feet below the surface of the sea was selected, and with heavy cables the "Investigator" was made secure to it. Throughout the winter she remained moored to it, though not without more than one experience of danger.

These experiences were repeated at the breaking of the ice on the coming of spring, the "Investigator" drifting towards a shoal upon which a huge mass of ice was stranded. For a time the ship was in imminent danger of being crushed, a peak of ice thirty feet high hanging perpendicularly above her and threatening each moment to fall. Fortunately the suspense was relieved by a mass falling from the great bulk in another direction, while the pressure on the floe carried it away from the ship. Later on the "Investigator" was in peril of being caught between the grounded mass and the moving floe, in which case she would inevitably have been crushed. A blast of powder, which cracked the ice, relieved the strain, and the vessel escaped without serious injury, though several sheets of her copper sheathing were stripped off and rolled up like scraps of paper. Progress, however, was slow, the only open water being near the land, beyond which the pack ice was heavy and close.

They rounded Cape Lambton on Banks' Land, a promontory which they found rose a thousand feet precipitously. The land beyond gradually lost the bold character of the rugged cape, the island presenting a view of hills in the interior which gradually sloped to the shore, having fine valleys and extensive plains, over and through which several small and one considerable sized stream flowed. A great deal of drift-wood lay along the beach, and the land was covered with verdure upon which large flocks of geese were feeding, while ducks were flying in great numbers. Two small islands were passed off the coast, one of which afforded an example of the force exerted by a drifting Polar Sea ice-floe. The island rose about forty feet above the surface of the sea, and broken masses of ice, which had formed a floe, had been driven entirely over it.

The pack still presented an impassable barrier to their course away from the land, and as the season was getting late they decided that they would make winter quarters. A suitable bay was found on the north of the island, and there they spent, not one, but two winters, for the ice remained so thick during the ensuing short summer that it was impossible to move. In the summer, however, if they could not get to sea, they could travel on to the land, and as game was plentiful they were able to keep themselves well supplied with fresh meat. But when winter again came upon them with its cold darkness, the game was scarcer, and, what was worse, the ship's stores were decreasing, so that it became necessary to reduce the rations that the stores might be made to last as long as possible, since another year might need to be passed in the ice.

The ship was little the worse for the straining she had received, but some of the men were showing signs of sickness, and Captain McClure decided to send out a party of the more robust to travel overland to the nearest station of the Hudson Bay Company, and thence press on to England with a request for a relief expedition. Everything was ready for this journey when, on April 10th, an incident happened which rendered it unnecessary.

On that day the captain and first lieutenant were walking on the ice near the ship discussing the serious state of affairs and depressed by the fact that one of the men had just died from scurvy, while others were in a bad state of health. As they walked onward they saw a man coming towards them over the ice. He was hastening so fast that they thought he must be flying from a bear, and they went forward to meet him. But as they approached him, they saw that he was not one of their own ship's company, for he was of a different build to any of their men, in addition to which his face showed black from between his furs, and he was waving his arms wildly. They stopped, doubtful what to make of him, and he rushed up, still gesticulating and articulating wildly.

"Who are you, and where do you come from?" McClure exclaimed.

"Lieutenant Pim, of the 'Resolute,' Captain Kellett," the strange figure managed to reply, as he seized McClure's hands and shook them frantically.

The story told by Pim was the following: In the winter of 1851-52 McClure had made a journey across the ice to Melville Island and left a record at Parry's winter harbor. To this island the "Resolute," entering by way of Baffin Bay, came in the following year and found McClure's record, learning from it where the "Investigator" might be found. Accordingly, Lieutenant Pim was sent across the straits with a sledge party on March 10th. For a month they had been wandering in search, and he happened to be on ahead of his men when he caught sight of the "Investigator" in the distance. He had pushed on to his expected goal, when he saw and recognized Captain McClure. His excitement overmastered him and he could only halloo and shout and jump about in his glee.

The noise of his shouts reached the vessel, where the crew, hearing a strange voice, came tumbling up from below to see who it was that had arrived. The sight of the "Resolute" sledge-party, who soon afterwards came up, completed their surprise and gratification, for it meant that close at hand was all the help they needed to insure their liberation. The whole ship's company journeyed across to where the "Resolute" lay, and, in the interchange of yarns and the assurance of abundance of food and rest till the ice broke up, they found the requisite stimulus to overcome all the evil effects of their past trials and privations.

The remainder of Captain McClure's adventure may be briefly told. The "Investigator" was abandoned, as in hopeless straits, and her captain and crew wintered on the "Resolute," which was obliged to remain in the pack until the following year. In the spring of 1854 a remarkable journey was made. Captain Collinson, of the "Enterprise," who had parted with McClure at Bering Strait four years earlier, remained like him in the ice, having come within a few miles of Point Victory, where the record of the Franklin party was afterwards found.

Several expeditions were sent out from the "Resolute" in the spring, one of which, under Mecham, made a most remarkable journey, in the hope of discovering the locality of Captain Collinson. In sixty-one and a half days of travel he journeyed 1,336 miles, his average speed on his return trip being 23½ miles a day, a record of interest in view of the recent controversy concerning the possible speed of Arctic travel. During that year Collinson got out of the ice and brought the "Enterprise" back to England.

McClure and his men returned on the "Resolute" by way of Baffin Bay. They had thus not only found, but traversed, the Northwest Passage, though not in the same ship, and partly by traveling over the ice. The carrying of a ship through this passage was reserved for Amundsen, fifty years later. For his great feat McClure received the honor of knighthood, while Parliament voted him and his officers and men a reward of £10,000. He had succeeded in a quest which began with Frobisher, nearly three centuries before.

CHAPTER XXI

Dr. Kane's Famous Arctic Voyage

THE search for the Sir John Franklin expedition was not confined to Englishmen. Americans shared strongly in the sympathy that in time grew world-wide, and a wealthy shipowner of New York, Henry Grinnell, fitted out a series of expeditions with the object of joining in the search. One of these, that of Dr. Kane, won a place among the most famous of polar expeditions. The first American voyage for Arctic research, financed by Grinnell, was under the command of Lieutenant Edwin J. De Haven, a Philadelphian who had served for years in the navy and had taken part in the celebrated Wilkes expedition to the Antarctic seas. Picked out by Grinnell as the best man he could find for the purpose, he took with him a physician, Dr. Elisha Kent Kane, who was afterwards to achieve distinction as a polar explorer for himself.

De Haven left New York May 24, 1850, with two small sailing vessels, the "Advance," of 140 tons, and the "Rescue," of but 90. The tiny submarine "Plunger" has a displacement of 168 tons, and the torpedo-boats of our navy average 200, so that it can be imagined with what frail cockleshells De Haven ventured into the frozen North. As might have been expected, the ice-pack proved an insurmountable obstacle to his little boats. They got no further than the mouth of Wellington Channel, whence they drifted through Lancaster Sound and down the western shore of Baffin's Bay, a distance of more than a thousand miles. They did not shake themselves free from the enclogging ice until the 16th of June, 1851, when De Haven returned to New York.

The second Grinnell expedition, which left New York two years later, was under the command of Dr. Kane, also a native of Philadelphia and a graduate of the Medical School of the University of Pennsylvania in the class of 1842.

The Kane expedition sailed from New York on May 30, 1853, in Mr. Grinnell's brig, the "Advance," one of those used by De Haven, the total party consisting of eighteen officers and men. Dr. Hayes, of later Arctic fame, was the surgeon, August Sonntag the astronomer, and Henry Brooks the first officer. On the 1st of July they reached Fiskernæs, a Danish settlement on the west coast of Greenland, to take on board fifty dogs and an Eskimo driver. By the end of July the little brig was among the floes in Melville Bay, and with the wind blowing half a gale the intrepid voyager made his vessel fast to a huge iceberg. As with its strange convoy the ship approached Cape York, the great ice mountain began to crack and shower down small fragments on the deck, the mariners cast off, and no sooner had they done so than the whole face of the berg gave way and a mighty crystal avalanche slid into the sea where the vessel had been moored only a short time before.

On the 1st of August the ship was moored to another large berg, "a moving breakwater of gigantic proportions,'" and under its floating lead they moved steadily to the north. Finally, the danger from drifting ice being passed, they got under way, sailing to the northwest through a fairly open channel, over a sea lit with the glory of the midnight sun, the ice-fields glittering with jeweled radiance and presenting the hues of blazing carbuncles, rubies, and molten gold.

As they faced northward, fresh meat for the dogs became almost impossible to obtain. The famished animals eagerly devoured two birds' nests with the contents, and a dead whale provided a series of luxurious banquets for the poor brutes.

On Littleton Island Dr. Kane determined to establish his first depot of stores, for use on the return voyage. The life-boat was loaded with provisions, blankets, and other articles, and then buried. Along her gunwale were placed the heaviest rocks the men could handle; and after the interstices had been filled up with smaller stones and sods of andromeda and moss, sand and water were poured among the layers. All this, frozen at once into a solid mass, would be hard enough, it was hoped, to resist the claws of the Polar bear.

Continuing his adventurous course, he passed through the drifting ice to some distance beyond Cape Lifeboat Cove and took shelter in a beautiful little bay, landlocked from east to west, and accessible only from the north, which he named Refuge Harbor. It was some time before the ice broke up sufficiently to permit of his effecting his escape; and even after he had once more got out into the channel, he had a daily fight with bergs and floes. At one time, while anchored off a rocky island which he called "Godsend Ledge," a perfect hurricane came on; and though he had three hawsers out, they snapped one after the other, like mere threads, and the "Advance" drifted to and fro at the mercy of the "wild ice." His only hope of safety lay in mooring close to a berg; and this effected, the brig was towed along by a gigantic courser—"the spray dashing over his windward flanks, and his forehead plowing up the lesser ice as if in scorn." Drifting masses, broken up and hurtled together by a tremendous storm, threatened them with destruction; and the explorers were thankful when, on the 22d, the gale abated, and they carried their little vessel into comparatively smooth water, sheltered by the ice-belt which lined the rocky and mountainous coast.

Having secured a haven of safety for the "Advance," Dr. Kane resolved to make a personal inspection of the coast, in order to select a convenient winter-station from which he might start on his sledge-journeys in the following spring. For this purpose he had caused his best and lightest whale-boat to be fitted with a canvas cover, that rendered it not less comfortable than a tent. A supply of pemmican was packed in small cases, and a sledge taken to pieces stowed away under the thwarts. The boat's crew consisted of Brooks, Bonsall, McGary, Sonntag, Riley, Blake, and Morton. Each man had buffalo-robes for his sleeping gear, carried a girdle full of woolen socks to keep them dry by the warmth of the body, and slung a tin cup and a sheath-knife to his belt. A soup-pot and lamp for the mess, and a single extra day suit as common property, completed the outfit.

Such were the difficulties of the route, consisting of waterways, gullies and hummocks, that it took them five days to advance forty miles, at the end of which they were forced to abandon the sledge and proceed on foot. Their journey led to an open bay, due, as he found, to a rushing stream, about three-quarters of a mile wide, flowing, as was afterwards observed, from a melting glacier.

Here, in the heart of the dreary snowscape, the travelers met with an Arctic flower-growth, of considerable variety of form and color. The infiltration of the melted snows fed its roots, and the reverberation of the sun's heat from the rocks fostered its delicate life. Amid festuca and other tufted grasses, brightened the purple lychnis and sparkled the white stem of the chickweed; together with a graceful hesperis, reminding the wanderers of the fragrant wallflower of our old English gardens.

After fording the river, Dr. Kane climbed a lofty headland, the view from which was most impressive. It extended beyond the eightieth parallel of north latitude. Far off on the left lay the western shore of the sound, receding towards the dim, misty north. To the right a rolling country led on to a low, dusky, wall-like ridge, which he afterwards recognized as the Great Humboldt Glacier; and still beyond this, reaching northward from the north-northeast, lay the land which now bears the honored name of Washington—its most projecting headland, Cape Andrew Jackson, bearing about fourteen degrees from the farthest hill on the opposite side, Cape John Barrow. All between was one vast sheet of ice. Close along its shore, almost looking down upon it from the crest of their lofty station, the explorers could see the long lines of hummocks dividing the floes like the trenches of a beleaguered city. Farther out, a stream of icebergs, increasing in numbers towards the north, presented an almost impenetrable barrier; but beyond these the ice seemed less obstructed and obstructive, and patches of open water glimmered on the distant horizon.

On their return to the brig preparations were made for the coming winter, which it was decided to pass in the secure haven they had reached, since known as Rensselaer Harbor. By the 10th of September the thermometer had fallen to 14 degrees Fahrenheit and the ice-floes had been welded into a compact mass by newly-formed ice. About sixty paces north of the ship an iceberg had been caught in the toils and remained as their gigantic neighbor as long as they occupied that harbor. The long winter passed slowly enough, with what alleviations they could find in their contracted quarters and with such labor as seemed necessary in preparation for the coming spring.

The first traces of returning light were observed at noon on the 21st of January, when a tint of orange lighted up, very briefly, the southern horizon. Necessarily, the influence of the long and intense darkness was very depressing, and was felt even by the lower animals, many of the dogs dying from "a mental disease," clearly due to the absence of light. The symptoms of this disease were very peculiar, and deserve to be indicated. The more material functions of the poor creatures went on, it would appear, without interruption,—they ate voraciously, retained their strength, and slept soundly. But, otherwise, they acted as if suffering from lunacy. They barked frenziedly at nothing, and walked in straight and curved lines with anxious and unwearying perseverance. They fawned on their masters, but without seeming conscious of the caresses lavished upon them in return. Their most intelligent actions seemed automatic; sometimes they clawed you, as if seeking to burrow into your seal-skins; sometimes they remained for hours in moody silence, and then started off howling as if pursued and ran up and down for hours.

A terrible adventure lay before the explorers. On the 20th of March a party was sent out to establish a depot of provisions, and Kane and the rest of his followers waited only for their return to begin the transit of the bay. Late at night on the 31st, they were working cheerfully by the glare of their lamps, when a sudden noise of steps was heard above, and immediately afterwards Sonntag, Ohlsen, and Petersen came down into the cabin. If there was something startling in their unexpected arrival, much more startling was their appearance. They were swollen, haggard, and scarcely able to speak.

Where were their companions? Behind in the ice,—Brooks, Baker, Wilson, and Pierre—all frozen and disabled; and they themselves had risked their lives to carry the pitiful news. Where were their comrades lying? With cold white lips they muttered that they could not tell; somewhere in among the hummocks to the north and east; the snow was drifting round them heavily when they parted. "Irish Tom" had gallantly remained to feed and care for them, but of their recovery there was little hope. It was useless to put additional questions; the men were too exhausted to be able to rally their ideas.

A rescue party was quickly organized and set out on the trail of the lost explorers, Ohlsen being taken with them on a sledge as a guide to the locality in which they had been left. Finally they were obliged to leave their tent, cache their pemmican, except a small allowance for each, and proceed through a temperature of nearly —50 degrees.

It was indispensable, then, that they should move on as rapidly as possible, looking for traces as they went. Yet when the men were ordered to spread themselves, so as to multiply the chances, though they all obeyed heartily, some painful impress of solitary danger kept them closing up continually into a single group. The strange manner in which some of them were affected must be attributed as much to shattered nerves as to the direct influence of the cold. Men like McGary and Bonsall, who had stood out the severest marches, were seized with trembling fits and short breath; and, in spite of all his efforts to keep up an example of sound bearing, Kane fainted twice on the snow.

"We had been nearly eighteen hours out without water or food, when a new hope cheered us. I think it was Hans, our Eskimo hunter, who thought he saw a broad sledge-track. The drift had nearly effaced it, and we were some of us doubtful at first whether it was not one of those accidental rifts which the gales make in the surface-snow. But as we traced it on to the deep snow among the hummocks, we were led to footsteps; and, following these with religious care, we at last came in sight of a small American flag fluttering from a hummock, and lower down a little masonic banner hanging from a tent-pole hardly above the drift. It was the camp of our disabled comrades. We reached it after an unbroken march of twenty-one hours."

They found the little tent almost buried in the snow. When Dr. Kane came up, his men, who had outstripped him, were standing in silent file on each side of it. With a delicacy of feeling which is almost characteristic of sailors, and seems instinctive to them, they expressed a desire that he should enter alone. As he crawled beneath the tent-curtain, and, coming upon the darkness, heard before him the burst of welcome gladness that came from the poor prostrate creatures within, and then for the first time the cheer without, his weakness and gratitude almost overcame him. "They had expected him," was their exclamation; "they were sure he would come!"

The return was made with all the haste available. Nothing was carried but what was indispensable, everything else being abandoned. A great part of the track lay among a succession of hummocks, fifteen or twenty feet high and too steep to be ascended.

The sledge had to pursue a winding course around these obstacles, frequently driving through gaps filled with recently-fallen snow, which hid the fissures and openings in the ice beneath. These, says Kane, were fearful traps to disengage a limb from, for every man was painfully aware that a fracture or even a sprain might cost him his life. In addition, the sledge was top-heavy with its load, which weighed not less than 1100 pounds, while the maimed men could not bear to be lashed down tight enough to secure them against falling off.

Yet, for the six hours, the progress of this undaunted band was cheering. They advanced nearly a mile an hour, and reached the new floes before they were absolutely weary. "Our sledge," says Kane, "sustained the trial admirably. Ohlsen, restored by hope, walked steadily at the leading belt of the sledge lines; and I began to feel certain of reaching our half-way station of the day before, where we had left our tent. But we were still nine miles from it, when, almost without premonition, we all became aware of an alarming failure of our energies."

Bonsall and Morton, two of the most robust of the party, besought permission to sleep. They declared that they did not feel cold, and that all they wanted was a little repose. Presently Hans was found frozen almost into rigidity under a drift; and Thomas, standing erect, had his eyes closed, and could scarcely articulate. Soon afterwards, John Blake threw himself on the snow, and refused to rise. They made no complaint of feeling cold; but it was in vain that Dr. Kane "wrestled, boxed, ran, argued, jeered, or reprimanded;" he found that an immediate halt was unavoidable.

We must condense the remainder of this story of Arctic terrors. The tent was at length reached and found in good condition, though a bear had overturned it and made havoc to some extent with its contents. After several hours of sleep they set out once more, in good spirits considering the circumstances. Yet their hard labors soon told on them again. As they grew weaker and weaker, their halts necessarily became more frequent; and they would fall, in a semi-somnolent condition, on the snow. Strange to say, these brief intervals of slumber proved refreshing, so that Dr. Kane was induced to try the experiment in his own person, taking care that Riley should arouse him at the end of three minutes. Afterwards he timed the men in the same way. They sat upon the runners of the sledge, and fell asleep immediately, but were startled into wakefulness the moment their three minutes had elapsed.

At eight in the evening the wayfarers were clear of the floes, and gained some new hope at the sight of the well-known Pinnacly Berg. Brandy, which sometimes proves an invaluable resource in emergencies, had already been administered in tablespoonful doses. After a final and stronger dram, and a longer rest, they resolved on a last effort to reach the brig, which they attained at one hour after noon.

But words are inadequate to describe their sufferings in this last stage of their journey. They were completely delirious, and no longer entertained any clear apprehension of what was transpiring. Like men in a dream they staggered onward, blindly, uncertainly. From an inspection of their footprints afterwards, it was seen that they had steered a bee-line for the brig, guided by a kind of instinct, for they remembered nothing of their course.

When about two miles from the brig they were met by Petersen and Whipple, with the dog-traces, and a supply of restoratives, for which Kane had sent a message in advance by Bonsall. As soon as the frozen, wayworn creatures were safe on board, Dr. Hayes took them under his charge. All were suffering from brain-symptoms, functional not organic, and to be rectified by rest and abundant diet. Ohlsen was for some time afflicted with blindness and strabismus; two others underwent amputation of parts of the foot, but without dangerous consequences; and two died, in spite of every attention. The rescue-party had traveled between eighty and ninety miles, dragging a heavy sledge for most of the distance. They had been out for seventy-two hours, and halted in all eight hours. The mean temperature of the whole time, including the noontide hours of three days, was about —41 degrees, or 70 degrees *below* freezing-point. Except at their two halts they had no means of quenching their thirst, and they could at no time intermit vigorous exercise without freezing.

Dr. Kane's purpose, as we are aware, was not that of seeking to reach the pole or to make a great northward record, but to search for the Sir John Franklin party or relics of its passage. As many expeditions had entered the channels opening west from Baffin Bay, he had gone farther north, hoping to find other channels leading east or west from the upper extremity of Smith Sound. He believed that, at least, some of the hardier members of the Franklin party might be alive, dwelling perhaps with the far northern Eskimos, or living on the proceeds of their own skill in hunting.

In pursuance of this purpose, at the end of April, 1854, Kane and seven of his men—ten of the party being left on the brig—started north on an exploring excursion, proposing to follow up the ice-belt to the Humboldt Glacier, there to replenish their food supply from the cache of pemmican they had made in their trip of the previous October, and then attempt to cross the ice of the sound to the opposite shore. This was to be the crowning effort of the expedition, to measure the frozen waste which lay between Greenland and the unknown land to the west, and make a search for an opening into the mysterious regions which lay in the higher north. This purpose, while not completely carried out, led to geographical results of much interest. Smith Sound here opens into a wide landlocked sea, since known as Kane Basin, on which fronts the enormous Humboldt Glacier, the greatest probably in existence. Its curved face, from Cape Agassiz to Cape Forbes, measures fully sixty miles in length, and presents a grand wall or front of glistening ice, kindled here and there into dazzling glory by the sun. Its form is that of a wedge, the apex lying inland, at perhaps "not more than a single day's railroad travel from the Pole." Thus it passes away into the center of the Greenland continent, which is occupied by an unbroken sea of ice, twelve hundred miles in length and of great depth, that receives a perpetual increase from the constantly falling snows. A frozen sea, yet a sea in constant motion, rolling onward slowly, laboriously, but surely, to find an outlet at each fiord or valley, and to load the seas of Greenland and the Atlantic with mighty icebergs.

This great glacier effectually terminated the labors of the explorers in that direction, and Dr. Kane decided that their future search should be made to the north and east of Cape Sabine,—so named by Captain Inglesfield,—on the coast of Ellesmere Land, which lay on the opposite side of Smith Sound. The expedition above mentioned was one of severe labors and much suffering upon the part of the explorers. The heroic leader, indeed, almost succumbed to the terrible hardships of this adventurous journey, and was carried back to the sledge in so prostrate a condition that recovery seemed hopeless. It may be doubted, indeed, whether his strength was ever thoroughly recruited, though the skill and attention of Dr. Hayes, and his own undaunted spirit, rescued him from the jaws of death. All the men were more or less afflicted, and in the middle of June only three were able to do duty, and of the officers Dr. Hayes alone was on his feet.

During the succeeding spring and summer other expeditions were sent out, the most important being under the lead of William Morton and comprising McGary, Bonsall, Hickey, Riley, and Hans, their Eskimo companion. Its orders were to push forward to the base of the Humboldt Glacier, there replenish their provisions from the cache, and while some of the men attempted to scale and survey the glacier, Morton and Hans were to cross the bay in the dog-sledge and follow the northwest coast, in the hope of discovering a northern outlet from the extensive Kane Sea.

Some interesting results were obtained by the latter party.

Their progress across the ice was not unattended with danger; but these explorers were men not easily daunted. They clambered up hillocks, and bridged broad chasms, and wound in and out of towering bergs, with equal skill and intrepidity; well seconded by their dogs, which showed as much sure-footedness as mules. At Cape Andrew Jackson they reached what appeared to be the farthest limit of the ice; and, looking northward, up what is now known as Kennedy Channel, they saw a broad expanse of open water. The landscape was also of a brighter character than any they had recently seen; a long low plain spreading between large headlands, and relieved here and there by ranges of rolling hills. Down the valley came a flock of brent geese with whirring wings; and the waves were darkened by the shadows of ducks and dovekies. Tern abounded, and the air literally echoed with their shrill cries.

The great channel of open water continued to spread to the northward. Broken ice was floating in it, but with passages fifteen miles wide, and perfectly clear. "There would have been no difficulty," they said, "in a frigate standing anywhere."

Pushing forward boldly Morton and his companion entered upon a bold deep curve in the eastern shore, which they designated Lafayette Bay. Beyond it lay two islands, which Dr. Kane afterwards named in honor of Sir John Franklin and Captain Crozier. The *ne plus ultra* of their adventurous journey was Cape Constitution, in latitude 80 degrees 10 minutes north, where the ice-foot seemed nearly to terminate. Here the cliffs were about two thousand feet in height, nobly guarding the water-way which apparently led to the enchanted region of the North Pole. Morton attempted to pass round the cape, but as there was no ice-foot his efforts were in vain; and he found it impossible to ascend the lofty cliffs. So he fastened to his walking-staff the Grinnell flag of the "Antarctic" —a well-worn relic, which had already fluttered in two Polar voyages—and rearing it on high, its weather-worn folds floated freely "over the highest northern land, not only of America, but of the

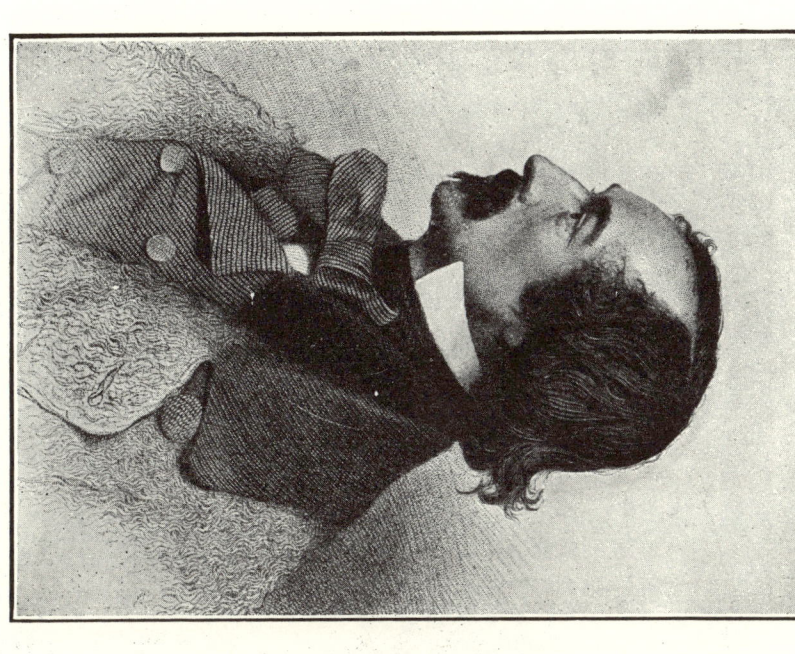

DR. ELISHA KENT KANE

One of the most famous American Arctic Explorers. Born in Philadelphia February 20, 1820, served on the First Grinnell Expedition of 1850, and Commander of the Second Grinnell Expedition in 1853, to search for traces of Sir John Franklin. He discovered the position of the Polar Sea through Smith's Sound, which was used by Dr. Cook and Commander Peary.

SIR JOHN FRANKLIN, CAPT. R. N.

The famous English Arctic Explorer. Born 1786. After serving in the British Navy at Trafalgar, and in other engagements, he led three Arctic expeditions, on the last of which, starting 1845, he perished in the winter of 1850-51. The fate of Franklin's Expedition, comprising 135 men, was the object of search of many following Polar Expeditions.

MacCLINTOCK FINDING SKELETONS OF SIR JOHN FRANKLIN'S MEN

Sir John Franklin's party, numbering one hundred and thirty-five souls, perished on Franklin's third expedition of 1845-47. Captain MacClintock, sent by Lady Franklin to search for proofs of their fate, found these ghastly relics at Erebus Bay, King William Land. Captain Hall, an American, nearly twenty years later, learned from the Eskimo that the skeletons of Franklin's men were scattered over King William Land, that the Eskimo had refused to aid the lost explorers, had stolen everything they had of value, and even suffered their dogs to eat them. It was said, but never proved, that some of Franklin's men had eaten their companions.

THREE MEN SAVED FROM DEATH

The commander had sent Rice, Frederick, Elison and Lynn to Cape Sabine to obtain meat. The Arctic night enveloped them. Getting the meat they started on their return, and on reaching one of the camps Elison's hands and feet were frozen. The men threw away the meat in order to drag and carry their comrade. Finally they broke up their boat to build a fire to save him. Rice staggered twenty-five miles to bring Brainard and Christiansen to their succor. Two of the men were frozen in their sleeping bags by the time the relief party reached them. None of these men except Brainard and Frederick lived through the ensuing privations.

[From DeLong's "Voyage of the Jeannette." Houghton-Mifflin Co.]
A PARTY'S BOATS NIPPED IN THE ICE

The launch and three boats were caught between the moving ice pack and a wall of ice ten feet high. The launch could have withstood direct pressure, but she was ground along the ice foot so that she was nearly lost. One of the boats was pulled out on the moving ice pack, but the others were saved as they lay.

globe." Straining his gaze into the misty distance, Morton could dimly see, far away on the western shore, a bare truncated peak, which they supposed to be 2,500 or 3,000 feet in height and to which Kane gave the name of the great pioneer of Arctic travel, Sir Edward Parry.

The summer advanced, August came, and efforts were made to release the brig, which for eleven months had been imprisoned in the ice. These efforts proved useless, the young ice began to close in all around the harbor, and it was evident that another winter lay before them in the ice, unless they should attempt to escape in their boats and seek the Danish settlements on the Greenland coast Dr. Kane determined to stand by the ship until the following spring, but left it to the others to decide if they would remain with him. Eight concluded to do so, while the remainder started on August 28th in one of the boats, under the leadership of Dr. Hayes, determined to push their way south, if possible. It did not prove possible. One of them returned in a few days after the start and the others in December. For three months they had been frozen up in an Eskimo hut, built in a rock crevice, within three hundred miles of the brig. Here they lived almost without fire and light and on such small supplies of walrus meat as they could procure from natives living fifty miles away. In the end starvation drove them back to the vessel, traveling by moonlight, with the aid of Eskimo dogs and sledges. In the journey Dr. Hayes fell into a space of open water and was wet to the skin. His body was badly frozen in many places, and he was only kept alive by the driver pounding him with his whip-stock.

The winter passed away with distressing slowness. All the precautions they could take did not prevent them from suffering from the terrible cold of an Arctic winter, while the want of proper and sufficient food and the appearance of scurvy among them aggravated their pains. Their location was north of the Eskimo village of Etah—now so well known as a starting point for Arctic expeditions—the nearest settlement being that of Annootok, with the natives of which they kept in communication.

As the winter advanced their condition daily grew worse, scurvy bringing the most of them to the verge of the grave. In December not more than three were capable of active work and to add to their trouble the supply of fuel ran short, so much so that it was necessary to resort to the outside oak sheathing of the vessel.

On February 25, 1855, the sun once more rose above the long, deep, gloomy night of an Arctic winter. Early in March they obtained a supply of walrus meat, which probably saved the lives of the whole party. A brief entry in Dr. Kane's journal, under the date of April 22d, clearly indicates the wretched condition of these brave men. Here it is: "I read our usual prayers; and Dr. Hayes, who feels sadly the loss of his foot, came aft and crawled upon deck to sniff the daylight. He had not seen the sun for five months and three weeks!"

Dr. Kane now undertook a sledge journey to Etah, in order to effect the purchase of a fresh supply of sledge dogs. Here he was hospitably received. A visit to an Eskimo hut, however, is not one of pleasure. Such an "amorphous mass of compounded humanity" is nowhere else to be seen: men, women and children, with little but their native dirt to cover them, crowded together in a close, stifling cell, fifteen feet by six! As Kane failed to obtain the dogs, he was forced to abandon the further exploration he had meditated on in search of traces of the Franklin expedition. Without dogs this was impossible, and out of sixty-two only four were left. Nothing remained but to prepare for their homeward journey, and as they were hopeless of extricating the "Advance" from its icy prison, it became necessary to make the effort in their boats.

These were three in number; but all were well worn by exposure to ice and storm. Two were "cypress whale-boats," twenty-six feet long, with seven feet beam, and three feet deep. These were strengthened with oak bottom pieces, and a long "string piece" bolted to the keel. The gunwale was fortified, and additional depth obtained, by means of a washboard of light cedar, about six inches high. A neat housing of light canvas was stretched upon a ridge-line sustained fore and aft by stanchions, and hung down over the boat's sides, where it was fastened (stopped) to a jack-stay. Each boat carried a single mast, stepped into an oaken thwart in such a manner that it could be readily unshipped and carried, with the oars, boat hooks, and ice poles, alongside the boat. The third boat was the little "Red Eric," which was mounted on the old sledge; not, indeed, with any intention of using her for purposes of navigation, but to cut her up for firewood, in case the supply of blubber should fail.

Powder and shot, on which the lives of the travelers depended, were carefully distributed in bags and tin canisters. The percussion caps Dr. Kane himself took charge of, as more precious than gold. To Mr. Bonsall were entrusted the arms and ammunition. Places were arranged for the guns, and hunters appointed for each boat. Mr. Petersen looked after the cooking gear. In fact, for each man a special duty was found, and nothing was neglected that could contribute in any way to the safety of the party. The completeness and thoughtfulness of these preparations had the best effect on the spirits of the men; and though some of them still doubted whether escape was possible, all braced up their energies to make the attempt. As most of them were invalids, some little preliminary training was needed; but this required to be very gradual. "We made but two miles the first day," says Kane, "and with a single boat; and, indeed, for some time after this I took care that they should not be disheartened by overwork. They came back early to a hearty supper and warm beds; and I had the satisfaction of marching them back each recurring morning refreshed and cheerful."

They bade farewell to the brig, which had been their home for upwards of two years, with much solemnity. The whole company assembled in the dismantled winter cabin to assist in the ceremony. It was Sunday. They read prayers and a chapter of the Bible. Then Dr. Kane addressed them in a few manly words. He did not attempt to disguise the difficulties that lay before them; but he declared that they could be overcome by energy and subordination to command, and that the thirteen hundred miles of ice and water that lay between them and North Greenland could be safely traversed by the majority—and that, indeed, there was hope for all. He added that, as men and mess-mates, it was their duty—and a duty enjoined upon them alike by religion and true courage—to postpone every consideration of self to the protection of the sick and the wounded; and this, under all circumstances, and by every one of them, must be regarded as a paramount order. In conclusion, he desired them to reflect upon the trials they had experienced and surmounted, and to remember how often an unseen Power had rescued them in the hour of danger. In Him it was for all of them to put their trust, confident that He would shield and save.

For the first part of the journey all went well and favorable progress was made, though on many days their labors were severe and at times disheartening, as the following extract from Dr. Kane's journal will show:

"From this time," he says, "we went on for some days, aided by our sails, meeting with accidents occasionally—the giving way of a spar or the falling of some of the party through the spongy ice—and occasionally, when the floe was altogether too infirm, laboring our way with great difficulty upon the ice belt. To mount this solid highway, or to descend from it, the axes were always in requisition. An inclined plane was to be cut, ten, fifteen, or even thirty feet long; and along this the sledges were to be pushed and guided by bars and levers with painful labor. These are light things, as I refer to them here; but in our circumstances, at the time I write of, when the breaking of a stick of timber was an irreparable harm, and the delay of a day involved the peril of life, they were grave enough. Even on the floes the axe was often indispensable to carve our path through the hummocks; and many a weary and anxious hour have I looked on and toiled while the sledges were waiting for the way to open. Sometimes, too, both on the land ice and on the belt, we encountered heavy snow drifts, which were to be shoveled away before we could get along; and within an hour afterward, or perhaps even at the bottom of the drift, one of the sledge runners would cut through to the water."

On the 12th of June Littleton Island was reached and the supplies they had formerly left there were found in excellent order. Ohlsen, one of the bravest and most intelligent of Dr. Kane's crew, at this point succumbed to disease, and was buried decently in a little gorge; his remains being duly protected from fox and bear. After this sad ceremony the march was resumed; but as they neared the Eskimo settlements it became less toilsome, assistance being freely given by the children of the Arctic world. They volunteered their aid at the drag ropes; they carried the sick upon hand sledges; they poured in abundant supplies of fresh food, the quantity of little auks they brought being characterized as "enormous." They fed the explorers and their dogs at the rate of eight thousand birds a week, all of them caught in their little hand nets. No wonder that, under such favorable circumstances, Dr. Kane and his followers threw off their gloom for a time. The men indulged in their old forecastle songs; the sledges began to move merrily ahead; and the old moody silence gave way to laugh and jest.

Their progress was somewhat remarkable considering the scanty supply of food to which they were reduced, the daily allowance consisting of only six ounces of bread-dust and a lump of tallow about the size of a walnut, to which was added, when fresh water could be procured, a cup of that great restorative, tea. Of this stimulating beverage they drank immoderately and were greatly benefited by it.

At times, too, they had the opportunity of a very acceptable feast, as when on one occasion they heard the welcome sound of a large flock of eider ducks. Knowing that the breeding place of these birds must be near at hand, they sought and found it. Here they remained for three days, gorging themselves on eggs, of which they found as many as twelve hundred in a day, and unheeding a tempest which was then howling over their heads.

After Cape York was reached and passed the birds failed them and they were reduced to their scanty diet again, their stock of provisions being diminished until they had only about thirty-six pounds per man. Of fuel they had a three weeks' supply, to which they added by cutting up the "Red Eric," and proceeding in the other two boats, on which its wood was loaded.

Under the influence of insufficient food the strength of the wayfarers steadily declined. Five ounces of bread-dust, four of tallow and three of bird-meat was all that could be allowed for a day's rations, a very small supply in that severe climate and under circumstances of incessant toil.

Dr. Kane remarks as curious that the effect of insufficient food is not, as might be supposed, the pangs of hunger. The first symptom is loss of power, often so imperceptibly brought on that only an accident reveals its extent. "I well remember," he says, "our look of blank amazement as, one day, the order being given to haul the 'Hope' over a tongue of ice, we found that she would not budge. At first I thought it was owing to the wetness of the snow-covered surface in which her runners were; but as there was a heavy gale blowing outside, and I was extremely anxious to get her on to a larger floe to prevent being drifted off, I lightened her cargo, and set both crews upon her. In the land of promise off Crimson Cliffs, such a force would have trundled her like a wheelbarrow: we could almost have borne her upon our backs. Now, with incessant labor and standing hauls, she moved at a snail's pace."

It was on this occasion that the little company nearly lost their best boat, the "Faith," which drifted away from the ice-floe. The sight produced an almost hysterical impression, for she had on board all their stores. Happily, before they could fully realize all the consequences of her probable loss, a flat cake of ice eddied into the vicinity of the floe. McGary and Dr. Kane sprang upon it, and succeeded in floating it across the chasm in time to secure the boat. Then the rest of the crew rejoined her, with emotions of thankfulness which the reader may well imagine.

In this extremity, the discovery of a seal asleep upon a field of ice filled them with joy. They approached it with extreme care, and as it raised itself in its fore-flippers, preparatory to a plunge, a well-aimed rifle shot brought it down.

With a wild shout both boats charged full upon the floes. Eager hands seized the precious booty, and lifted it upon safer ice. The men, as if lost in a delirium of joy, ran over the ice, crying, laughing and brandishing their knives. Never was animal more quickly prepared for the table; never were viands more keenly relished. A grand cooking fire was kindled, and the famished voyagers enjoyed that night a strange, almost a savage orgie.

It is unnecessary to dwell minutely on the later incidents of the journey. On the 1st of August Dr. Kane sighted the Devil's Thumb, and was soon in waters that are familiar to every whaler. Passing to the south of Cape Shackleton, the voyagers followed up the quiet water channels that run parallel to the coast, occasionally killing a seal or some birds, and at night encamping upon the rocks.

Two days later, as they were slowly rowing through the mist, a familiar sound—the cadence of a "halloo"—came to them over the waters. With joyous hearts they pulled in the direction of the sound, and in about half an hour could make out the single mast of a small shallop. "'Tis the Upernavik oil-boat!" cried Petersen, half laughing, half crying. And such, indeed, it proved to be. In a few minutes they were on board of her, and in the embraces of old friends.

"Here," says Kane—and the conclusion of his narrative is best given in his own words—"here we first got our cloudy, vague idea of what had passed in the big world during our absence. The friction of its fierce rotation had not much disturbed this little outpost of civilization; and we thought it a sort of blunder as Carlie Mossyn told us that France and England were leagued with the Mussulman against the Greek Church! He was a good Lutheran, this assistant cooper, and all news with him had a theological complexion. . . .

"But 'Sir John Franklin?' There we were at home again. Our own delusive little speciality rose uppermost. Franklin's party, or traces of the dead which represented it, had been found nearly a thousand miles to the south of where we had been searching for them. . . . And so we 'out oars' again, and rowed into the fogs.

"Another sleeping-halt has passed, and we have all washed clean at the fresh-water basins, and furbished up our ragged furs and woolens. Kasarsoak, the snowy top of Sanderson Hope, shows itself above the mists, and we hear the yelling of the dogs. Petersen had been foreman of the settlement; and he calls my attention with a sort of pride to the tolling of the workmen's bell. It is six o'clock. We are nearing the end of our trials. Can it be a dream?

"We hugged the land by the big harbor, turned the corner by the old brew-house, and in the midst of a crowd of children hauled our boats for the last time upon the rocks.

"For eighty-four days we had lived in the open air. Our habits were hard and weather worn. We could not remain within the four walls of a house without a distressing sense of suffocation. But we drank coffee that night before many a hospitable threshold, and listened again and again to the hymn of welcome, which, sung by many voices, greeted our deliverance."

Dr. Kane and his party remained at Upernavik until the 6th of September, when they embarked on board the "Marianne" for the Shetland Isles. But putting in at Godhavn, they caught sight

DR. KANE'S FAMOUS ARCTIC VOYAGE

of an American squadron, under Captain Hartstene, which had been despatched in quest of them, and soon afterwards found themselves under the shelter of the national flag. At New York Dr. Kane received the honorable welcome to which his courage, his fertility of resource, his patient resolution and his noble purpose had entitled him. And though he had failed to discover Sir John Franklin, he had deserved well of the civilized world, having considerably enlarged its knowledge of the Polar regions.

Yet his suffering and exposure had fatally undermined his constitution. In 1856 he went to England and thence to Cuba to recuperate, but his health was broken beyond recovery and he died at Havana in February, 1857, two years after his return.

CHAPTER XXII

Hayes, Hall and other Hardy Adventurers

IN 1860 began another of the American expeditions to the Pole, under the command of Dr. Isaac I. Hayes, who had accompanied the Kane expedition as surgeon, had discovered Grinnell Land in 1855, and had traversed the icy seas to a latitude beyond 80 degrees. On the 6th of July, 1860, he set sail on an expedition under his own command, in which he hoped to pass the ice belt in Smith Sound and reach the open polar sea—he firmly believing, from past experiences, that the sea about the North Pole was not frozen. He was accompanied by Messrs. Sonntag and Radcliffe as astronomer and assistant astronomer, and by a crew of twelve officers and men.

On the 30th of July they crossed the Arctic Circle, and on the second day of August, as they lay becalmed off the Greenland coast, they beheld a scene which Dr. Hayes describes for us in the following glowing language.

"It seemed as if we had been drawn by some unseen hand into a land of enchantment. Here was the Valhalla of the sturdy Vikings, here the city of the sungod Freya; Alfheim, with its elfin curves, and Glitner, more brilliant than the sun, the home of the happy; and there, piercing the clouds, was Himnborg, the celestial mount."

His eloquent diary gives further details of the scene before his enraptured eyes. His description is well worth reproducing, as a pen-picture of the beauty often to be seen in the northern seas:

"The air was almost as warm as that of a southern summer eve; and yet before them were the icebergs and the bleak mountains, with which it is impossible, in this land of green hills and waving woods, to associate any idea other than that of cold repulsiveness. Bright and soft was the sky, and as strangely inspiring as that of Italy. The bergs had lost their cold, frozen look, and glittered in the glow of the brilliant heavens like masses of solid flame or burnished metal. Those near at hand seemed to have been wrought out of Parian marble, and incrusted with shining gems of pearl and opal. One in particular challenged attention by its grandeur. Its form was not unlike that of the Roman Coliseum, and it lay so far away that half its height was buried beneath the rim of the 'blood-red waters.' As the sun, in its course along the horizon, passed behind it, one might have thought that the old Roman ruin had broken out into a sudden conflagration.

"Where the bergs cast their silent shadows the water was a rich green; and nothing could be softer or more tender than the gradual coloring of the sea as it shoaled on the sloping tongue or spur of each floating mass. When the ice overhung the water the tint deepened, and a cavern in one of the nearer bergs exhibited the solid color of the malachite mingled with the transparency of the emerald; while, in strange contrast, a broad streak of cobalt shot diagonally through its body.

"The romantic character of the scene was increased by the numerous tiny cascades which leaped into the sea from these floating islands; the water being discharged from lakes of melted snow and ice which tranquilly reposed far up in the valleys separating the icy ridges of their upper surface. From other bergs large pieces were occasionally detached, crashing into the water with deafening roar, while the slow ocean-swell resounded hoarsely through their broken archways."

But they were soon to find that the beauty of the iceberg may conceal imminent peril. Shortly after leaving Upernavik they had such an experience, having come near a nest of icebergs, on which the current rapidly carried their vessel. An eddy threw them upon one of these huge masses, great blocks falling which would have crushed the ship if they had struck her.

This peril escaped, another threatened them. A long tongue from the berg projected immediately beneath the schooner, and the keel slipped and grinded upon it until it seemed probable that the ship would be hurled into the air, or else capsized. Here again the berg proved their safety. A loud report was heard; another and another followed in swift succession; the roar seemed to fill the air with a thousand echoes. The opposite side of the berg had split off, piece after piece, tumbling a vast volume of ice into the waves, and sending the revolving berg careening back upon the ship. The movement now was quicker; fragments began again to fall; and, already sufficiently alarmed by the dissolution which had taken place, Dr. Hayes and his followers were in momentary expectation of seeing the whole side nearest to them give way, and crash down upon the steamer.

They escaped this danger by planting an ice-anchor and drawing the vessel away from the berg. They were barely in time to escape destruction. Scarcely were they twenty yards distant when the expected disruption occurred. The side nearest them split off and crashed wildly into the sea, raising a tremendous swell and covering the tossing waters with fragments of ice. Luckily for them they were beyond its reach, and they hastened to get away from that scene of peril.

September had arrived when they at length crossed Melville Bay and entered Smith Sound. The young ice was forming fast and the season near its close, and it became necessary to seek winter quarters. A place was selected in a sheltered cave about twenty miles by latitude, but eighty miles by the coast line, south of Dr. Kane's wintering place at Rensselaer Harbor. On their way thither they had picked up Hans, the Eskimo, who had done such good service for Kane and his party. With him were his wife and child, who did not prove welcome additions to the ship's crew.

The sun sank out of sight behind the southern hills on the 15th of October; and the little company of brave men were face to face with the long winter darkness of the Polar World. At first a kind of soft twilight prevailed, and the golden glow of the unseen orb of day rested on the mountain tops; but surely and steadily the partial radiance lessened, and slowly and surely came on the sad obscurity of the Arctic night.

Dr. Hayes occasionally amused himself with taking his team of dogs on an excursion. They were twelve in number, healthy, strong and swift of foot. They would carry the sledge over the ice at a tremendous speed, accomplishing six miles in twenty-eight to thirty-three minutes. But to manage them is quite an art, for they are guided solely by the whip and voice.

On the outside are placed the strongest dogs; and the team sways to right and left, according as the whip falls on the snow to the one side or the other, or as it touches the leading dogs. The voice aids the whip, but the experienced driver relies more upon compulsion than upon persuasion. This whip is a wonderful instrument. Its lash is about four feet longer than the traces, and tipped with a "cracker" of hard sinew, quite capable of phlebotomizing a refractory animal. Its material is simply raw seal-hide, and it is attached to a light whip-stock only two feet and a half in length. Hence, to roll out the lash to its full length is a truly difficult undertaking, and in this, as in other arts, it is practice only that makes perfect.

Driving an Eskimo team, take it all in all, seems to be, as Dr. Hayes describes it, the very hardest kind of hard work. Incessantly must the driver ply his whip, and ply it mercilessly as well as incessantly, or it will avail him nothing. The least hesitancy or weakness on the driver's part is immediately detected by his dogs, and they act accordingly. Unless fully convinced that the soundness of their skins is at his mercy, they will indulge in the greatest liberties. "If they see a fox crossing the ice," says Dr. Hayes, "or come upon a bear-track, or 'wind' a seal, or sight a bird, away they dash over snow-drifts and hummocks, pricking up their short ears and curling up their long bushy tails for a wild, wolfish race after the game. If the whip-lash goes out with a fierce snap, the ears and the tails drop, and they go on about their proper business; but woe be unto you if they get the control. I have seen my own driver sorely put to his mettle, and not until he had brought a yell of pain from almost every dog in the team did he conquer their obstinacy. They were running after a fox, and were taking us toward what appeared to be unsafe ice. The wind was blowing hard, and the lash was sometimes driven back into the driver's face; hence the difficulty. The whip, however, finally brought them to reason; and in full view of the game, and within a few yards of the treacherous ice, they came first down into a limping trot, and then stopped, most unwillingly. Of course this made them very cross, and a general fight, fierce and angry, now followed, which was not quieted until the driver had sailed in among them and knocked them to right and left with his hard hickory whip-stock."

Slowly the winter passed, with its long hours of monotony and its few alleviations. Some amusement was afforded by the conjugal vagaries of Hans and his wife. The Eskimo lady was singularly disinclined for work, and when invited to assist in replenishing the men's winter wardrobe obstinately refused. Dr. Hayes describes her as the most dogged of her sex. She was indifferent to everything and everybody, and about once a fortnight indulged in a fit of ill temper, in which she was wont to declare her intention of abandoning Hans and the expedition, and returning to her own people. She essayed the experiment on one occasion, and, with her baby on her back, dashed away towards Cape Alexander. Hans, however, came out of his tent, as calm and impassive as ever, and stood leisurely smoking his pipe, and surveying the receding form of his wife and child with the most provoking unconcern. Dr. Hayes thought it desirable to call his attention to his wife's strategic movement.

"Yes, me see."

"Where is she going, Hans?"

"She no go; she come back all right."

"But she will freeze, Hans?"

"She no freeze; she come back by-by, you see."

And he continued to smoke his pipe with a quiet chuckle and a complacent conviction of his knowledge of the ways of womankind in general, and of his wife in particular. And in about two hours the Eskimo Xantippe came back, looking very blue and cold and evidently much subdued.

A disagreeable incident of the winter detention at Port Foulke was the outbreak of an epidemic disorder among the dogs, resembling mania or delirium. Of the character of this we have previously spoken. The mortality was dreadful. In the first two weeks of December eighteen died; three more deaths occurred in the following week; and Dr. Hayes found himself reduced to nine animals. As all his plans of exploration in the coming spring depended upon the efficiency of his teams as a means of transportation across the ice, his anxiety was great; and in order to obtain a fresh supply, he determined on sending Mr. Sonntag, with Hans as driver, to the nearest Eskimo settlement on Northumberland Island, if necessary, or to Whale Sound, if haply any station should be found upon its shores.

The expedition proved an unfortunate one. After several months of absence, Hans came back alone, with the bad news of the death of his companion and without the dogs for which he had been sent. The story he told was that Mr. Sonntag had incautiously stepped on some thin ice covering a recently closed tide-crack. It gave way and he fell in. Hans hastened to his rescue, and the two then turned back for Sorfalik, where a snow hut could afford them shelter. Unfortunately, Mr. Sonntag did not change his wet clothing; and when the sledge halted at Sorfalik, Hans discovered that his companion was stiff and speechless. Removing him into the hut as quickly as possible, he placed him in the sleeping bag, administered some brandy, and having tightly closed the hut, lighted their alcohol lamp, for the double purpose of elevating the temperature and making some coffee. His efforts were in vain; Sonntag never recovered consciousness, and in a few hours died.

Hans continued his journey alone, but found it difficult to discover any Eskimos, and from those he met at length no dogs were to be had. When he returned his team was reduced to five miserable attenuated dogs, while the unfortunate trip had resulted in the death of one of the most esteemed members of the party.

With the approach of spring, however, Dr. Hayes succeeded in purchasing some good dogs from Eskimos who visited his camp, until he got together a group of seventeen hardy animals. With these he set out on a preliminary trip northward, of which we need only say that one morning, when he emerged from his sleeping cave in the snow, he found the thermometer to record the bitterly low temperature of 68 degrees below zero, or 100 degrees below the freezing point. We find few records surpassing this, though Dr. Cook in his recent polar trip reports the extraordinary low temperature of —83 degrees Fahrenheit. During this excursion Rensselaer Harbor was reached and traces of Dr. Kane's ship, the "Advance," were sought. None were found, and it became probable that the deserted ship had sunk before the onset of the ice-floes.

Returning from this preliminary excursion, preparations were made for a more extended one, and on the 3d of April the party, twelve in number, set out merrily with two sledges, "The Hope," drawn by eight dogs, and "The Perseverance," by six. It did not go on merrily, for difficulties and obstacles beset the explorers, so that in twenty-two days they advanced only thirty miles. Four more days passed, and then, on April 28th, being half-way across the Kane Basin, Hayes sent back eight of his men, proceeding with three companions in his dash towards Grinnell Land, on the opposite side of the water. This was not reached until May 11th, after thirty-eight days of exhausting labor.

From this point the energetic explorers pushed northward, though only twelve days' allowance of dog food remained. Onward they went until Kennedy Channel was entered, and a point beyond that attained by Morton, in Kane's expedition, was reached. At this point Jansen, the strongest man in the expedition, broke down. He was left in charge of Macdonald, and Hayes pushed on with Knorr, the remaining member of the small party.

His progress was checked at length by the rotten ice, which proved to be impassable. Hayes had reached his *ne plus ultra;* he had not attained latitude 82 degrees, but he had actually advanced to the shore of that northernmost gulf, into which Kennedy Channel opens through a broad bay. Here the ice was broken up, and waterways ramified across it, and led into the free ocean which, it may be, lies beyond. Climbing to the summit of a rugged cliff about 800 feet in height, Hayes was rewarded for his labors and suffering by a glorious prospect. Standing against the dark "water-sky" at the north, rose, in dim outline, the white sloping summit of a noble headland, the northernmost known land upon the globe. He calculated it to be in latitude 82 degrees 30 minutes, or about four hundred and fifty miles from the North Pole. Nearer, another bold cape stood forth; and nearer, a third headland towered majestically above the sea, as if pushing up into the very skies a lofty mountainpeak, on which winter had dropped its diadem of snows.

Nothing remained for him but to return as quickly as possible to Port Foulke; as quickly as possible, for the summer was rapidly approaching, the ice was yielding to the solar influence, and the open water was eating from Kennedy Channel into the ice-masses of Smith Sound in the north, as well as through Baffin Bay in the south. But before turning his back on the unexplored Polar Sea, he desired to erect some memorial of his adventures. Some flags which he had brought with him were suspended by a whip-lash between two tall rocks; and the following record, enclosed in a small glass vial, was deposited beneath a hastily-reared cairn of stones:

"This point, the most northern land that has ever been reached, was visited by the undersigned, May 18, 19, 1861, accompanied by George F. Knorr, traveling with a dog-sledge. We arrived here after a toilsome march of forty-six days from my winter harbor, near Cape Alexander, at the mouth of Smith Sound. My observations place us in latitude 81 degrees 35 minutes, longitude 70 degrees 30 minutes west. Our further progress was stopped by rotten ice and cracks. Kennedy Channel appears to expand into the Polar Basin; and, satisfied that it is navigable at least during the months of July, August, and September, I go hence to my winter harbor, to make another trial to get through Smith Sound with my vessel, after the ice breaks up this summer.   I. I. HAYES.

"May 19, 1861."

It must suffice here to state that no further discovery was made, and that in the following summer the explorer brought his vessel, the "United States," back to the country whose name it bore. Dr. Hayes made another voyage in 1869, but on this occasion confined his trip to Southern Greenland.

At the time of Hayes's first voyage north another American explorer of note was making his pioneer trip to the Arctic seas. This was Charles Francis Hall, a man who from boyhood had made the polar regions the goal of his desires. His means were very limited, but he succeeded in interesting some friends in his project, which at first was confined to a search for relics of the Sir John Franklin expedition. Henry Grinnell, the patron of the Kane expedition, was among those who aided him, and he set out in 1860 on a voyage which yielded no notable results except the discovery in Frobisher Strait of relics of the visit of Martin Frobisher, three centuries before.

A second voyage was made in 1864, it being 1869 before he returned to the United States. During this long absence he devoted himself to an enthusiastic search for relics of the Franklin party, pushing westward as far as King William's Land, and finding or obtaining from the Eskimos many articles which had belonged to Franklin and his men, about one hundred and fifty in all.

Hall set out on a third voyage in 1871, this time with the ambitious purpose of seeking the North Pole. He had the support of the government in this expedition, and was instructed to explore and survey the passage between Greenland and Grinnell Land and, if possible, to reach the Pole. Setting out on June 29, 1871, in a steam vessel, the "Polaris,'" with a crew of thirty-three, he had the good fortune to carry his ship readily through the seas which had baffled Kane and Hayes, sailing past the highest points they had reached in sledge journeys and passing through Robeson Channel to where it opens into the waters of the Polar Sea. The highest point reached was in latitude 82 degrees 16 minutes, about two hundred miles north of Kane's highest and fifty miles beyond that of Hayes.

It was now the 7th of September, and it was decided to lay up for the winter, this being done in a sheltered cove in latitude 87 degrees 38 minutes, which Hall named Thank God Harbor. While preparations for "wintering" were being made, Captain Hall started on a sledge-journey, which occupied from October 10th to October 24th. On his return he was suddenly taken sick. At first it was supposed to be only a temporary bilious attack, but on the following day the symptoms became alarming, and he was frequently delirious. His illness continued, and gradually assumed the appearance of paralysis.

Early on the 8th of November, the heroic explorer's adventurous career was terminated. "Last evening," says Tyson, "the captain himself thought he was better, and would soon be around again. But it seems he took worse in the night. Captain Buddington came and told me he 'thought Captain Hall was dying.' I got up immediately, and went to the cabin and looked at him. He was quite unconscious—knew nothing. He lay on his face, and was breathing heavily; his face was hid in the pillow. It was about half-past three o'clock in the morning that he died. Assisted in preparing the grave, which is nearly half a mile from the ship, inland; but the ground was so frozen that it was necessarily very shallow—even with picks it was scarcely possible to break it up."

On the 11th he wrote: "At half-past eleven this morning we placed all that was mortal of our late commander in the frozen ground. Even at that hour of the day it was almost dark, and I had to hold a lantern for Mr. Bryan to read the papers. It was a gloomy day and well befitting the event. The place also was gloomy and desolate in the extreme."

Thus ended Hall's ambitious project of conquering the secret of the North Pole; and thus was quenched the enthusiasm of a singularly ardent nature. Though better fitted for a volunteer than a leader, to act alone than to govern others, he undertook his work with a boundless energy and an untiring perseverance; and had he lived, it is certain he would have advanced as far to the northward as man is able to go. We cannot but regret so sudden and disastrous a termination of a chivalrous enterprise. Yet there is something appropriate in his place of burial; and that lonely grave amid the peaks and icebergs of the Polar World is surely a more suitable sepulchre for such a dauntless explorer than one in the crowded city cemetery, or even the village churchyard. On no man was the strange magical spell of the North more powerfully laid than on Charles Francis Hall; and it is well that he should sleep where the cold northern winds blow across his grave, and the weird radiance of the aurora falls upon it.

Fortunate as had been the northward passage of the "Polaris," through easy channels and open seas, on her return in the summer of 1872 the ice demon lay in wait for her and played havoc with the gallant ship. Caught in the floes off the southern entrance of Kennedy Channel, in latitude 80 degrees, the vessel drifted southward in the ice to 78 degrees 28 minutes. Here a furious gale assailed her, the grinding ice crushing in her strong sides until the crew believed that she was wounded beyond hope and would sink with the opening of the floe.

The only hope seemed to be to take to the ice, and the crew began getting out stores, tents, clothing, boats, everything they could lay hands on. Nineteen of the ship's company, including two Eskimos and their wives and children, scrambled out on the pack, while the others passed them the articles as rapidly as possible. Through the wind and the cold they worked, clouds of snow driving past them and finally thickening until they could barely see. The force of the gale in time grew so great that those on the pack crouched behind the stores they had rescued, waiting for it to abate.

As they lay thus, the sound of cracking ice came to them from the direction of the ship. Peering through the gloom, a cry of despair broke from their lips. The ice had parted in the gale, and down the long line of open water that lay before them they saw the dark hull of the "Polaris" vanishing in the gloom. She was gone —probably to sink with all on board. They were left adrift on an ice-pack that at any moment might split asunder and drop them into the freezing water. Or if held together death from cold and starvation threatened them. Never had men been in a more terrible situation.

The story of these castaways is a long and distressing one, but must here be dealt with briefly. In the morning, when the storm had abated and the air was clear, they looked eagerly for some sign of the "Polaris." She was visible, but miles away, and as the day went on vanished from sight, leaving them stranded on floating ice in the Arctic Sea.

Fortunately for the party, Captain Tyson was with them on the floe and at once took charge of affairs. The others included Mr. Meyers, the meteorologist, the steward, cook, six seamen, and Joe and Hans, two Eskimos, with their wives and children, one of these being an infant born on the ship and only two months old.

The separation from the ship had taken place on October 15th, and during the night of the 16th, another disruption of the floe occurred, Tyson and his companions finding themselves adrift on one part, with one of the two boats, while the other boat and part of the provisions remained on the main body of the floe. On the 21st, however, they succeeded in recovering these precious and necessary articles; and, afterwards, in removing to a larger and firmer floe which lay much nearer the shore. Then they built up their snow-houses, forming quite a little encampment: one hut for Captain Tyson and Mr. Meyers, a second for the men, others for the Eskimos, for Joe, Hannah, and Puney and for Hans and his family; a store-hut for provisions, and a cook-house,—all united by arched galleries or corridors made of snow. These were true *igloës,* and made in the regular Eskimo fashion.

Their hope was to get to the shore, where their ammunition might provide them with some species of game. On the 30th of October the day's allowance for the whole company consisted of two pounds of pemmican, six pounds of bread, and four pounds of canned meat. On such scanty rations everybody's strength rapidly declined; and though the natives continued hunting, no success atended their efforts. In fact, it is very difficult to find the seal in winter. They live principally under the ice, and can be seen only when the ice cracks. Being warm-blooded animals, they cannot long continue under the ice without breathing. Consequently, for the purposes of respiration, they make air-holes through the ice and snow; but at the surface these holes are so small—not more than two and a half inches across—that they are scarcely distinguishable, especially in the dim uncertain light of an Arctic winter-day. A native will sometimes remain watching a seal-hole for thirty-six or forty-eight hours before getting a chance to strike; and if the first stroke misses, the seal is gone for ever. Barbed spears are used by the hunter; and as the seal's skull is exceedingly thin, a well-aimed blow is sure to penetrate, and then the prize can be held securely until the hole has been sufficiently enlarged for the body to come through.

Two seals were captured on the 21st of November, and proved a temporary alleviation of the distress of the castaways. All the dogs but four had been sacrificed, and everybody was suffering pitifully from weakness. The ice-floe, meantime, continued to drift to the southward. And so the dreary record continues day by day: other seals being occasionally caught, but the situation of the wanderers growing daily more critical and distressing. For eighty-three days the sun was lost to sight while the cold was intense. Huddling in their snow-houses, with lamps for their only source of heat, hope almost abandoned them during those wearisome days.

Never, perhaps, was the return of the sun more welcomed than by the desolate castaways on the floe. But its appearance and the commencement of spring was not entirely an unmixed blessing. The rising temperature naturally caused the ice to break up, and as the floe upon which they were marooned gradually decreased in size, fresh anxiety was caused to them by the possible danger of their haven being broken up. This was realized on March 11th, when their ice raft broke up in a gale, leaving them on a piece less than one hundred yards square. Fortunately it was of great thickness and solidity.

As March merged into April things grew worse and their position more perilous. A violent gale, which continued, with little intermission, for several days, reduced the storm-beaten company to great distress from the impossibility of capturing any seals. They began to suffer the pangs of hunger, and at one time it seemed as if death by starvation would be the termination of their miseries. Nay, worse results were to be apprehended. "Some of the men," wrote Tyson, on the 15th of April, "have dangerous looks; this hunger is disturbing their brains. I cannot but fear that they contemplate crime. After what we have gone through, I hope this company may be preserved from any fatal wrong. We can and we must bear what God sends without crime. This party must not disgrace humanity by cannibalism." Fortunately a seal was killed on the 18th, and this supply came like a direct blessing from Heaven to recruit their strength.

Just as it was needed! For at night, on the 20th, a heavy sea suddenly arose, and sweeping in violent billows over the ice-floe occupied by the castaways, carried off their tent, their skins, most of their bed-clothing,—everything, in fact, that was movable,—and plunged them into destitution. Only a few articles were saved, which they contrived to stow in the boat; the women and children were already in it, or the little ones must certainly have perished. It required all the efforts of the men to save the boat. They knew that their lives depended on its preservation, and this knowledge inspired them to exertions which, in their enfeebled condition, were almost superhuman. For twelve hours they held on to it, "like grim Death;" scarcely a sound was uttered, save and except the crying of the children, and Captain Tyson's order to "Hold on," "Bear down," "Put on all your weight," and the responsive "Ay, ay, sir," which, in this terrible crisis, came readily enough. Discipline was temporarily restored under the influence of danger.

We find them, on the 22d of April, half drowned, half frozen, without shelter, and without food! Had the end come? Not yet: Heaven again came to their rescue; a bear was sighted, pursued, killed, brought back to the "camp" in triumph, and speedily devoured. On the 28th, three young seals fell to the hunters' rifles, and abundance reigned. On the same day they were cheered by the appearance of a steamer working her way through the ice to the southwest; and though she did not see them, it infused new hope into their hearts, as it was a sign and a token that they might now expect to be relieved. And, indeed, on the following day another steamer was seen. Then volleys were fired; colors were hoisted; loud shouts were raised; but these combined efforts failed to draw her attention to the little company on the ice-raft. A third steamer afterwards came in sight, but did not bring them deliverance.

However, it was not far off. On the 30th, a fourth steamer was discovered through the fog, and so near them that Hans leaped into his kajak and paddled towards her. Meantime, she perceived Captain Tyson's signals, and, to the intense joy of all these storm-beaten, wan, attenuated, suffering castaways, bore down upon them. In a few minutes she was alongside of their piece of ice.

"On her approach, and as they slowed down," says Captain Tyson, whose words we shall here adopt, "I took off my old Russian cap, which I had worn all winter, and waving it over my head, gave them three cheers, in which all the men most heartily joined. It was instantly returned by a hundred men, who covered her top-gallant-mast, forecastle, and fore-rigging. We then gave three more, and a 'tiger;' which was appropriate, surely, as she proved to be the sealer 'Tigress,'—a barkentine of Conception Bay, Newfoundland."

They found that in the 196 days they had spent on the floe they had drifted over 1500 miles from the latitude in which the "Polaris" was beset on October 12th. For the time they believed they were the only survivors of the expedition, but in this they were wrong. The remainder of the party also escaped, though without undergoing quite the same hardships as themselves.

When the "Polaris" broke away from the ice, she did not sink, but drifted rapidly before the gale through the open channel. Captain Buddington, who had assumed command when Captain Hall died, and the twelve men who remained on board, managed to keep the disabled vessel afloat, but they could do no more until she again became involved in the ice. By that time all hopes of returning to the place where the other men were on the ice was abandoned, and, as the water was fairly open, the efforts of the crew were mainly directed to warping the ship towards the coast. By good fortune she managed to escape from the crushing packs, and, with tireless effort and great care, she was at length brought within sight of land. Then she was caught in the ice along the shore and so severely nipped that her ruin was complete. She, however, did not sink, and her crew were able to reach the land.

Selecting a site for an encampment, they removed thither enough timber from the broken-up vessel to construct a house, to which they also removed enough stores to last them. When these necessaries were secured, they brought more timber ashore, and, during the longer winter night, they employed themselves in constructing a couple of boats. It was a laborious task, and but slow progress was made until daylight returned. Then they were able to carry on the work faster; but it was the middle of May before they had them finished and seaworthy.

As soon as the ice began to break up, they launched the boats, which were fully provisioned from the wreck, and on June 3d they sailed away to the south. Three weeks later they sighted a whaler, the "Ravenscraig," who took them aboard, and within a few months of their comrades, whom they thought had all perished, landing in America from the "Tigress," the boat party also landed, having saved, in addition to themselves, all the records of the surveys and observations made by the expedition. These were of great geographical value, making known much of the neighborhood of the straits between Greenland and Grant's Land. The expedition, although attaining to a high latitude, did not succeed in reaching the Pole, but their adventures made a fascinating chapter in the history of Polar research.

There is one more expedition fitted to speak of in this chapter, as it bore a certain resemblance to those of Hayes and Hall in character. It was an enterprise sent out by the English government in 1875, under the command of Sir George Nares, its purpose being to reach the Pole if possible. It comprised two ships, the "Alert" and the "Discovery."

Pursuing the same course as that of Hall in the "Polaris," they reached the high latitude in which the Robeson Channel opens into the Polar Sea. Here the "Discovery" wintered, while the "Alert" went farther north, taking with her an officer and a sledge team of men from the "Discovery," to be sent back overland when winter quarters were selected.

On the last day of August the "Alert" met a particularly heavy floe, the ice forming it being of the massive character which denoted that its origin was the Polar Sea. Once the grinding mass of hummocks, rising higher than the vessel's decks, threatened to enfold her. There would have been no hope of escape if they had, and only by persistently ramming her way through some of the looser ice did she escape in towards the shore. Next day a strong gale sprang up from the southwest, and the "Alert" went along at ten miles an hour in an open channel between the land and the heavy pack which was drifting about three miles out. By midday they reached latitude 82 degrees 24 minutes north, and the flags were run up to the mastheads amid general rejoicing, for it was the farthest point north to which a ship had yet sailed.

With the channel showing clear ahead of them and the spanking breeze astern, expectation was high on board that they would be able to sail right up to latitude 84 degrees, but within an hour their hopes were suddenly and thoroughly checked. On hauling to the westward they rounded a promontory and found that the land trended away to the west. The wind veered round to the northwest and drove the ice in upon the channel, which gradually became narrower until, when off Cape Sheridan, the main pack was observed to be touching the grounded ice and effectually barring all further progress. The "Alert" was run close up to the end of the channel, and then, when it was certain that there was no chance of getting through the barrier, she was anchored to a floe which rested aground off the cape. The next day, as the heavy ice of the pack was grinding against the stranded floe, and an opening just large enough for the vessel to get in was observed in the floe, she was warped into the basin.

She was barely inside when a solid hummock crushed against the opening, forming a great barrier between the vessel and the outer moving pack. Had it struck there a few minutes earlier the vessel would have been severely injured by the "nip," but as it was the hummock formed an admirable shelter from the pressure of the pack. This was often so severe that masses over 30,000 tons in weight were broken off and forced up the inclined shore, rising twelve and fourteen feet higher out of the water as they crunched along the ground.

With the opening of the next spring a sledging party was sent out, taking with it two whale-boats in case open water should be reached. There proved no need of these boats, the supposed "open polar sea" of Kane and Hayes proving a vast sheet of ice, seemingly of such ancient origin that Nares gave it the title of "palæocrystic ice."

As the days went on the toil of dragging the sledges over the endless ice field grew intensely wearisome, and although the men stuck to their task with true British obstinacy, it began to tell upon them. One man fell sick, growing weaker and weaker until he was no longer able to pull, and then was unable to walk. One of the boats was abandoned, and the sick man laid on a sledge. His condition was more than disquieting to the leaders, for it was evident he was suffering from scurvy, and no one could say who would be the next to develop it.

On April 23d they added only a mile and a quarter to their distance, for they had come upon clumps of ice hummocks which made their progress so difficult that they had to combine forces to haul first one sledge and then another over the obstacles. On April 28th, when they were seventeen miles from the shore, they found the track of a hare in the snow, going towards the land, but with the footprints so close together that the animal was evidently very weak. Where it had come from, or how it had got so far from the shore, were riddles they could not solve.

As May came in signs of scurvy made themselves only too evident among the members of the crew, and on May 11th the leaders decided that the next day they would have to turn south once more. They started with a light sledge in the morning and pushed on till noon, when they took their bearings. They had reached latitude 83 degrees 20 minutes 26 seconds north, and were then only 399½ miles from the Pole itself, having beaten all other records of Arctic explorations.

The return to the ship proved exhausting in the extreme. One of the men died and the others were so utterly worn out that hope of reaching the ships was almost abandoned. Lieutenant Parr was the strongest, yet even he was pitiably weak, and when he volunteered to set out alone for the ship in quest of relief few dreamed that he would be able to reach his goal.

They could scarcely accept the evidence of their ears the next morning when the shouts of men's voices came to them in their sleeping bags. The gallant Parr had reached the ship, and the bold fellows who had conquered the "farthest north" were saved when on the brink of death.

Other surveying parties were sent out and on their return the vessels started for home, reaching England without misadventure on November 2, 1876, with the proud consciousness of having surpassed Parry's record of 1827 and approached nearer the pole than any man had before done.

CHAPTER XXIII.

Nordenskiöld and the Northeast Passage

IN the preceding chapter we have been principally concerned with expeditions to the seas north of America, and with polar researches by the route lying through Smith Sound. Later Arctic ventures have proved that this is the best road to the Pole, and as we now know it is the only one by which the Pole has been reached. But the course of history leads us to other seas, those lying north of Europe and Asia, the seas in which Parry made his famous 1827 record of 82 degrees 45 minutes and which became the seat of important discoveries in the latter part of the nineteenth century.

Readers of the chapters of polar history so far given will have perceived that the main objects of explorations were the discovery of a northwest passage from the Atlantic to the Pacific north of America, and the rescue of the unfortunates who were lost in this effort, especially of the Sir John Franklin party. Those which made the discovery of the North Pole their chief object were few in number, the most important being the expeditions of Parry, Hayes, Hall, and Nares.

Meanwhile the problem of the Northeast Passage—that from the Atlantic to the Pacific by way of the seas north of Europe and Asia—remained unsolved. After the long ago Willoughby expedition little attention was paid to it until very recent times, when Baron Nordenskiöld made his famous and successful voyage in that direction. We must, however, briefly consider an unsuccessful attempt in this field preceding that of Nordenskiöld. This was the Austrian expedition of 1872 under Lieutenant Payer.

This expedition was supported by the enthusiastic approval of the whole Austro-Hungarian empire, great results being looked for from it. Its commander, Lieutenant Payer, was a seaman of proved ability, familiar with the difficulties and dangers of Arctic navigation, he having served in a German expedition of some importance in 1868, and executed a map of its discoveries notable for beauty and accuracy.

It was his intention to round the northeastern point of Nova Zembla and pass eastward to the most northern point of Siberia, where he would pitch his winter camp. He hoped in the following year to continue the voyage to Bering Strait; while, during the spring, sledge-parties would be engaged in exploring the unknown coasts of Wrangell Land, and otherwise advancing the bounds of geographical discovery in that remote and desolate region.

As it proved, the season of 1872 was one of exceptional severity, and ice was encountered in seas which, under more favorable conditions, were generally free from obstruction. Lieutenant Payer, however, bated not one jot of hope, and kept his course to the eastward with resolute intrepidity; hoping to reach Cape Chelyuskin, the farthest north Siberian promontory, where he proposed to pitch his winter-camp.

He was baffled, however, as so many had been baffled before him, by the forces of the Arctic winter. He was compelled to winter among the ice; using his sledges when opportunity offered, for the purpose of exploration, or to obtain fresh provisions.

Both the summers of 1873 and 1874 were spent off the Siberian coast; but though many interesting discoveries were made, Lieutenant Payer did not succeed in effecting a passage through the Icy Sea to Bering Strait. This navigation of the Asiatic mainland remained to be accomplished.

In August, 1873, Payer's ship, the "Tegethof," drifted northward to the highest point yet reached in those eastern seas, land being sighted at 79 degrees 43 minutes north latitude, and the drift continuing until the eightieth parallel was passed. Here the ice-floe in which the vessel had been immovably fixed for fourteen months was driven upon an island, by the shore of which the long polar winter was passed, the cold becoming so severe that the quicksilver in the thermometer remained frozen for weeks, while the midwinter darkness was intense.

Several sledge journeys were made to explore the new land, which Payer named Franz Josef Land in honor of the Austrian emperor. It lay north of the latitude of Spitzbergen, which it closely approached in area. It was a land of desolation, with mountains 5000 feet in height, the vast cliffs between them being filled with gigantic glaciers. At latitude 81 degrees 37 minutes the explorers reached a territory which they named Crown Prince Rudolf Land, the cliffs of which were covered with thousands of ducks and auks, while seals, bears, hares and foxes abounded. In April, 1874, the coast was followed to 81 degrees 57 minutes north, while land was visible in the distance which seemed to stretch beyond the eighty-third parallel, being the most northern then known upon the globe. This region has since been explored by Leigh Smith and others and found to consist of an archipelago, composed of numerous islands, which are divided into two large masses lying east and west, the group extending between 80 and 83 degrees north. In the autumn of 1874 the expedition returned home, unsuccessful in its main object, but with very important discoveries to its credit.

The work of Payer was in a sense preliminary to that of Baron Nordenskiöld in 1878-79, with which we are here principally concerned. This notable discoverer, Adolf Erik Nordenskiöld by name, was born at Helsingfors, Finland, in 1832, was educated in his native land, and in 1857 became a professor of mineralogy at Stockholm. He took part at various times in no less than eight Arctic expeditions, and was made a baron of Sweden in 1880 after his feat of traversing the Northeast Passage.

The solution of this important geographical problem was the

RESCUE OF THE GREELY PARTY, JUNE 23, 1884

Three years after the start of his expedition Greely and his men, encamped near Cape Sabine, Grinnell Land, had been reduced to the direst extremities. By June 21, 1884, death had decimated their numbers, and the commander himself was so weak that he discontinued his journal. The next day Frederick and Brainard obtained some water, and this with a few square inches of soaked seal skin was all the food the men had for the ensuing forty-two hours. When vitality was at its lowest ebb, and hope was nearly gone, Greely heard the whistle of the "Thetis" blown by order of Captain Winfield S. Schley, who had been sent to search for Greely and the Lady Franklin Bay Expedition.

CROSSING A BROKEN ICE FIELD

This illustration gives some idea of the difficulties which Arctic explorers must endure in making progress over the ever-moving floes. Crushed and jagged from the enormous pressure of the vast ice pack, the surface rises into hills and valleys over which the men must haul their entire outfit, often when reduced by cold and lack of food to weak shadows of themselves.

DeLong.   Chipp.   Melville.

[From DeLong's "Voyage of the Jeannette," Houghton-Mifflin Co.]

THE "JEANNETTE'S" BOATS SEPARATED BY THE STORM

DeLong and twelve men in the first cutter, Chipp and nine men in the second cutter, and Melville with nine men in the whale boat, started to sail from the edge of the Polar ice floe to the coast of Siberia. They had traversed successfully about four-fifths of the voyage when the boats were separated by a heavy gale on September 12, 1881, and September 17th DeLong's boat reached land, which they supposed to be the "Lena Delta." During the month of October every man who had started in DeLong's boat, except two, had perished. Melville was fortunate enough to reach native settlements and brought his party through. Chipp and his men were never heard of again.

[From DeLong's "Voyage of the Jeannette," Houghton-Mifflin Co.]

THE "JEANNETTE'S" CREW DRAGGING THEIR BOATS OVER THE ICE

The men had to go over the same ground four times each way at this stage of their perilous journey. The first trip they brought two sledges forward one mile; at the second trip two more sledges; at the third trip one of the boats, a cutter; at the fourth trip the second cutter and whale boat. One mile progress, therefore, meant seven miles of travel by men and nine miles by the dog sledges. At this point the nearest island off the coast of Siberia was one hundred and twenty miles distant.

result of a carefully devised plan, based on the experience and study of its projector, who had devoted years of thought and investigation to the enterprise, collecting information from whalers and other Arctic navigators as well as employing the results of his own voyages. Two of these, made in 1875 and 1876, were to the mouth of the Yenisei River, in Western Siberia, the expense being borne by merchants and landholders having interests in Siberia, to whom a trade-route from Europe to the great Arctic rivers of Asia would have been of much advantage.

The comparative ease with which these two tentative voyages were made led Nordenskiöld to push on with new vigor and enthusiasm towards the great object of his ambition, and he began eagerly to prepare for the great voyage he projected. It involved an expense of about $100,000, three-fifths of which sum was provided by Mr. Oscar Deikson, of Gothenburg, a merchant who had helped to finance his former voyages, and the remainder by King Oscar II, in behalf of the government of Sweden.

With this aid a screw steamer, the "Vega," was provided, built expressly for use in the Arctic waters and equipped in the most complete manner available for a three years' scientific voyage. The total force of the expedition, embracing botanists, zoologists, meteorologists and crew, numbered only thirty men, Captain Polander, of the Royal Swedish Navy, being second in command and the actual captain of the vessel. There were also some officers of foreign navies, taken on board at the request of their respective governments, among them Lieutenant Bove, of the Italian navy, who had been selected to command a projected Antarctic expedition. It was a picked company throughout, and in this respect no expedition had ever been better equipped. The steamer "Lena" was added as a consort to the "Vega" for most of her course, its goal being the Lena River, on which stream it was to be used for trade purposes.

On the 21st of July, 1878, the company of explorers left the harbor of Tromsö, Sweden, and sailed for the North Cape, the most northerly point of Europe and the true starting point of the adventurous voyage. Progress was slow on account of adverse winds, the ships heading for the island of Nova Zembla. Here it passed through the Yuger Schar, the strait that lies between Vaygatz Island and the mainland, and entered the great Kara Sea, the vast expanse of Arctic waters which lies between the extreme north of Nova Zembla and Cape Chelyuskin, the northern point of the continent of Asia. At the end of July the several ships of the expedition met in Ehabarook, the appointed rendezvous.

Besides the "Vega" and "Lena" there were two others, the "Frazer" and the "Express," which bore cargoes of iron-ware and bar iron for the Yenisei River. This they were to ascend and to return the same season to Norway. It will suffice to say that this was successfully accomplished, these vessels reaching Hammerfest in September with full cargoes of tallow, wheat, rye and oats, the first shipments ever made by sea from the Yenisei region to the European markets.

Deikson Harbor, near the mouth of the Yenisei, had been entered on the 1st of August, and the "Vega" and "Lena" lay there till the 10th, when the voyage was resumed. For two days all went well, then great masses of floating ice were encountered and heavy fogs made progress slow and dangerous. The fact that the Taimyr Peninsula lies farther to the west than had been supposed added to their difficulties, small islands being encountered where the charts promised open sea.

On the 19th of August the "Vega" came to anchor off Cape Chelyuskin, Asia's northern extremity, a new fact in the history of navigation, and one which was duly celebrated by hoisting flags, firing salutes, and other demonstrations of triumph. The only party to observe these demonstrations was a large white bear, and he plainly did not approve of them. The next day the vessels steamed onward and in a week more the mouth of the Lena River was reached. Here the little "Lena" parted company with its consort and steamed away up the great Siberian river, reaching Yakutsk, its destination, on the 21st of September.

The region in which they now were, that since known as Nordenskiöld Sea, is that of the New Siberian Islands, a group famous for containing great quantities of mammoth ivory and other remains of the mammoths which once evidently were very numerous in this region. These islands were reached on the 26th. Ice was now forming fast and the "Vega" met with much obstruction, being detained at North Cape for a week. The opportunity was taken to make several land excursions, which led to some interesting discoveries, among them the finding of ruins of habitations like those of the Eskimos, indicating that a similar people had dwelt here in the past.

As the "Vega" went on much trouble and delay were caused by fogs and ice, it being the 227th of September before the east side of Kolintschin Bay was reached and the anchor dropped. They were now in the vicinity of Bering Strait and warm hopes of completing their journey before the season ended were entertained, it being fully expected that the voyage could be resumed on the next day.

But nature decided otherwise, the night proved bitterly cold, and the floes were frozen so firmly together that on the next day the "Vega" found it impossible to break through them. It was hoped that the ice would soon break up, but north winds prevailed, packing heavy masses along the coast, while the growing chill formed new ice with great rapidity. Before November ended all chance of escaping vanished and the explorers were forced to admit that they were frozen in for the winter. Thus, by what Nordenskiöld regarded as a most unfortunate accident, their hopeful expectation of completing the voyage in one season was defeated and nature clasped them in her wintry fetters for another year.

It was certainly unfortunate. Had they reached and left that point one day earlier they would undoubtedly have entered the strait and reached the Pacific, then little more than a hundred miles away, and escaped ten months of weary detention. As it was, navigation closed more than two weeks before the date at which whaling ships were usually able to leave those waters.

There was nothing, however, to do but submit to the detention, which continued until July 18th of the following year. The time was spent in making meteorological observations of interest and value, in digesting the results of the voyage and in visiting the natives, one village of about two hundred Eskimos being in the vicinity. They were also sufficiently far south as to have a visit from the sun for some time every day.

On July 18th the ice was found to be in motion. The fires were once more lighted under the boilers of the vessel and at 3.30 P. M. the "Vega" glided away from her place of imprisonment. Two days later the Northeast Passage, for which Willoughby began the search 326 years before, was an accomplished fact. Again the Swedish flag was raised and a salute was fired. The point had been reached at which, as Nordenskiöld expressed it, "the Old and the New World seem to shake hands."

The homeward voyage was made by way of Japan, Ceylon and the Suez Canal, the successful navigator being received in Europe with enthusiastic demonstrations and distinguished marks of honor for his signal triumph.

CHAPTER XXIV

The Horrors of the "Jeannette" Expedition

DURING the summer of Nordenskiöld's return to civilization from his fortunate expedition, another, destined to a far more unfortunate fate, set out for the same seas, though with a different purpose. This was an American expedition, under the command of Lieutenant George W. DeLong, of the United States Navy, its principal purpose being the discovery of the North Pole and the exploration of the Arctic region. A secondary purpose was to search for Professor Nordenskiöld, who had now been absent a year, his fate unknown. DeLong's instructions to make this search were due to the fact that he proposed to take the Bering Strait route, near which the Swedish navigator might possibly be found.

This route was chosen from reliance on two theories—both of which proved unsound. One was that the Japan current made a way for its warm waters through the strait and might keep open a passage to the pole. The other was that Wrangell Land, instead of being the small island it has since proved, might be of vast, perhaps of continental, area, stretching across the polar space and connecting with Greenland. This was the theory entertained by Dr. Petermann, an eminent German geographer, the validity of which DeLong was to test by following the coast line of this supposed Arctic continent and making sledge expeditions along the ice foot. He proposed to reach Wrangell Land the first season, spend the winter there in exploration, and the next season fight his way as far north as possible.

"If the current takes me to the west," he wrote before starting, "you will hear of me through St. Petersburg; but if it takes me eastward and northward, there is no saying what points I may reach; but I hope to come out through Smith's or Jones' Sound." He further wrote, "It is our intention to attack the Polar regions by the way of Bering Straits, and if our efforts are not crowned with success, we shall have made an attempt in a new direction and examined a hitherto unknown country."

At a later date he thus expressed his intentions:

"If the season is favorable to an advance northward I shall make for Kellett (or Wrangell) Land, and follow along its east coast as far as we can go. If everything is all right with Nordenskiöld, and I hear of it, there will be no necessity for our going to St. Lawrence Bay at all. In this case I shall push through Bering Strait at once and make for the east side of Kellett Land, following it as far as possible, and getting to as high a latitude with the ship as we can before getting into winter quarters. If our progress is uninterrupted for some distance, I shall content myself with one landing, at first on the southeast point of Wrangell or Kellett Land, where we will build a cairn and leave a record of our progress to date. If our progress is interrupted, we shall no doubt make frequent landings on Kellett Land, and build several cairns; but, generally speaking, I shall endeavor to build cairns and leave records every twenty-five nautical miles of our track."

On the 8th of July, 1879, the "Jeannette," DeLong's ship, sailed from San Francisco for the north. It was heavily laden with supplies for a long voyage and had thirty-two persons aboard. A stop was made at St. Michael's, Alaska, where forty dogs were procured, also some Indians who were to act as drivers and hunters. Bering Strait was soon afterwards reached, and on the last day of August it was learned that the "Vega"' had passed the winter in Kolintschin Bay and had sailed thence to the south. In proof of this Swedish, Danish and Russian buttons were found in a hut on the shore, while papers were recovered written in Swedish and having on them the word "Stockholm." This confirmed the story of the natives, for it was sure that no other Swedish vessel had been in that locality, and DeLong, this part of his mission fulfilled, headed the "Jeannette" for Wrangell Land. As it proved, the delay of the "Jeannette" in this search prevented their reaching Wrangell Land before the ice-pack closed in upon them, a fact which led to disastrous results. On September 6th DeLong made in his journal the following entry:

"I am hoping and praying to get the ship into Herald Island (a small island east of Wrangell Land) to make winter quarters. As far as the eye can range is ice, and not only does it look as if it never had broken up, but it also looks as if it never would. Yesterday, I hoped that to-day would make an opening for us into the land; to-day I hope that to-morrow will do it. I suppose a gale of wind would break up the pack, but the pack might break us up. This morning shows some pools of thin ice and water, but as they are disconnected and we cannot jump the ship over obstructions; they are of no use yet to us."

On the 8th he again wrote: "I consider it an exceptional state of the ice that we are having just now, and count upon the September gales to break up the pack, and perhaps open leads to Herald Island. I want the ship to be in condition to move without delay. Besides, I am told that in the latter part of September and early part of October there is experienced in these latitudes quite an Indian summer, and I shall not begin to expect wintering in the pack until this Indian summer is given a chance to liberate us."

The liberation, as is too well known, was not to come. Yet DeLong at this very point did, in the judgment of the Naval Court of Inquiry, the best that could be effected. "Either he had to return to some port to the southward, and pass the winter there in idleness, thus sacrificing all chances of pushing his researches to the northward until the following summer, or else he must endeavor to force the vessel through to Wrangell Island, then erroneously supposed to be a large continent, to winter there, and prosecute his explorations by sledges. The chances of accomplishing this latter alternative were sufficiently good at the time to justify him in choosing it; and indeed, had he done otherwise, he might fairly have been thought wanting in the high qualities necessary for an explorer."

His efforts, however, proved in vain. Herald Island could not be reached, and till the end of the month the vessel drifted on in the pack, held between the floes as in a vise. It was the same through the month of October; land was seen from time to time, but it could not be reached and the imprisoned vessel and crew drifted helplessly on. The "Jeannette" was caught never to escape. Land seen on the 28th DeLong believed to be the north side of Wrangell Land, but he no longer thought it a continent, writing that "it was either one large island or an archipelago."

A night of great beauty followed the 28th. "The heavens were cloudless, the moon very nearly full and shining brightly, and every star twinkling; the air perfectly calm, and not a sound to break the spell. The ship and her surroundings made a perfect picture. Standing out in bold relief against the blue sky, every rope and spar with a thick coat of snow and frost,—she was simply a beautiful spectacle. The long lines of wire reaching to the tripod and observatory, round frosted lumps here and there where a dog lay asleep; sleds standing on end against the steam-cutter to make a foreground for the ship; surrounded with a bank (rail high) of snow and ice; and in every direction as far as the eye could reach, a confused, irregular ice-field—would have made a picture seldom seen."

During the first half of November the danger increased. Large cracks opened in the floe, huge masses of ice were thrown near the ship, and she was in imminent peril of being crushed. On the 24th she got afloat for the first time for weeks, and in a few days a gale set her adrift; but soon the pack closed in and she was frozen fast again.

Lieutenant Danenhower says: "It was dark, in the long night, and there was no chance of working the pack had it been good judgment to do so. We reckoned that she had drifted at least forty miles with the ice in her immediate vicinity. Previous to this time the ship had stood the pressure in the most remarkable manner. On one occasion, I stood on the deck-house above a sharp tongue of ice that pressed the port side just abaft the forechains, and in the wake of the immense truss that had been strengthened at Mare Island, by the urgent advice of Commodore William H. Shock. The fate of the "Jeannette" was then delicately balanced, and when I saw the immense tongue break and harmlessly underrun the ship I gave heartfelt thanks to Shock's good judgment. She would groan from stem to stern; the cabin-doors were often jammed so that we could not get out in case of an emergency, and the heavy truss was imbedded three-quarters of an inch into the ceiling. The safety of the ship at that time was due entirely to the truss."

Recording the experiences which have been just named, De Long says: "This steady strain on one's mind is fearful. Seemingly we are not secure for a moment, and yet we can take no measures for our security. A crisis may occur at any moment, and we can do nothing but be thankful in the morning that it has not come during the night, and at night that it has not come since morning. Living over a powder mill, waiting for an explosion, would be a similar mode of existence. . . . Sleeping with all my clothes on, and starting up anxiously at every snap or crack in the ice outside, or the ship's frame inside, most effectually prevents my getting a proper kind or amount of rest, and yet I do not see anything else in store for me for some time to come."

Christmas day was passed, drearily enough, and at midnight on the 31st all hands were called together on the quarter-deck to give three cheers for the New Year and for the "Jeannette." But the New Year brought no good fortune in its trail. On the 19th of January there was a loud noise, as if the ship's frame was cracking, the pressure of the groaning and grinding floes being immense. The ice moved to the eastward, piling up large masses under the ship's stern and breaking the fore-foot so that the ship leaked badly.

Water now began to flow in rapidly, standing three feet deep in the fore-hold, and it was necessary to set the deck pumps at work. This was accomplished, after some hours of severe labor, by the indomitable energy of Mr. Melville, the engineer. The steam pump made forty strokes a minute, pumping out 2,250 gallons to the hour, while by packing with plaster of Paris and ashes the inflow was largely decreased. The pumping went on constantly through the four following months, and as the decreasing coal stock excited apprehension, a windmill pump was arranged by the skill of Melville and his assistants which rendered valuable service.

Meanwhile the ship was drifting about in such a varying way that DeLong lost all faith in theories of Arctic currents, thinking that the movements of the water were the local creation of the varying winds. Lieutenant Danenhower later gave his evidence to the same effect:

"The important point of the drift," he said, "is the fact that the ship traversed an immense area of ocean, at times gyrating in almost perfect circles, her course and the observations of her officers proving that land does not exist in that area, and establishing many facts of value as regards the depth and character of the ocean bed and its temperatures, animal life, etc."

During the period in question they added to their food supply by killing several large bears and an immense walrus, so heavy that thirty of the dogs and four of the men were unable to drag the carcass over the rough ice until cut in two. Its weight was estimated at 2,800 pounds, a valuable prize for dog food.

As for the drifting ship, her gyrations continued, with the discouraging result that observations on the 30th of March placed her in almost the same position she had occupied four months before, a fact that did not well accord with the theory of polar drift.

At the end of May the log was headed "one hundred and ninety miles northwest of Herald Island." Thus after nine months of floating to and fro in the pack-ice she was less than two hundred miles distant from the spot where she had been locked in an icy prison in September, 1879.

Summer was upon her again and strong hopes were now entertained of breaking loose. A fall of rain on the first of June and a rise in the thermometer to 37 degrees gave vitality to their hopes, and they looked eagerly forward to a quick escape. Yet the summer proved inclement, fogs, snows and gales being almost the daily entry in the ship's log. From the crow's nest, at the end of the month, the ship was seen to occupy the center of an island of ice, which was surrounded by a lane of open water a mile distant. But the ice around her continued thick, and during the months of July and August her position remained unchanged, while every effort to liberate the screw proved unsuccessful. DeLong's journal for August 17th contained the following entry:

"Our glorious summer is passing away; it is painful beyond expression to go round the ice in the morning and see no change since the night before, and to look the last thing at night at the same thing you saw in the morning. . . . High as our temperature is (34 degrees), foggy weather a daily occurrence, yet here we are hard and fast, with ponds here and there two or three feet deep, with an occasional hole through to the sea. Does the ice never find an outlet? It has no regular set in any direction north, south, east or west, as far as I can judge, but slowly surges in obedience to wind pressure, and grinds back again to an equilibrium when the pressure ceases. Are there no tides in this ocean? . . . Full moon or new moon, last quarter or first quarter, the ice is as immovable as a rock. . . . It is hard to believe that an impenetrable barrier exists clear up to the Pole, and yet as far as we have gone, we have not seen one speck of land north of Herald Island."

"A Frozen Summer, June-August, 1880," such is the significant title of the ninth chapter in Mrs. DeLong's "Voyage of the 'Jeannette.'" On September 1st the ice gave way sufficiently to allow the ship to rest on an even keel, but she remained immovably locked in the floe, and after sawing through the ice under the forefoot with the hope of setting her afloat, the water came in so freely that this work had to be stopped. It was evident that the stern was badly broken, and the prospect of keeping the ship afloat if open water were reached became very questionable.

Before the end of September it was evident that the "Jeannette" could not be freed and preparations were made for spending a second winter in the ice. It was necessary to make ready to abandon the ship suddenly in case of any disaster, but they preferred keeping in its shelter to trusting themselves to the ice, DeLong writing that he could "conceive no greater forlorn hope than to attempt to reach Siberia over the ice with a winter's cold sapping one's life at every step." If he had had before him the experiences of later voyagers, a different fate might have awaited him.

There was no lack in the food supply, several more bears having been shot. And the crew continued in good health with the exception of Lieutenant Danenhower, who had been under the surgeon's care for nine months in consequence of a serious trouble with his eyes. Otherwise he was well, and scurvy, the bane of polar adventure, had not shown itself in any instance.

The situation was not without its alleviations. DeLong writes thus of the beauty of an Arctic night:

"October 16th. I have heretofore made several attempts to describe the beauty of these Arctic winter nights, but have found my powers too feeble to do the subject justice. They must be seen to be appreciated. It is so hard to make a descriptive picture of moon, stars, ice and ship, and unluckily photography cannot come into play in this temperature to supply a real picture. Imagine a moon nearly full, a cloudless sky, brilliant stars, a pure white waste of snow-covered ice, which seems firm and crisp under your feet, a ship standing out in bold relief, every rope and thread plainly visible, and enormously enlarged by accumulations of fluffy and down-like frost feathers; and you have a crude picture of the scene. But to fill in and properly understand the situation, one must experience the majestic and awful silence which generally prevails on these occasions, and causes one to feel how trifling and insignificant he is in comparison with such grand works in nature. The brightness is wonderful. The reflection of moonlight from bright ice-spots makes brilliant efforts, and should a stray piece of tin be near you, it seems to have the light of the dazzling gem. A window in the deck-house looks like a calcium light when the moonlight strikes it at the proper angle, and makes the feeble light from an oil-lamp within, seem ridiculous when the angle is changed. Standing one hundred yards away from the ship one has a scene of the grandest, wildest and most awful beauty."

And the Arctic prisoners succeeded in keeping up their spirits, celebrating Christmas and New Year with some of the home enthusiasm, and enjoying the amusements necessary for health in the polar solitudes. Yet with all they could do to make the time pass cheerily, the monotony was depressing and the coming of spring was hailed with gladness.

May came and with it a hopeful sign. On the 16th of May land was sighted, the first they had seen for fourteen long months. It was an island, a small one apparently, but as the commander wrote: "Fourteen months without anything to look at but ice and sky, and twenty months drifting in the pack, will make a little mass of volcanic rock like *our island* as pleasing to the eye as an oasis in the desert."

On the 24th more land was seen, while large lanes of water opened in the ice, and on the 31st Engineer Melville with several companions set out with a dog team to visit this second island, then fifteen or twenty miles away. They christened it Henrietta Island, the first seen having been named Jeannette Island. The journey proved a severe and dangerous one, but it was a welcome break in their monotonous life. DeLong wrote of it: "Thank God, we have at last landed upon a newly-discovered part of this earth, and a perilous journey (Melville's) has been accomplished without disaster. It was a great risk, but it has resulted in some advantage."

The discovery of these islands, in about latitude 77 degrees north, longitude 158 degrees east, was but a passing moment of cheer in their life, the prelude to disasters far greater than they had yet experienced, a momentary ringing up of the curtain upon a scene of life to let it descend upon a scene of death. The time was at hand for the ship to be released from her two winters of imprisonment and to enter upon an imprisonment more hopeless still, that of the ocean depths. Scarcely had the excursionists returned from the new-named islands when the ice around the ship began to break up into huge masses, leads opening and closing with force enough to grind her to powder had she not still remained in the center of a small island of ice. This protected her sides, but her bottom was continually hammered by ice cakes floating below.

On Sunday, June 12th, at midnight, the floe in which she lay split in a line with her keel, and she suddenly righted, the concussion sending all hands in alarm to the deck. As the day went on the ice began pressing upon her sides, and at 3.40 P. M. it was reported as having broken through into the starboard coal bunkers. She was keeled over more than 20 degrees to starboard. At four o'clock she lay perfectly quiet, but with her bows lifted high into the air, sufficiently to show the injury to her forefoot made on January 9, 1880. It was evident that she was hopelessly wounded and that no effort could keep her afloat when the ice left her free.

Mr. Melville went on the floe to take a final photograph of the hapless "Jeannette," and on his return heard the order given to prepare to leave the vessel by taking chronometers, rifles, ammunition and other articles to the floe. Lieutenant Chipp was sick in bed, but was notified to come on deck, and the captain carefully supervised the operations, quieting down all haste or consternation among the men and moving about the deck in a manner as unconcerned as if they were in the midst of an ordinary operation. The necessary articles, including the personal effects of officers and men, were safely landed on the ice, but there was difficulty in getting out a barrel of lime-juice, an article necessary to prevent scurvy on the proposed march. To rescue it seaman Starr waded into the forward store-room at the risk of his life.

By eleven o'clock that night the situation had grown perilous in the extreme. The ship's water-ways had been broken in and the iron-work around the smoke-stack buckled up and its rivets sheared off, so that it was supported only by the guys. The order was now given to leave the ship, three boats being lowered—the first and second cutters and the first whale-boat—while the ship's company of thirty-three landed on the floe, where they encamped in six tents.

Here they were far from safe. Shortly after the watch was set and the order given to turn in, and as they were getting into their sleeping bags, the ice cracked under Captain DeLong's tent, and it became necessary to move the stores and boats to another part of the floe. Erickson, one of the captain's party, would have gone into the water but for the fact that the Mackintosh blanket on the middle of which he was lying was held up by the weight of others who lay on its sides.

At 4 A. M., June 3d, a loud cry came from the watch: "There she goes; hurry up and look; the last sight you will have of the old 'Jeannette'!" The ice so far had held together sufficiently to prevent her sinking. It now opened and down went the gallant ship, with her colors flying at the masthead, the ice stripping her yards upwards as she sank. A visit on the next morning to the spot where she was last seen, showed nothing afloat but a cabin chair, a signal chest, and some smaller articles.

The watery grave of the poor "Jeannette" lay in latitude 77

degrees 14 minutes 57 seconds north, longitude 154 degrees 58 minutes 45 seconds east, in a depth of thirty-eight fathoms.

Hopeless was now the situation of Captain DeLong and his officers and crew, fearful the fate that faced them. At the dread distance of three hundred and fifty miles from the Siberian coast, with long and toilsome marches over rough hummocks before them, and a desolate coast to land upon, and with a subsequent journey of over fifteen hundred miles to Yakutsk, the nearest Russian city, the outlook was sadly discouraging. Some of the men also were sick, suffering from lead poisoning due to the tins of canned goods, while Lieutenant Chipp had just risen from a sick bed and Danenhower had long been an invalid from the condition of his eyes.

Yet with fortitude and hope they faced the situation before them. They had three good boats, had sledges, clothing and ammunition, and a large supply of provisions, including nearly five thousand pounds of American pemmican in canisters, about fifteen hundred pounds of other canned provisions and an equal weight of bread, while their guns could be depended upon to bring them an occasional supply of fresh meat.

On June 16th the order was given that a start should be made at 6 p. m. on the following day, a night march being decided on to avoid blindness from the intense glare of the sunlight on the ice. Dinner was to be at midnight, supper at 6 a. m., and sleep during the hours of day. The day's delay was made to give the sick a chance to recuperate. Before setting out DeLong prepared a record of the loss of the "Jeannette" and the southward start, sewing it up in a piece of black rubber enclosed within an empty boat breaker and trusting it to the waves. It was their purpose, he said, to seek to reach the New Siberian Islands and from them make their way by boats to the coast of Siberia.

Yet the work before them was slow and toilsome. Their boats and provision sledges had to be drawn over the hummocky ice, each officer and man being provided with a harness fashioned to go across the chest and one shoulder and attached to the sled by a lanyard. It was a terrible strain, through softened snow knee-deep and ice rough and full of fissures, over which the boats had to be jumped or ferried, while the sledges were dragged over large hummocks.

Taking the first cutter to a point marked by ice-pilot Dunbar, they had to return several times for the others, so that it took three hours to make the first mile and a half, and in the succeeding days a mile or mile and a half a day was the limit. The men had to go over the road thirteen times—seven times drawing loads and six times empty handed—so that twenty-six miles of travel were necessary to make an advance of two. And so many of them were invalided that twenty-one had to do the work for the whole.

This was bad enough, but worse was known to the captain and kept secret by him. Observations taken at the end of a week showed him that the ice drift had more than robbed them of the fruits of their labor. They had drifted twenty-seven miles to the northwest farther than they had marched to the south! Near the end of June the snow melted and traveling grew easier, their thirteen daily journeys over the same ground being reduced to seven. But the pools of thaw water kept their feet constantly wet.

On the 11th of July their eyes were gladdened by the sight of land in the distance, but the steady ice-drift made their progress so slow that it was the 28th before they were able to set foot on it. Its shore was so steep that a landing proved hard to make, yet by 7 P. M. everybody was on shore, the silk flag was unfurled and possession was taken in the name of the President of the United States. The island was christened Bennett Island, in honor of Mr. J. G. Bennett, the patron of the expedition.

The ship's company encamped here for several days, glad of a period of rest and a change of diet, sea-birds being numerous on the small volcanic island and easily caught. But a surfeit of bird meat brought on sickness and they soon had to go back to pemmican. They left the island on August 6th and on the 20th reached Thaddeus Island, one of the New Siberian group, among which they were imprisoned by the ice for nearly ten days.

Navigable water was found at the end of this time and the party distributed themselves among the three boats, Captain De-Long taking command of the first cutter, Lieutenant Chipp of the second, and Engineer Melville of the whale boat. The second cutter was a bad sea-boat and had little room for provisions, the first cutter having the greatest capacity of the three and being an excellent sea-boat. The whale boat was also well built and strong.

Onward with hope the castaways now went, knowing that the coast of Asia was not far distant. On the 10th of September it came in sight, about twenty miles away, and on the 11th a landing was made on the small Semenovski Island and hunting parties sent out. An old hut was found there and footprints made by a white man's boot—a very encouraging indication.

But their good fortune was quickly at an end. Leaving the island on the 12th, they soon found themselves in the clasp of a gale, which grew so severe as to set all hands in the whale-boat to pumping and baling out water. The boats kept close together until about 7 P. M., when the gale increased in force and they were separated, never to meet again. Their destiny differed. The first cutter reached land, but only to leave its party to the sad fate of death by cold and starvation. The second cutter vanished, leaving no record of its fate, it having probably swamped in the stormy sea. Those in the whale-boat alone escaped death, reaching shore by the successful use of a drag or sea-anchor and keeping the boat afloat until land was reached by incessant baling.

We shall end here this chapter of the adventures of the hapless ship's company of the "Jeannette," leaving the record of the adventures of those who reached shore for the following chapter, in which the story of the escape of Melville and his boat's crew will be described, with his subsequent search for the fated DeLong and his companions.

CHAPTER XXV

Melville Finds the Remains of the DeLong Party

WE have followed the unfortunate ship's company of the "Jeannette" from their start at San Francisco to the time they were frozen in the pack ice off Herald Island; thence through their long and wearisome drift in this sea of ice for two winters and one summer until the crushed and hopelessly wounded "Jeannette" sank in the Arctic sea; followed by their brave and disheartening journey over the ice to the far-off Siberian coast. Off this coast, as has been stated, the three boats containing the hapless wanderers parted in a gale and never came together again. Of their inmates, only those of the whale-boat, commanded by Engineer Melville, survived the perils of sea and shore, death claiming as victims, with two exceptions, all those on the other boats. It is our purpose here, therefore, to follow the fortunes of Melville and his comrades and tell the story of their return to safety and of their subsequent search through the Siberian wilds for their lost companions.

George Wallace Melville bears a record worthy of some brief mention before we describe this crucial portion of his career. Born in New York City in 1841, he was educated in the Brooklyn Polytechnic School and entered the naval service of the United States in 1861 as third assistant engineer. As such he took an active part in the work of the navy during the Civil War, frequently volunteering for dangerous and desperate service. He became chief engineer in 1881, and as such aided greatly in the building up of the new United States Navy, in which he became engineer-in-chief in 1887. He was given the rank of rear admiral in 1899.

Mr. Melville strongly interested himself in polar research and has taken part in three separate expeditions to the Arctic seas. Of these the most important is that in connection with the "Jeannette" enterprise, which he joined as engineer. His heroic conduct in this unlucky voyage was fully recognized in this country and was rewarded by Congress in a special act in 1890, by which he was advanced one grade in the service. It is the detail of this part of his career with which we are here concerned.

Melville's comrades in the whale-boat cruise were nine in number, comprising Lieutenant Danenhower and eight of the crew, among the latter being the Chinese steward and one of the Alaska Indians, named Aneguin. The whale-boat was twenty-five feet four inches long and strongly put together. Like the cutters, it was clinker-built, copper-fastened, and with inside lining. And like the others, its draught was deep, this being due to the heavy oak keel pieces put upon the boats to strengthen them for the wearing work of hauling over the ice.

The severe gale which had separated the boats off the Siberian coast gave exhausting labor to Engineer Melville's crew, who were kept busy pumping or baling out the water which poured in from the combing waves. The pocket prismatic compass they had was here of no avail, and they had to steer by the sun or moon, in which work the professional skill of Lieutenant Danenhower, still on the sick list, was of great service. He carried the chronometer and chart and could lay the proper course of the boat very closely by the bearings of the sun. By this means he was fortunate in bringing the wave-tossed craft safely to land at one of the eastern mouths of the Lena River on September 15th, three days after they had left Semenovski Island.

Favoring fortune had brought them ashore in an inhabited region, the river was still open, and a Tungus Indian whom they met and engaged as pilot took them in safety up its course for the following eleven days, at the end of which a village was reached.

Here they found several Russian exiles, who took great interest in the arrival of the castaways, the coming of whom was a welcome break in the dreary monotony of their existence. One of them, Kopelloff by name, served them a good turn by teaching Lieutenant Danenhower a number of Russian phrases, likely to prove very useful in their later intercourse with the Siberian officials.

The young ice was now forming in the river, rendering further progress by the boat unavailable, and they were detained until it should be thick enough for sledding. But tidings of their arrival were sent ahead, another of the exiles, Koosmah Gernymahoff, with the chief of the village, going forward to Bulem, the most northern Russian station in Siberia, to acquaint the authorities there with the fact.

On the 17th of October Danenhower set out with a dog team on a search for the two other boats, but the surface conditions proved unfavorable for the work, and he was unable to proceed far in any direction. The young ice which covered the broad-channel lower river was too thick to permit the passage of boats and too weak to bear sledges, and ignorance of the language of the natives prevented any useful intercourse, so that they were unable to learn the resources of the vicinity as to reindeer or dog teams.

The messengers who had been sent south to Bulem returned on the 29th with the report that they had met natives with deer sleds, these bringing with them two rescued seamen of De Long's party, Nindemann and Noros, whom they were taking to Bulem. They brought also a note given them by these sailors in which it was stated that the captain's party had reached land, but were starving and in need of immediate assistance.

This news, communicated by Koosmah to Engineer Melville, roused him to the most earnest endeavors, active efforts being at once made to reach and rescue Captain DeLong's party. Danenhower was left in charge of the whale-boat crew with orders to conduct them as soon as possible to Bulem, while Melville set out with a native guide and a dog team in search of the castaways. On November 1st he received from the commandant at Bulem a good supply of bread, deer-meat and tea, and also a paper written by the two rescued seamen and addressed to the American Minister at St. Petersburg. These were forwarded by the lieutenant to Melville, and he quickly followed his messenger, overtaking Melville at the first deer station.

We may finish here the story of Lieutenant Danenhower, who was now directed by Melville to proceed to Yakutsk, twelve hundred miles away. This place he reached on December 17th, and received there three despatches from the Secretary of the Navy. In return he advised the Secretary of the state of affairs and requested permission to search for Lieutenant Chipp's party. This permission was granted, but was afterwards revoked on account of the condition of his health, and he was directed to return to the United States. He reached there in February, 1882.

Before proceeding with the account of Melville's search, the story of Nindemann and Noros, as related to him by them, must be told. On the 9th of October DeLong had sent them out in advance, saying to Nindemann: "I think you have to go only twelve miles to a settlement called Kumarksurka, and you and Noros can find it in three days, or, at the longest, four. Do the best you can; if you find assistance come back as quick as possible; and if you do not, you are as well off as we are."

Starting off with a cheer from their comrades and a copy of the captain's chart, the two men pushed forward with all possible speed. On the first day they dined on a ptarmigan, killed by them; on the second their food consisted of a bootsole soaked in water and burned to a crust, with tea made from the Arctic willow. The remaining bootsole served them on the 11th, but on the 12th they were more fortunate, for, while gathering some drift-wood, Noros found beneath it two fishes and Nindemann caught a lemming. During the next eight days they had little to eat beyond portions of a pair of sealskin pants, soaked and burned to a crust, but on the 20th they found in a hut fishes enough to keep them alive for several days. But their diet had induced dysentery, from which they were growing very weak.

While resting in an abandoned hut on the 22d they had the good fortune, looking through a crack in the hut, to see a native, to whom they lost no time in making their presence known. The native, whose sympathy was aroused by their condition, brought some others that evening, and putting the exhausted and half-starved men on their deer sleds, they drove with them to their tents, which were reached at midnight. Here they were given food. Their rescuers proceeded with them the next day until they fortunately met a Russian, to whom they succeeded in making known their situation and the fact that they wished to be taken to Bulem. They reached the place on the 29th.

On the 3d of November the two men heard the door of their hut in Bulem opened and to their glad ears came a familiar voice speaking American words. It was Engineer Melville, who exclaimed, "Noros, are you alive?"

The meeting was a joyful one, and the rescued seamen eagerly told their story, Melville making a chart of the route described by them and marking on it the location of the huts they had found, as a guide in his intended immediate search for DeLong and his party. The privations of the two men, however, gave him gloomy anticipations as to the fate of those they had left, the seamen themselves being very sick from exhaustion and the dysentery caused by their eating decayed fish. The very great probability was that those left behind had perished.

On November 5th Melville set out on his search of the Lena delta, taking two dog teams, two natives and a ten days' supply of food, and following the route he had charted from the account of the two seamen. He had no difficulty in finding the route, some of the huts described by them being reached, while from several native hunters he received some of the records left by Captain DeLong. These records indicated where he should look for the log-books, chronometers and other articles that had been abandoned, and these he quickly found in a cache erected on the ocean shore, its location marked by a tall flagstaff.

For three weeks afterwards the search was diligently continued, not without much suffering on the part of the searching party, the weather being very severe, but no traces of the lost men were found. The natives knew nothing of them, and it became certain that they had ceased to live, in view of the fact that their food supply had been practically exhausted when the two seamen left them. Further search, with the hope of finding any of them alive, was plainly useless. That they had all perished was beyond doubt, and Melville sadly returned, having done all that it was possible to do in the wintry conditions then prevailing.

He brought the relics he had found to Bulem, and from there proceeded with them to Yakutsk, the nearest place where the supplies needed and the requisite orders from the Russian authorities to its subordinates could be procured. The logs and papers were placed in charge of Lieutenant Danenhower, to be taken to the United States, and under orders telegraphed from the Navy Department Melville prepared for a search for the remains of his late companions.

Setting out again in the midwinter season, he proceeded north, and, accompanied by seamen Nindemann and Bartlett, the latter having picked up some knowledge of Russian speech, he resumed his search. It was March 16th when he first came upon the track of his lost companions. On that date he found the hut in which they had slept before crossing the river. On the 23d he reached the location of their sad death.

The resting place of the unfortunate voyagers was indicated by four poles lashed together and projecting from the deep snow drift, while the muzzle of a Remington rifle stood eight inches above the snow, its strap hitched over the poles. A few hundred yards further on he came upon the remains so long sought, the dead bodies of Captain DeLong and Surgeon Ambler. With them was that of Ah Sam, the Chinese cook. By the side of DeLong lay his notebook with the last feebly indicated words he had been able to write, while under the poles were found the books and records which he had carried with him to his sad end. The bodies of the others were also found, with the exception of those of Erickson, one of the seamen, and Alexai, an Indian, which were sought for in vain. The journal afterwards showed that they had died and been buried in the river.

The natives who accompanied Melville could with difficulty be induced to aid in getting the bodies out of the snow. It was necessary to pry them up with sticks of wood, as they were frozen to the ground. One arm of Captain DeLong had been seen lifted above the snow, but his body was covered.

After digging in the snow and finding a few small objects and taking from the bodies all articles found upon them—except a small bronze crucifix found upon the person of Mr. Collins, which Melvilled ordered to be buried with him—the preparations for return were made. All the bodies were carried over the mountain to the southward of Mat-Vai, where a tomb was dug on a high bluff, and the bodies reverently interred. They were laid side by side in regular order, as their names had been written on the vertical shaft of a cross erected over the tomb.

The tomb was covered with seven-inch plank and a pyramid of large stones built over it, arrangements being subsequently made to have it covered with a deep layer of earth to prevent the possibility of the sun thawing the bodies below. Above this pyramid rose the cross, twenty-two feet high and with an arm twelve feet in length. Standing, as the cairn and cross did, on an eminence, they formed conspicuous objects, which could be seen at a distance of twenty miles. On the cross was the following inscription:

"In memory of twelve of the officers and men of the Arctic steamer "Jeannette," who died of starvation in the Lena Delta, October, 1881—Lieutenant G. W. DeLong, Dr. J. M. Ambler, J. J. Collins, W. Lee, A. Görtz, A. Dressler, H. H. Erickson, G. W. Boyd, N. Iverson, H. H. Kaack, Alexai, Ah Sam."

Melville made a subsequent search for the party of the second cutter, commanded by Lieutenant Chipp, but not a trace of them could be discovered, though the search was very thorough. And though the first cutter was found, frozen in the ice and badly stove, there was no trace of Chipp's boat. At a later date other searching parties were sent out, but with like negative result, and it became evident that the second cutter had gone down in the gale, with all on board. It may further be stated that the bodies of DeLong and his men were subsequently taken from their lonely tomb in the Siberian wilds and brought to the United States, where they were reinterred with reverent and appropriate ceremonies.

This story of the fate of the "Jeannette" and of Captain DeLong and most of his officers and crew can justly be completed only by suitable extracts from the captain's journal, in which the details of their sufferings and wanderings are given. Our extracts begin with their losing sight of the whale-boat, as follows:

"At 9 P. M. September 12th, lost sight of whale-boat ahead; at 10 P.M. lost sight of second cutter astern; wind freshening to a gale. Step of mast carried away; lowered sail and rode to sea anchor; very heavy sea, and hard squalls. Barometer falling rapidly.

"13th, very heavy northeast gale . . . At 8 P. M. set a jury sail made of a sled cover, and kept the boat away to the westward before the sea;—17th, grounded at a few hundred yards, landed at 8 P. M.; dark and snow storm, but Collins had a good fire going; at 10.20 had landed everything, except boat oars, mast, sled, and alcohol breakers;—18th, had fires going all the time to dry our clothes, we must look our situation in the face, and prepare to walk to a settlement.

"September 19th, ordered preparations to be made for leaving this place, and as a beginning, all sleeping bags are to be left behind. Left in instrument box a record, portions of which read thus:

"LENA DELTA, September 19, 1881.

"Landed here on the evening of the 17th, and will proceed this afternoon to try and reach, with God's help, a settlement, the nearest of which I believe is ninety-five miles distant. We are all well, have four days' provisions, arms and ammunition, and are carrying with us only ship's books and papers, with blankets, tents, and some medicines, therefore our chances of getting through seem good. . . . At 2.45 went ahead, and at 4.30 stopped and camped. Loads too heavy—men used up—Lee groaning and complaining, Erickson, Boyd, and Sam, hobbling. Three rests of fifteen minutes each of no use. Road bad. Breaking through thin crust; occasionally up to the knees. Sent Nindemann back with Alexai and Dressler to deposit log-books. . . . Every one of us seems to have lost all feeling in his toes, and some of us even half way up the feet. That terrible week in the boat has done us great injury; opened our last can of pemmican, and so cut it that it must suffice for four days' food, then we are at the end of our provisions and must eat the dog (the last of the forty) unless Providence sends something in our way. When the dog is eaten ——? I was much impressed and derive great encouragement from an accident of last Sunday. Our Bible got soaking wet, and I had to read the Epistle and Gospel from my prayer-book. According to my rough calculation it must have been the fifteenth Sunday after Trinity, and the Gospel contained some promises which seemed peculiarly adapted to our condition. (The passage is in Matthew v. 24.)

"September 21st, at 3.30, came to a bend in the river making south, and to our surprise two huts, one seemingly new. At 9 P. M. a knock outside the hut was heard and Alexai said, 'Captain, we have got two reindeer,' and in he came bearing a hind quarter of meat. September 24th, commenced preparations for departure from the hut at seven o'clock. . . . At 10 P. M. made a rough bed of a few logs! wrapped our blankets around us and sought a sleep that did not come; 27th, made tea at daylight, and at 5.05 had our breakfast—four-fourteenths of a pound of pemmican. . . . At 9.45 five men arrived in camp, bringing a fine buck. Saved again!! September 30th, one hundred and tenth day from leaving the ship, Erickson is no better, and it is a foregone conclusion that he must lose four of the toes of his right foot, and one of his left. The doctor commenced slicing away the flesh after breakfast, fortunately without pain to the patient, for the forward part of the foot is dead: but it was a heart-rending sight to me, the cutting away of bones and flesh of a man whom I hoped to return sound and whole to his friends. October 1st, the doctor resumed the cutting of poor Erickson's toes this morning, only one toe left now. And where are we? I think at the beginning of the Lena River at last. My chart is simply useless. Left a record in the hut that we are proceeding to cross to the west side to reach some settlement on the Lena River.

"October 3d, nothing remains but the dog. I therefore ordered him killed and dressed by Iverson, and soon after a kind of stew made of such parts as could not be carried, of which everybody, except the doctor and myself, eagerly partook, to us it was a nauseating mess. . . . Erickson soon became delirious, and his talking was a horrible accompaniment to the wretchedness of our surroundings. During the night got his gloves off; his hands were frozen. At 8 A. M. got Erickson (quite unconscious) and lashed on the sled under the cover of a hut, made a fire and got warm. . . . Half a pound of dog was fried for each one, and a cup of tea given, and that constituted our day's food. At 8.45 A. M., our messmate, Erickson, departed this life. October 6th, as to burying him, I cannot dig a grave, the ground is frozen, and I have nothing to dig with. There is nothing to do but to bury him in the river. Sewed him up in the flaps of the tent, and covered him with my flag. Got tea ready, and with one-half ounce alcohol, we will try to make out to bury him. But we are all so weak that I do not see how we are going to move.

"At 12.40 P. M. read the burial service, and carried our departed shipmate's body down to the river, where, a hole having been cut in the ice, he was buried; three volleys from our two Remingtons being fired over him as a funeral honor.

"A board was prepared with this cut on it:

In Memory,
H. H. ERICKSON,
October 6, 1881.
U. S. S. Jeannette.

And this will be stuck in the river bank abreast his grave. His clothing was divided up among his messmates. Iverson has his Bible and a lock of his hair. Kaack has a lock of his hair. . . . Supper, 5 P. M., half pound of dog meat and tea. October 9th, sent Nindemann and Noros ahead for relief; they carry their blankets, one rifle, forty pounds ammunition, two ounces alcohol. . . . Under way again at 10.30, had for dinner one ounce of alcohol; Alexai shot three ptarmigan. Find canoe; lay our heads on it and go to sleep.

"10th, eat deer-skin scraps. . . . Ahead again till eleven. At three halted, used up. Crawled into a hole on the bank. Nothing for supper, except a spoonful of glycerine. 17th, Alexai died, covered him with ensign, and laid him in a crib. 21st, one hundred and thirty-first day, Kaack was found dead at midnight. Too weak to carry the bodies out on the ice; the doctor, Collins, and I carried them around the corner out of sight. Then my eye closed up. Sunday, October 23d, one hundred and thirty-third day—everybody pretty weak—slept or rested all day, managed to get enough wood in before dark. Read part of divine service. Suffering in our feet. No foot gear.

"Monday, October 24th, one hundred and thirty-fourth day. A hard night.

"Tuesday, October 25th, one hundred and thirty-fifth day. No record.

"Wednesday, October 26th, one hundred and thirty-sixth day. No record.

"Thursday, October 27th, one hundred and thirty-seventh day. Iverson broke down.

"Friday, October 28th, one hundred and thirty-eighth day. Iverson died during early morning.

"Saturday, October 29th, one hundred and thirty-ninth day. Dressler died during the night.

"Sunday, October 30th, one hundred and fortieth day. Boyd and Görtz died during the night. Mr. Collins dying."

With this entry of death the doleful record closes. The captain, surgeon, and the last one of the crew must have quickly followed their comrades to the grave. Thus ends this saddest of all Arctic journals.

CHAPTER XXVI.

Greely's Arctic Winter of Starvation

AMONG the many disasters to which Arctic expeditions have been exposed, there have been three instances of extraordinary misfortune and suffering, three cases in which starvation and death claimed victims in numbers, the three most terrible visitations of calamity in all Arctic history. With two of these, the frightful misfortunes of the Franklin and the De Long expeditions, we have dealt. The third remains to be described, that of the heroic Greely, in its way one of the worst of the three, since its record of starvation extended through a whole winter, to close with death for most of the party in the end and a sensational rescue of the few survivors when they had gone through all the horrors of death. The narration of this record of disaster and suffering is given in the present chapter.

The origin of the Greely expedition was the following: An international conference had decided on a plan to establish a chain of stations around the border of the Arctic Circle for the purpose of exploring, of collecting specimens in natural history, and of taking meteorological, magnetic and other observations for the benefit of science. Of these stations the United States established two, one in Alaska and one in Grinnell Land. It is the latter with which we are concerned.

Lieutenant Adolphus W. Greely, of the United States Army, was chosen as the leader of the Grinnell Land expedition, which consisted of four officers and twenty-one men, and left New York in the early summer of 1881 in the "Proteus," a steamer chartered for the purpose. Congress had voted $25,000 for the expenses of the expedition, which was to proceed to Lady Franklin Bay, on the shores of Grinnell Land, and from there send out exploring parties, by dog sledge and steam launch, as far north as possible. A ship was to be sent each year with supplies, and if these should fail to reach him, Greely was instructed to begin a retreat not later than September 1, 1883.

The expedition left St. John's, Newfoundland, on the 7th of July, stops being made at various points on the Greenland coast to obtain dogs and complete the preparations for a long sojourn in a land of desolation. At Upernavik a number of dogs were obtained, and two Eskimos, Jens and Frederick, were taken on board as drivers. The season was unusually mild, and they were able to make excellent progress through the unimpeded water. On the way they stopped at Cary Islands and examined the records left there by Sir George Nares in 1875, and which had been examined once before by Sir Allen Young, in 1876. The sea was full of white wales, narwhals, and grampus. The latter has the reputation of being a voracious feeder, one authority stating that a dead grampus had been found, choked by a seal he had attempted to swallow, although, when he was opened, his stomach was found to contain no fewer than thirteen porpoises and fourteen seals.

On August 4th the "Proteus," for the first time during the voyage, was stopped by the ice. Being built specially for navigating the ice-covered seas, she was very powerful in the bows, which were further embellished by a strong iron prow. Thus she was able to force her way through the ice which would have been impassable to a lighter craft. Her method, when she was faced by moderately thin ice which was yet thick enough to stop her ordinary progress, was to steam astern for a couple of hundred yards and then rush full speed at the ice. The strength of the iron prow and the force of her powerful engines drove her into the floe, but the operation was one that required great care. As she approached the floe, the crew, running from one side of the deck to the other, caused her to

LEADERS OF FAMOUS ARCTIC EXPEDITIONS

Captain George E. Tyson Dr. Isaac H. Haye
Captain Charles F. Hall William Scoresby

FAMOUS EARLY ARCTIC ADVENTURERS

Baron Wrangel. Henry Hudson
Sir John Ross Sir Edward Parry

[From DeLong's "Voyage of the Jeannette," Houghton-Mifflin Co.]

THE "JEANNETTE" CRUSHED AND SUNK BY THE ICE

After drifting frozen in an ice floe for twenty-two months the "Jeannette," Captain George W. DeLong, commander, was crushed and sunk by the ice on June 13, 1881. The ship had been frozen in the ice. Suddenly a lead opened alongside; the pack closed in again nipping the ship, and then, while the stern was held fast, raising the bow of the vessel, the pressure was renewed with tremendous force, the ship cracking all over. The spar-deck buckled up; the starboard side caved in. All the boat's provisions were quickly hauled away on the ice to some distance, and the crew watched their ship slip through the ice to the bottom before starting on their march to what proved to be one of the most frightful and memorable marches of Arctic history.

RESCUE OF THE REMNANT OF HALL'S EXPEDITION

THE FUNERAL OF CAPTAIN CHARLES F. HALL IN THE ARCTIC REGIONS

roll as she struck, the engines being reversed directly her prow penetrated the ice, so as to prevent her wedging herself in. This exciting operation was repeated several times when she met the floe in Lady Franklin Bay, and only by its means was she able to ram her way through and reach the destination of the expedition.

A site for landing was selected on the north of Discovery Bay, where the "Discovery," of the Nares expedition, had wintered in 1876. Proceeding a little distance from the spot where the "Discovery" winter quarters had been erected, a suitable situation was marked out for "Fort Conger," which was to form the base of the operations pending the time when the relief ship was due to take the expedition home again.

During the following week every one was hard at work erecting the frame house which was to form their home during the next two years, unloading stores and other articles belonging to the expedition, arranging the heavy casks and cases of imperishable provisions near the house, and exploring and hunting over the surrounding country.

On August 18th, all the stores belonging to the party were landed from the "Proteus," and that vessel got up steam and bade farewell. The men of the party worked with such a will that they had their house built, the recording instruments erected in proper localities, the provisions stacked, and everything in order sufficiently early to permit them to carry out some surveys while the weather was yet mild enough for sledge traveling. Attention was also given to obtaining as much game as possible, and by the time that the temperature was cold enough to warrant their going into winter quarters, they had obtained for their larder twenty-six musk oxen and ten ducks, besides hare, seal, and ptarmigan, in all 6,000 pounds of fresh meat for their own food, and an equal amount for the dogs.

In the middle of September they were visited by a large pack of wolves. These were first discovered prowling over the ice on the harbor in front of the encampment, and, fearing the loss of some of the dogs, as well as provisions, a hunting party went out to shoot them. But the wolves were too cunning, keeping out of range until the men were tired out. They were frequently fired at, but none fell, although this might not have been due to bad marksmanship. The Arctic wolves, as was discovered later, are perhaps the most tenacious of life of any of the northern animals.

One was seen, a day or so later, within a hundred yards of the house. It was immediately fired at, and rolled over with a bullet through the body; but before the marksman could get over to where it lay, the apparently dead creature scrambled to its feet and made off, bleeding profusely. The trail left by the blood was distinctly visible on the snow, although the wolf itself, being covered with pure white fur, was quite invisible. For over an hour the trail was followed, and when at last the dead body was found, it lay practically bloodless, having struggled on while there was a drop of blood in its veins.

In view of the difficulty of shooting them, the men resolved to poison them. But here, again, the wolves were not to be caught. The first time that poisoned meat was put out it was left untouched. Some good meat was added, and at once disappeared, though the pieces containing poison were still left alone. The poisoned baits were then taken up, and only good meat put down, the wolves always taking it until, their confidence being gained, a few poisoned baits were mixed with the others. The experiment succeeded so well that when the baits were next visited four wolves and one fox were found dead. The others, evidently alarmed, made off and did not again return.

Winter passed away in the drear and monotonous way that winter in the Arctic does and with the coming of spring the work of exploration began. The growing power of the sun as the months passed on is described in striking terms in the records of the expedition. An exploring party led by Greely himself found decidedly wintry conditions late in April. A large river was reached covered with thick ice and leading to an enormous glacier five miles wide and 175 feet high, completely blocking up the valley. Everywhere the ground was covered with ice and snow, with no signs of life and no sound other than an occasional gurgle of running water under the river ice.

When, early in July, the valley was again visited an extraordinary difference in conditions was observed. They might have doubted the existence of what they had seen before but for the sparkling glacier. The river now flowed along, glittering in the bright sunlight, between banks covered with flowering plants. Bright yellow poppies gleamed all over the verdure-clad slopes, with sturdy heath blooms, daisies, and other blossoms mingling, and over them were flitting innumerable white and yellow butterflies. Bumble-bees droned, and flies, as well as the familiar daddy-long-legs, were everywhere present, and also their arch-enemies, the spiders. Ptarmigan, their white plumage somewhat speckled with dark feathers, plovers, and birds of smaller size, were seen on the wing; while over the verdant sides of the valley and along the banks of the river, large herds of musk oxen were browsing, with calves following the cows. The sky was brilliantly blue and almost free from clouds. In the face of so much that was beautiful and full of life, it was difficult to realize that a few months later the valley would again be desolate and deserted, owning once more the supremacy of the icy grip of the frost and snow.

Sledging parties were sent northward, one of them reaching the spot where the "Alert," of the Nares expedition, had passed the winter of 1875. It had been intended to go farther, but the ice proved impassable, and they were obliged to return after reaching a latitude of 82 degrees 56 minutes. Another party, under Lieutenant Lockwood, second in command of the expedition, had better fortune.

Setting out in the early spring, a course was laid across the frozen strait towards Greenland, the party consisting of thirteen men and five sledges. Advantage was taken of the experience of the members of the Nares expedition, and in laying the plans for this trip provision was made for a series of food deposits and relief parties along the route. This is the method that has generally been since pursued and has proved of great advantage.

Some of these food caches had been made before the party set out, while the last was placed when in sight of Cape Britannia, the northwest extremity of Greenland. At this point the party divided, three continuing the journey while the others were sent back. The three consisted of Lieutenant Lockwood, Sergeant Brainard, and the Eskimo Frederick, one of the dog teams being taken with them. This team saved them an enormous amount of labor by dragging the sledge for them, but even then they found the traveling exceedingly difficult. Their sleeping-bags were damp, and consequently they were always compelled to rest in great discomfort. As they approached Cape Brittania the route became more difficult, and their best march was sixteen miles in ten hours. Beyond the cape an island was reached, to which the name of the leader, Lieutenant Lockwood, was given, and the extreme point of which furnished their "farthest north." They had succeeded in reaching the most northerly point that had yet been discovered, not only on the coast of Greenland, but also in the Arctic regions. The latitude recorded was 83 degrees 24 minutes north, being 4 minutes beyond that of the Nares expedition, and thus the honor which for three hundred years had been the boast of the British, that of having attained the nearest point to the North Pole reached by man, was wrested from the British Lion by its cousin, the American Eagle.

The coast line still showed beyond, and to the most distant point the name of Cape Washington was given. Then the small band turned back, having succeeded in reaching a few miles nearer the pole than Commander Markham, of the Nares party, whose journey, however, was over the frozen sea, whereas the other was along the Greenland and Peary Land coast.

The summer of 1882 came and passed without an appearance of the relief ship promised by the government. One had been sent out with a load of supplies, the "Neptune," under William Beebe, but ice and storms prevented its reaching the Fort Conger station and it returned, after leaving supplies of provisions at several points on the route. Its failure to appear caused no alarm, as food was still plentiful, but the coming on of another winter was, as usual, one of the unwelcome events of Arctic life. Comfort, however, was prepared for by carrying the snow, which in the preceding winter had been piled against the sides of the house, over the roof, a precaution which added considerably to the warmth of the interior.

When winter passed and spring came again—the spring of 1883—Lieutenant Lockwood and Sergeant Brainard made an exploration of the interior of Grinnell Land, covering 437 miles in one month's sledging, and adding much to the knowledge of that large island, hitherto unexplored in its interior. Summer at length arrived and anxiety about the promised relief ship arose. If it should again fail to come it would not be safe to remain another winter at Fort Conger, and preparations for a retreat in their boats was made. These consisted of a steam launch twenty-seven feet long, an ice-boat which had been abandoned by Lieutenant Beaumont, of the Nares party, in 1876, and two whale-boats. A depot of forty days' full rations was placed at Cape Baird and another of twenty days' rations at Cape Collinson, as soon as the ice was open enough to allow the launch to proceed. Then when it had returned and all the survey parties were in, a decision was come to that if no steamer arrived by July 31st the retreat would be commenced.

July passed and August arrived, but there were no signs of the approach of any relief steamer. They could not risk a longer wait, and on August 9th, with the boats loaded with the records of the work done and as much food as could be stored in them, the party bade farewell to Fort Conger and started on what was destined to be a tragic journey. The lateness of the season made navigation extremely difficult for such small craft, and they were frequently impeded by ice which would have offered no obstacle to a big steamer. The adventurers had scarcely got out of sight of the house where they had passed the two long dark winters before they were so beset with loose ice that progress was almost impossible. Then new ice formed round them, and they were hard and fast. The fact that they only carried a limited supply of fuel made their position more serious, and when, on August 18th, a temporary breaking in the floes enabled them to move forward, there was a general rejoicing. But it was soon checked on discovering that they were forced inside of a huge mass of ice over fifty feet high and extending right up to the solid floe. It was impossible to turn back and fight through the drifting ice behind them, and the only hope of escape seemed to be to steam on in case there might be a channel through the floe ahead.

As they passed along the great wall of ice they were amazed at seeing a crevice run into it. Arriving opposite to it, they found that it was a cleavage which went right through the mass, and they turned into it. The enormous berg had grounded and had split asunder, leaving a passage a hundred yards long and barely twelve feet wide, the sides of which were sheer fifty feet high on either hand. Such a formation was unique, even in the Arctic regions, and the steaming through it was an adventure without a parallel.

The passage led into fairly open water, and they pushed on until Rawlings Bay was reached. Here the floes closed in on them so quickly that the boats were caught before anything could be done to save them. Hasty efforts were made to lift the lighter boats on the ice and to unload the food supplies from the others. The nip had not been severe enough to injure the boats seriously, but the ice held them captive, and the journey south was now restricted to the slow drift of the floe. By August 26th they had traveled 300 miles from Fort Conger and were within fifty miles of Cape Sabine, a headland where Sir George Nares had left a store of provisions in

1876. The present hope of the wanderers was to reach this point before the winter night set in.

Meanwhile, what had become of the government relief expedition? Two ships had been sent out, the "Proteus" and the "Yantic," well laden with supplies, but they had experienced much difficulty with the ice. The "Proteus" finally succeeded in reaching Cape Sabine, but for some reason unexplained it left there without depositing a supply of provisions, despite the fact that Greely would be almost certain to reach that point if forced to retreat from Lady Franklin Bay. Whatever the cause of this remissness, it proved fatal to most of the retreating party and nearly to all.

The "Proteus" left Cape Sabine after a short stay, but ice was soon again encountered, and on the 23d of July the vessel was surrounded by heavy floes. In the afternoon the ice closed in upon her in immense masses, crushing in the ship's sides. In the early evening a change in the tide opened the ice and set her free, but the "Proteus" was incurably injured and at once went down. Recognizing their peril, the crew had taken to the ship's boats, with what provisions they could save. A month was spent in reaching Upernavik, where the "Yantic" soon arrived and took them on board. This was a small and weak craft and at once sailed south with the rescued crew of the "Proteus," Greely and his party being abandoned to their fate.

When the "Yantic" reached St. John's it was the 13th of September, too late to make a further effort to reach the ice-bound explorers. The best that could be done was to prepare a relief expedition for the following summer, this consisting of the "Thetis" and the "Bear," two ships purchased for the purpose and put under the command of Commander W. S. Schley, of the American Navy. The British government also donated for the same purpose the "Alert," one of the two ships of the Nares expedition. These set out in April and May, 1884, reaching Littleton Island near the end of June.

Meanwhile Greely and his companions were passing through a terrible experience. We left them in the drift ice near the end of August. When the 1st of September came they were still beset, with barely fifty days' rations. They were in doubt what to do, whether to remain in the boats with the chance of drifting nearer to Cape Sabine, lying now about twenty miles away, or to push over the rough ice for the shore. Their commander was in favor of the former alternative, and they kept in the boats until September 10th, when it became evident that they would have to make a sledge journey to the shore.

Unfortunately, severe weather now came upon them and their journey became a struggle. They had tried to drag two of the boats with them, but one had to be abandoned, and on September 28th they were still struggling over the rough ice with the other. Only by the most persistent exertion were they able to reach the shore with their stores, this being at a point some distance from Cape Sabine.

They had now traveled 500 miles since they left Fort Conger, and not only were the men considerably exhausted by their recent struggle, but winter was setting in very rapidly with constant and heavy storms. It was therefore decided to form a camp where they were, while the snow had not frozen too hard for them to get some stones for a shelter. They had been compelled, on their journey over the ice, to abandon everything in the way of covering save their sleeping-bags, and unless they built a hut of some description the rigor of the winter would inevitably be fatal to all.

Such stones as could be found were collected and built into a low wall forming a square of about sixteen feet. The stones were difficult to obtain, and the wall could only be made three feet high. An opening was left in one of the sides of the square and a passageway constructed, so that the entrance to the interior did not open directly on to the frozen exterior. Across the top of the walls the boat they had dragged with them over the ice was laid keel uppermost, the oars being laid under it so as to maintain it in position, the open spaces between the sides of the boat and the walls being covered with such canvas as they had. Around the stone walls and over the top, snow was piled, and their living house was complete. It sheltered them from the wind and from the extreme bitterness of the cold, but beyond that nothing could be claimed for it. Every one had to enter it on hands and knees, and, once inside, no one could stand up, while the taller men of the party were only able to sit up in the middle of the hut where the boat made the roof slightly higher.

The men arranged their sleeping-bags against the walls with the feet towards the middle of the floor, and when they had crept in through the narrow entrance, they groped their way into the bags. Then, half lying and half sitting, with their shoulders against the stones behind them, they made themselves as comfortable as they could during the long period of darkness. They divided themselves into messes for the purpose of feeding, and two cooks prepared the food, an operation that was always difficult and unpleasant. It had, of necessity, to be carried on inside the hut, and when the two men were kneeling in a cramped-up position over the make-shift for a stove in the middle of the floor, there was no room for any one else to stretch his legs. Every one had to huddle up as closely as possible, and as all the smoke from the stove had to find its way out of the hut the best way it could, the atmosphere during cooking time was far from refreshing. The heat from the stove also thawed the ground immediately under it and the snow on the canvas over it, so that the cooking of every meal meant a wetting and a choking for the cooks.

The hut finished, a party set out for Cape Sabine in search of the provisions supposed to be stored there. They returned on October 9th, having found a record of the sinking of the "Proteus" just off the cape and the starting of its crew in boats to the south in search of the "Yantic." Some provisions were found and their whale-boat, which had drifted ashore near the cape, was recovered. At a later date it served them for firewood when their other fuel was exhausted.

The news brought was a serious blow to the wanderers. They knew now that no help could reach them till the following spring or summer. And it was found that the party from the "Proteus" had used much of the stores upon which the Greely party had depended. When they obtained what was left, part of the bread was found to be a mass of green slimy mildew. Yet so hungry were the members of the band sent to convey the stores from Cape Sabine to the hut that when the green moldy stuff was thrown out by the officer in charge, the men seized and devoured it despite all he could do to persuade them from such a course.

The question of the strictest economy in the management of the food supplies was now a matter of life or death, and very seriously the leaders debated it. On October 26th the sun sank beneath the horizon, and in the ensuing darkness, which lasted for 110 days, there would be no chance of obtaining any game. A few blue foxes had been killed since the camp was formed, and half the number were set aside for subsequent consumption, those consumed at once being devoured to the bones, every part being put into the stew.

Meagre as the rations were, it was necessary to reduce them still further if the food was to last until the spring. By a further, reduction it was calculated that the party could exist until March 1st, when the available supplies would amount to ten days' rations. But no relief could possibly reach them until a couple of months later than that, and how were they to live after March 10th, when the last crumb of their supplies had been consumed.

There was only one course open for them, and that was explained by the leader. On November 1st the allowance for each man would be fourteen ounces, given out every twenty-four hours, and on March 1st, as soon as there was light, they would take their remaining ten days' supply and set out across the frozen straits in the forlorn hope of reaching an outlying camp of Etah Eskimo on the Greenland coast.

The terrible prospect of such a scheme to men situated as they were can scarcely be imagined. For four months they would have to face that rigid diet, suffering the pangs of starvation constantly, almost entirely in the dark, and always huddled up in the sleeping-bags against the walls of their low-roofed hut. Yet they accepted the scheme without a murmur.

Seldom have men shown themselves so absolutely courageous, for at the best it was merely slow starvation so as to be able to make an almost hopeless dash for freedom and food in four months' time. The suffering during those four months was terrible. Men, as soon as they got hold of their day's rations, were tempted to devour them at once, and so still for a time the ceaseless gnawing of hunger; but to do so meant that in an hour's time the pain would be back again with no means of staying it until twenty-three hours had passed. Calmly and bravely they faced the ordeal, dividing their scanty store into regular meals, and when, by an accident one of them upset his can, spilling his few mouthfuls of tea on the ground, the others contributed from their share so that he should not go entirely without. Nothing could exceed the touching fidelity which characterized their bearing, one to the other, during this period of unexampled suffering.

At Cape Isabella, a stock of 140 pounds of meat was known to have been left by Sir George Nares, and a party of four set out in the hopes of securing it. For a week before they started they were allowed an extra ration in order to strengthen them for the trial of a journey in the dark over rough ice and with the temperature at 34 degrees below zero. The extra ration consisted of two ounces a day.

For five days they battled their way through the darkness against a heavy wind laden with snow, and at last found the food. Piling it on their sledge, they turned back home, and for fourteen hours labored with it, consuming only a little warm tea during that time, for they had no means of heating more. One of the four was badly bitten by the frost, and was soon so stricken that he could not even stagger along. A piercing wind was blowing, and to save their comrade's life, the others abandoned the sledge and tried to support him. Soon two of them became exhausted, and the remaining one, Sergeant Rice, pushed on alone to the camp in order to bring help. For sixteen hours he fought his way over the twenty-five miles that lay between him and the hut. When he arrived there his lips were too frozen for him to be able to speak at once.

Weary and weak as the whole party was, eight of the strongest at once started out to the rescue. When they reached the spot, they found the men lying under the sleeping-bag, which was frozen so hard over them that it had to be cut open before they could be got out. Then they resumed their way to the camp, which they reached after forty-four hours' absence, in which time they had covered forty miles.

The frost-bitten man, Elison, was almost dead, his face, feet, and hands being absolutely frozen, but so determined were they all to survive as long as possible that he was tended with all the care they could command. He was kept alive in spite of his sufferings, which, during the first week after his rescue, were so severe that he daily called on his comrades to end his misery.

Meanwhile the memory of the abandoned sledge laden with meat was constantly in the minds of the starving men, whose hunger was now so great that in the darkness after the lamp was put out—economy compelled them to use it only for cooking—men crept to the stove and devoured any rancid fat left in the lamp. The success of the journey across the ice on March 1st was what they looked forward to, and with the arrival of that date they believed their sufferings would be over.

On January 18th the first one of the party to die passed away, really of starvation, although the men, to keep the ugly word away from their minds, accepted the doctor's statement that it was of an effusion of water at the heart that the man had died.

Sergeant Rice, accompanied by the Eskimo Jens, now made a plucky effort to reach Littleton Island, where an outlying camp of Eskimo might be found; but Jens could not stand the journey, and, five days after starting, they returned. Every one was now impressed with the necessity of husbanding their energies for the great effort to be made on the first day of March, and as February slowly passed away, the emaciated creatures grew enthusiastic as they sought to cheer one another up by detailing the tremendous feasts they would have when they returned to civilization. At length the 1st of March dawned, and the brave hearts, which had kept up so long against starvation and despair, shrank before the terrible blow they received. The ice had broken, and open water rolled where they had planned to cross on the ice. Nothing was said, for the courage of the men was only equaled by their consideration for one another, but the effect of the great disappointment sank deep into the minds of many.

The food remaining was eked out through the month with the aid of some blue foxes and a ptarmigan, which were eaten to the bones, and April found them with only a few days even of the starvation rations remaining. Several of the men were so weak that they could barely turn over in their sleeping-bags. The Eskimo Frederick was found dead in his bag, and another of the little party followed the next day. Then Sergeants Rice and Fredericks insisted on making an effort to reach the meat abandoned when Elison was frost-bitten. It is difficult to understand why the effort had not been made before; but many errors of judgment are conspicuous after a campaign which are not so apparent in the moment of struggle.

Now that it was made it failed, through the freezing wind penetrating the starved bodies of the two men. Rice, who throughout the terrible ordeal of their captivity had never spared himself, was the first to feel it. A strong wind was blowing, bringing down heavy snow squalls. Suddenly Rice began to talk wildly and then staggered. Fredericks grasped him by the arm and tried to keep him up, but the cold and starvation had too tight a hold upon their victim. He vainly endeavored to pull himself together, but only for a moment; then he sank down on the snow, babbling about the feast he was going to enjoy.

His comrade tried to restore him by giving him some of the stimulants they had with them, and did not hesitate to strip off his own fur coat to lay upon him, sitting the while, holding his hands, and exposed to all the biting fury of the Arctic wind, in his shirt sleeves. But everything was useless; Rice was too worn out and too weak to fight further, and died as he faintly talked of the food he fancied he was eating.

The shock to Fredericks was almost overwhelming, for he was miles away from the camp, chilled to the bone, and with only a little coffee and spirits of ammonia to revive his own drooping vitality. Yet he would not leave his dead comrade until he had reverently laid him in a shallow resting-place in the snow, though it almost cost him his life to pay this last tribute.

When he at last managed to reach the camp with his sad tidings he was almost gone, and the news he brought plunged every one into the lowest depths of sorrow, for Rice had always been one of the bravest and best of the party. Those who were able to do so, attended Fredericks and revived him.

To those who were weakest the end of Rice was a fatal blow, and the next day or so saw three or four pass away, one of whom was the intrepid Lockwood. A very few more days and all would have gone but for a gleam of good fortune. A young bear was killed, and the 400 pounds of meat obtained from it was the salvation of the survivors.

Several seals were seen in the straits and a few walrus, and all who could still handle a gun were daily striving to obtain fresh supplies for the larder. Eskimo Jens, who hunted assiduously, succeeded in killing a small seal; but in a chase after another his kayak was injured in the ice and he was drowned.

After his death only misfortune attended the hunting, and, failing to replenish their stock of game, they were reduced to such a terrible plight that they had only the thick skin of the seal on which to subsist. Even this fare was carefully divided and measured, so that life might be maintained as long as possible in case a relief vessel came. One day it was found that somebody was stealing. All the party was assembled, but no one would admit the theft. It was decided that the thief should be shot, if discovered. One man, being suspected, was watched. He was caught and executed.

A fortnight later, the last few square inches of the seal's skin was gone, and the men, now little more than living skeletons, lay in their sleeping-bags looking at one another with hollow eyes, wondering, perhaps, who would be the last to go, when a steamer's whistle sounded over the straits.

It was the "Bear," of the expedition commanded by Winfield S. Schley, with whom came George W. Melville, late of the "Jeannette," for engineer. They had left St. John's on May 12th, and pushed north through the ice of Baffin's Bay and Smith Sound, sending a party ashore on June 22d to search for signs of the missing explorers. On Brevoort Island a letter written by Lieutenant Lockwood was found, giving their location and stating that their food supply was nearly gone. As this was dated eight months before, the dismayed officers lost hope of finding any of them alive. Before sunset of the next day Greely's camp was discovered. Greely was seen on his knees, muttering the prayer for the dying over one of his comrades. He looked up, dazed, bewildered, unable to read the meaning of what met his eyes.

"Greely, is this you?" asked Colwell, one of the party of rescue, as he took the emaciated hand.

"Yes," answered Greely, in a scarcely audible voice. "Yes—

seven of us left—here we are—dying—like men. Did what I came to do—beat the record."

Seven there were. Death had taken its toll of all the rest. A day or two more and not a man would have been alive. The careful use of restoratives saved the survivors from death, and Adolphus Greely still dwells among us, a man of high honor among his countrymen.

CHAPTER XXVII

Nansen's Memorable Voyage in the "Fram"

THE cruise of the "Jeannette," of which we have elsewhere spoken, had one unexpected result. It was the inspiring cause of one of the most memorable of polar voyages. This arose from the fact that relics from the lost ship were found in 1884 frozen in floating ice off the coast of Greenland. This fact led to much discussion among geographers and the belief arose that a strong and steady current flowed along the course over which the "Jeannette" had drifted and along that afterwards taken by the floating relics. This belief was not sustained by the experience of DeLong and Melville, of the "Jeannette," but it was held by many others.

Here was something worth proving. A theory is of no value until it is demonstrated. As the belief that the world is round was not proved until the adventurer Columbus undertook to demonstrate it, so the theory in question remained an academic opinion until a man was found willing to test its accuracy. The man appeared in the hardy Norwegian, Fridtjof Nansen.

Nansen was by no means a beginner in Arctic work. He had already made a daring journey across Greenland, he being the first man to cross its frozen interior. This was done in 1888, when he started in at a point on the east coat of Southern Greenland and emerged at a point on the west coast, having traversed the great central ice-field of the island.

As a student of Arctic phenomena, he became firmly convinced of the existence of a drift current across the polar region and grew eager to demonstrate it. It seemed to him that if a vessel were built of sufficient strength to withstand the pressure of the winter ice, and provisioned for a sufficiently long period, there was every chance of its drifting along the entire course of the current, perhaps to within a measurable distance of the pole, and certainly well within that region which had hitherto been unexplored. The area affected by the current would have to be entered as near the outside edge as possible, so as to participate in the full sweep of its curve, and, in order to avoid the terrible crushing pressure of the winter ice, the vessel would have to be so built as to cause it to be lifted by the ice, when the pressure became too severe, and thus rest on the top.

His views, when published, did not meet the support he hoped for. Some of the veterans in polar research argued that it was impossible to build a ship that could withstand the terrible pressure of the northern ice-fields. But Nansen was not discouraged and he found a shipbuilder willing to build such a vessel as he desired, while the Norwegian government voted a sum of over $55,000 towards the expense. Other support was obtained, and the building of the "Fram'" ("Forward"), as the proposed vessel was called, was at once begun.

She was built of wood and of tremendous strength, her beams and sides being of great thickness, while on the outside of the hull not a single angle was allowed to remain. Every projection was carefully rounded off and smoothed, so that there should not be as much as half an inch protruding and capable of affording the ice a holding place. Even the keel was sacrificed to the general idea of avoiding possible holding places for the ice. The lines of the ship were necessarily different from those of the ordinary vessel. Her sides bulged outwards and the stern and stem sloped away, so that whichever way the ice exerted the pressure, the "Fram" would present a smooth surface to it, inclined in such a way that the tendency of the ice would be to get under it and lift the vessel up. This did not improve her qualities as a sea boat, and the way in which she afterwards pitched, plunged, and rolled, whenever she came into a moving sea, tried the sea-faring capacities of every one on board.

She was fitted with engines and a screw, and was rigged as a three-masted fore-and-aft schooner. Electric light was laid on all over her, the power being generated by a windmill when the engine was not working. Every available crevice was utilized for the storing of coals and provisions.

By the middle of June, 1893, the thirteen men who formed the expedition had succeeded in finding a place for everything, though not without some difficulty, for the quantity of the stores which had to be packed was enormous. By a delay in delivery, just as they were congratulating themselves that everything was stowed away, a shipment of dog biscuits arrived. The ship was full already, but the biscuits had to be stored somewhere, so one of the men wriggled right up into the bows, and between the beams and the ribs he packed away the troublesome late arrivals. Everything was at last on board and stored, and on June 24, 1893, the "Fram" started on her memorable journey.

It is not here proposed to give in full detail the story of this memorable voyage, but to confine ourselves to its more salient points, avoiding the repetition of many features of Arctic life given in former chapters. It must suffice then to say that the route lay up the coast of Norway and from North Cape through the Arctic Ocean until Chabarowa, in the Yugor Straits, was reached on July 29th. Here thirty-four Siberian sledge dogs were obtained, the boilers cleaned and other preparations made, and the "Fram" put to sea again, reaching the Kara Sea on August 4th.

Here ice and adverse winds caused delay, and the men occupied themselves in hunting, game being plentiful. The result was the gathering of an abundant supply of fresh meat, consisting of reindeer, seal and duck. A bear was also shot and a large quantity of walrus meat obtained, though in shooting the latter Nansen lost his favorite rifle, which dropped overboard and could not be recovered.

Cape Chelyuskin, the most northerly point of Asia, was reached on September 10th. They were now nearing the region in which it was thought the current turned northward, and after steaming a week further east the course was changed and the "Fram" headed northward. As long as there was open water ahead the energetic crew kept working their vessel so as to get her as high up as possible into the area affected by the current; but when they had passed the line which marks the limit of the floes, they soon found that further navigation was impossible. The "Fram" was soon fast in the ice and, with winter upon them, the crew made themselves and the ship as comfortable as they could.

The builder of the "Fram" had given attention not alone to the exterior of the vessel; he had also made the internal arrangements as complete as possible for the comfort of the explorers during the prolonged period they were to remain in the ice. Now that they were in the pack, they realized how well their comfort had been considered. For the matter of that, they had always found their quarters cosy, even when the "Fram" displayed her capabilities of rolling and tossing. The main cabin, in which they lived, was always warm, and the passage-ways leading from it to the outside were so skilfully arranged that those on board did not experience the distressing moisture which was so troublesome on the "Alert" and "Discovery." The electric light as a substitute for lamps was also an admirable innovation, for the interior of the cabin was always brightly lit without the air becoming heavy, as would have been the case with exposed lamps. A great deal of thought had also been given to ventilation, with the result that the cabins were never close.

Over the deck a large screen was erected, tent shape, and above it there was reared the windmill which drove the electric motor and generated the electricity for the lights. As the ship was to remain in the ice until it drifted out again, everything was made snug for a long stay. On the ice alongside various observatories were erected and scientific instruments placed to make complete records, and later, a row of comfortable kennels was made for the accommodation of the dogs.

These animals at first had been somewhat troublesome. They were so savage that it was necessary to keep them all tied up on deck, and during the voyage along the coast they were frequently wet and miserable, and incessantly howling. Once, rope muzzles were made, and when each dog was fitted they were allowed loose; but an Arctic dog requires something stronger than a rope to keep its jaws closed when let loose among a lot of other Arctic dogs. The result of the experiment was not a success, except from a dog-fight point of view; when at length the struggling, snarling, snapping pack were separated, they were tied up again to the deck until the ship was fast in the ice. By that time they were somewhat reconciled to one another; when they had been allowed to have a scamper or two, with plenty of opportunity to find out who were the kings and who were not, they settled down into a big happy family.

It was in latitude 78 degrees 50 minutes north that the "Fram" was first frozen in, and her course was watched with much anxiety to see in what direction she would drift. To their dismay the course was toward the southeast, and they feared that they had missed the northward drift looked for. A few days later, however, the course turned north and all were happy again.

As for the ice, it steadily increased in thickness and there was constant movement in the mass, the pressure causing it to heave upward and pile into great rugged hummocks. The "Fram" had vastly more resisting power than the "Jeannette;" but could any work of man's hands withstand those jagged masses, which lifted before the pressure behind them until they stood forty and fifty feet high? Sometimes they were forced up so high that they overbalanced and crashed down upon the lower masses with the roar and rattle of thunder.

It was during their second winter in the ice, on January 4 and

5, 1895, that the "Fram" was subjected to the greatest pressure experienced. The ice was now thirty feet in thickness, a fact which was ascertained by boring, and immense masses of it came gliding and pressing with tremendous force against the port side of the ship. It piled itself up above the gunwales and high up the rigging, threatening, if not to crush the imprisoned ship, at least to bury her beneath its mass. Scarcely a man aboard believed she could live through this terrific assault.

All the boats were taken out on to the ice and filled with provisions; the dogs were put in kennels also on the ice where they would be free to escape if necessary, and every one was constantly on the alert for the first sign of the "nip." All hands were ready to leave ship and no one was allowed to sleep unless fully clothed.

At last it came. They were all at meals when the increased uproar of the moving ice told them that the movement was nearing the vessel. Then, for the first time, they heard the ominous sounds of creaking timber. The "Fram" was being "nipped."

Every one hurried out of the cabin to see to the boats and the dogs and the stores. For the moment it seemed that nothing could save her, and that the stupendous weight of the gliding wall would soon grind her solid timbers into splinters. There was a sound of rending; a groaning crash; the "Fram" shivered till the breathless watchers thought they saw her spars tremble. Then, with a mighty wrench, she broke from the bonds that held her, and slowly rose from her nest in the ice, slipping upwards and away from the crushing force. A cheer burst from the lips of every one as she moved, for it meant not only the realization of the hopes and ideals of those concerned in her construction and the complete vindication of their faith in her, but also the guarantee that the explorers were safely and securely housed, whatever might transpire.

When the movement in the ice had subsided, it was found that the "Fram" had slipped out of harm's way in a marvelous manner. So firmly had she been frozen in that the spot from whence she had been driven contained a complete mold of her shape, every seam and mark being reproduced in the ice. This proved that the test had not only been a severe one, but conclusive as well, since the vessel had really been frozen so solid into a mass of ice as to be a part of the mass. Her escape was an overwhelming disproof of the adverse theories expressed against her, and an entire victory for Nansen.

The existence of this constant movement of the Arctic ice, which is everywhere found, calls for some explanation. It might be imagined that the vast field of thick ice in the polar seas, extending for some two thousand miles between the northern shores of America, Asia and Europe, would rest in one vast, moveless plain, resisting storms and all other disrupting forces. And so it might but for a constant movement in the water itself, that of the tides, with their daily rise and fall.

The ebb tide, in the shallower waters, leaves wide tracts of ice, previously afloat, straining on the ground, cracking so as to form enormous fissures and weakening the surface resistance. On the other hand, the flood tide wells and presses against the overlying barrier of ice, lifting it up until it cracks and opens, the pressure underneath raising the separated masses upon their neighbors, which in turn resist with all their weight and grind back upon the masses beyond. With the turn of the tide the forced-up masses gravitate down again, tumbling, crashing, bounding and rebounding one upon the other.

It is a battle between the energy and the resistance of nature, and usually energy wins along the line of least resistance. Here, when once a point gives way, the accumulated force concentrates. The "point" may be an area of ice a hundred miles square and fifty feet thick, and this tremendous mass, moved by the immeasurable force of the water pressure beneath it, grinds upon its surroundings and upon itself. Huge masses are pushed upon the surface of the pack, crushing, grinding, and splintering as they go, their weight causing the under ice to bend and crack, and so add to the confusion of the struggle. Mass meets mass in a test of strength, and, failing to climb over one another, crush together, closer and higher, until there is a diminution of the pressure from below and they surge back, shattering themselves in the commotion and yet binding themselves into a single unit strong enough to resist the next onslaught of the tidal energy.

This is the kind of conflict that was going on around and beneath the "Fram," the sturdy vessel braving every nip by slipping upwards from the pressure; the crew, confident in her capabilities, living in merry good-humor in her cabin. What the confusion of the ice was like may be gathered from the opinion of those who saw it when the return of the sun enabled them to do so, and also relieved the pressure. "Imagine a stormy sea, all broken waves and flying billows, suddenly frozen solid into ice, and you have some idea, on a small scale, of the piled-up hummocks on the pack."

During their second winter in the ice Nansen determined on a bold experiment. Believing that the "Fram" would soon reach the highest latitude to which the current was likely to carry her, the drift then tending westward through the sea north of Franz Josef Land and towards Spitzbergen, he conceived the plan of leaving the ship under the efficient care of Captain Sverdrup and taking to the ice himself in a sledge journey farther north. He proposed to take but one companion, with provisions sufficient for a dash northward and a return to land at the Franz Josef islands, as it was hopeless to expect to reach the "Fram" again. For companion he selected Lieutenant Hjalmar Johansen, of the Norwegian navy, who had joined the expedition as stoker and had subsequently become Nansen's meteorological assistant.

A start was made on February 26, 1895, with six sledges and provisions for men and dogs for several months. But they found themselves too heavily equipped and were obliged to return to the "Fram" again, to reduce the weight of their convoy. The next start was made on March 14th, this time with three sledges, two kayaks and twenty-eight dogs, the quantity of provisions being considerably reduced. The "Fram" had now reached the eighty-fourth parallel of latitude, the highest northing so far made, and the route of the adventurers lay along the one hundredth parallel of east longitude.

For the first few days traveling was slow, heavy, and laborious, the ice being rough and rugged. But it grew smoother as they advanced, and always, at the end of each period of travel when they formed their camp, the Pole was nearer. On March 22d they reached 85 degrees 10 minutes north latitude. The ice they were journeying over now was not only rough but was constantly moving, the drift being against them. But still they pushed northward and on the 29th reached the latitude of 85 degrees 30 minutes.

Progress now became slow, the southward drift growing stronger while the ice grew very rough. The labor was severe, the ice being piled up in ridges and hummocks, over which the heavy sledges had to be drawn. In these cases the dogs were of no assistance, they patiently resting until the obstacle was passed, and then drawing the sledges over a short stretch of level ice until a new ridge was reached. On April 7th they were at 86 degrees 14 minutes north latitude, the highest northern point attained by man up to that time, and only about two hundred miles from the Pole.

It was unsafe to venture farther. If they should meet equal obstacles on their return they would have great difficulty in reaching the nearest land. This was Franz Josef Land, lying to the southwest of where they were. They had unluckily left their midwinter clothing on the ship, thinking that it would not be needed in the spring weather, but in a temperature ranging from 49 to 4 degrees below zero they felt the want of it severely, the perspiration of the body converting their woolen clothing every day into an icy coat of mail, which had to be thawed out by the bodily heat at night when they crept into their sleeping-bags. As a result they would shiver for an hour and a half before they felt at all comfortable.

The food for the dogs daily grew scarcer, and they were anxious to get on as far as possible before it was finished. When, therefore, they came upon a stretch of fairly smooth ice, they made the most of it, and only when they and their dogs were dead tired did they stop. It was their custom to always wind up their watches when they crept into their sleeping-bags, but on one occasion, after they had kept afoot for thirty-six hours at a stretch, when they took them from under their heavy clothing they discovered that both had stopped. In their anxiety to push forward they had forgotten to wind them up and the springs had run down. There was nothing to do but guess at what the time ought to be, and it became difficult to estimate their position.

Their next trouble was the failure of the dog food. When the first dog died they kept him, for unless they fell in with a bear and killed it, the bodies of the weaker dogs was all that they could give the stronger ones to keep them alive.

They expected to reach land by the end of April, but April and May passed, and still only the rugged ice was in view. One by one the dogs had to be sacrificed until only two remained. The weight of the sledges was also very considerably reduced by this time. The third sledge had been abandoned, and now each man, assisted by one dog, dragged a sledge on which rested his kayak, his *ski*, firearms, and other necessaries, as well as a moiety of the remaining stores.

June came in and still no land was in sight, but the character of the ice was changing, though not very much for the better. It was not so rugged and hummocky, but it was frequently intersected by channels mostly full of floating pieces. It was useless taking to the kayaks to cross them, and often impossible to go round, so they adopted the method of jumping from piece to piece, and drawing their sledges after them. On June 22d they came upon a seal, which they succeeded in shooting and securing, a fact which was so memorable that they rested for a day, giving the dogs an ample supply of the meat. But the rest was scarcely idleness, for they were visited by three bears, all of which also fell under bullets. They now had abundance of food, both for themselves and the dogs, to last a few weeks if they did not come in sight of land. Two days later, however, they saw it, lying ahead of them, and they pushed on till a wide, open channel stopped them.

It was evident that the kayaks would have to be used in getting across, and they were taken from the sledges and examined. The result of the rough handling they had undergone in the journey over the ice was manifest in many a crack and hole in the skin-covering, but how to repair them was a question which taxed even the ingenuity and enterprise of the two intrepid Norsemen. They had enough skins to make patches, and twine with which to stitch them on. It was the making of some waterproof coating for the stitch-holes that puzzled them. They possessed a little train-oil, and by fixing up an arrangement over their spirit cooking stove, they obtained a little soot, which was mixed with the oil and used as paint. It was not a very artistic compound, but it was the best they could make, and it kept the water out. Then the kayaks were carefully fastened together by the *ski,* and upon them was laid the sledges and the stores.

When everything had been made fast, the explorers prepared to launch them. Johansen was behind Nansen, and stooping down, when he heard something moving at his back. Thinking it was one of the dogs, he did not look round, and the next thing he knew was that something hit him beside the head, so that, in his own words, "he saw fireworks." He fell forward, and immediately felt a heavy body upon him. He managed to turn partly round, and saw just above his face the head of a huge bear.

Nansen, ignorant of what had occurred, was bending over his end of the kayak, when he heard Johansen exclaim, "Get a gun." Glancing round, he saw his comrade lying under the bear, gripping its throat with both hands. With everything securely tied to the kayaks, it was no easy matter to extricate the weapon, and while he was seeking to get it he heard Johansen quietly say, "You will have to hurry if you don't want to be too late."

The two dogs, all that were left of the twenty-eight, were standing snarling at the bear, and as Johansen spoke the one which always traveled with him approached nearer. The bear, having his attention for the moment distracted, stepped off Johansen, who immediately wriggled away and scrambled to his feet. Just as the bear turned on to the dog, Nansen got the gun out of its case. Swinging round, he found the bear close beside him, and he pulled the first trigger he touched. It fired the barrel loaded with shot, but so near was the bear that the charge entered behind the ear without having time to scatter, and brought him down dead between Nansen and Johansen.

The former was terribly afraid that his companion had been seriously injured, but the only mark the bear had left was a streak across the face where the dirt had been scraped away. As they had not washed their faces since they left the "Fram," there was a thick covering of dirt on them, and the bear's claw, as it passed over Johansen's face, had scraped this away, leaving the white skin to show through.

Though land had been seen in June, they had a long struggle over the ice and water before it came in sight again. Through the remainder of the month and the whole of July they battled with the broken ice and difficult channels, making little progress with great toil, and it was August 6th before land was once more seen, what they saw being one of a group of four islands. They continued, however, upon the ice, following it downward until August 26th, when they were in about latitude 81 degrees 13 minutes north and longitude 55½ degrees east. They had been hoping to reach Spitzbergen, where a ship might have been found, but the season was now so far advanced that they felt it necessary to winter where they were. In crossing the open water to the shore they found it impossible to bring their two dogs across in the kayaks and could not abandon the poor brutes on the ice. They therefore mercifully shot them to save them from the painful death of starvation.

As soon as they came to a place which recommended itself to them, they ran ashore and landed the kayaks and stores. The place was merely a barren, rocky coast, sheltered somewhat by the high ground behind, but without a trace of vegetation. On the beach one piece of drift-wood was found. In addition, there were plenty of small boulders, but such material was scarcely sufficient for the building of a hut in which to pass the dreary, cold, dark winter.

They overhauled their stores, and found they possessed two guns, some cartridges, a small hatchet, and two knives. With the hatchet, after considerable labor, they cut through the piece of driftwood, and rejoiced in the possession of a suitable ridge-pole for the center of the roof. Stones were collected and built into a low wall, within which all their property, except the guns, kayaks, and knives, was placed. Then, with the unstored articles, they set out along the coast and the floating ice to seek the wherewithal to complete the house.

Walrus was what they especially needed, for the hide would afford a covering for the roof, the blubber would furnish fuel for the stove, and the meat would be useful as food. They spied two lying at the edge of a piece of ice and, approaching with the utmost caution, succeeded in shooting both. Their weight, however, as they fell over, caused them to slide from the ice, and they were in the water before the men could reach them. They secured the carcases, so as to prevent them from either sinking or drifting away, and essayed to haul them up on the ice again so as to remove the hides and blubber. But the combined strength of the two men was insufficient to pull one of the huge carcases up on to the ice again, and they were compelled to strip the skin and blubber off as the walrus lay in the water. This necessitated lying upon the floating carcases, and by the time the operation was completed, their already travel-stained clothing was rendered still more uncomfortable by being saturated with blood and fat.

Returning to the camp with their walrus hides and blubber, they explored the ridge lying behind the spot, and were fortunate in finding some moss, which they carefully gathered and carried away to assist in the building of the hut. The walls they had made of the stones allowed for an internal space of about ten feet long by not quite six feet wide. The crevices between the stones they filled in with moss and gravel, and then stretching the walrus hides over the ridge-pole, they weighted them down with more stones. Over all of it they heaped snow and ice and, in order to avoid suffocation by the smoke of their blubber cooking stove, they constructed an ice-chimney. This, however, did not always carry off the smoke, while it frequently thawed at the base, and made the interior very draughty. Their guns and other articles and stores they placed inside the hut, leaving the kayaks outside; and when everything was stored conveniently, they built a wall before the door as a screen to break the wind, and hung a curtain of skins across the doorway. The floor of the hut was composed of stones which no ingenuity of theirs could render smooth or even, and upon these their sleeping-bag, the fur of which was almost worn entirely away, was stretched.

The hut finished, a hunting expedition for winter provisions was in place. Bears proved to be sufficiently abundant, and they soon succeeded in getting meat enough to last them through the winter and well into the following summer. They had put this in cold storage on the top of the hut, and though during the winter they often heard foxes gnawing at the frozen mass over their heads, they let them feed in peace, knowing that they had more than they needed for themselves. Bear's meat, fried at night and boiled in the morning, was about all the food they had, and during the long winter night, when the temperature within the hut was often near the freezing point, they would frequently lie in their sleeping-bag, side by side, twenty-two hours out of the twenty-four.

A picturesque glimpse is given by Nansen of their life in his diary entry made on December 24, 1895, when the temperature inside the hut was 11 degrees below zero.

"And this is Christmas Eve; cold and blowy out of doors, and cold and draughty indoors. How desolate it is here! We have never had such a Christmas before. The bells are now ringing in the Christmas festival at home; I can hear the sound of them swinging out through the air from the church towers. How beautiful it sounds! Now the candles are being lit on the Christmas trees, and flocks of children are let in and dance round in exuberant glee. Must have a Christmas party for children when I get home. We, too, are keeping the festival in our little way. Johansen has turned his shirt, and has put the outer one inside. I have done the same, and have changed my drawers as well, and put on the others which I had wrung out in warm water. And then I have washed myself in a quarter of a cup of warm water, using the discarded drawers as sponge and towel. I feel like a new being; my clothes do not stick to my body as much as they did. Then for supper we had fish 'gratin,' made of potted fish and Indian meal, with train-oil for butter—fried or boiled both equally dry—and as sweets we had bread fried in train-oil. To-morrow morning we are going to have chocolate and bread."

Time passed on monotonously enough, the night being dismally long and dreary, but at length the approach of the sun became manifest by the gradually brightening twilight, and the arrival of a flock of little auks reminded them that spring was at hand. They celebrated the occasion by boiling their clothes, one article at a time, in the only pot they possessed, and then scraping the grease and dirt from them by the aid of a knife, so as to render them soft enough for traveling, as it was beyond the question to get them clean. The sooty smoke from the winter's cooking had thoroughly begrimed their faces, and all they could do to get clean was first to try and scrape the dirt off with the knife, and then rub themselves all over with bear's grease and wipe it off with moss.

By the middle of May the water along the shore was sufficiently open to permit of their starting in the kayaks on the journey which they expected would end at Spitzbergen. On May 19, 1896, they bade adieu to their winter camp, having packed everything on the kayaks, which they fastened together for convenience and stability. Sometimes they had to get out on the ice which blocked the channel and drag the kayaks over to the open water on the other side; sometimes they sailed and sometimes they paddled. They passed numbers of walrus lying on the ice, the great monsters paying no heed to them whatever. Once they landed on a mass of ice which rose high out of the water, in order to climb to the top of it and examine the coast line, for they were still in very great doubt whether they were off the shore of a hitherto undiscovered island or not.

They made the kayaks fast to a projecting piece of ice, and together climbed up to the top of the hummocks. As they reached the summit they looked back to the spot where they had left the kayaks, and were horrified to see them adrift. Already they were some distance away from the ice, and, being tied together, they were going rapidly down the channel. For a moment the sight held the two men motionless, for the kayaks represented their only means of escape. Everything beyond the clothes in which they stood was stored on board, and to be left on the ice without food, arms, or shelter, was almost certain death.

There was only one desperate means of salvation, and that Nansen took. Dashing down the hummock, he plunged into the ice-cold water and struck out after the retreating kayaks.

Weighted by his stiff, heavy, grease-sodden clothes, he had the utmost difficulty in swimming at all; but there was a greater handicap even than his clothes in the low temperature of the water. It struck through him with a chill which reached to his bones, numbing his muscles, and making his joints lose their suppleness. The breeze which was blowing helped the kayaks along, and increased his discomfort. Soon he felt that the fight was only a matter of min-

[From DeLong's "Voyage of the Jeannette," Houghton-Mifflin Co.]

MELVILLE FINDS THE BODIES OF DELONG AND HIS MEN

Mr. Melville, now retired Rear-Admiral, who was in command of DeLong's whale boat after the "Jeannette" broke up, made his way to villages in Siberia and organized a party to search for Captain DeLong and his men. Retracing the route of the two men who had saved themselves out of DeLong's boat, he came upon records and traces of the party at various stages of their progress, and, though obliged to return to his starting point, discovered the dead bodies of DeLong and his companions on March 23, 1882, half a year after their deaths. DeLong and two men lay at some distance from the main camp, where seven other bodies were found. He searched in vain for traces of Chipp and the crew of the second cutter.

A FEARFUL STRUGGLE FOR LIFE

Captain Tyson and part of his crew, having lost their ship, had dragged their boat upon a small ice floe, when at 9 P. M. huge waves began to wash over the floe. The tent and bed clothing were swept away, and all hands seized the boat to try to hold it on the ice. Finally it was made fast with ropes to some projecting pieces of ice, and the men and women stood from nine o'clock in the evening to seven o'clock the next morning unceasingly trying to keep the boat, which was their only means of salvation, from being washed away and crushed in the raging sea. With almost every wave came an avalanche of loose ice from a foot square to the size of a bureau, which bruised and crippled the crew. All through the night the waves came every fifteen or twenty minutes, until the almost exhausted men managed to get the boat to a larger piece of ice which was riding more easily in the heavy sea.

> Tuesday October 25th
> 135th day.
>
> Wednesday October 26th
> 136th day.
>
> Thursday October 27th.
> 137th day, Iveson broken down
>
> Friday October 28th.
> 138th day. Iveson died during early morning.
>
> Saturday Oct 29.
> 139th day — Dressler died during night
>
> Sunday Oct 30 —
> 140th day — Boyd & Ioertz died during night — Mr Collins dying

FAC-SIMILE OF LAST PAGE OF JOURNAL OF LIEUTENANT-COMMANDER GEO. W. DeLONG

[From DeLong's "Voyage of the Jeannette," Houghton-Mifflin Co.]

In the six days covered by this historic and awe-inspiring document, which was found by Melville, the deaths of four men are recorded. Another was dying, and but three remained. DeLong, Dr. Ambler and Ah Sam were found dead a thousand yards from the rest of the bodies. The laconic manuscript record of this very extremity of terrible suffering gives only a faint idea of the frightful privations which these men endured. Not less impressive is the fact that the commander of the expedition faithfully recorded the performance of his work until, perhaps, only a few hours before he himself, too, was frozen into an endless sleep. Nothing can more vividly exemplify the courage of the men who have braved the awful perils of the Polar regions than such an insight as this page gives. More than five hundred Arctic expeditions have been made. All have endured discomfort, most acute suffering, and many have laid down their lives in efforts to reveal to the world the mystery and terrors of the Polar ice.

A DEATH ON THE ARCTIC ICE

While in winter quarters near Cape Sabine, Grinnel Land, Rice and Frederick started to obtain meat abandoned the previous November. Their footgear froze solid and they were caught in a drifting snow storm. On reaching the spot where the meat had been left no traces of it were to be found. They started back, and Rice began to show signs of exhaustion. He became delirious, and Frederick in a temperature of thirty degrees below freezing stripped off his jumper in which to wrap his comrade's feet. For four hours he held Rice in his arms, thinly clad, until the wretched man died. Frederick not only brought back to the starving party's headquarters everything that the two men had taken away, but also turned in Rice's unconsumed rations.

utes, for as the coldness numbed him more and more, he realized that unless he overtook the kayaks quickly he would go to the bottom like a stone. The cold penetrated to his lungs, so that he gasped for breath; his hands and feet lost all feeling, and his eyes were growing blurred as he nerved himself for a final desperate struggle.

Swimming as hard as his strength of will and muscle could command, he succeeded in coming within touch of the light-drifting craft. The fact that the two were fastened together was of the utmost importance under the circumstances, for had they been separate he could never have clambered into one in his benumbed and exhausted condition. As it was, he managed to get one arm over the *ski* which formed the coupling between the kayaks. His hands were too cold to grip and he hung for a few seconds resting, till the growing chill in his limbs warned him of the danger he was in of becoming frozen. With a superb effort of determination, he raised himself until he was able to lift a leg over the side of one of the kayaks, and then struggled on board, where he lay for a minute or so trying to recover his breath.

Still fearing the cold, he grasped a paddle and set to work vigorously to force the kayaks back to the ice on which Johansen was standing. The exertion caused his blood to circulate once more, and, by the time he had reached the ice, the deadly chill was out of his frame. There were no dry clothes to put on in place of his wet ones, and all that could be done was to wring them out, and then, working hard to keep up his circulation, wait till they dried on his back.

In order to prevent another such occurrence, the kayaks were freed from each other, Nansen occupying one with half the provisions and stores, and Johansen the other. Two days after the break away they had reason to be thankful they had made this arrangement. They were skirting along the ice at the time, and suddenly came upon a herd of walrus. Instead of quietly watching them go past, as was usually the case, a huge bull slid off the ice with a roar, and swam rapidly towards Nansen's kayak.

Diving as he came near to it, Nansen anticipated that he intended rising immediately underneath it, and so capsizing it. He therefore paddled as hard as he could, when the walrus rose by his side. It reared high out of the water, towering over the kayak and its occupant, and only by the quickest of manœuvres was Nansen able to avoid having it fall upon him. Balked in that attempt, the walrus swam alongside and, plunging its tusks through the frail covering of the kayak, strove to upset it with its flipper.

Nansen swung his paddle in the air, and bringing it down with all his strength on the monster's head, caused it again to rear in the water. Paddling furiously directly the brute's tusks were withdrawn, he managed to elude it till it sank, when he made for the ice, reaching it just in time, the water having almost swamped the kayak through the holes the walrus had made with his tusks.

When the damaged kayak was taken out of the water, the injury was found to be more extensive than at first supposed. The two explorers determined to stay where they were for a few days, so as to thoroughly overhaul and repair their kayaks, and have a good rest before commencing the difficult journey, which was to be made before they could arrive at Spitzbergen. They made as comfortable a camp as they could on the ice, and, after supper, got into the sleeping-bag and rested peacefully. Nansen was first awake, and, having crept out of the bag, set to work preparing breakfast. It was ready before Johansen was, and not wishing to disturb his comrade, Nansen put on his *ski* and set out for a "constitutional" over the ice. He had not proceeded far when he heard a sound which made his heart jump. It was the bark of a dog.

Hurrying back, he told Johansen, who, however, did not catch the meaning of his words, and then set out in the direction whence the sound had come, in search of, as he believed, a whaling ship. He had not gone very far when he saw in the distance two moving specks. There was evidently a whaler in the neighborhood, he told himself, and redoubled his efforts. As he approached the two specks became clearer, until he saw distinctly that one was a man and the other a dog.

The man noticed him and waved his hat, to which Nansen replied by waving his; as they came nearer, he heard the man speak to his dog in English.

"How do you do?" he said to Nansen when they met.

"How do you do?" Nansen answered, as they shook hands. "Are you wintering near here?"

"Yes; our camp is over there. Won't you come across?" the other replied. "I think we can find room for you, if you will."

Nansen, never dreaming but that he was recognized, assented, although he wondered why the man did not ask him about the "Fram." Presently his companion looked at him closely and said: "Are you Nansen?"

"Of course I am," the explorer answered, and at once both his hands were clasped in a hearty grasp as his companion quickly expressed his congratulations.

"I was not certain," he explained. "When I saw you in London you were a fair man with light hair, but now your face and hair are black, and for the moment I did not know you. My name is Jackson."

Nansen had forgotten that his face and hair were still begrimed with the dirt and grease of months of travel, and that his own family might have been forgiven for not recognizing in the unkempt, travel-stained, long-haired man, the smart, well-set-up Norwegian doctor. Now, however, that he was known, he listened with great interest to the information that his companion was able to give him.

This was to the effect that he was the leader of a party, known as the Jackson-Harmsworth expedition, which had left England for Franz Josef Land in 1894, its purpose being to make a thorough exploration of that group, and prove whether it was the southern portion of a great polar continent or a collection of islands. He had found the latter to be the case. Instead of it being comprised of two large bodies of land, as believed by the original discoverers, it was found to be an archipelago of small islands. The probability of there being a polar continent was largely set to rest when Nansen told him that he had sounded the sea to the north and found it to be from 1,600 to 1,900 fathoms deep.

As he and Mr. Jackson talked another member of the party joined them, and close behind him came four others, all of them giving the wanderer a hearty greeting. When the encampment of the party on Cape Flora was reached Nansen was photographed as he stood, in his winter garb. Then they took him into the house and supplied him with a luxury he had not known for more than a year—a cake of soap and a change of clothes.

While he was enjoying his bath, his hosts exchanged opinions. The fact that he had arrived on foot and alone suggested to them the idea that he was the only survivor of the thirteen who had set out in the "Fram," and they decided to make no reference to what might be a very unhappy memory. Consequently, when Nansen reappeared, clean and comfortably clad, they had a meal ready for him, and urged him to set to at once. He looked at them and asked where his comrade Johansen was. Had they not brought him in? Of course they knew nothing about Johansen; they believed Nansen was the only survivor, and he had been so long out of the world that it had never occurred to him it was necessary to tell them Johansen was waiting for him to return to breakfast. When two men see no one else but themselves for more than a year, it is not to be wondered at that they forget the rest of the world is not in touch with them.

As soon as he mentioned the fact that Johansen was in the neighborhood, a party at once started off to fetch him, and the worthy lieutenant was as much surprised as they had been when they came upon him. They at once took charge of him and his belongings, and a few hours later he and Nansen, well washed, well clad, and well fed, were smoking cigars in comfortable chairs in the dining-room of the hospitable Jackson's quarters, the heroes of the occasion.

Three weeks later they were sailing south to Norway in the "Windward," and arrived at Vardo on August 13, 1896. A week later the "Fram" entered the same port, with all her crew in good health, and with nearly three years' supplies still on board.

The record of her voyage, after the departure of Nansen and Johansen on March 14, 1895, was very satisfactory. She drifted steadily in the ice towards the northwest until she touched as high as 85 degrees 57 minutes north. At the end of February, 1896, she became stationary, and remained so until the middle of July, when the crew forced a passage through the ice into open water, and from thence the "Fram" sailed to Norway. The first news the crew received on arrival at Vardo was that Nansen and Johansen had reached there just a week before. They had had some misgivings as to the safety of their two adventurous comrades, and the news of their return cleared away the only sign of uneasiness from the otherwise happy minds of the men who formed one of the most successful expeditions that has ever set out in search of the North Pole.

CHAPTER XXVIII

Andrée's Fatal Flight Northward in a Balloon

WE have dealt with many methods of seeking the Pole, by ship, by boat, by sledge, by floating in the ice; there is still another to be considered, that of flying through the air, one by which all the difficulties of ice ridges, ice drift, and open water caused by splitting of the ice, can be avoided. But in avoiding these there are other difficulties to be met, some of them perhaps insuperable, and the first attempt to reach the Pole by an air voyage could scarcely be expected to be more successful than the first one by the water voyage. It is this first—perhaps also the last—air voyage with which we are here concerned. The fact that the air, if it could be traversed in safety for the necessary distance, offered a field in which all the perils and delays of ice-navigation could be avoided, and the great journey could be completed, if at all, in days or weeks instead of years, and with a minimum of suffering and hardship, was one very likely to appeal to adventurous spirits.

To maintain the feasibility of such an excursion, however, was one thing; to attempt it was another. In the degree of development of navigation of the air up to the end of the last century such an enterprise did not commend itself to the judgment of the cautious. Yet a Columbus is rarely wanting when a new continent is to be discovered or a great feat of any kind to be performed, and the Columbus in this instance was S. A. Andrée, a Swedish engineer, who set out in the summer of 1897 on a singular and daring enterprise, one which, despite its promise, was filled with perilous elements and threatened by all the terrors of the unknown.

This daring attempt was one of so much interest that an account of it will doubtless be read with interest, despite its failure to attain its end. Solomon August Andrée was born in the town of Grenna, Sweden, in 1854, was educated in the technical college of Stockholm, and after engaging in the iron business, entered the field of engineering. He next became a teacher of physics at the college at Stockholm from which he had graduated and subsequently chief engineer of the Patent Office of Sweden.

During this period he was active in other ways. In 1881-82 he joined an expedition to Spitzbergen under Dr. Ekholm, with the purpose of making scientific observations, and at a later date crossed the ocean to Philadelphia to study the oceanic conditions of the atmosphere. He was gathering information likely to be of use to him in his later career. One thing that struck him in this voyage was the regularity of the currents of air near the ocean surface. From this he deduced that the upper currents would be still more uniform and that it might be possible, by taking advantage of them, to cross from Europe to America in a balloon. Such was the primary step toward the famous enterprise which he was afterwards to undertake.

He continued his study of atmospheric conditions, his brother Ernst, a sea-captain in the merchant service, making observations for him in all parts of the world. To study the currents of the upper air he made a number of balloon ascents with Coelti, a prominent Norwegian aeronaut, in this way gaining useful experience in the art of ballooning.

We have said that Andrée had the spirit of a Columbus, and that not without warrant, for he had conceived the daring plan of following in the air the path of Columbus through the waves, his project being to cross the ocean in a balloon from the Cape Verde Islands to Venezuela. This was for the purpose of proving that long voyages in the air could be safely made.

Spending the summer of 1893 with his sailor brother at Göteborg, the details of the plan and the probable aid of the air currents were worked out between them, their calculations leading to the conclusion that the distance could be traversed in ninety-seven hours. Their study was as thorough as it could be made with the imperfect data at their command, and the results were submitted to several of the Swedish scientists, including the explorer Nordenskiöld, one of whom said:

"If you have faith in such an undertaking, why not rather set out from Spitzbergen and try to reach the North Pole?"

This first put the great project in which he afterward engaged into Andrée's mind, a project among the most daring and adventurous that man had ever undertaken, considering the state of aeronautical science at that period. Full of his new scheme, which appealed strongly to his enthusiastic soul, he began a series of experiments in aeronautics, obtaining a sum of $1,400 from a memorial fund at Stockholm to assist him. In one of his ascents he crossed the Baltic, with great peril to his life, in a small balloon.

His great project was first publicly made known in a lecture before the Royal Swedish Academy of Sciences in 1895, printed with the title of "Proposed Plan of an Expedition to the North Pole in a Balloon." In this lecture he said, referring to the fact that so far the polar explorer had used only one means of travel, the sledge:

"The fact remains that in attempting to push on over the polar ice we have lost numbers of men, ships, and money, and several hundred years of time, without having succeeded in crossing the icy desert and reaching the Pole. Is it not time to examine this question and look about for some other means of transportation than the sledge? Yes, it is time, and we will not have to look far to find the means that is particularly adapted for such purposes.

"This means is the balloon. Not the ideally perfect steerable balloon that is dreamed of and worshipped but has never been seen, but the balloon that we really possess and that is judged so unfavorably while only its weak points are noticed and emphasized. Such a balloon is good enough to carry the explorer to the Pole and back again. With such a balloon the voyage across the icy desert *can* be accomplished.'"

Had he waited some ten years more he would have found the steerable balloon to which he referred developed to a state of considerable perfection, but his enthusiasm was too great to permit delay.

Andrée was a delegate to the Geographical Congress at London in July, 1895, and presented to it his plans with much elaboration. His arguments were received with considerable favor, some of the delegates becoming quite enthusiastic. One of these was Markham, the leader of the exploring party of the Nares expedition, who supported him strongly and said that he would like to go with him himself. Nordenskiöld also remained a faithful supporter of the project, and also Nils Ekholm, one of the ablest meteorologists of Europe, who showed his faith in the scheme by agreeing to go with him. On the other hand, many men of experience in Arctic affairs descried the daring project, predicting certain failure and the inevitable death of the adventurer and all who joined him in the rash attempt.

He found the necessary financial support, however, without difficulty, the required sum, $36,000, being quickly raised by a public subscription, the King of Sweden heading it with $8,000. Meanwhile Andrée continued his experiments, spending the winter of 1895-96 in France and England and making many ascents with French aeronauts. The balloon for his enterprise was constructed at Paris under his close supervision, it costing about $10,000. It was about seventy-five feet in height and had a capacity of 6,000 cubic meters of gas, it being intended to lift a weight of three tons, consisting of the aeronaut and two companions, provisions for a year or more, scientific and other apparatus, and the requisite mechanism and chemical materials to manufacture a new supply of gas in the polar regions, if necessary. The balloon was enclosed with heavy cordage, so as to enable it to resist the action of the sun. An ingenious contrivance for direction motion was added. This consisted of a rubber sail secured to the apex of the balloon, with a rope leading to the car. In addition was a guide rope, which was intended to drag on the ground or in the water, arrangements being made to adjust it to different positions for 180 degrees of the circumference of a ring attached to the car.

In the manufacture of the balloon three thicknesses of silk were used, with varnish to bind them together and three thicknesses of varnish on the outside. The gondola or car, which hung about twenty-five feet below, was about five feet deep and six and a half feet in diameter. It was made of wicker-work lined with varnished silk, and was capacious enough to allow one of the aeronauts to sleep while the others were on the alert. A lid of basket-work covered it, with a trapdoor in it by which the car could be entered or left. While at work the men were to stand upon this lid, having a large ring, waist high, to protect them.

The cooking apparatus was ingeniously devised to prevent danger of firing the inflammable gas of the balloon. It was done in a copper cylinder let down from the car, an alcohol lamp supplying the heat. This could be lighted by a mechanism in the car and blown out by means of a rubber tube, while a reflecting glass enabled the cook to see if it was burning.

The guiding and steering apparatus represented the best means that could be devised for this purpose before the advent of the dirigible air-ship. The guiding ropes were of different lengths, the shortest measuring about one thousand feet and the longest about twelve hundred. These were intended to hang from a bearing-ring just outside the car, and, when the balloon was not too high, to drag on the ice or the ground. Experiments with this device in July, 1895, showed that when the rope was attached to the central eyelet the balloon moved in the line of the wind, but when attached to one or the other side its course was changed by a considerable number of degrees. The sail could be adjusted to aid materially in this result, and it was thought that by its use and the rudder-like effect of the dragging rope a tack of thirty degrees could be made. It was intended to so manipulate the gas and the basket as to keep the balloon about five hundred feet above the surface.

A large number of carrier-pigeons were taken along to be sent back with any important news. A supply of cork buoys was also taken, each having a vertical shaft with a small Swedish flag attached to it. In the center of each buoy was a small water-tight metal box, in which a letter could be placed before it was thrown overboard. Such buoys might float for months or even years before they came ashore or were seen and picked up at sea.

The locality chosen for the start was Danes Island, one of the northwestern islands of the Spitzbergen group, the proposed time for the start being the month of July, 1896. Andrée's chosen companions were Dr. Nils Ekholm, a meteorologist of high standing, and Nils Strindberg, an amateur photographer who was eager to take part in the trip. These two had made many of the instruments taken in the balloon.

The spot chosen for the ascent was Pike's house, built by an English sportsman in the northern part of the island. Here an octagonal building was erected and the balloon inflated by its maker in the latter part of July, 1896. All was ready by the 27th, but the favoring south wind desired failed to blow. They waited impatiently for the wind to change to the right quarter, but it blew steadily from the north, and at the end of the first week of August it was decided that the season was too far advanced to warrant a start. The disappointed explorers accordingly sent their materials and apparatus to Tromsö to be stored and returned to Stockholm to wait the coming of another summer.

The necessary funds for a new expedition were easily obtained and the king now placed a Swedish gunboat at Andrée's disposal to aid him in his effort. But during the winter Ekholm withdrew from the party, either fearing the result or on account of being recently married and in response to his wife's fears. He was replaced by Knut Frankel, an able engineer, whose aid Andrée was glad to obtain.

The new start for Danes Island was made early in June, 1897, and on the 19th the work of inflation of the balloon began. Its surface was thoroughly examined to check any leakage or repair any weak spots that might appear, all the work being pressed forward with great rapidity. Last of all, the inflation being finished, the car was attached to the balloon, which was held down by three strong ropes. All was ready for the great ascent.

Andrée's last act on the 11th of July, the day of the ascent, was to write two messages, which were taken to Tromsö and telegraphed to Stockholm. One read:

"*To Aftonblast:*

"To-day, Sunday, at 10.35 A. M., we began preparations for departure, and are ready now, 2.30 P. M. We shall probably be going in north and northeast direction and expect by and by to come into regions with more favorable wind conditions than here. In the name of all my associates I send warmest greeting to fatherland and friends. ANDREE."

The other was to the king:

"VIRGOS HARBOR, July 11, 2.35 P. M.

"*To King Oscar:*

"In the moment of departure the members of the polar expedition beg your majesty to accept our respectful greeting and warmest thanks. ANDREE."

Everything ready and the moment arrived, the members of the expedition shook hands cordially with those who were there to see them off, the latter showing more emotion than the three explorers themselves, of whom only Strindberg manifested any signs of anxiety. Entering the car and examining to see if everything was in order, the leader called, "Strindberg!" Strindberg stepped upon the car. "Frankel!" Frankel followed. "Come!" said Andrée in a cheerful tone. The sailors appointed to cut the holding cords first released those that held the center of the balloon. It immediately began a rolling motion, and they had to wait until it should come to a partial rest. "Cut!" then cried Andrée. The knives were plied; the ropes parted; the balloon shot up three hundred feet into the air.

A loud cheer and cries of "Happy Voyage" came from those left behind as they watched the course of the great balloon. Its first movement was a swoop downward until it nearly reached the surface of the water, then it rose again before the violent wind that was blowing and shot away at great speed, the three explorers waving their handkerchiefs as it swept from the land out over the Arctic Sea. In about half an hour it vanished from the view of the spectators, though they continued to wait for some time longer in hope that a last glimpse might be obtained, some of them, doubtless, fearful that they had gazed for the last time upon their late companions.

An incident of an unfortunate character happened at the start. As the balloon bounded upward two of the guide ropes, a considerable length of which trailed upon the ground, yielded to the tension caused by the quick bound and friction with the surface, and broke. Only that this possible accident had been provided for, these indispensable aids would have been lost at the very start. Foreseeing such a mishap, Andrée had the ropes constructed in sections of about one hundred yards each, joined with screws. It was the lower sections that gave way, so that fortunately the accident did not prove serious.

The utility of the guide ropes was evident to the spectators, since, though the wind was south-southwest, the explorers succeeded in laying their course nearly due north. They also aided in keeping the height uniform. The only peril encountered was from an ice-clad hill, six hundred feet high, which lay in their path. But when the balloon neared this it rose and soared over it like an enormous bird, keeping steadily to its distance from the surface. When finally all hopes of catching another glimpse of the balloon were at an end, the spectators turned away, glad that the opportunity had been theirs of seeing so unusual an event.

The explorers had set out prepared to face a possibly long detention in the frozen world. In the car of the balloon they carried weapons, ammunition, and material suitable with which to build a shelter, should the balloon collapse and leave them on the ice. An aluminium boat was also carried, so that the party could escape by sea if necessary. Of the carrier pigeons taken with them, to be liberated at intervals on the passage, nothing certain was afterwards known. Although one pigeon is said to have been shot in the far north, it is doubtful whether it was one of the Andrée birds.

The balloon, when it went out of sight, was traveling at a speed which would have carried it over the Pole in a few days, and probably have enabled it to descend in Siberia or America in about a week. For the first fortnight after it had started, therefore, interest all over the world was keenly excited for further news. But the fotnight passed without any reliable intelligence being received, and a month followed, and so on until a year had gone by. Then relief and search parties were talked about, and the Swedish Geographical Society sent one out to look for the missing balloonists in Siberia. It did not meet with Andrée, nor did it obtain any reliable information respecting him.

News was published to the effect that some outlying hunting tribes had come upon a huge bag, having a mass of cordage attached to it, together with the remains of some human bodies. The Russian, Swedish, and Norwegian governments immediately sent forward auxiliary search parties, but their only success was to trace the origin of the report, and find that a Siberian trader had, in a moment of mischievous humor, hoaxed a too confiding telegraph agent.

Later, on September 12, 1899, a Swedish sloop, the "Martha," reached Hammerfest with the information that a buoy, branded with the name of the Andrée expedition, had been found to the northeast of King Charles Islands. The buoy had lost the screw-plug from the top, and had been so damaged by coming in contact with some hard substance that the interior cylinder was too dented to permit of an examination being made of the inside.

It is still possible that one of the buoys taken by Andrée may be discovered containing a record of his doings from the moment he disappeared with his balloon sailing towards the north. But it is very unlikely, and it is scarcely probable that any sign will ever be discovered of the balloon or its occupants. For years the frozen north held all traces of the Franklin expedition from the eyes of the searchers who were able to conduct their operations along the route they knew Franklin had followed. No search party can knowingly follow the route Andrée and his comrades took. Their fate will probably be forever a mystery, for so many things might have happened that no one theory can claim for itself more probability than another. All that is certain is that the party went out of sight drifting towards the north. They carried their lives in their hands, and knew that they did so. Had they succeeded, they would have achieved a mighty triumph; they failed, and in doing so set their names as indelibly on the scroll of Fame as any hero who has laid down his life in the contest with the measureless mystery of the Pole.

In a lecture delivered by Andrée in April, 1896, he had used the following words: "If our expedition should return home without success, or even if we should perish, it will not be long before a new balloon expedition will be started for the same purpose as ours. This idea has taken so mighty a hold on the human mind that it cannot be quieted. It will necessarily appear again with the full strength of a natural law."

In this conjecture he was not astray, for in less than ten years after his venture a similar project was devised by an American explorer. This was Walter Wellman, an enterprising western journalist, who had made an unsuccessful polar expedition by the Franz Josef Land route in 1899. A few years later he proposed to take advantage of all the progress made in ballooning and air-ship experiment since Andrée's unfortunate effort in an attempt to reach the Pole, and was very hopeful of success.

The air-ship, or dirigible balloon, built for him at Paris, was the largest which had been constructed to that time, and was taken by him to Danes Island, Spitzbergen, in 1906. He had selected this island, as Andrée had done, as the most available starting point for such a voyage. His air-ship was 183 feet long, 52½ feet wide, had a 20 horse-power engine and two propellers, one on each side. It had also a complete sledging outfit and a combined boat and car, these to be used in case of accident to the balloon. It was supplied with fuel and food sufficient to last five persons for a considerable time.

He proposed to start in the summer of 1906, hoping to reach the Pole in a few days. But before the time of starting arrived serious mechanical defects were found in the apparatus, of a character that would have exposed the explorers to great danger. The air-ship was accordingly taken back to Paris for reconstruction, the expedition being delayed for another year.

In 1907 the air-ship, with its defects remedied, was taken again to Danes Island. But the weather proved seriously detrimental to the enterprise, furious gales blowing and the general conditions being so unfavorable that a second postponement was felt necessary. In the following year further improvements were made, and the great air-ship, capable of carrying 19,000 pounds and making twenty miles an hour by the aid of its powerful engines, was again got in order for a flight, a trial trip, which proved its efficiency, being made. It was then too late in the year to start for the Pole, and 1909 was fixed for the date.

Copyright 1909 by Doubleday, Page & Co.

COMMANDER ROBERT E. PEARY AND HIS ESKIMO DOGS

At the time when Dr. Cook's report of the Discovery of the Pole electrified the world, Peary, the great Arctic explorer, had already been many months beyond human knowledge in the great Unknown. Dr. Cook said it was to anticipate Peary's expected success that he made his dash for the northern axis of the earth, and the consequent excitement was at fever heat when Peary's cablegrams arrived.

PEARY'S SHIP CAUGHT IN A GREAT ICE FIELD OF THE NORTH

To have the ship surrounded by a great expanse of broken ice, or to be frozen in by the formation of new ice, is the common experience of the Arctic explorer. Peary's vessel is seen here in this hazardous predicament. The view also gives some idea of the grandeur and extent of Arctic scenery.

Photograph, Underwood & Underwood, N. Y.

ESKIMOS ON THE ICE IN NORTH STAR BAY

This is the spot where the crew of Sir John Franklin's expedition perished from scurvy and starvation. In the distance is seen Peary's relief ship, "The Erik."

MRS. ROBERT E. PEARY
As she dressed when accompanying her husband on Polar expeditions.

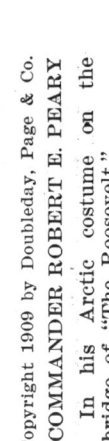

Copyright 1909 by Doubleday, Page & Co.
COMMANDER ROBERT E. PEARY
In his Arctic costume on the bridge of "The Roosevelt."

MRS. ROBERT E. PEARY
Wife of the great explorer.

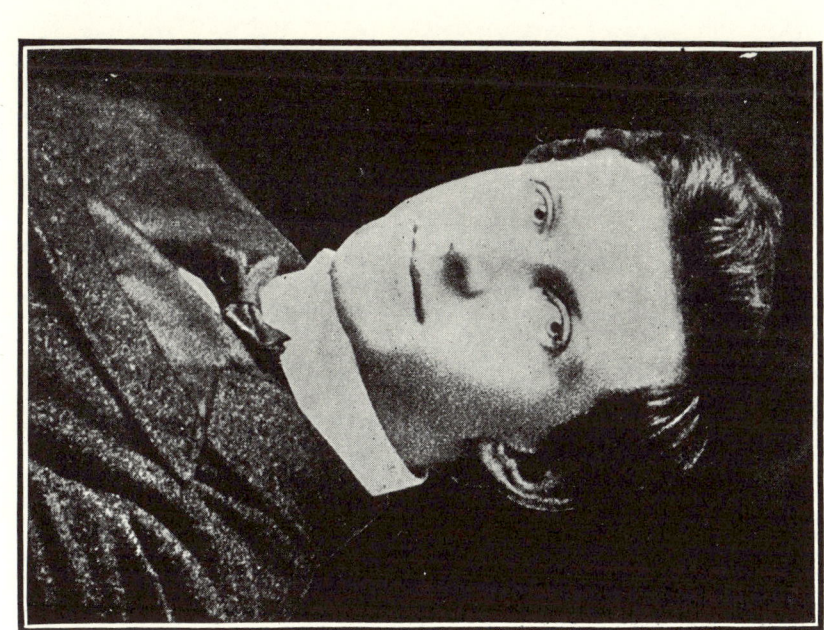

ANTHONY FIALA
Leader of the Ziegler Polar Expedition, who was rescued by the Arctic steamer "Terra Nova."

GENERAL A. W. GREELY
One of the most celebrated of living American Arctic explorers.

REAR ADMIRAL WINFIELD S. SCHLEY
An American Arctic explorer who went to the relief of the Greely Expedition.

DR. FRITJOF NANSEN

The celebrated Northern explorer, whose voyage in the "Fram" brought him world-wide fame.

THE DUKE OF THE ABRUZZI

His Royal Highness, Luigi Amadeo, cousin of the King of Italy, who brought fame upon himself and his country by his daring attempt to reach the North Pole.

THE GJOA

Which under the guidance of Captain Amundsen sailed through the passage north of the American Continent in 1905

CAPTAIN RONALD AMUNDSEN

On the deck of his vessel, "The Gjoa," with which he navigated the Northwest Passage for the first time in history.

In the summer of 1909 Mr. Wellman for the first time succeeded in getting a send off for the Pole. He did not go far, the journey suddenly ending for a reason like that which had imperilled Andrée's voyage at its start, the breaking of his guide rope. Wellman had a long and very heavy rope attached to his car, not as a rudder but as a drag to counterbalance the ascending power of the balloon. It was intended to trail on the ice, so that, if the air-ship should rise and lift it upward, the weight of the part in the air would increase so as to limit the degree of ascension and keep the height practically uniform. The drag-rope weighed about 1,400 pounds, its weight being increased in an ingenious manner. It was a hollow tube of leather in which a considerable part of the food supply was packed. Outwardly, in its lower part, it was covered with overlapping steel scales, so that it could slip easily over rough ice.

It was this weighted rope that provedd disastrous to the expedition. The strain of the first sudden rise of the air-ship caused such a tension that the rope parted near the car, its total length being lost and the balloon darting rapidly upward into the air. The often deferred expedition was again at an end. To venture onward without the drag rope would be like a ship venturing to sea without its rudder, and it became necessary to bring the apparatus to land again, a feat which was accomplished with some trouble and risk.

It may be said with some assurance that this project is now at an end, for the announcement from Cook and Peary some two months later that they had reached the Pole by the method of sledging, put an end to the need of such an expedition. Even if Wellman had reached the Pole in the summer of 1909, he would have ranked only third in the roll of polar discoverers. It will probably be the same with Count Zeppelin's projected polar voyage in his great air-ship, one that has proved itself capable of making an eight hundred mile excursion within a few days, unless he should venture upon the voyage for the purpose of showing what an air-ship is capable of doing.

CHAPTER XXIX

Modern Vikings in the Arctic Seas

THE reader will remember that the first of modern navigators to venture upon the seas of ice were the daring Vikings, or Sea-Kings, of Scandinavia. It is now more than a thousand years ago since these fearless mariners, in their open craft, reached and named Iceland, and a century later landed upon Greenland's icy shores. They completed their work at that time by discovering the continent of America, five hundred years in advance of Columbus.

In our own times descendants of the Vikings have turned their prows to the same waters again and taken an active part in the work of polar research. Two of these we have mentioned: Nordenskiöld, the first to achieve the Northeast Passage, and Nansen, whose dash toward the Pole was marked by great brilliancy of conception and measurable success. We have now to tell the story of some other adventurers of the Scandinavian realm, who have inscribed their names on the roll of Arctic heroes.

Notable among these was Nyglius Erickson, who in 1906 with two companions set out to explore the unknown portion of the east Greenland coast, from Cape Bismarck on the south to Cape Bridgman in the far north. The northern and western part of Peary Land, which lies north of Greenland, had been explored as far east as Cape Bridgman, and the east coast of Greenland as far north as Cape Bismarck, but between these two points lay a stretch of coast hundreds of miles in length of which nothing was known south of Independence Bay, which Peary had reached in his journey across Greenland. The survey and mapping of this unknown region, so as to complete our knowledge of the Greenland coast, was the object of the intrepid Erickson and his equally brave companions.

We can only say of this expedition that it was successful in its results, but fatal to the explorers. Their failure to return gave rise to fears of their safety, and searching parties were sent out which found their dead bodies. They had perished from cold and hunger on their return. But in a bottle, attached to the neck of one of the dead heroes, were the full records of their expedition, showing that they had surveyed the whole line of unknown coast and completed the survey of the entire Greenland coast. It was a splendid result, which they had paid for with their lives.

The course of our narrative now takes us to another Viking enterprise, that led by Captain Sverdrup, of the "Fram," who remained four years in the far north and added greatly to our knowledge of the great group of islands north of the American continent. Of Sverdrup it need only be said that he had been associated with Nansen in all his enterprises, being one of his companions when he crossed South Greenland in 1888 and going with him as captain of the "Fram'" in his great drifting voyage in 1893-96.

Nansen's stout ship had not only survived its encounter with the ice, but was little the worse for its desperate battle with the Arctic floes. With a little renovation it was in order for another voyage to the frozen seas, and in 1898 Sverdrup set out again in the hardy "Fram" on another voyage to the north. The expedition was equipped by private enterprise, Sverdrup's patrons on this occasion being two brothers named Ringnes.

The expedition in question sailed from Larvick, Norway, on June 24, 1898, the day known in Norway as St. Hans Day. The party consisted of sixteen, all told, the plan of operations being to sail along the western coast of Greenland to Smith Sound, where the ship was to push as far north as possible and form a headquarters, whence sledge expeditions were to be sent out in all directions. As to the localities to which chief attention was to be paid, the commander of the expedition was to use his own judgment; but on one point the instructions were definite and emphatic—there was to be no attempt at a dash for the Pole.

On the way along the Greenland coast dogs for the sledge teams were procured and a large amount of walrus meat to feed them was obtained. The floating ice checked them in Smith Sound, and on August 21st a locality was chosen for winter quarters in Rice Strait, on the coast of Ellesmere Land.

As Peary was then in the north, engaged in mapping out the land in that direction, the Norwegians decided to give their attention to the land lying on the western side of the strait, in the vicinity of Hayes Sound, where Nares, in 1875, had done considerable work. They completed the survey of the coast line running round Robeson Channel, and, during their stay, not only mapped out an area of one hundred thousand square miles in Ellesmere Land, but also located hitherto undiscovered land, which was named after King Oscar of Norway and taken possession of in his name. Valuable additions were also made to the zoological, geological, meteorological, and botanical records, while the story of the expedition abounds in interesting experiences.

Two expeditions were sent out in a southwest direction across this region, finding a large glacier district in the southern part of Ellesmere Land. The sun set on October 16th for the remainder of the winter. A party was out taking observations over some mountains behind the bay in which the "Fram" was anchored, and had returned to camp for the evening meal as the sun was going down. One of the party drew the attention of the others to it, and they gathered at the door of the tent and watched it in silence.

"We were looking at the sun for the last time that year," Captain Sverdrup wrote in his account of the expedition. "Its pale light lay dying over the 'inland ice'; its disc, light red, was veiled on the horizon; it was like a day in the land of the dead. All light was so hopelessly cold; all life so far away. We stood and watched it till it sank; then everything became so still that it made one shudder—as if the Almighty had deserted us and shut the gates of Heaven. The light died away across the mountains and slowly vanished, while over us crept the great shades of the polar night, the night that kills all life."

The winter passed without any fatality among them, although there was an occasion when one of the members nearly came to his end. Various trips were taken when the moon was up to try and locate the site where Greely made his historic camp on Pim Island, which was in that vicinity. In February two men set out to look for it, and, as they did not intend to be long away, they took neither food nor sleeping-bags with them. The weather was clear and cold, with the thermometer at —40 degrees Fahrenheit, but the men experienced no ill effects from it on their journey. They found some pieces of rope and sail-cloth scattered about at a spot on the north side of the island, and came to the conclusion that this must have been the site of the camp. Having examined the place, they were about to return to the "Fram," when one of them sank to the ground. His companions strove to lift him up, but without avail; he had suddenly become exhausted, and his strength gave out so entirely that he could not remain on his feet. It was a serious situation. A few hours of inactivity in such a temperature, without an excess of fur clothing and warm food, meant freezing to death. His companion was in doubt whether to wait and strive to rouse him, or to run to the ship for help. He adopted the latter course, and sped away as fast as his legs could carry him. Arrived at the "Fram," he raised the alarm, and every one turned out and hastened to the rescue. A sledge was quickly harnessed to a dog team, and on it were placed furs and food. The place where the man had collapsed was about a mile away, and the rescuers were soon at his side. He lay in a heap on frozen snow, too far gone to recognize any one. He was pushed into a sleeping-bag, placed on the sledge, and driven off at top speed to the ship, where he was promptly put into his bunk and restoratives administered to him. Soon the efforts were successful, and he sank into a sleep from which he awakened, many hours after, little the worse for his adventure. He escaped without even a touch of frost-bite.

A few days after this episode the temperature fell rapidly, until the thermometer registered as low as —58 degrees Fahrenheit. Explorer Peary was at the time some fifteen miles to the north of the "Fram," and the temperature in his locality went down to —67 degrees Fahrenheit, a cold so intense that, hardened as he was to the rigors of Arctic weather, he had seven toes so severely frost-bitten that they had to be amputated.

Yet the way in which mankind can adapt themselves to all varieties of climate, by use and custom, was shown by a visit they had from one of Peary's Eskimos. He reached the "Fram" on a day when the temperature was at —40 degrees Fahrenheit. Invited on board, he said he must first change his traveling clothes, and, in the open air, he stripped to the waist to remove his heavy furs and put on a lighter suit. He was apparently as unaffected by the intense cold on his naked flesh as one of the Norwegians would have been had the thermometer stood at 40 degrees above instead of 40 degrees below zero.

During the sledge journeys numerous indications were found of musk oxen being in the neighborhood of the sheltered valleys in the interior of the islands. As a supply of fresh beef was always desirable, considerable attention was paid to these animals, and, from time to time, the larder was kept well supplied with their meat. On these hunting expeditions some interesting observations were made on the habits of the oxen. One of the most interesting was as to the manner in which they met attack. When they were disturbed in feeding, the herd would retreat slowly and in order; but if they saw they were being pursued, they moved towards any vantage ground, such as a rise or hill summit, there to form themselves into a square. Each animal took up its position as though by word of command, until they stood, shoulder to shoulder, with their heads outward and so close together that their horns often linked, while within the square were sheltered any young calves there might be with the herd.

As the enemy approached one of the oxen, usually the oldest bull in the herd, dashed out from his place in the square and bounded towards the foe, with head down, horns brandished with sidelong tosses of the head, snorting and bellowing defiance. As he left the square the ranks closed up and remained so until he returned, when the ranks opened enough for him to back into his place, while another charged out to carry on the combat in front of the square. These movements were executed with lightning rapidity, every animal dashing out in turn to seek single combat, the one to advance being always the one to the right of the returned champion. Usually the advance was for a distance of a dozen yards, but there were occasions when the explorers saw the challenging ox advance over a hundred yards from the main body.

When there were sufficient bulls in the herd to form the outer lines, the cows were placed, with the calves, inside the square; but if the bulls were not numerous enough to complete the outer ranks, then the cows took their places beside the bulls. In one instance, where the herd consisted of cows and calves only, the cows formed the square and caried on the fight while the calves were sheltered within.

When the square was once formed it never broke. Every beast in it might be killed, one by one, but there was never a sign of a break-away or a stampede. If only a few were killed, the square stood its ground until the attackers retreated, when, with an open field, the square slowly retired, still in formation, and still ready, at the first signal, to halt and renew the fight. In one instance, where every beast had been shot save one, that one made a sortie, pranced round in defiance, and retired to the heap of slain, all that remained of his gallant comrades. Their method of defense was capable of repelling the attack of any animal inhabiting the Arctic regions, and more complete in its system than appeared to be needed to repel any of the animals likely to attack them.

The return of summer, during the first year of their stay, was marred by the death of the doctor. Early in June the shores of Hayes Sound were being surveyed. The ice still covered the sea and the land was deep in snow. One night, when the surveying party had returned to their tent and were sitting round the oil stove eating their supper, they heard a man outside asking if he might come in. They opened the tent flap and discovered the doctor standing outside. He was evidently ill, and, as they soon realized, snow-blind. He had missed his way while out after specimens and had accidentally stumbled on the camp. He was taken in and given warm food, which revived him somewhat, afterwards being put in a sleeping-bag and made as comfortable as they could make him. In the morning he pronounced himself much better, and said he would stay at the camp, resting, for the day. The party left him with no misgivings, but on their return in the evening they found him dead in the sleeping-bag.

Camp was struck the following morning, and with the body of the doctor on the sledge, the party started back to the ship. It was a sad journey. Not only was it the first time in the history of the "Fram" that a member of the ship's company had died, but the loss of the doctor was a serious matter to the explorers, who were thus left without any qualified expert to attend to them in the event of either sickness or accident occurring. The procession reached the ship on June 15th, and the next morning the whole company formed up in funeral array to convey the remains of the doctor to their last resting-place. They gave him a sailor's burial. The national flag covered the body and bier, and the explorers, walking slowly, two and two, proceeded down Rice Strait over the ice to a spot where a hole had been cut through the ice to the open water.

The body was lowered to the water's edge, where it was held while prayers were read and a hymn sung. In the words of Captain Sverdrup: "The followed the moment when he slowly slipped into the deep. We shall never forget it. We sang a hymn and said the Lord's Prayer."

In 1899 the "Fram" was taken southward to Jones Sound, a channel dividing Ellesmere Land from North Devon Island to the south. Surveying parties were sent westward along the sound, but not without difficulty, they meeting with rough pressure ridges in the ice, which they had to cut through with pick and spade to make a path for the sledges. At other places the ice was fairly smooth.

In this vicinity game was found in the greatest abundance, musk oxen, reindeer and wolves being plentiful. The larder was in need of being replenished, and the members of the party secured as much beef and venison as they could for their winter supply. By the time they returned to the ship they had enough fresh meat, not only for themselves but also for the dogs, to last until the following spring.

As the survey work advanced to the west of the sound, the discovery of several inaccuracies in former maps led to the hope that new land might be located in that direction. Advantage was taken of the opening of the ice in the summer season to push the "Fram" farther to the west, so as to enable the sledge parties to reach still greater distances over the ice in that direction. It was by this means the crowning triumph of the expedition was achieved, though at the time of its achievement an event happened which very nearly brought a tragic ending. This was no less than a fire on the "Fram."

There were, at the time, only nine men on board. For the winter, an awning had been spread over the deck, below the shelter of which numerous articles were stored, including the ammunition and powder-boxes, a number of kayaks, spare wood for repairing sledges and making *ski,* the oil barrels, and an iron tank full of spirits. The chimney from the galley rose above this awning, and one day a spark fell upon it. At once the canvas burst into flame.

On the first alarm, the mate, who was in charge, gave his attention to the removal of the oil and explosives; but while these were being dragged out of danger the flames spread rapidly from the awning to the rigging, reaching the mainsail, which also became ignited. Then the fire reached the kayaks, the coverings of which were all saturated with grease. The blaze that followed set all the spare wood alight. The iron tank, full of spirits, was thus surrounded by flames. It was impossible to beat them back, and the men realized that if the tank burst and the spirits caught fire, the ship was doomed. With despairing energy they attacked the fire with buckets of water, and, despite the primitive nature of the weapon, they succeeded in subduing the flames before irreparable damage was done. The tank, fortunately, withstood the heat, though it was badly warped. The kayaks were destroyed, as well as all the spare wood, the rigging and sails on the mainmast, the awning and some stores on the lower deck, where the flames also penetrated. But the ship was saved.

On October 13, 1900, the news was brought to the ship that the hopes of discovering new land were likely to be realized. A party who had been far out to the west had seen in the distance what appeared to be land at a place where none was shown on the maps. Five days later, with a picked band, Captain Sverdrup was hastening to the place indicated. As the winter was near at hand, they could not do more than verify the news. In the distance they saw what appeared to be new land, but it was impossible to proceed with the survey of this before the spring.

On April 8, 1901, Sverdrup and his picked companions set out again to explore the new territory. After pushing on as far as the outer limit of the coast, they came upon what appeared to be a large bay, one hundred miles wide, with broad and deep fiords penetrating the land on its eastern side. The land they had descried lay on the far side of it, and for the moment they feared that, after all, it was only a portion of Ellesmere Land, though making the area of that much larger than had hitherto been believed. To prove or disprove their fears they commenced to cross the ice in the bay. As they proceeded, the land at the head of the bay was seen to suddenly open out and reveal a sound running between two islands. It was new land which lay before them, and with great jubilation they named the channel Eureka Sound. The position was 78 degrees 50 minutes north latitude and 84 degrees west longitude.

Close examination of this island led to the discovery of remains of extensive Eskimo settlements, showing that at one time there had been a considerable population where now not a single Eskimo was to be found. The presence of whale bones among the ruins of the huts told of a still further change that had occurred, for whales are now quite extinct in that part, and have been so for a long period.

Sverdrup pushed his exploration farther north, along the western coast of the extensive island variously known as Ellesmere Land in its southern portion, Grinnell Land in its central, and Grant Land in its northern. Its northern and western portion had been surveyed by the various expeditions of Nares, Greely and Peary, whose surveys had extended to its northwest extremity, but Sverdrup completed the survey of its eastern side, his expedition reaching the northwest cape and completely demonstrating its insular character.

He continued his explorations to the westward, tracing the coast line of Axel Helborg Island, discovered by him west of Eureka Sound. Westward still, north of the group of Parry Islands, he located and surveyed the coasts of three other islands, two of which he named Ellef Ringnes Land and Amund Ringnes Land, in honor of the patrons of his expedition. The third, lying southwest of these, was given the name of King Christian Land, after the Danish King, the strait separating it from Ellef Ringnes Land being named Danish Sound.

Sverdrup returned in 1902, after a four years' absence. The chief results of his expedition were the discovery and mapping of the southwest and west coast of Ellesmere Land and of the islands named, together with valuable meteorological observations and a representative natural history collection.

Leaving Sverdrup's record, we now take up that of another Norwegian explorer, Captain Roald Amundsen, who won the distinguished honor of being the first to carry a vessel through the Northwest Passage, and thus completed the work of McClure more than fifty years before.

Captain Amundsen had been on various polar voyages before the one in question. A second lieutenant in the Norwegian Navy, his Arctic experience began with observations in the East Greenland current in 1891. In 1897 he was granted leave of absence to join the Belgian Antarctic expedition, and was first officer of the "Belgica" during its two years in the Antarctic ice fields. But his chief experience in the polar seas, that on which his future fame will rest, was his daring expedition of 1903-06. In this expedition he had Dr. Frederick A. Cook as a shipmate.

Leaving Christiania, Norway, on June 17, 1903, in a tiny sealing vessel, the "Gjoa," driven by gasoline engines, he made his way northward to Baffin Bay and Lancaster Sound, his purposes being two in number, to re-locate the Magnetic Pole and to endeavor to navigate the Northwest Passage.

Following Amundsen's track, we make our way through Lancaster Sound and Barrow Strait, its western continuation, and thence southward through Peel Sound and Franklin Strait, separating the Princess of Wales Island on the west from North Somerset Island and Boothia Peninsula on the east. The latter is the most northerly extremity of the American continent, which here sends a tract of land far northward into the Arctic Sea. He was now in the vicinity of King William's Land, the scene of Sir John Franklin's fate.

Amundsen had not reached this locality in his little ship without many adventures with the ice. He was now in the vicinity of the Magnetic Pole, as located by Sir James Ross in 1831 on the peninsula above named, then supposed to be an island and named Boothia Felix. The locality of the pole, as then determined, was 97 degrees west longitude, 70½ degrees north latitude. It was Amundsen's desire to locate it more exactly and discover if it had shifted its position during the years that had elapsed.

Seeking winter quarters at a point on the coast of King William's Land, about one hundred miles from the location ascribed to the Magnetic Pole, he began a series of careful observations in magnetism, continued day and night for the long period of nineteen months, including two winters in the sea of ice. He finally located the pole in King William's Land, at a point not far removed from that assigned to it by Ross in 1831.

In the spring of 1905 two members of the party, Amundsen and Hansen, explored and charted the east coast of Victoria Land as far north as the seventy-second degree of north latitude, naming the coast charted King Haakon Land in honor of the King of Norway. Here he discovered an unknown tribe of Eskimos. In the following summer the "Gjoa" was taken from the quarters in which she had passed two winters and the work of completing the task of traversing the Northwest Passage was resumed. The course now followed kept closely to the northern coast of the continent, traversing the channel between the mainland and the islands.

Onward through the realm of ice went the adventurers, traversing in the opposite direction the route followed by McClure in 1850, until Point Barrow was passed and the waters of Bering Strait reached. The difficulties of the route were such that the little "Gjoa" had to pass another winter in the ice. But in December the adventurers succeeded in reaching an Alaskan telegraph station, and on the 5th a message was cabled to Alaska that the "Gjoa" and her crew were safe, and that they had succeeded in locating the Magnetic Pole and carrying their ship through the Northwest

Passage, a feat which had been attempted in vain for four centuries. The news spread rapidly round the world, as a new and great victory by man over the Arctic problem, a further step in the conquest of the earth.

With the coming of a new summer, the "Gjoa" was taken farther on her record-making voyage, and in October, 1906, King Haakon received a telegram from the explorer that his ship had safely arrived at Cape Nome, Alaska. Little more time was needed to bring him and his crew safely home, where an enthusiastic reception awaited them, as having won for Norway one of the world's great geographical prizes.

CHAPTER XXX

Abruzzi, the Royal Italian Explorer

IN the year 1899 a new nation entered upon the work of polar exploration. Hitherto the work had been confined to the Americans, English, Scandinavians and Russians and the people of the south of Europe had taken no part in it. But now Italy stepped into the field, in the person of the ambitious and adventurous Duke of the Abruzzi, a cousin of King Victor Emmanuel of Italy. In 1897 the duke had begun a career of exploration by proceeding to Alaska and climbing to the lofty peak of Mount St. Elias, which he was the first to reach. He now grew eager to reach another peak, that of the earth at its northern extremity.

Realizing, however, that the Italians had had no experience in the ice-clad seas and had no vessels specially adapted to the kind of navigation before him, he wisely availed himself of the experience and equipment of the Norwegians. Buying the old sealing steamer "Jason," of Norwegian build, he had it refitted for polar work, giving it the new name of "Stella Polare"—"Polar Star." He also availed himself of the valuable aid of Dr. Nansen in arranging his plans and preparing his equipment and very wisely added a quota of Norwegians to his crew, it being composed of ten of the sons of Italy and ten of those of Norway. His plan of action was to sail as far north as possible, establish winter quarters upon some far northern coast, and seek in the spring to reach the vicinity of the Pole by sledge journeys.

Abruzzi was availing himself to the utmost of the work of his predecessors. In addition to the valuable advice and aid of Nansen, he took advantage of the camp established in Franz Josef Land by the Jackson-Harmsworth expedition, and in his purpose of making sledge dashes northward he was following the plan laid down by Peary and Nansen.

Reaching Archangel, in Northern Russia, the "Stella Polare" was headed northward for Franz Josef Land, and in August, 1899, reached Cape Flora, Jackson's headquarters, in latitude 80 degrees north. It was here that Nansen had been rescued and entertained. The huts of the former occupants were found standing intact, and Abruzzi stocked them with provisions for a food depot and pushed northward through the British Channel.

On reaching latitude 80 degrees 30 minutes the "Stella Polare" was met by the "Capella," Walter Wellman's ship, then sailing southward after an unsuccessful voyage north. Wellman, however, had done some good work in exploring and mapping the Franz Josef archipelago. The two exploring parties exchanged visits, after which each set out on its special course, the one southward to civilization, the other northward to desolation. The British Channel and the waters north of it proving unusually free from ice, the "Stella Polare" was enabled to steam beyond the eighty-second degree of latitude to a position near the shores of Crown Prince Rudolph Land, the western coast of which had been visited by Payer in 1883 and the eastern coast by Wellman in 1899.

The ship was now at or near the northern extremity of land in that region, and as the plan of the expedition was to establish headquarters on some suitable coast, making this the base for sledge journeys northward, Teplitz Bay, on Prince Rudolph Island, in latitude 81 degrees 53 minutes, was selected as a suitable place for wintering, and the ship was taken in and anchored near enough to the shore to permit the easy landing of stores.

Teplitz Bay is open towards the south and west, the land on the north being level but rocky. A leader of more experience in Arctic navigation would have had doubts as to the security of the situation as a place for a ship to lie exposed to the winter movements of the ice. With the bay open on two sides, it was scarcely possible for it to escape from the pressure of moving floes outside; but the opinion was held that the ice along the shores was strong enough to withstand any pressure from the open sea, and so the "Stella Polare" was moored to the shore. Their trust was nearly to prove fatal.

Brief journeys along the coast and over the highest land which could be reached, an elevation of 2,900 feet, effectually disposed of the claims of Peterman Land and King Oscar Land, islands placed on the map by the Payer expedition. Nansen also had failed to find these islands, and it seemed certain that the former explorers had been deceived by massive bodies of ice, resembling land.

By September 7th the work of preparation for wintering in this situation was completed and the explorers made merry over their success to this date and hopefully discussed the prospect before them. The difficulties which beset other explorers, often from the very commencement of their journeys, had not been experienced by them, and now, with their vessel almost as high to the north as any vessel had yet been, with their complete outfit at one of the most northerly stations yet established, and with everything snug and secure for the winter, it is not surprising that they should have allowed their enthusiasm to run away with them. It was the first time that Italy had entered into the contest of winning fame from the mysteries of the Arctic, and the outlook was so rosy that they were not without dreams of carrying the flag to the Pole itself and showing to the world that the all-conquering spirit of ancient Rome still animated the race. Their Norwegian comrades, men of colder temperament, felt like postponing the triumph until the battle was won, but the enthusiasm of the southern nature could not be repressed.

They were soon to gain a truer idea of the task before them, and to learn the unsafe conditions of their situation. An ice-floe, drifting in the sea beyond the bay, caught the edge of the shore ice, in which the "Stella Polare" lay at rest, as it passed. The ice yielded to the strain, and along its length was uplifted a ridge of hummock ice. The line of pressure passed through the spot where the "Stella Polare" was made fast. The hummock rose against her bows and forced her ninety feet away from where she had been, while, at the same moment, an increase in the pressure caught her by the sides, heeled her over, and cracked her timbers till those on board rushed to the deck under the belief that the vessel was about to collapse. The rigging of the foremast was torn away, the planks of the exposed side showed spaces of three inches between them, and water poured into the hold so rapidly that it was feared the ship would go down. The hand-pump was manned and worked, while the fires were lit so as to get up steam and set the steam-pump going, every one who was not required for these jobs working vigorously to get all stores out of the ship and on to the ice, lest she should go down and leave them stranded and foodless. The Arctic was giving a characteristic and rugged greeting to the visitors from the South.

The stores were landed with the greatest rapidity, the activity with which every one worked being still further stimulated by the news from below that the hand-pump, which was being worked by four men, could not keep the water back, and that already it was almost touching the bars of the furnaces. At one time it looked as though there would be no chance of saving the fires, and had the water once reached them and so prevented steam being got up, the plight of the explorers would have been critical in the extreme. As it was, the Norwegian engineers worked like heroes, and managed to make enough steam to start the steam-pump just as the water touched the fires in one of the boiler furnaces. The steam-pump, assisting the hand-pump, was sufficient to keep the water from rising further, but not enough to keep it back altogether. Neither the steam nor the hand pump, by itself, could prevent the water from rising. Both had to be kept going, since if the water should reach the fires and put them out the effort to save the ship might have proved hopeless.

They worked on with a brave persistence, Italian and Norwegian alike, until they had all the stores out on the ice, together with spars, ropes, sails, and all other things needed for the construction of a shelter in which to pass the winter, if it should become necessary. This was only completed after twenty-four hours of toil, and when it was finished the worn-out party sought a brief respite in sleep. As soon as the pumps ceased working the waters rose rapidly in the holds and over the furnace bars, putting out the fires. Contrary to expectations, the ship did not go down, the ice being sufficiently strong to sustain it from sinking, so that the water stopped rising when it had covered the furnaces.

Although the ship was now secure from sinking, it had heeled over to such an extent that it was impossible to remain on board, and a hut was erected on shore, around which the stores were stacked for the winter. For ten days the entire party labored at this work, and when it was finished it was realized that all the plans for the preliminary sledge trips must be abandoned. Instead of giving attention to reaching the Pole, it was first of all necessary to see what could be done in the way of repairing the ship so as to keep it afloat when the supporting ice should give way.

A close examination revealed the fact that the severe pressure had considerably affected the form of the ship. The crank shaft was bent out of the straight, and the heavy iron beams which had been put in to strengthen the vessel amidships were all bent and twisted. The planks at the sides were started and gaped open in many places. The water which had made its way in had frozen, so that the furnaces were covered by a sheet of solid ice, while the same thing existed in the hold. As the hand-pump could not lower the water alone, it was decided to use a boiler and pump which formed part of the balloon equipment. Although the use of these articles effectually terminated any hopes of balloon experiments, it enabled them to get the water down sufficiently to permit of repairs being effected. From the beginning of October to the middle of

November the work of repairing fully occupied the crew; but they succeeded in making the ship water-tight and available for departure when the winter should pass. The bay, by this time, was frozen over sufficiently to preclude any fears of further nips occurring.

On November 20th the last vestige of daylight vanished, and thenceforward the explorers were in the gloom of the Arctic night. A heavy snow-storm entirely covered the dog kennels, so that the animals had to run loose for a time. This was not satisfactory, for those of the creatures which were unable to squeeze into shelter near the hut, were frozen to the ice as they slept. To overcome this, big holes were dug in the ground, the dogs were driven in, and the entrances walled up. But the Arctic dog is a creature of resource, and when the men in charge of them went in due time to feed the animals, it was found that they had made an outlet for themselves by burrowing through the snow, and were again at liberty. A wall of biscuit tins was now built round the inside of the holes, and the entire mass frozen by pouring water over the tins. But the dogs again burrowed their way out, and they were then left to their own devices, the holes being left open, so that there should be some shelter available for the dogs if they liked to use it. This most of them did not like, preferring to squeeze in between the sides of the hut and the kitchen, where they contributed their share to the entertainment by occasional howling choruses during the long dark hours of the winter.

During the long night the plans for the sledge expeditions to the North, which had been so effectively interrupted by the nipping of the ship, were further considered. As the original scheme could no longer be carried out, a modified plan was adopted. Under this, it was determined to send out three parties, which were to start about the middle of February and press forward towards the Pole. Each party was to consist of three Italians. One was to carry provisions for thirty days, the second for sixty days, and the third for ninety days. The second and third parties were to carry kayaks. An advance party had been sent out early in the month to establish depots of supplies on the proposed route. It returned in a few days, having accomplished its purpose.

It had been intended that the Duke of the Abruzzi should lead the detachments as the head of the third party, the one which would have the honor of proceeding the longest way; but early in January he had two fingers of his right hand frost-bitten so severely that the two top joints had to be amputated. This debarred him from taking his place at the head of the enterprise, and he appointed Captain Cagni to the lead in his stead. The other parties were commanded, the first by Dr. Cavalli, and the second by Lieutenant Querini. A fourth party was to follow the other three for a couple of days, as an auxiliary, so as to allow of a saving in the consumption of provisions carried by the others. It was also arranged that twenty-five days after the start of the expedition, those of the company who remained behind at Teplitz Bay should send a watch party to Cape Fligely, in order to be ready to set out and meet, and, if necessary, render any assistance which the returning members of the first detachment might require. From the top of Cape Fligely a distance of eight miles could be seen over the ice to the north, and a signal-post, erected on the cape, would be visible as a guide to the returning explorers as they approached over the ice. The watch party was to be on the cape again fifty-five days after the departure of the third detachment.

The date of departure was ultimately fixed for the 18th of February. The detachments, when ready to start, numbered, in all, twelve men, with thirteen sledges, drawn by one hundred and four dogs, each sledge weighing, with its load of provisions, six hundred and seventeen pounds. The weather, at the time of the start, was intensely cold, there having been a gale blowing for some days before. When all was ready for the march to begin, the detachments set out, after hearty farewells from those who remained behind, and who watched them slowly pass out of sight over the ice and into the cold mysteries of the white region lying towards the north.

The camp at Teplitz Bay was strangely quiet after their departure, the absence of the dogs, no less than the absence of the men, rendering the place lonely and deserted. It was not expected that the auxiliary detachment would be back again for some days, and it was with very great surprise that the Duke, while walking near the hut one day, heard the sounds of dogs barking near at hand. He hastened in the direction whence the sounds came, and was astounded to see Lieutenant Querini coming towards him. Immediately he came to the conclusion that disaster had overtaken the expedition soon after starting, and that the lieutenant was the bearer of ill news, if not the only survivor of the detachment.

The facts were, however, not so bad as this. What had happened was that the cold had become so intense, after leaving Cape Fligely, that not only the men, but the dogs also, suffered severely, and were almost incapacitated. The experience of a few days revealed many points where improvement could be made in the arrangement of the sledges and their loading, and the commander, realizing that only valuable time would be lost, and perhaps the entire expedition jeopardized, by pushing on under the circumstances, decided to return to the main camp, so as to overhaul the arrangements, and reorganize the detachments in the light of their experience.

By the time the detachments were again ready to start, February had passed and March 10th had arrived. The loss of time, consequent on their return, necesitated an alteration in the program of all the parties, and when they set out the second time the order of march was for the first detachment to return after twelve days' march, the second in twenty-four, and the third in thirty-six. The detachments were also varied, so that the main detachment should number four instead of three men. A Norwegian, the engineer of the ship, was included in the first detachment at his earnest request.

The second start was made on Sunday, March 11th, and this time there was no turning back. On March 28th, Abruzzi went, with the watch party, to Cape Fligely, and constructed a shelter in which they could remain in readiness to greet the first detachment on its return, the date of which was expected to be April 4th. On that date, and for some days before, an anxious watch was kept from the lookout point towards the north, but no signs were seen of the returning explorers. For a day or so this did not cause any grave anxiety, as it was quite possible that there might be a brief delay, but as the days went by without a sign, and the days grew into weeks, there was serious uneasiness at the continued non-appearance of the men.

The time arrived when the second detachment was due, and still the watchers saw no signs of the returning men. Uneasiness gave place to grave anxiety, and the few who remained at the camp were beginning to wonder whether they would be obliged to return home alone, with only a tale of loss and disaster to bear to their country, when a man of the second party reached the camp in a state of great exhaustion. His story was that his detachment, the second, had parted with the third on March 31st, and had been successful on the return journey up to April 15th, when an open channel in the ice near the island had stopped their march. For days they had sought a way round it, but, failing, the leader had despatched the man in the kayak to reach the watch station, and summon the assistance of a boat party, to convey the remainder over the channel. The man had attempted to land at a point where the ice was some fifteen feet high, but while he was testing it to see if he could clamber up, the kayak slipped away from him and left him clinging, with no hope of escape if he should slip into the water below.

He was one of the Alpine guides, and with his ice-axe he

managed to cut a way up the ice to the summit, though the struggle was a terrible strain on his strength and skill. When, at last, he reached the summit, he was met by a new difficulty. He did not know where he was, nor in which direction the camp lay. He was without food, or refreshment, but he made his way to a higher point, from whence he was, fortunately, able to see the top of the ship's masts showing over the ice. This gave him the direction of the camp at Teplitz Bay, and he made his way thither, with as much speed as he could. When he arrived, he had been battling his way for over twenty-four hours, from the time he lost his kayak, a feat of very great endurance.

In answer to anxious questions as to the first detachment, he said he and all the rest believed the first detachment was in the camp, for it had left the main body in time to reach Cape Fligely by April 2d. At the time it started back, owing to the drift of the ice, the island could be distinctly seen, so that there could be no difficulty as to the men knowing which way to go. Moreover, a change had been made in the command, and the first detachment had left under the command of Lieutenant Querini, Dr. Cavalli having been placed at the head of the second detachment owing to his showing greater staying powers on the march than the lieutenant.

As soon as the rest of the detachment had been conveyed from the ice pack to the camp, Dr. Cavalli corroborated the story and shared, with the rest of the expedition, the anxiety at the non-arrival of the little band. His detachment, he said, had parted with the main party on March 31st, and had seen Captain Cagni and his companions continue their way to the north, with a train of six sledges and forty-eight dogs. The first detachment might, he suggested, have been carried away to the east, and, as they had no kayak with them, they might have been cut off by an open channel and so prevented from reaching the island. Relief parties were immediately sent out to search the ice in that direction, and also to see whether the men had taken refuge on the islands further to the northeast, where Nansen and Johansen had passed their winter. The search was continued until May 10th, when the parties returned, having searched far and wide but without finding any trace of the missing detachment. It was then hoped that they had made their way to Cape Flora, where there was an abundance of food and other necessaries, but when the "Stella Polare" touched there, on her way home, no signs were found of the missing men, and it was then realized that they were lost. How, or when, or where, they had met their end, no one could form any opinion. A break in the ice may have precipitated them into a channel; cold may have overcome them as they slept; moving hummocks may have overwhelmed them, or a sudden snow-storm may have caused them to lose their direction, and have led them into dangers they were not able to escape. When no trace could be found of them, and no vestige of their outfit discovered on the ice, or the islands, there was only one thing the survivors could realize, and that was that their comrades had gone out of the world in silence, in mystery and in sacrifice to the knowledge of humanity.

As the month of May gradually passed, the members of the expedition gathered at Cape Fligely so as to maintain a steady watch for the return of the main detachment. In addition to the watch party there was also a party at Teplitz Bay, and word was sent from one place to the other as the days went by, while short journeys were constantly being taken along the shores on the lookout for the return of Captain Cagni and his companions. The provisions they had with them were calculated only to last until May 26th, but the leader had expressed his intention, if he had not succeeded in reaching far enough to the north, of proceeding on reduced rations so as to attain as high a latitude as possible before returning.

On the reduced scale they would be able to subsist until June 10th, but when that date arrived and still there was no sign of them, the remainder of the expedition became alarmed. The disappearance of Lieutenant Querini and his companions did not tend to alleviate their anxiety. A week passed without any sign; June 20th came and went, and the next two days saw the little community depressed and sad at what they regarded as the fatal silence. On the 23d they barely exchanged words with one another, lest they should add to each other's sorrow by expressing the almost hopeless fear that every one felt.

On the evening of that day the watch party at Cape Fligely had retired to their shelter when they heard the barking of dogs. Hastily going outside, they saw a man, with a sledge, advancing from the direction of Teplitz Bay. They waited in silence for him to come up, fearing he brought news of disaster. But their fears were turned to joy when he shouted the news that the third detachment had safely returned to camp, having penetrated as far as 86 degrees 34 minutes north, and so established the "farthest north" record of any expedition yet despatched to the Arctic. It was twenty geographic miles farther north than Nansen had reached.

The story Captain Cagni had to tell was one of persistent courage and determination. The straits to which he and his companions were reduced were shown by the condition of their equipment. They had a single sledge in a very damaged state, a bottomless saucepan, a broken cooking lamp, and a ragged tent. Their dogs were reduced to seven, the others having been killed to feed the survivors as well as the men. On the return journey the drift of the ice had carried them to the west, so that when they reached the latitude of Teplitz Bay they were many miles to the west of it. The condition of the ice had compelled them to go still further away before they were able to turn and head direct for the camp.

From March 11th to April 24th they marched steadily towards the north, and covered something like six hundred miles in ninety-five days. For the whole period of 104 days they marched 753 miles. During the first stage of the journey they maintained a speed of five miles a day, but during the second stage they doubled that, and covered, on an average, ten miles a day. From their experience they argued it was impossible to reach the Pole from any such base as that at Teplitz Bay while dog sledges were the only available means of transport.

With the return of this detachment the work of the expedition was at an end. The vessel was freed from the ice after a little difficulty, and, proving to be seaworthy, steamed out of the bay on August 14th. They arrived at Hammerfest without mishap on September 5th. They were given a most enthusiastic reception on their return to Italy, having given that country the honor of reaching the "farthest north."

CHAPTER XXXI

The Problem of the Antarctic Zone

WHILE so much attention was being given to the Arctic problem, that of the Antarctic was long neglected, and only within recent years has any determined effort to solve it been made. It was not until 1600 that the first contact was made with the southern world of ice. Dirk Gerritz, a Dutch navigator, sailing with a squadron for the East Indies, was separated from his other ships while passing through the Straits of Magellan and was driven as far as 64 degrees south. He discovered, in that latitude, a rocky coast line covered with snow. The discovery did not excite any great interest at the time, and, for a period of nearly two centuries, nothing was done to probe further into the mysteries of the south. In 1769 an expedition was sent out under Captain Kerguellen to explore the regions lying to the south of the Cape of Good Hope. He was successful in locating the group of islands, still known as Kerguellen Islands, and sailed thence to Australia, demonstrating that no land, other than these islands, existed between the Cape of Good Hope and Australia.

The first to make a vigorous effort to learn the secrets of the far south was the famous Captain Cook, a polar explorer, the predecessor of his namesake of our own days. His first voyage of discovery in the southern sea of ice was in 1772-73, in which, after various efforts, he reached only 61 degrees south latitude. In 1774 he made another voyage and now attained 71 degrees 10 minutes, further progress to the south being barred by a line of lofty ice cliffs. With unyielding persistence, he went again in 1775, discovering in latitude 59 degrees three high rocky islets, with a lofty peak which he named Freezeland Point. Far to the east was seen a long coast-line with snow-capped mountains, while other lands were sighted farther to the south. The ships proceeded to explore the seas in the neighborhood of these new lands, but a repetition of the trials and difficulties of the previous year met the explorers. Whichever way they sailed they encountered ice, either in massive bergs, or lines of cliffs, miles in length. On February 6, 1775, the cold hostility of the region daunted even the brave heart of Captain Cook. He decided to turn back, writing in his log: "The risk one runs in exploring a coast in these unknown and icy seas is so great, that I can be bold enough to say that no man will ever venture further than I have done, and that the lands which lie to the south will never be explored."

Modern exploration has shown that Cook was hasty in this assertion, but his opinion carried weight enough to check for many years all attempts to solve the mystery of the Antarctic. In 1819 Captain William Smith, driven southward by a storm, discovered and named the South Shetland Islands, and these were soon afterwards explored by a British war-ship, and found to form a scattered group between 61 and 63 degrees south. Powell, an English skipper, met with land farther south in 1821, naming it Trinity Land; Palmer, an American, sailed along a coast to which he gave the name of Palmer's Land; and Bellinghausen, a Russian, soon after located Alexander's Land, still farther south.

The seas in which these finds were made were well filled with whales and seals, and oil-seekers soon began to make their way to that region, while Captain Weddell was sent out by an English trading firm on a voyage of discovery and reached latitude 74 degrees 15 minutes. Other discoveries in this period were of Enderby's Land, Graham's Land, and Adelaide Islands, but Weddell's record remained the "farthest south."

These private excursions to the south were followed somewhat later by three important government expeditions, a French one under D'Urville in 1838, an English one under Sir James Ross in 1839, and an American one under Captain Wilkes in 1840. These added materially to our knowledge of the far south. D'Urville was checked by a bank of ice extending for three hundred miles east and west; but Ross, who made three voyages in 1839-43, discovered and named Victoria Land and traced its coast from 71 degrees to 78 degrees 10 minutes south, the highest latitude reached to that time in the Antarctic. On this land was a lofty range of mountains containing two volcanoes, which he named after his ships, "Erebus" and "Terror." Wilkes discovered a long coast line, which apparently extended from Enderby's Land to Ringold's Knoll, being of such extent that he described it as an Antarctic continent. His discovery, long questioned, has since been confirmed.

For fifty years after the work of these expeditions the Antarctic region was neglected by explorers, the first attempt after those named to discover its mysteries being made by a Belgian expedition in 1897. The story of this expedition, on which Dr. Cook went as surgeon, is told in an earlier chapter, and we must pass on to a British expedition which set out in 1898, under the leadership of Captain C. E. Borchgrevinck, a Norwegian, who had voyaged into the Antarctic on a whaler in 1894, and had landed on South Victoria Land and Possession Island. He was one of the first to set foot on Antarctic soil, and reached as far south as 74 degrees 10 minutes. He had also discovered a lichen growing on the rocks of Cape Adare, the first living thing found in the Antarctic.

His present expedition, financed by Sir George Newnes, an English capitalist, whom he had infected with his enthusiasm, set sail in the "Southern Cross," a small barque-rigged steamer of 276 tons, built by the builder of the "Fram," under the command of Captain Bernhard Jensen. With stores and equipment for some years, a crew of Norwegians, an efficient scientific staff, and a large kennel of Arctic dogs, she left St. Katherine's Dock on August 22, 1898, amid much popular demonstration, and sailed for Tasmania.

We cannot go into the details of this voyage, and shall only say that the ship left the ten members of the expedition at Cape Adare, in Victoria Land, and returned to New Zealand, to come back for them the following year. Here they spent the winter of 1899, being fortunate in discovering that fish were abundant in the deeper waters of the bay and that these were nearly all edible. Numbers of them were caught through holes cut in the ice and proved a welcome addition to their diet. They also discovered at the approach of summer that insect life exists on the Antarctic land, several specimens being found.

The "Southern Cross" returned on January 29, 1900, and four days later steamed away with all on board. Following the coast southward to the vicinity of Mount Terror, a sledge party was landed which made a rapid push to the south, and on February 16th reached the latitude of 78 degrees 50 minutes south, the highest Antarctic latitude attained up to that time.

While the party remained ashore at Mount Terror one of the most exciting incidents of the whole journey occurred. The party landed at a small beach which lay under cliffs towering five hundred feet above. In order to get photographs of it, the boat was despatched back to the ship for a camera, while Borchgrevinck and Jensen remained ashore. The boat had not gone very far when a great roar sounded in the air. Those on shore feared for the moment that a slide had begun in the cliffs over their heads; but it was not the rocks that were moving. A mighty glacier, which entered the sea near where they were standing, was shedding an iceberg from the parent mass, and the noise was caused by the rending of the ice as the millions of tons mass tore itself free. The beach was barely four feet above the water, and, as the berg crashed into the sea, it sent up a great wave that swept along the coast. The men on the beach barely saw it coming before it had reached them. Pressing themselves against the face of the cliff at the highest point they could reach, they held on for dear life while the icy water surged up and over them. After the first wave had passed, others followed, though these only reached up to their arm-pits, and had it not been for a projecting point of rock, which served to break the force of the waves, there is little doubt but that both would have been swept away. The full force of the waves was shown only a few yards away from where the two had stood, stones being torn loose and the mark of the water being left twenty feet up the face of the cliff.

Having reached "farthest south," the homeward journey was begun on February 19th, and three days later the "Southern Cross" steamed into Port Ross, in the Island of Auckland. The expedition was then practically at an end, having succeeded so well in its objects that it was able to claim that it had located the Southern Magnetic Pole as being in latitude 73 degrees 20 minutes south and longitude 146 degrees east; had discovered insect and plant life on the Antarctic continent; had reached the farthest south, and had added very considerably to the geographical and scientific knowledge of the world.

The interest in Antarctic research had now decidedly revived, and in 1901 three nations, England, Germany and Sweden, despatched expeditions to the far south. Each was to have its distinct field of operation, the British to explore the region south of Australia, the Swedes that south of Cape Horn, and the Germans the Bouvet Island district. This island, first seen by Captain Cook, had been revisited by a German steamer, the "Valdivia," in 1898, and evidence found of extensive land nearer the Pole.

The German expedition sailed from Kiel on August 11, 1901, on board the "Gauss," and was under the command of Professor Erich von Drygalski. Their objective was Kerguellen Island, and the chief work carried out was of a purely scientific character. It was originally intended that all the expeditions should return to Europe after passing one winter in the Antarctic. The Germans did so, but both the Swedes and the British were unable to carry out this part of the program, the former in consequence of the loss of their ship in the ice, the latter because their ship was hard and fast in the southern ice. The Germans were more fortunate in escaping the ill effects of what was an unusually severe ice season; but the expeditions of the other nations, by the longer stay they had in the frozen regions, were able to return with a much more comprehensive collection of information.

The principal result achieved by the German expedition was to prove that Knox Land and Kemp Land, which appear as separate coasts on the old maps, are really continuous areas. Forcing a way through the pack ice, the "Gauss" found a stretch of open water, rapidly shoaling, and leading to a rugged, steep coast line, in the position which Ross had charted in 1841 as "ice cliffs." Here the ship became frozen into the ice and winter quarters were established. Little work of importance was done, and in the following summer the explorers freed their ship from the ice and returned to Germany.

The Swedish expedition, sailing in the "Antarctica,'" commanded by Captain C. A. Larsen, was headed by Professor Otto Nordenskiöld, the plan being to leave a party of six on the Antarctic shores, the ship returning for the winter to the Falkland Islands. The final return was to be in 1903. As it proved, the summer of 1902-3 was the coldest and worst for ice conditions ever recorded in the south polar region, and instead of one winter, the Swedes were compelled to spend two in the ice.

On February 10, 1902, the vessel was in Sydney Herbert Bay, which formed the hitherto unvisited part of Erebus and Terror Gulf. As it was obviously impossible to get farther to the south, Nordenskiöld decided to establish the winter station on one of the islands in this vicinity. A brief visit to Seymour Island did not reveal the wealth of fossil-bearing strata that was expected. Paulet Island was visited and an interesting circular lake was discovered, lying in a circular range of hills. The banks of the lake bore ample evidences that at one time there had been great volcanic activity at the place, and the lake was evidently formed in the hollow of the extinct crater. The place did not appeal to them as a site for the winter station, and, as further journeys revealed another island on the other side of Seymour Island, where there was a beach which appeared to be sheltered from the southward, the point whence the most violent winds blew, it was decided to build the hut there.

The "Antarctica" anchored in the bay opposite the beach and rapidly unloaded the camp equipment. When everything was almost landed, a movement in the ice at the mouth of the bay compelled the ship to stand out into open water, so the party of six, who were to spend the winter on the island, hastened ashore, where they had their hut to build and all preparations to make without the help, which had been counted upon, of the crew of the vessel. But this did not weigh heavily upon them, and they set to work with a will. In the course of a week, the "Antarctica" was able to get into the bay again and to land the remaining stores; but by that time the hut was up and the adventurous six were almost settled down to their routine work.

A day or so after landing, Nordenskiöld discovered that the island they were on—named by them Snow Hill Island—was peculiarly interesting from a geological point of view, for he found fossils of ammonites, a token of ancient life of the region which alone would have made the expedition memorable.

The position proved to be badly chosen, as it was exposed to gales of great violence, the wind at one time being strong enough to lift a whale-boat, carry it over a second one, and dash it against an ice cliff, twenty-one yards away, with such violence that its side was smashed in. As winter approached, the storms obscured the sky and the sun was not often seen. They were not far enough south to lose it altogether, and all through the winter they had the benefit of its presence, though not for many hours at a time. When it did come, however, it came with great magnificence. After a series of storms they saw it rise one morning, and the spectacle is described as gorgeous and beautiful.

The winter passed without misfortune, and with the approach of spring preparations were made for the first long sledge journey. On this, and other journeys, they succeeded in traveling long distances over what was often heavy ice, on two meals a day. The first, which was the more substantial of the two, consisted of pemmican made into a thick porridge-like soup, the nutritious qualities of which were felt even as it was being eaten. This was followed by coffee, meat biscuits, butter and sugar. On such a meal the men existed and traveled all day, making no stop until the evening, when they had their dinner, consisting merely of pea or lentil soup, meat, chocolate, bread, butter, and, sometimes, bacon. Immediately they had eaten this frugal repast they were in their sleeping-bags and asleep.

Meanwhile the "Antarctica" had proceeded north to Tierra del Fuego and South Georgia, picked up some members of the party who had been left there, and sailed south again with the purpose of reaching the winter station early in January. As she advanced, however, she found the sea so blocked with ice that she could not follow the course she had traversed the previous year. When she arrived at Hope Bay, some miles to the north of the station, Professor Andersson and two companions landed with sledges and sufficient provisions to last nine men for two months. It was their intention to proceed over the ice to the station, while the "Antarctica'" steamed away to the west, in the hopes of finding an opening through the ice which would enable her to reach the station. If, on the arrival of the relief party at the station, the "Antarctica" had not appeared, they were to return, with the other six, and wait for the ship at Hope Bay.

As it proved, they were not able to traverse the intervening region, and were compelled to stay where they were, and as the summer passed without the ship being seen, they decided to return to Hope Bay and await her. The original party had also looked for the "Antarctica" in vain. The farthest south they penetrated was to 56 degrees 48 minutes, but they had been fortunate in finding fossil remains of unknown animals, and the fossil leaves of several kinds of pine trees and ferns.

The "Antarctica" was, like her two parties, ice bound. She had steamed away to the west, and then, a chance offering itself, had stood to the south until she was in the latitude of Paulet Island. She turned to the east, heading in the direction of the station on Snow Hill Island, when the ice caught her. For days she remained in the pack, those on board chafing at the delay and trying every device to get her free. But the ice was too strong, and at last they were forced to admit that they were caught for the winter. This was bad enough, but there was worse to follow. A movement began in the pack, and a pressure-ridge started directly for the ship. It was upon them almost before they realized it, and the crash with which she heeled over told its own tale. The ice had torn a length of her keel away, and had made a hole in her which it was impossible to repair.

Everything that could be got out was thrown on to the ice, and the ship's company formed themselves into sledge parties to convey as much as they could to the nearest land. This was Paulet Island, where they arrived after an arduous march and at once set to work to construct a shelter for the winter, which was now upon them. There they stayed, within a few miles of the station, and of the other party at Hope Bay, but all in ignorance of the proximity of one another, and quite unable to communicate.

With the first sign of approaching spring the men at the original station made arrangements to resume their expeditions and complete the survey of the islands in their immediate vicinity. The first trip was in the direction of Hope Bay, and the party had been out some days when, in the dim light, one of them thought he saw a dark patch on the ice in the distance. He drew his companion's attention to it, but neither cared to trust their eyes. As they approached nearer, the dark patch resolved itself into the figures of men, and a still nearer view revealed two such extraordinary creatures that one of the men from the station thought it would be as well to have a revolver ready in case of emergency. The two figures were in black garments, with black caps on their heads, and their hands and faces were as black as their clothes, while the upper parts of their faces were hidden by curious-looking masks. Beside them was a sledge.

With considerable uncertainty the men from the station approached, and were not reassured when they were asked, in English, how they were. "Thanks; how are you?" they replied. "Don't you know us?" one of the strange-looking creatures asked. "We're the relief party. Have you seen the ship?" Then a third figure appeared from behind an ice hummock where he had been preparing a meal. They were Professor Andersson and his companions, who were on their way, for the second time, to the station.

Without loss of time the reunited comrades made their way to the station, where soap and water and a fresh supply of clothes soon transformed the appearance of the three who had had so trying a time in the little stone hut at Hope Bay. But the situation was still fraught with anxiety, now that they realized that something very serious had happened to the "Antarctica." It was impossible for them to determine whether she had gone to the bottom, or had been beset in the ice. Only one thing was clear, and that was that they would all have to stay where they were until some help came to them. While they were still debating what chances there were of any coming before another winter went by, they were startled, one day, by the arrival of visitors. These proved to be a search party from the Argentine cruiser "Uruguay," which the Argentine government had despatched on account of the "Antarctica," not having returned at her appointed time. Help had come at a time and from a quarter least expected.

But the news that the cruiser brought added very much to the fears the explorers entertained as to the safety of the "Antarctica" and her crew. If she had been beset, some of her company could have reached the station over the ice while it was still compact, or, if she was still afloat, she ought herself to have been able to reach them. The absence of all news made the members of the expedition gathered at the station more than uneasy as to the fate of their comrades.

The morning after the Argentine officers arrived, one of the men, looking out of the hut, exclaimed that eight men were coming over the ice. Under the impression that they were some of the cruiser's crew sent to assist in removing the baggage from the station to the ship, he went out to meet them, walking slowly, as he tried to decide what was to be done if they could not speak any language he knew. The others in the hut, watching him, saw him suddenly leap forward and then turn to them and wave his arms. "Larsen! Larsen is here!" they heard him shout.

With one accord they rushed out after him, and in a few moments were eagerly shaking hands with the eight men, who were a detachment sent out from the camp on Paulet Island to ascertain whether the party at the station was still intact or whether it had been rescued. The news was sent to the cruiser, and soon all the members of the expedition and their baggage were on board and the ship was steaming for Paulet Island.

On arrival off the coast no signs of the remainder of the crew of the "Antarctica" were to be seen, so the whistle was blown. The men at the time were all in the shelter, sleeping, and the sudden sound of the whistle roused them. For the moment they could not believe their ears. Then one of them looked out and saw the ship, and the shout with which he and his companions greeted the sight rang far out over the water.

Professor Andersson and his two comrades had left the "Antarctica" on December 29, 1902; the ship was nipped on January 10, 1903; and the castaways arrived at Paulet Island at the end of February. They had lived in the shelter they constructed, subsisting mostly on penguin, until November, when the Argentine cruiser arrived. Only one man had died.

The expedition reached Buenos Aires on November 30, 1903, having, during the time they had been in the Antarctic, collected a mass of interesting and valuable scientific information.

We have next to tell the story of the British expedition. This set out in August, 1901, in the "Discovery," a vessel specially built for the purpose, under Captain Robert F. Scott, of the British Navy. Victoria Land, their destination, was reached on December 24th, in the summer of the south. Sailing along this land, a good harbor was found as far south as 76 degrees 31 minutes. Thence the coast line was followed to 174 degrees east longitude, and here a sledge party crossed the ice to 78 degrees 50 minutes south, the latitude previously reached by Borchgrevinck.

Winter quarters were selected at a point within sight of Mounts Erebus and Terror, the ship being worked in as close to the shore as possible. She was built to withstand the ice pressure, and remained in this position unharmed for two winters. As soon as all was made snug sledge trips were taken along the coast and over the ice, the longest of these, in the following September, being by Captain Scott, Lieutenant Shackleton and Dr. Wilson. They had dogs with them at the start, but the animals grew sick and weak, and were, at last, quite useless in dragging the sledges. The three men harnessed themselves to the sledges in place of the dogs, and, handicapped with this weight of 240 pounds each, they pushed on until they reached 82 degrees 17 minutes south, the farthest south then made, being about two hundred and fifty miles nearer the Pole than any other explorers had reached. From the position they then occupied they were able to see as far as 83 degrees 20 minutes south, and would have gone as far, if not farther, but for an insuperable obstacle that confronted them. The route they followed was over rough ice, often yawning with deep crevasses, down which the sledges had to be lowered and then hauled up on the other side.

Some of them were veritable chasms, but they faded into insignificance when compared with the one which opened before the explorers at the end of the march. For a time they examined this mighty ice ravine to see if it were not possible, one way or another, to get across. The descent might have been possible, and there was no great difficulty in crossing the floor of it, but the far side rose in an unbroken precipice, and they recognized it as insurmountable, even to such daring and intrepid climbers as themselves. They therefore returned to the ship. The greatest speed made by them was as high as thirty-two miles in a day, a speed unsurpassed except by one of their own parties, which, with heavy sledges and without dogs, made thirty-three miles in a day over the inland ice.

During the second year of their stay, a discovery was made, which, from a geological point of view, exceeded in value all the others put together. It was in October that a sledge party set out to penetrate into the interior of Victoria Land. They traveled over the ice plain at an average altitude of 9,000 feet until, in 78 degrees south and 146 degrees 30 minutes east, they were at a distance of 270 miles from the ship. The interior of the land seemed to stretch in a vast continental plateau continuously at a height of 9,000 feet. In one of the many ravines examined, sandstone strata were discovered, in one of which there was a narrow seam of fossil plants. The "coal measure" was only one-eighth of an inch in thickness, but within it were found specimens of plants belonging to the Miocene period.

In February, 1904, the relief ship "Morning" arrived at the station, and, with the explosives she brought with her, the "Discovery" was freed from the ice and commenced her homeward journey. She had completed a stay of two winters in a latitude 500 miles further south than any other ship had wintered, while the expedition had reaped a success such as no previous expedition had achieved in the Antarctic region.

CHAPTER XXXII

Shackleton on the Threshold of the South Pole

THE year 1909 ranks as a record one in polar research. Early in that year the word was flashed north that a daring investigator had gone far to rob the far south of its mystery, approaching almost within touching distance of the South Pole. And in September of that year was flashed south still more startling news, to the effect that two equally daring investigators had knocked at the door of the far north, and stood upon the spot where the North Pole should penetrate the earth, if there were any visible form to this geographical figment.

We are here concerned with the first of these discoveries, that relating to the South Pole. That both these extremities of the earth's axis would before long be reached was as certain as anything could be. For a generation explorers had been approaching the North Pole step by step, learning the best methods and the necessary equipment for the enterprise, and tracing the most suitable starting place. The problem had reached that stage in which a bold dash was alone needed for its completion.

In the south progress towards the Pole had been much slower. Not until the closing years of the nineteenth century had a human foot been set on the land adjoining the polar region. But important discoveries had been made. There was much reason to believe that a continental area of land surrounded the Pole, instead of an ocean of water, as seemed the case in the north. This, if it should prove a fact, would vitally change the conditions. The ice ridges and open leads of water which formed the great difficulty in the north could not exist on a land surface, and though this might present difficulties of its own, those which troubled the north polar explorer would not be met.

There were, doubtless, wide stretches of ice and snow to traverse, there was a fearfully low temperature to endure, there might be mountainous elevations to climb and cross, but the lessons learned in the north could be applied in the south, the best kind of Arctic dress could be worn, the sleeping-bag could be used, the dog sledge could be employed, the most easily carried food could be taken, and besides these only pluck and endurance seemed needed to win victory in the great battle with the hostile forces of ice and cold.

The first step in this work was taken by Borchgrevink in 1900, in his pioneer sledge journey over the southern ice. He was followed two years later by Captain Scott, whose journey over the ice occupied ninety-four days and covered not less than a thousand miles. With him on this daring excursion was Lieutenant Ernest H. Shackleton, like himself an officer of the British Navy, and a man of inflexible will and courage. An instance of this was shown on the trip in question, in the latter part of which the three men of the party had to take the place of the dogs in pulling the loaded sledges. In this severe work Lieutenant Shackleton ruptured a blood-vessel, which unfitted him for pulling and even for walking. Yet the other two were quite unable to add his weight to the load they already had to drag, and if they were to reach the ship alive he would have to walk. With heroic determination the brave fellow nerved himself to this painful task, heroically trudging after them on foot, and complaining only that his injury prevented him in taking his part in their work. Of such metal as this heroes are made.

Shackleton was not long home before the Antarctic problem called him again, and he began to prepare for a south polar expedition under his own leadership. The experience gained in his former journey was of the greatest value to him and he believed that he had learned the true way to attain the Pole. He proposed, as before, to make his final dash with a party of three, and to add to the dogs a number of the hardy Manchurian ponies, of which ten were taken with him. But the great innovation of his proposed journey was the use of a motor car, one especially adapted to rough traveling in a cold climate. Having no hummocks or ridges to deal with and no open water to cross, he believed that such a car could be successfully used, and felt sure that it would add greatly to the ease and progress of his journey. King Edward VII Land, near the point of Borchgrevink's farthest south in 1900, was selected by him as a starting point and the expedition set sail in 1907, fifteen men composing the party. As in the two former expeditions, it was proposed to have the ship land the exploring party at the desired locality and return to warmer climes, coming to seek them again during the following summer.

Setting out in the "Nimrod" in 1907, the explorers on reaching the Antarctic Seas found themselves subjected to hostile polar weather. While seeking a suitable place to land their ship was assailed by fierce winds, through which it labored with difficulty, the party suffering great hardship in this encounter. As it proved, pack ice prevented the "Nimrod" from reaching King Edward VII Land, and they were obliged to seek winter quarters at Cape Royds, on Victoria Land, in the vicinity of Mt. Erebus, twenty miles from where the "Discovery" party had wintered. Here their stores, implements and animals were unloaded, a terrific blizzard assailing them during three days of this time, by which so much sea-water was thrown ashore, freezing as it fell, that the stores landed were buried in five or six feet of ice. The work of landing completed, the "Nimrod" steamed away on February 22, 1908, leaving the little party to its winter duties and diversions, if any could be found.

While the work of preparing for the coming season of cold was in progress a party of three, with a supporting party of three more, provisioned for ten days, was sent out to try the ascent of Mt. Erebus. After several days of hard climbing, in which a violent wind storm added to their difficulties and dangers, the whole six reached the summit of the volcano and gazed over the crater's edge. Here they found themselves on the lip of a huge and steaming abyss, while the air was filled with the fumes of burning sulphur. The steam was hurled up in great, globular volumes, preceded by a low, hissing sound and then a booming roar. A breeze sweeping away the steam for a few minutes, the depth of the crater—eight to nine hundred feet—lay revealed, while its width seemed about a half mile. On the crater's floor the steam puffed upward from three well-like openings.

In their return the party made progress by sliding down the ice slopes, traversing five thousand feet in four hours; but their clothes were much the worse for this hasty descent. They had found the height of the mountain to be 13,350 feet.

This conquest of Mt. Erebus, whose huge sides had previously been ascended only about nine thousand feet, was one of the alleviations of the long southern winter. Another was the exercising and finding the pulling capacities of the ponies, the sledges being loaded and drawn two miles daily up and down on the sea-ice. It was found that 650 pounds for each pony was the best weight for their pulling powers, while the exercise brought them into excellent condition for their coming work. The sledges were also got in the best order, and as spring approached the ponies were hardened for their coming duties by more active exercise, such as hauling the coal supply and other work. The dogs also were got into condition for their coming duties, and the motor car was tried upon the sea-ice, where it worked satisfactorily, alterations being made in it to reduce its weight, all superfluous gear being taken off. Before testing this car upon the land surface, however, a party of three started on a brief journey south to examine conditions, and concluded then that they were such as to render the car unavailable. This was owing to the very heavy snowfall, which was much greater than on Shackleton's former experience in the "Discovery" expedition. This intended adjunct of the expedition, therefore, had to be given up.

The first step towards the polar dash was taken in September, it consisting in the forming of a food depot. There were six persons on this trip, the sledges being hauled by hand and each man's load being about one hundred and seventy pounds. The depot was formed in latitude 76 degrees 36 minutes, at a distance of about one hundred and forty miles from the winter camp.

On September 22d a party of three set out on an expedition as important in its way as the search for the Pole, its purpose being to locate the south megnetic pole, whose position had never been definitely fixed, though a close approximation to it had been made. This party consisted of Professor David, the geologist of the expedition, with two others of the scientific corps.

It was mid October before everything was ready for the main expedition, that having the South Pole for its goal. The food supply had been fixed, consisting of pemmican, biscuits, cheese, chocolate, sugar, tea and some other articles, the daily ration to be thirty-two ounces per man. Of the ten original ponies only eight had been landed and of these four had died from a proclivity for eating sand—leaving but four of the original number.

The party for the Pole finally got off on October 28th, it consisting of four persons, Shackleton himself, Dr. Marshall, the surgeon of the expedition; Lieutenant Adams, the meteorologist, and Frank Wild, who had charge of the dogs and sledges. Provisions were taken for ninety-one days, with a smaller supply for the ponies, with the idea that they might find it advisable to use some of these animals for food. A supporting party provisioned for fourteen days accompanied them.

Troubles soon assailed them, one of the ponies laming itself and a blizzard keeping them prisoners for several days. The next trouble came when one of the ponies sank through the snow cap of a hidden crevasse, carrying Adams down with it. An apparently bottomless cavern lay below, and though Adams and the pony were rescued, their escape from death was very narrow.

Day after day they trudged onward, with no small trouble and hardship, the seemingly level plain being on all sides seamed with crevasses, often lightly covered with new snow, so that the utmost vigilance was needed to avoid them. A second depot was made in latitude 81 degrees 4 minutes, and here one of the ponies was killed. This was done from the fact that the animal rations were running short, and fresh meat was needed, both for the depot and to carry with them. A sledge was left to mark the spot, it being sunk in the snow so that eight feet projected above the surface. To it a bamboo pole with a black flag was attached. But the surrounding viewpoints of the country were chiefly trusted to for finding the depot, careful observations of them being taken. Two other ponies were subsequently killed for the same purpose, and new food caches made.

On November 22d a range of ice-clad mountains was seen, with a bare peak at intervals. Their position was such that some way up them would have to be found if the Pole was to be reached. As they went on towards them the snow grew very soft, the ponies at times sinking in it to their bellies. On they marched, gradually ascending, and finally reaching a glacier which they hoped might lead to the Pole itself. Up this their subsequent course lay.

On December 2d they very nearly met with a tragedy, a shout for "Help" from Wild calling them in haste to his assistance. When they reached him they saw that the forward end of the pony sledge projected over a crevasse, Wild grasping it and hanging over the gulf. No sign of the pony was visible. Wild was aided to escape from his dangerous position, but the pony was gone, and the man's escape was almost a miracle. The loss of the sledge with its load would have been almost fatal to them, and though they now had to draw it themselves, they were thankful that they had it to draw.

By December 9th they were in a perfect nest of crevasses, some covered with snow so as to be very deceptive. Marshall went through one of these and was only saved by his harness, and soon after Adams and Shackleton had similar experiences. The glacier they were ascending seemed everywhere seamed with cracks, many of them probably a thousand or more feet deep.

On and on they went, constantly beset with difficulties and frequently with dangers. On December 17th the plateau they were seeking—here about 6,000 feet high—came in sight, and their difficulties seemed over. And here Wild found some geological specimens that, on their return to the ship, proved to be coal. There were several seams of this useful mineral, from four inches to eight feet in thickness. Still on they marched, dragging their sledges and ascending steadily, their food in time running so low that they had to reduce themselves to nearly starvation rations.

On January 6, 1909, they reached latitude 88 degrees 7 minutes south, and camped in a blizzard. For the next sixty hours the wind blew with a speed of seventy to eighty miles an hour, while the thermometer at times went down to 70 degrees below freezing point.

The situation was serious. To advance in the face of that wind was impossible, and with their rapidly diminishing food supply it was almost suicidal to venture farther. But on the 9th, when the blizzard began to break, they made another desperate rush forward, and at 9 A.M. reached latitude 88 degrees 23 minutes. Here the British flag was hoisted. The end was reached, with the Pole only one hundred and eleven miles away. Before them stretched still the endless white plain which they had traversed so many days, and they could but conclude that the South Pole was situated on this immense plateau, more than ten thousand feet above the sea level. A photograph of the party and of the floating flag was taken; they took possession of the plateau in the name of the British king; then they turned their faces north again, having done all of which flesh and blood was capable.

With the return of Shackleton and his companions we shall deal far more briefly. They had simply to follow the path traversed in going out, with a blizzard now blowing at their back and helping them to the rapid progress of from twenty to twenty-nine miles daily. Their ponies were all gone, the one that fell down the crevasse being the last, and for a month they had been obliged to draw the sledges by hand. On the return there was but one sledge to draw and this became lightened by the gradual exhaustion of the food supply. Several times on the return trip their food gave out, but in each case they fortunately reached a food cache in good time to restore it. Yet the continual dependence on horse meat produced dysentery, which by February 4th prostrated the entire party. The southern blizzard, however, continued to help them onward, and on March 4th they succeeded in reaching the ship, which was now awaiting them. The length of the entire journey, including relays, was 1,708 miles and the time occupied 126 days. The results, in addition to the polar record, were the discovery of coal measures, the making of a complete meteorological record, and the discovery of eight distinct mountain ranges and more than a hundred mountains.

Meanwhile the party sent in search of the Magnetic Pole had succeeded in locating it in the vicinity of latitude 70 degrees 25 minutes south, longitude 15 degrees 4 minutes east. The "Nimrod" had reached the camp in time to meet the two parties on their return, and they soon set out for home. On the voyage northward they discovered a new range of coast mountains on what was apparently an extension of Victoria Land towards Wilkes Land. Thus the disputed discovery of Captain Wilkes was confirmed. Shackleton had blazed a track to the vicinity of the South Pole, which cannot remain much longer a *terra incognita.*